A Survey of Human Communication

Michael A. Griffin

UNIVERSITY PRESS OF AMERICA,® INC.
Lanham · Boulder · New York · Toronto · Plymouth, UK

Copyright © 2016 by
University Press of America,® Inc.
4501 Forbes Boulevard
Suite 200
Lanham, Maryland 20706
UPA Acquisitions Department (301) 459-3366

Unit A, Whitacre Mews, 26-34 Stannary Street,
London SE11 4AB, United Kingdom

Library of Congress Control Number: 2015952399
ISBN: 978-0-7618-6689-3 (paperback : alk. paper)
eISBN: 978-0-7618-6690-9

The paper used in this publication meets the minimum
requirements of American National Standard for Information
Sciences—Permanence of Paper for Printed Library Materials,
ANSI Z39.48-1992

Contents

Contents

Acknowledgments

I would like to thank Joanne Schlub and Pauline Blair for their editing work, and Moses Francisco for securing inter-library book loans for me. I again thank Madeline Horinouchi for the use of her speeches. John Macagba deserves the credit for convincing me to enroll in those first, and in retrospect, fateful, speech courses with Bob Bailey, a wonderful, humanistic teacher.

CHAPTER ONE

The Basics of Human Communication

Definition, Purposes, and Conceptualization

DEFINITION

People form varying ideas when they see or hear the word *communication* used. They may think of the communication conveyed by traditional media such as television or radio, or even through the newer medium of the Internet. They may read a journalist's printed communication text in a morning newspaper or online magazine about some topic of information, which could include an interview or a portion of a speech delivered by someone. They may even think about the communication they had with someone earlier in the day, when they said "Hi" to someone or a person asked them what they were going to do that evening. In all of the contexts above, there is a transmission of messages. Information is conveyed. Some communication has occurred. This book will focus on what is termed *human communication*, which has some distinction with media and mass communication technology.

Human communication is an attempt by people to create meaning in and for their experience, circumstance, or larger environment, both for themselves and for others. Effort is required since people have to make some response to the available stimuli in order to gain meaning from the stimuli. To accomplish this, we must differentiate among the features of the stimuli (which could be a verbal message). The effort encompasses a process since it elicits a series of mental actions which occur over time, albeit a relatively instantaneous one in normal circumstances given how quickly our brain processes information. The meaning of effort could include what occurs during personal reflection as well as interaction with other people. Overall, the goal and essence of human communication is for people to share meaning. Two or more people understanding the communicated message create a shared meaning within and between themselves for that message.

We create our meaning through our use of symbols (language being our primary system of symbols), so we might say that our human communication results from symbolic interaction.

Notice that communication is not the sending and receiving of meaning between people. We state a word or use a gesture, symbolizing a meaning that we have in our mind, that someone can hear or observe, and he or she, in turn, interprets the symbols that we have said or gestured. We are not in someone else's mind making up the meaning of our communication for them. They do it. Thus, as Berlo noted long ago, "Communication does not consist of the transmission of meaning. Meanings are not transmittable, nor transferable. Only messages are transmittable and meanings are not in the message, they are in the message-users."[1]

If communication is the sending and receiving of messages that exist as stimuli for us and are cognitively interpreted by us as representations of some phenomena, then if people do not have a response to a message, either through their ignoring it or being unaware of the message stimulus, then there is no communication.[2] Meanings have to be shared.

PURPOSES OF COMMUNICATION

People spend a great deal of their waking hours communicating. People also believe that through a thorough examination of their human communication behavior, they can improve that behavior. It is not an overstatement to claim that effective communication benefits an individual in every aspect of his or her life in which they apply that skill. Furthermore, the people who interact with that effective communicator also benefit.

1. *Predict and Control Our Environment.* Barnlund and Verderber suggest that we communicate to influence people in our environment, and we can benefit from more accurate predictions about the influence we expect to attain.[3] This is not primarily about being self-centered at the expense of other people. We cannot fault someone for simply attempting to satisfy their needs. The accuracy of our predictions is problematic, of course, since all aspects of human behavior are not known. Still, people find that they can, with increased knowledge and practice, succeed in their human relationships and in their professional jobs.[4] Despite acknowledged lapses, people feel confident about their ability to anticipate communication outcomes, and they can increase the likelihood of those outcomes.

2. *Self Knowledge.* We gain a sense of who we are through our communication with others. Mead suggests that we become aware of ourselves through

our interaction with others.[5] Personal introspection about the messages others give us about their view of us can provide us some insight into ourselves. This does not mean that others' perceptions of us should be accepted without examination. If there is personal comfort in those conclusions, fine. We probably have not liked everything we have done in our lives nor every aspect of how we regularly communicate, but people can and do make adjustments and realize their humanness. Knowing who you are allows you to better predict what you are likely to do in a variety of situations, and gain some comfort in that knowledge.

3. *Establish Relationships With Others.* As social beings, nearly everyone feels a need to interact with others. People spend a great deal of time communicating with friends and loved ones just to satisfy their emotional needs, particularly the desires to be loved and liked.[6] Other social needs we attempt to fulfill through our communication with others include: pleasure, inclusion, escape, relaxation, and control.[7]

4. *Everyday Needs.* We communicate in part with others to satisfy our on-going physical and safety requirements. We need our health, which depends on (among others) sufficient food, water, shelter, and sleep. We speak with others to learn about safety hazards that can endanger our lives, property, and freedoms, or simply to share information about everyday topics that arise. Overall, we use joint and group problem solving and decision making to seek solutions for the numerous everyday concerns we face, and other people seek such help from us.[8]

CONCEPTUALIZATION OF HUMAN COMMUNICATION

Human communication is commonly thought of as a *transaction* so the basic conception of this perspective is termed the *transactional model* of communication.[9]

A transaction in its basic application to communication means that two or more people involved in a personal interaction affect each other. Barnlund stresses that there is a reciprocal relationship (an interdependence) among the elements as they interact in a "… dynamic, continuous, [and] circular" process.[10] There exist simultaneous responses between the communicators and within each of them. While communication is occurring between two (or more) people, each person's message influences the meaning that both (or all) of them create within themselves. For this reason, Pearson and Nelson describe this as co-creation of meaning.[11]

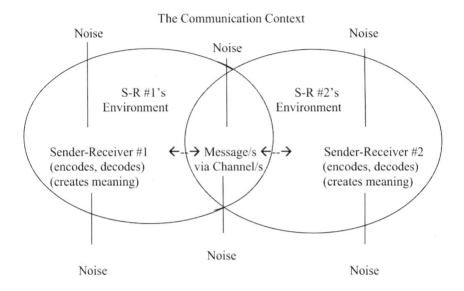

FIGURE 1.1

   While communication is a complex, non-linear process, for the nature of this text the visual figure at the top of the next page will suffice to provide a basic view of the elements included in the Transactional Model of Communication. A discussion of each element follows. Bear in mind that any analysis of someone's communication with another person or a group would have to consider each of these parts, although one or a few of them may prove to provide more insight and/or a basis for improvement in the event of a communication problem.

   1. *Sender-Receiver.* All people involved in a given communication act are both senders of messages and receivers of messages. One person may be orally and nonverbally communicating at a given moment with one or more people in his/her presence, but the other individuals are at least providing nonverbal communication. During a subsequent moment, a person who had been previously listening and responding nonverbally may suddenly and vocally say something (at which point the earlier speaker may respond as a nonverbal sender of messages). In short, we are all senders and receivers in a communication act.
   The term *sender* is being used here for conventional understanding and as a reflection of common communication interaction. It is recognized that the

term *source* can also be used since it takes into account the idea that not all messages are necessarily sent but are available to be perceived or picked up on by another person (discussed further below).

2. *Message/s.* According to Pearson and Nelson, "The message is the verbal and nonverbal form of the ... thought, or feeling that one person (the source) ... communicate[s] to another person or group of people (the receivers)."[12] This suggests that the message might be thought of as the content of discussion that provides a focus for what the communicators want to emphasize. Stated in a more limited sense, the message is the substance suggested by words or other means which the communication source sends to the receiver. Based on this idea, one person may say to another, "Did you get my message?" or "I got your message."

Given that people are not fully aware of all of their own thoughts and feelings at a given moment and that they may even be unaware of messages they are creating, we cannot limit as messages those that are "intended" or simply "sent" to the receiver/s. Messages may be either intentional or unintentional. Chapter Three (Perception) will add further insight to this.

In an interaction between two people, there is a constant and simultaneous flow of messages in each direction. Some of the messages sent will be in direct response to messages received so they are labeled *feedback*, or responses by one person to the other person's communicated messages. This feedback can be a combination of verbal words and a set of nonverbal responses (e.g., tone of voice, facial expression, or posture) or simply a nonverbal message. People often use the modifiers *positive* or *negative* in conjunction with *feedback*. These simply mean that someone likes or does not like a response given, or that the response is complementary or uncomplimentary about the person or phenomenon under discussion.

In review of the previous discussion (p.1-2), any message provided does not convey meaning but provides an opportunity for the receiver of the message to create meaning in response to the stimuli of the message.

3. *Encode, Decode.* When and while we communicate, one or more parts of our brain are responding to the stimuli it receives.[13] This response is typically created by a combination of both emotional (reflexive) and logical (reflective) impulses, one of which may be stronger at a given time. It may be more apt to say that the response *is* one and the same as the co-impulses being referred to. Creating a code or message for conveying the meaning of this mental response is termed *encoding*. In a sense, we translate our mental impulses and put them into some symbolic, external message form (such as a word or a nonverbal gesture) that others can respond to. For example, we see a good friend get out of a nearby car. An impulse inside our brain has been created.

We may instantly smile and feel good about seeing our friend. Assuming our friend sees us and our smile (the smile being a code, perhaps for we like him and are happy to see him), he is going to have a mental impulse in response to that coded message. He will translate it, called *decoding*, giving meaning to his own mental impulse (reaction) that might be translated as: "My friend sees me and is smiling at me, he (or she) is happy to see me." Notice that what starts out as a mental impulse for the one friend ends up as a mental impulse for the other friend, and we have used a symbolic code (such as a smile) to interact and co-create meaning for that event. This is an example of what Adler and Rodman describe as *symbolic interaction* (the symbols, or codes, are the means by which we interact).[14]

The above encoding and decoding example is at least a little simplified. When we have a mental reaction to some stimuli in our environment, perhaps to some smell we perceive emanating from the person standing next to us, we also decode, or translate our own impulses that we put into a message. We react to (translate) our codes even as another person next to us translates our codes (they may see our facial scowl and raised nose). As Barnlund suggests, "[e]ncoding and decoding ... may be combined in a single person [or] may occur simultaneously in speakers and listeners ...."[15] The coded message being decoded is the translation, the meaning derived from the perceived code. Since communication is a process, our decoding influences the form of the subsequent code (message), and so on.

Thus, we are all continually encoding and decoding most of what we encode. We translate and give meaning to our own coded messages. The descriptor *most* is used since we do have impulses for which we recognize an extant meaning, without putting those impulses into symbolic form, as in thinking an actual word. Of course, we decode the messages, or codes we perceive that others create (not that we perceive more than a fraction of them).

Sometimes we notice that our encoding is not accurate. Many people have had the experience of telling someone else their idea or feeling about something, then, upon hearing the second person's description or evaluation of that same thing, say, "That's what I meant." While this could be a falsification, most, if not everyone, have had this legitimate experience. It is fortunate that by others' communication we can become clear about our own ideas.

4. *Meaning.* Verderber suggests that meaning is "[t]he pure ideas and feelings that exist in a person's mind ...."[16] According to Zweig, we have both emotional (reflexive) and analytical (reflective, "thinking") circuits in our brain. Emotional processing occurs mostly in the basal ganglia and the limbic areas while our cognitive "thinking" operations occur in the cerebral cortex, which is itself "... part of the emotional system ...."[17] Meaning, in its raw

form, is the electro-chemical response of one or both of these and other areas of the brain responding in tandem. These responses may exist at or below our level of consciousness and they can lead to a physiological response and/or mental thought. Our meaning may simply be a fear response or the conscious thought "this is good."

Additional explanations of meaning have been provided in the earlier definition of communication and the encoding/decoding sections. Further discussion will occur in Chapter Three relating to the perception process.

5. *Channel/s.* The channels of communication are the routes by which message a travels from one communicator to another. We communicate our messages through our senses. Person to person communication commonly emphasizes our use of sight and hearing. People in intimate relationships increase their use of touch and smell.

The question raised about communication channels is, which sense or senses is predicted to be most effective in which situation? Sometimes people think a defense-arousing statement is best made by avoiding the face-to-face visual channel and only using the oral channel by calling the person on the phone. Today people may omit the phone and use the visual, but not face-to-face, printed form of an e-mail or text message channel to communicate something. People know that some things are either easier said or best conveyed via one channel or another.

6. *Environment.* Communication occurs in a physical context that influences both our topics of conversation and how we speak about them. These settings can vary from sitting in a church pew listening to a sermon to reporting on a business issue to a boss while walking down a hallway to standing next to someone in line at the bank, and so on. We know that some topics and word use are appropriate in some settings but not in others. The status relationships between the communicators and the existing social norms influence the interaction, as do cultural rules. These determine who speaks first, how respect is conveyed, to what extent individuality or collectivity is emphasized, and so on. Time is also an element in the environment, including the influence the time of the day has on what is or is not said as well as the timing of a comment in an ongoing interaction. Communicators also bring their personal experiences and communication skills to the interaction.

All of the above elements significantly influence the communication that occurs and the meaning that each participant generates from that interaction. The key question about the communicators' environments is. To what extent do they overlap? The more they overlap, the easier the communication becomes and the more likely the communicators will understand each other.

The less the environments overlap, the increased likelihood the communicators will experience misunderstandings and conflicts.

7. *Noise*. Noise is anything that reduces the clarity of a message or impedes a person from receiving a clear message. A clear message received is one that has what might be termed high fidelity, an accurate reproduction of the original. According to Berlo, "In analyzing communication, we are interested in determining what increases or reduces the fidelity of the process."[18]

Noise can be external, physical noise, such as the sound of a lawnmower in the background that prevents us from hearing everything that someone says or even the physical distraction of seeing a rainbow that momentarily diverts out attention from someone speaking to us. It can be internal, physiological noise, such as the physical pain of a headache or even an earache that overrides our reception of someone else's words. Other internal noise can be psychological, as when someone is in a bad mood and does not pay enough attention to what someone else says to them. Noise can also be semantic in nature when the listener is not familiar with the vocabulary of the speaker. An extreme example of this is when the other person is speaking a foreign language unknown to the listener. This is the stimulus for the phrase, "That's Greek to me." Verderber concludes that "[m]uch of our success as communicators depends on how we cope with external, internal, and semantic noises, each of which can create blocks in the sensory channels and interfere with the decoding process."[19]

CONCLUSION

Human communication has been defined as the attempt by people to create meaning within others and within themselves for their personal and shared experience. Communication is described as transactional in nature since the messages in the communication interaction are shared, as is the meaning created from the individual messages. We influence each other in the interaction. It was suggested that meanings are not in messages (such as words) but in the message users. Therefore, in order to gain insight into and overlap with the meaning of messages, we have to know something about the person with whom we are interacting in addition to how they use their messages. The larger purpose of communication is to use our knowledge about life and communication as well as our communication skills to more accurately predict and significantly influence what is likely to occur on a moment-to-moment basis in our interactions with others. The Transactional Model of Communication and its elements were diagrammed and explained. Communication understanding requires that each part of the process, as well as their combined interaction, be examined.

CHAPTER 1 HOMEWORK
(as assigned by your instructor)

1. Give one written example of a message (write it out) someone provided for you that you interpreted differently than did the sender of that message.

2. Give one example of an accurate prediction you made of someone's expected communication response to a message you provided them. Provide the prediction and the messages.

3. Give one example of a specific noise that reduced the quality or completeness of the message content (words) you received from someone.
   a. Describe the noise occurring.
   b. Write down the words—the message—you thought you heard.
   c. Describe what you said and/or did thereafter, based up the meaning you formed.
   d. Briefly explain the problem/s that occurred as a result of what you said or did.
   e. What was the complete message (words) you missed receiving as a result of the noise?

REFERENCES

1. D. Berlo, *The Process of Communication* (New York: Holt, Rinehart and Winston, 1960), p. 175.
2. D. Barnlund, *Interpersonal Communication: Survey and Studies* (Boston: Houghton Mifflin Company, 1968).
3. Ibid; R. Verderber, *Communicate!* (7th ed.) (Belmont, CA: Wadsworth Publishing Company, 1993).
4. J. Pearson and P. Nelson, *An Introduction to Human Communication* (8th ed.) (Boston: The McGraw-Hill Company, Inc., 2000).
5. D. Miller, *George Herbert Mead: Self, Language and the World* (Chicago: The University of Chicago Press, 1978).
6. J. DeVito, *Human Communication: The Basic Course* (10th ed.) (Boston: Pearson Education, Inc., 2006).
7. R. Adler and G. Rodman, *Understanding Human Communication* (10th ed.) (New York: Oxford University Press, 2009).

8. DeVito, op cit.
9. Barnlund, op cit.
10. Barnlund, op cit., p. 23.
11. Pearson and Nelson, op cit.
12. Ibid.
13. J. Zwieg, *Your Money and Your Brain* (New York: Simon & Schuster, 2007).
14. Adler and Rodman, op cit.
15. Barnlund, op cit., p. 26.
16. Verderber, op cit., p. 8.
17. Zwieg, op cit., p. 14.
18. Berlo, op cit., p. 40.
19. Verderber, op cit., p. 9.

CHAPTER TWO

Principles, Misconceptions, Competence, and Contexts

PRINCIPLES

Communication between people is significantly influenced by certain principles. Some of these have already been referred to or discussed in some form in Chapter One. The list here is introductory, rather than comprehensive.

1. *Communication is a Transactional Process.* It is the sharing of messages between two or more individuals that are both or all affected by the interaction. In a simplistic way, think of the transaction that occurs when you buy something from a store. You ask for or put the merchandise you want to purchase on the counter. You see or are told the price; you give the clerk the money, and the clerk hands the item back to your with any change that is due. There is an ongoing, give and take between the two of you. Communication is an interaction over time, of senders and receivers sharing messages and creating meaning. It is a process, changing as people and their environment change. People influence both each other and themselves as they communicate. Communication elements (The Communication Context, Chapter One) are interdependent—a change in one element leads to changes in others. Human interaction can be understood as a system[1] and is thus circular in nature.[2] One change (one message) in one part of they system affects the rest of the system.

2. *Communication is Self-Reflective.* As explained in Chapter One, in the initial phase of communication, we have a mental impulse or reaction to some stimuli or message in our awareness, which we then encode (translate). This provides some meaning for us. We may then send our response to this meaning to the person with whom we are communicating. In addition, we

have an internal response to our own message even as we send it and our subsequent messages may be altered by that reflection. We know of occasions when we have changed the direction of a point of view we were expressing (our thought stream) due to our evaluation of it even as we expressed it, let alone the reaction we have to listener's reaction to that point of view. We form an image of our message meaning and react to that meaning even as the receiver does. Levinson labels this a *self-reflexive* relationship.[3] As we are aware of our message sent and our perceived interpretation of the receiver's response, we compare our reaction (or second meaning) with the initial encoded meaning; and this, in turn, influences what we communicate next (the messages-in-process).

In other words, the message we send to someone else comes instantaneously right back to us even as we speak (technically, it never leaves us), a full circle from our brain to our mouth (for oral messages) then back to our brain via our hearing and other senses, to check for continuity (in an electrical sense), consistency, logic, and even affirmation. It is amazing to consider that our brain can perform at least four cognitive manipulations nearly simultaneously: our brain sends a message, we evaluate that message as we send it, we also evaluate the sender's response to that message as we send it, and we sometimes change the message about to be sent to fit what we think will fit the altered meaning we have of the communication moment. This reveals the self-reflective nature. Both our initial impulse meaning and our interpreted meaning about both our and our listener's responses influence subsequent messages that come out orally and/or through nonverbal communication. It is as if there is a tape recorder or mirror right in front of our face as we communicate, projecting our messages right back to us.

3. *Communication is Purposeful.* We have an intention when we communicate. We communicate to create and share meaning. We communicate to influence other's creation of meaning (the controlling of our environment). Communication is deliberative whether our interaction with someone is either important or unimportant to us. We may be aware or unaware of our purposes. We will not always know why we made a certain comment or made a particular facial expression but someone analyzing our communication can question our intention.[4]

4. *Communication is Inevitable.* Since our behavior provides messages, too, there is always behavior to examine, both our own and others', so we cannot *not* communicate. Whether we are active or inactive, there is a message with meaning value. Our behavior influences the meanings that other people form about us, who in turn cannot avoid responding to our behavior.[5] Thus,

communication can be intentional or unintentional. Someone sees us from afar gesturing avidly to another person or running to a car in the far part of a parking lot and there is an available message about us. There is a meaning response in their mind and we do not even know it.

5. *Communication is Irreversible* and *Unrepeatable*. As the saying goes, you cannot un-ring the bell. You cannot "take it back." The participants in the interaction have created a meaning for the individual message. There is no de-messaging the brain (outside a possible drug application, physical injury, Alzheimer's Disease, etc.). A communication receiver cannot just wipe the thought away. Many times people say things when they are upset and/or in a conflict with someone else that they later wish they had not said. The speaker may apologize but that does not clear the original meaning from the receiver's brain.

Once you or someone else has provided a message 'out there' for others to perceive and they have now created a meaning for that message, any attempt to restate that message, to "say it again," will lead to the creation of a different meaning for that second message even if the verbal content of both messages is identical. The receiver of the first message has already created and stored a distinct meaning for the first message. It is for this reason that you will not get the same reaction from your listeners when you try to retell a joke that you did not state correctly or your listeners did not "get." In most cases, the second telling will not get the listener response anticipated. Given the constant change in ourselves and others from moment to moment, our frame of mind, the dynamics of our relationships, and the contexts we are in, we cannot expect that the meanings we may intend to convey through our messages will be repeated.

6. *Communication is a Package of Signals*. At any one moment in an interaction between two or more people, multiple messages from one communication sender combine to provide the basis of a larger meaning for the receiver. The verbal content (words) and the nonverbal reactions need to be analyzed as a whole before a more complete and accurate evaluation of the meaning can be determined by the receiver of the communication. In some situations there may simply be a variety of nonverbal messages that need to be examined as a whole for the communication receiver to make sense of the unit of communication. Knowing that we cannot not communicate, the nonverbal package of messages is always going to be available for interpretation, and a variety of messages are more difficult to interpret than a singular one.. For example, there may be a combination of standing posture, distance between communicators, and length of eye contact that implies that Communicator

A is happy (or sad). An examination of just one of these individual messages may have been insufficient for the Communicator B to be sure of the Communicator A's thoughts, feelings, or intensity of those feelings.

Occasionally, people will notice that the meanings they infer from someone else's messages do not fit together as a consistent whole. On these occasions, there is a contradiction between one or more content and/or nonverbal messages. A co-worker could greet you in the morning at work with a "How are you?" but not smile and walk right passed you. You might ask someone to go to lunch and they could respond with a demure, head down, quiet voice, "No thank you." These are examples of the *mixed message*. There are multiple meanings and we may be unsure which one to believe. In the first example, our co-worker does not seem happy to see us despite the verbal content greeting. What primary meaning should we, the listener form? In the second example, the "no" does not seem firm. Which overall meaning should we, the asking person, form? In fact, the person responding "no" seems to be experiencing mixed feelings, which is why they are communicating a mixed message.

The overall point of communication being a package of signals is that we need to be mindful of the combinations of messages we receive from others so as to increase our potential accuracy of interpretation, and remind ourselves to seek additional messages to confirm our conclusion.

7. *Communication Requires a Process of Adjustment.* Mutual understanding can be achieved through communication if the communicators use the same verbal and nonverbal system of signals.[6] This is apparent, for example, when you hear someone refer to someone else as a "friend", yet this "friend" did not share their lunch with the speaker or loan the speaker one dollar. While you categorize such actions as unfriendly, you recognize that the speaker does not. You adjust your meaning of "friend" for the speaker according to the speaker's use, even if you do not agree with the speaker's application. We often use identical messages but do not have identical meanings for these. Thus, people invariably have to make some effort to discover what others seem to imply by their messages.

8. *Communication is Relational.* As noted in Chapter One, one of the purposes of communication is to establish relationships with other people. Thus, much of the communication in our interactions with others is focused on and conveys messages about how we view those other people. According to Watzlawick, our communication illustrates and defines our individual relationships.[7] The communication pattern occurring between two people reflects their relationship at that interaction moment. Our interaction patterns are said to be either *symmetrical* or *complementary*.

A *symmetrical* pattern reveals that each communicator perceives that the relationship status between the two of them is equal, so they speak as equals to each other. There is a matching style of communication. Differences are minimized. Two friends may both say "please" and "thank you" when requesting and receiving something. They both may take turns listening to the other person speak. They both may even express anger to the other one after the other person has been angry with them. On the other hand, what is often thought of as a symmetrical relationship between husband and wife can erupt in conflict when the one of them challenges the other one's presumed authority.[8]

A *complementary* communication pattern between two people reveals that they both accept the idea that one of them will have more say and power over how they will interact together. They speak to each other as non-equals. Differences are maximized. This is common in the relationships between parents and their children, between employers and their employees, and between military officers and enlisted personnel. One person may command and the other may respond passively and carry out the command, as between a boss and an employee. We would not be surprised to hear a sports coach berate the playing ability or motivation of one of his or her players. One person may be providing more information and the other one may be emphasizing listening, as between a teacher and student. Person A may have more to say and be able to do more about a certain subject so Person B may accept that. On another occasion and subject, Person B may be allowed the greater influence

While there is a content or literal message in the expressions of both communication patterns (a co-worker may say, "Let's go get a soda") both communicators also use that same communication to reinforce what they believe is or even should be the state of the relationship (the co-worker appears to think of the other co-worker as an equal). We may not disagree about the meaning of the content message or even the legitimacy for the other person to say it to us (e.g., the boss tells us in a commanding tone of voice to mop the floor) but we may not like the relationship implied by the other person's communication. For example, we may not like the boss reminding us that he is the boss and we are not, especially if we think we are smarter or better in some way than is the boss.

In summary, communication tells us something about the relationships between people. One type of relationships is not necessarily better or worse than the other ones. The people involved and even observers can evaluate the effectiveness and appropriateness of the existing interaction pattern. The communicators can be asked if they are fully aware of and comfortable with their relationship roles. If they desire to change their relationships within the confines of an established role (e.g. supervisor-employee), they can do so with their communication (e.g., get the boss to communicate more respect to them).

MISCONCEPTIONS

All textbooks attempt to increase the reader's learning of the subject matter. In discussing the subject matter, oversights and misconceptions of the subject may be implied or revealed. It is hoped that this book is no different. Aside from misconceptions that naturally arise in the topic areas discussed in each chapter, the following list is provided as more overarching in nature.

  1. *Communication will Solve (all of) our Problems,* and its corollary, *The More Communication, the Better*. While experience has shown that there is certainly a great deal of support for this, and this is the prime reason that people study communication, it is not this simple. Many interacting people have differing beliefs, values, and/or desires that no amount or quality of communication has resolved. For example, given the range of news accounts and books written since the 9/11 attack on the United States, it is apparent that there are numerous commandments and ideas in the *Koran* of the Muslim faith that are antithetical to those in the *Bible* of the Christian faith, and vice versa. While nations and people have sometimes agreed to disagree, not everyone leaves it at that. Whether someone agrees with it or not, since 1948 there have been many Muslims in the Middle East who have publicly said that Israel should not exist as a country, and countries there have made numerous physical efforts to bring about Israel's demise. No amount of talking before the separate wars changed that, nor has changed that up to the moment (yet we can hope). In what is western Europe, there has been talk and even some intermarriage between peoples and rulers for thousands of years, and there has been fighting between them for thousands of years (the last ended in 1945). There was talk between the governments of Germany, France, England, and others during the 1920's and 1930's but that did not stop Germany from attacking France, England, and the U.S.S.R. in what became World War II. America's talking did not stop the U.S.S.R.'s expansion into Eastern Europe and elsewhere following WW II. Many parents know of times when no amount or quality of communication has gotten their children to do or not do something. Friendly talk to the schoolyard bully in elementary school did not always get him to stop his bullying, but sometimes the threat of or actual physical force did. This discussion is not meant to favor physical violence as a solution, just to point out that communication does not solve everything. More is certainly not better if the communication is simply more of the same and more of the defensive-arousing type.

  It is easy for "Monday-morning quarterbacks" to expound, *after the fact* on what did occur or what should have occurred in the communication between two or more people or groups of people. Real people have real differences and it is not a statement in favor of divorce to say so. However, there is enough casual information about conflicts that reveals that some communicators reach an impasse about one or more issues important to each of them despite the best intentions and quality of communication from themselves and from professionals involved.

2. *Communication Can Break Down.* This idea makes some sense since most people have experienced a misunderstanding due to ineffective communication. Still, people frequently use this explanation when they actually mean that the other communicator does not agree or accept their point of view (presumably without a good reason). Yet those citing this misconception construe the idea that if only one or both people had communicated better there would have been a better ending to the interaction (quite possibly the one that suited the speaker using this expression). Communication itself does not "break down" but people at varying times are more and less effective in using it. The misconception also overlooks the communication principle that since we cannot not communicate, there is no ending to the communication.

Further, people often knowingly act contrary to the communication given. There was no "communication breakdown" in the movie *Cool Hand Luke* when a prisoner escaped from the prison after being told in advance not to. Once caught and returned to the prison, the warden said something to the effect of, "What we have here is a failure to communicate." This implied that failure meant misunderstanding. There was no misunderstanding. The prisoner knew full well that he was not supposed to escape and would be punished if caught escaping. That did not stop him from escaping (and getting caught) again.

3. *Communication is a Natural Ability.* Almost every person is born with the physical apparatus to speak and hear so it seems everyone naturally does so. This misconception oversimplifies the idea that speaking (the production of oral sounds, such as words) is the same as communication. It could be, but as Chapter One explained, human communication is the creation and sharing of meaning. If someone's speaking in a recognizable language does not result in shared understanding (meaning), there has been no communication. There has simply been *noise*.

Even among speakers of the same language, everyone is a different person with his or her own unique communication persona that requires our ongoing learning about and adapting to as we continue to interact with different people over a lifetime.

Fortunately, people can and do improve their communication skills. People can even become so skilled that observers may conclude the speakers seem to have natural communication ability without the observers realizing that communicators worked long and hard to make their communication effective. The following section of this chapter provides a short list of characteristics that have been found to be effective for communicators. Other, context-specific skills are referred to in the individual chapters.

COMMUNICATOR COMPETENCE

1. *Accurately Monitor Your Own Communication.* This means being aware of how you are communicating so you can use that information to guide how you communicate, both in the moment and in the future. As Adler and Rodman explain, it requires that you objectively observe and evaluate the effectiveness of your own communication as you communicate.[9] Knowing how you are communicating provides you with an option to change that communication if you so desire.

Adler and Rodman found other benefits of being a high self-monitor: increased accuracy in evaluating the communication partner's emotions, expanded memory of what occurred in the interaction (which aids future interaction), and added assertiveness as a communicator.[10]

2. *Gain the Perspective of the Other Communicator.* We need to have an idea about the other person and how they are likely to respond to us to even begin to communicate with them. This becomes more obvious when we are in a foreign country and do not know the culture or speak the language. To communicate, we typically (and largely unconsciously) put ourselves in their position and communicate to that person in terms of what we guess to be their sense of self, in combination with their sense of us. We infer what the other person's attitude is toward us and then speak to them according to that conclusion.[11] If we put ourselves in our boss's position at work and conclude from his or her interaction with us that he or she views us as an equal, we will speak to the boss as if we were equal. If we are wrong, our boss may become upset with us, illustratings the *reciprocal nature* of communication.[12]

Overall, we can increase our communication effectiveness with others the more we accurately gauge and respond to their view of us and to the communication situation we are in. This will increase the likelihood that we will create some shared meaning for the moment (e.g., "I sense from your anger that you think I did not work hard enough to get the job done. Still, I think that if you actually saw how quickly I did work, you would reach a different conclusion.").

3. *Adjust Communication to Fit the Situation.* Change the message, channel, and/or environment to fit the interaction circumstance and the other person, to increase the likelihood that your desired outcome is achieved. It may even include changing the communication source—yourself, which means having someone else deliver your message. There is no concrete list that fits everyone under similar circumstances. Still, people have to be flexible in their interactions with others. For example, on arriving at work you see your friend appear worried so you might ask what is wrong and possibly give him or her a sympathetic sigh. On leaving work, your friend may sport a smile so you smile in return. When our boss is mad we tend to be quieter around him or her. In general, the more flexible we are, the more we can fit into the changing communication interactions around us.

4. *Effectively Perform the Communication Skills.* Be able to put them into practice. Nearly every chapter provides directions and exercises for learning and employing a communication skill. Expect that practice will be necessary and mistakes will be made. People can always find something in communication to improve upon, so you should expect a lifetime of learning and improving. A list of skills is provided at the end of this chapter.

COMMUNICATION CONTEXTS

As the communication model in Chapter One indicated, human communication occurs in a context. The three major contexts or settings addressed in this book are: interpersonal communication, group communication, and public speaking.

1. *Interpersonal Communication.* Interpersonal communication normally refers to the messages occurring between two people but it can include the personal communication between three or more people in a small group. For our discussion, this term focuses on the communication interaction between two people. Most of our daily conversations take place in one-on-one situations with other individuals. We tend to share intimate communication with those we have a close relationship with and are less intimate with those who are strangers or acquaintances. We may speak with a family member at breakfast, use the phone to call a friend before lunch, be told by our boss to help a customer at work, or read a bedtime story to our child at night.

The primary goal of interpersonal communication is to establish and continually improve person-to-person relationships with people. Other goals (Chapter 1) include the ability to predict and control our environment. The topic areas and/or skills that especially relate to interpersonal communication include self-disclosure, perception, listening, interpreting verbal and nonverbal messages, and conflict resolution.

It also needs to be noted that *intra*personal communication, which refers to the dialogue people have within themselves—their thinking, reflection, talking silently or even out loud to themselves—creates the basis for how people perceive both themselves and the communication interactions in which they find themselves. Creating meaning is initially an intra-personal affair that can be transformed into an interpersonal process to create and share meaning with others.

2. *Group Communication.* A small group is one comprised of three to fifteen individuals who meet to achieve some common goal in a setting that allows everyone to interact with everyone else. In this circumstance, the communication purpose is to solve a problem or reach a decision about some issue. Group members often share information among themselves so there tends to be some intimate communication mixed in with formal, business-style talk. Such groups include: families, sports teams, a small town mayor's office, a group of students working on a school project, small businesses, and so on. Organizations are a much larger grouping of individuals, comprised of many small groups of people and can reach into the millions of members (like the U.S. military). Most of the organizations we belong to are work-related, religious, or social ones. Leadership communication, task and other role-related communication, communication intended to get us to conform, decision making, and group structure variables are distinct from the discussion of interpersonal communication (although interpersonal interaction is recognized). Cultural groups are even larger and typically represent the people of specific countries. Communication between people from different cultures is fraught with difficulties.

3. *Public Communication.* This often means a single person or a small group of individual people delivering typically formal messages to an immediate audience, with the additional possibility of the speeches being relayed to other people via television, radio, or the Internet. Public Debates, forums, or colloquiums may also provide for multiple speakers and points of view on a given topic. Religious sermons, given all of our places of worship and their weekly or bi-weekly meetings, may be our most prolific type of public speech. The public speaking purposes are to inform, persuade, or create good will. There is a high

degree of formality during this speech, although an informal question/answer period may follow. The speaker may provide an intimate examination of some aspect of his life and/or ideas. While audience members in attendance are limited in their oral interaction with the public speaker, they do provide nonverbal messages during the speech so the speaker can gain an idea about their evaluation of it. Audiences attend such events expecting to primarily experience the role of listener. Public speeches play a vital role in our communities and our nation in spreading a whole range of information about people, products, services, and ideas that affect us. This information can become the source of change, as we then decide to do or not do something in our personal, social, or public life.

CONCLUSION

This chapter provided an explanation of some of the commonly recognized communication principles and misconceptions, an overview of communicator competence, and a description of the over-arching communication contexts that will define the limits of human communication examined in this book. Few implications of these concepts were raised here since there will be more detail as each topic area is covered in the following chapters.

CHAPTER 2 HOMEWORK

1.a. Write about one communication interaction (incident) which recently occurred between you and someone else. Include all the dialogue and other pieces of information you can remember. For example, while walking across campus, let us assume that you saw your friend Bill approaching you. Maybe you stopped about three feet from him, smiled, and said "Hi Bill. Nice to see you. Where are you headed?" [and so on] Write down your communication interaction, continuing the description of what transpired between the two of you.

   b. Which principle (or principles) of communication listed at the beginning of this chapter is being illustrated by this interaction you just described, and explain how this (or these) principle fits the situation.

2. Provide 1 example you can find in a book, movie, play, or even your daily life that illustrates just one of the communication misconceptions noted in this chapter. List the misconception and briefly explain how your example portrays the misconception.

COMMUNICATION SKILLS

Accurately monitor personal communication.

Grasp the point of view of the other communicator/s.

Adjust personal communication to fit the situation.

Provide accurate and sufficient feedback.

Limit subjectivity and overgeneralization during the perception process.

Verify your perceptions with the other communicators: ask questions, ask for clarifying information, describe and explain your perception/s to the other communicators, withhold conclusions for a reasonable time.

Carefully observe people's interactions.

Listen carefully to what others say; focus attention on them and their communication; position yourself to listen effortlessly.

Be silent when the other person needs to formulate his/her thoughts, become aware of their body movements; identify emotions conveyed on people's faces in their voices

Do not interrupt; allow the other person to complete their speaking before responding.

Eliminate barriers to effective listening (distractions, noise, other)

Perform effective active listening: paraphrase the content, describe the conveyed feeling; speak in a tentative manner, and ask questions.

Effectively express sympathy and empathy.

As appropriate, listen objectively and critically, and at other times be nonjudgmental.

Disclose personal information when appropriate; refuse to be pressured to disclose.

Actively listen to people's disclosure; keep disclosure confidential; do not hurt someone with his or her disclosure.

Be descriptive, concrete, and specific with verbal messages, avoid bypassing.

Adjust direct vs. indirect language according to expectations and perceived effectiveness.

Avoid racism and sexism in language usage, polarization, and doublespeak.

Practice dating and indexing techniques to minimize stereotypes and other generalities.

Ask people what they mean by the words they use.

Improve personal vocabulary

Recognize a lie when you hear and see one.

Be expressive with your voice to complement your spoken words.

Monitor your nonverbal communication; accurately decode nonverbal messages

Use the appropriate (proxemic) space for the topic, person, relationship, and context.

Use your clothes and artifacts to enhance your communication

Follow the appropriate time that fits the communication situation; be flexible.

Communicate consistency of thoughts; alter thoughts when evidence shows an inconsistency; avoid imposing a consistency which does not exist.

Give constructive praise, blame, and criticism.

Describe what you perceive, then offer an evaluation.

Maintain effective conversations: take turns, signal turn-taking and yielding messages

Minimize the use of disclaimers and excuses.

Communicate honesty and openness.

Recognize communication noise

Recognize communication principles when they occur

Avoid communicating communication misperceptions.

Use implicit personality characteristics that fit the individual.

Be skeptical of first impressions; withhold judgment.

Be mindful of expectations of others; avoid using them to control others.

Do not be fooled by inferences—question the person using them; use them advisedly.

Do not be fooled or controlled by someone's doublespeak; seek the extensional reality.

Identify the three sets of attitudes expressed by nonverbal communication.

Use appropriate (and legal) touch.

Be able to initiate conversations with strangers.

Use communication to maintain relationships (be open, empathetic, positive, expressive, other-oriented).

If relationship withdrawal is sought, use communication that reveals that.

If relationship repair is sought, be able to: apologize, discuss harms, recognize causes, affirm the other person, negotiate solutions.

Vocally defend your friends in their absence.

Use a variety of communication roles in small group interaction that focus on achieving the task and improve member relationships; communicate as a team player, and network with your associates.

Communicate with your group members to solve important problems.

Be an effective group member[24]: center conflict on issues, be critically open-minded, ensure understanding, beware of groupthink.

Use productive communication to ensure effective meetings

Use effective leadership communication and encourage communication patterns that increase the quality of communication between organizational members.

If there is conflict, center communication on the conflict, not on the individual/s

Follow a win-win conflict strategy

When there is a conflict, be actively involved in resolving it. Talk about it, discuss the present circumstances, be spontaneous, use face-enhancing strategies, and be assertive.

Recognize the bases of conflict, discuss those with the participants

Develop a cooperative interaction climate with supportive communication.

Use "I" messages to ensure personal responsibility and avoid blaming other individuals

Use constructive criticism when criticism is appropriate.

Discuss differences in meaning associated with intercultural communication.

Observe intercultural communication differences; determine whether to discuss them.

Be flexible to fit the intercultural communication context.

In intercultural communication, minimize ethnocentrism and stereotyping.

Discuss intercultural communication differences.

Control speech anxiety when delivering public speeches.

Fulfill the basic steps in public speaking preparation (subject selection, etc.).

Use a loud, clear, and varied speaking delivery with a vocabulary fitting the audience.

Create an appropriate thesis statement and supporting ideas, with logical development.

Effectively integrate presentational aids into an organized speech pattern.

Ensure the speech introduction and conclusion fulfill their purposes.

Satisfy your basic speech purpose (inform, persuade, entertain/good will).

Speak to your audience's needs and provide solutions for those needs.

Enhance your speaker credibility.

REFERENCES

1. P. Watzlawick, J. Beavin, and D. Jackson, *Pragmatics of Human Communication* (New York: W.W. Norton & Company, Inc., 1967).
2. D. Barnlund, *Interpersonal Communication: Survey and Studies* (Boston: Houghton Mifflin Company, 1968).
3. M. Levinson, "Your most enchanted listener: GS wisdom from Wendell Johnson," in *ETC: A Review of General Semantics*, 65, 4, (October, 2008): 337-342.
4. D. Berlo, *The Process of Communication* (New York: Holt, Rinehart and Winston, 1960).
5. Watzlawick, op cit.
6. Ibid.
7. Ibid.
8. R. Verderber, *Communicate!* (7th ed.) (Belmont, CA: Wadsworth Publishing Company, 1993).
9. R. Adler and G. Rodman, *Understanding Human Communication* (10th ed.) (New York: Oxford University Press, 2009).
10. Ibid.
11. D. Miller, *George Herbert Mead: Self, Language and the World* (Chicago: The University of Chicago Press, 1978).
12. Barnlund, op cit.

CHAPTER THREE:

Perception and Communication

Chapter One began with a definition of human communication as an effort by people to create meaning in their environment and share that meaning with others. There was also a brief discussion about the formation of meaning in our brain. This chapter will discuss the role of perception as it relates to the process of communication, including its part in the formation of meaning. It is this meaning that we communicate to others in the form of messages.

DEFINITION

Perception is the process of assigning meaning to our sensory information. Through our senses (our channels of communication), we become aware of stimuli or data in our surroundings which become information seeking a meaning response from us. Our brain registers (either consciously or unconsciously) the world of our experience. Perception is the result and the response of our neural activity is our meaning; it is that which is of import to us. In brief, perception is the near-instantaneous process of experiencing meaning from our sensory reactions to stimuli in our environment. Since communication is the sharing of meaning, we need to investigate the creation of meaning occurring in the perception process.

PERCEPTION PROCESS, MEANING, AND COMMUNICATION

Meaning, or that which is thought to be something of significance, does not exist in a vacuum or spring from the brow of Zeus. It requires a substance or

external stimulus which people can use to draw and create internal significance from, something to be aware of. This substance is our physical act of
sensing stimuli and our response to that sensing is our meaning. Meaning is
the result of this perception process, and this meaning may be shared with
others.

There is a difference between *communication* and *perception*. People come
to share (communicate) their meanings with others through their communicated messages *after* they have experienced their initial acts of perception
and meaning formulation. The value and effectiveness of our communication
(shared meaning) is based upon and intertwined with the quality of the perceptions we have of the world around us.

Rather than give a few generalities about the perception process, this text
offers more detailed descriptions of facets of the perception process normally
in the typical survey text. Some of the material in this chapter draws on the
work of people in the field of behavioral economics, particularly the recent
publications by Ariely, Thaler and Sunstein, and Zweig.

Since there are a series of actions that occur, perception has been described
as a process. As Zweig explains, one or more of our senses (sight, smell,
sound, taste, and touch) first receives a signal.[1] This is then relayed to the
more reflexive parts of our brain sometimes referred to as System 1 which are
the first to record our sensory inputs. Zweig states that the reflexive areas "…
help evaluate [the inputs] on a basic scale from "bad" to "good" with blaz-
ing speed. Those evaluations, in turn, are transferred into emotions such as
fear or pleasure, motivating your body to take action."[2] From the instant of
sensing a stimulus to the experiencing of an emotion (e.g., fear), a time lapse
of a tenth of a second or less occurs before we are even consciously aware of
being afraid, elated, and so on. According to Zweig, it is our reflexive system
that both initially and to a much greater degree "… make[s] … sense of the
world around us—and we tap into our analytical system (System 2) only when
intuition can't figure something out."[3] Overall, this explanation implies that
the composition and physical capabilities of our reflexive system are extremely
influential in determining the meaning we come to have for a given phenomenon such as a smile on someone's face, the fragrance of a flower, someone's
presumed character, and so on. Mental strategies that influence this composition are explained later in this chapter.

PERCEPTION IS SUBJECTIVE

In as much as people think they "see" what is "out there" in the world to
be seen, they also notice that their observational reports often differ from
those of other people, such as their parents, friends, and neighbors. How can

that be? You might think that there would always be agreement about what Person A said to Person B or the way Person C smiled at Person D, and much agreement about what it meant (at least among speakers of the same language). Berlo suggests that these differences occur because perception is a subjective action resulting from an individual's own selection of what to perceive and how to interpret that which is perceived.[4] This is not to suggest that our perceptions are necessarily or even mostly inaccurate merely because they are subjective.

1. *People are Selective.* Since there are too many stimuli (bits of information) for any single person to observe at any given moment, no single person can observe all of them. Each person's senses will pick up some of the available stimuli, overlooking other stimuli. This is termed *selective exposure* since what we tend to notice is information that reinforces our beliefs. We are more likely to avail ourselves to points of view, actions, and other stimuli that are consistent with what is meaningful to us. Of that information sensed, some will get more attention from the perceiver, and not all those focused on are likely to be communicated to others. This is called *selective attention.* The perceiver will have had to select some of stimuli to be reported. The predispositions in section "D" to follow will discuss some of the factors behind what is selected and what is not selected. This selection then, is not objective. Rather, the person's reflexive and reflective (logical) cognitions have to discriminate among the available information because not everything can be reported nor is everything of significant importance to the perceiver.

2. *People Interpret What is Selected.* There is ongoing and differing research about how our brain processes information during the creation of meaning. It is much more complicated than we know.[5] Two of the recognized explanations of how we interpret sensory data are that we use schemata to structure such inputs and that we respond to stimuli on the basis of mental rules. Since it is individuals that are doing the interpretation, the interpretation is subjective.

First, it is suggested that we organize perceptions according to one or more of the *schemata* we have stored in our brains. Data, without being put into some recognizable form, would be meaningless. People create and then store in their brains mental representations of their experiences with life's phenomena (objects, people, concepts, and events) and then later refer back to these generic concepts for ordering and interpretation of new information. According to Zweig, "The pursuit of patterns in random data is a fundamental function in our brains—so basic to human nature that our species … might better be named … "man the pattern seeker."[6] We have an innate tendency

to find order whether it exits or not, and through this ordering find meaning in the situation.[7] This gives us a sense of what is going on. For example,
sometimes when we see clouds we do not just see a mass of white and gray
but find ourselves noticing caricatures of animals, scenes from nature, and so
on. We notice forms whether they exist or not.

It does not take much data for us to perceive a pattern emerging. Zweig
suggests that "Two in a row of almost anything ... will make you expect a
third."[8] Given a couple details or occurrences, formulate another person's
character, the shape of someone's body, the size of a house, the near-future
direction of the housing (or stock) market, who has a *hot hand* (so let them
keep shooting the basketball), and so on. There is a common description that
refers to this: connecting the dots. Further, this pattern-making impulse is
not only automatic as noted in the preceding paragraph, but it also operates
without our being aware of or having control over it.

The mental patterns people have stored in their mind give shape to otherwise incomplete information received, providing a meaningful whole.[9] It
is suggested that people tend to fill in what is otherwise incomplete patterns
so that, with the complete pattern, we may find something recognizable
for which we have stored meaning. People have been found to fill-in, for
example, what appear to be triangles not connected at the three corners, or
a circle from what are a series of unconnected straight lines. Many young
school children practice connecting the dots to complete various shapes such
as dogs, cats, pumpkins, and so on. Buckhout reports that people also fill
in incomplete shapes with the passage of time.[10] Subjects initially drew the
incomplete triangle pretty accurately, redrew it one month later with a longer
yet still incomplete third side, and after three months drew a complete triangle. Pearson states that people fill in both verbal and non-verbal information for the incomplete data they hear and see to provide mental closure. For
this complete picture we have some associated meaning that may satisfy our
understanding of the situation.

Based on the totality of our experience, we have created general ideas or
schemata. We do not store all of the information pertaining to each experience we have, just a pattern that is more compact. Having a general idea, we
can gain some meaning from the limited information we may acquire in the
moment about, say, soccer players or high school graduations. We have an
untold amount of these schemata at our disposal to apply to all sorts of situations, people, places, and so on. Notice that schemata give us something to go
on, even if they may be inaccurate representations or the application of them
unrelated to the information at hand.

In sum, schemata are a type of mental shortcut for framing sensory information to provide us meaning. For more accurate applications of stimuli
to schema, we can create more schema having finer distinctions between

themselves that increases the chance that we will find a close match repre-senting the existing stimuli. The next explanation of how people respond to and interpret sensory information is also a mental shortcut.

A second explanation for how we organize and interpret stimuli we perceive is that we apply ingrained *rules* to them. It is thought that our reflexive, emo-tional mental system operates by rules, some of which are innate and some that we develop through our experiences, that provide us with an explanation for the stimuli we perceive. People duck or turn away if they sense that something is about to strike their head. Experience may lead a financial investor with his money rules to not panic when the stock market drops by ten or twenty percent, but rather get excited about that being a good time to buy stocks that are now cheaper. Taleb explains, "We ... have a hunger for rules because we need to reduce the dimension of matters so they can get into our heads."[11] We learn the rules of an interaction, such as those involved in playing a game, and then with the rules we can respond reflexively, without really thinking.

Quick and dirty, on one hand, or fast and frugal on the other, could char-acterize the quality of our use of rules. With rules we can quickly respond to situations, be it to someone's sudden glaring face toward us, someone's gentle finger touch on our elbow, and so on. We have rules about all kinds of things, such as the Golden Rule, and for some people, the Ten Commandments. We also many communication rules, such as rules for greeting, politeness, sharing personal information, touching whom and on what body area, for speaking at the dinner table, holding informal or formal meetings, and so on. When we are in the act of perception, it is suggested that our rules primarily guide us.[12] Rules are especially useful in emergencies when there is insufficient time to carefully assess the situation and determine a plan of action.

The weakness of using rules in the quick and dirty way which occurs in the act of perception is that the outcomes are biased.[13] Considering the limita-tions of encoding and decoding messages, we can understand that our decod-ing of a given message may only represent a general idea of a sender's encoded message since the rule we used to interpret the message may be incomplete and/or ill fitting.

Emotional responses are not our only options during the perception process. People can and do learn to channel their sensory input into the more rational, normally termed *thinking* part (System 2) of their brain. This can be seen, for example, when people discussing an emotional-laden topic focus their con-versation on the logic and evidence presented as opposed to shouting at each other. Through sufficient experience and training, people can learn and react in an effective, calculated manner, as shown by some military people under combat situations or by some airline pilots when their planes need to make an emergency landing. System 2 thinking is used when a person mentally and/

or physically practices an operation. With repetition, future impacts of stimuli can be handled intuitively by automatic responses (System 1) from our brain.[14] This is the sought-after purpose and result of training. Unfortunately, as Taleb suggests, "Much of the trouble with human nature resides in our inability to use much of System 2, or to use it in a prolonged way ...."[15] Thus, the initial meaning we come to realize in the perception process is emotion-laden, but we can also use emotions to get our rational, reflective (System 2) brain working. In short, "One cannot make a decision without emotion."[16]

Thus, we have a *subjective I* which usually organizes and provides us with a meaning for the stimuli we encounter. In a larger sense, who and what we are, the entirety of our experiences, our values and beliefs, our physical sensing capabilities, our intelligence, and our alertness to our surroundings that we bring to the moment of perception, has the greatest impact and influence upon the evaluation (meaning) we make of each situation we are in, from the inception of processing the stimuli in our environment to the resulting meaning and feelings we form as a result of the perception process. The "I" has it. Everyone brings a different "self" to the perception moment, and that "self" has come to judge. We can expect differing perceptions of a given event. Subjectivity does not mean there cannot be agreement, though. Through the use of the scientific method, our observations of the world can be fairly objective. Through our use of logic and the avoidance of fallacious thinking, we can make fairly sound judgments about what we have observed. Through the use of the scientific method, people have been able to achieve a certain degree of objectivity, and with effective communication people have been able to reach a significant amount of agreement about any number of phenomenon and physical realities. These can aid us in overcoming common weaknesses in the reflexive predispositions typically hold. It is not easy because actual thinking takes a lot of time and energy.

Who and what we are, our past experiences and current persona, provide, in themselves, a predisposition to perceive a situation one way or another. This is modified by our selective attention and exposure, as Pearson explains it: "[We have ... the tendency to see, hear, and believe only what [we] want to see, hear, and believe."[17] Some more specific aspects of our mental processing are explored in the next section.

PREDISPOSITIONS OF OUR REFLEXIVE COMPOSITION

As noted earlier, Zweig finds that the reflexive, intuitive, emotional system in our brain makes the initial assessment of what we become aware of in our world.[18] We are largely unaware of most of this processing occurring in our mind. It is as if we are operating on autopilot as we make our way through the perception process. Further, we have an inclination to interpret the sensory information we contact according to (1) our innate mental responses and (2) the responses imbedded into the system that are distilled from our life's experiences and interpretation of those experiences. These provide us with a *predisposition*, a readiness to respond to stimuli absorbed. The total of these internal responses to external stimuli tend to become unchanged over our life.[19] Thus, our reflexive mental system is itself a predisposition.

There is one caveat here. Since the reflexive parts of our brain are connected to the reflective, analytical part of our brain, each section can influence (to a degree) the other. In fact, according to Zweig, emotional thoughts and logical reasoning are integrated in sound decision making.[20] This connection between the two suggests the possibility that people's conscious, thoughtful attempts to control their subsequent reflexive, non-thinking responses can be attained. In fact, this has been found to happen. For example, many people initially fearful of speaking before groups have, through training and experience, learned to control their anxiety (alter their predisposition about public speaking) and deliver very effective speeches. Some have even learned to enjoy it.

Our perception of a given person, place, event, concept, or "thing" is influenced (in part) by one or more of the reflexive actions discussed in the following section. Each action exhibits a predisposition to respond to someone or something according to the composition of the action, that is composed of both innate urges and individual responses to experiences that have been confirmed and become a habit. In a sense, our experiences are imprinted in our brain and our brain then reacts and creates meaning to future stimuli based on how the existing imprinting responds to that future stimuli. The two parts (both mental and physical along with the "software" connecting them) contribute to the forming of the meaning we come to experience from our interaction with people and phenomena in our surroundings. The remainder of this chapter explores some of our common predispositions.

It is also recognized that our perception of communication messages and other phenomena around us are dependent upon and influenced by the ability of our individual senses to register what exists to be seen, heard, touched, tasted, or smelled. People differ in their physical abilities in each of these areas so not everyone will notice the same or the entirety of existing information.

1. *Comparison.* We gain a sense, or meaning, for a new stimulus (e.g., a frown, a "hi," a firm handshake, and so on) by linking it with a pre-existing mental pattern that seems to have some similar characteristics (e.g., a frown from the past, a "hi" from the past, and so on). This provides a meaning basis

for the new experience. In brief, we compare the unknown with something known to gain a sense of it and have a basis for responding to it.

Reasoning by comparison is one of the well-known and common forms of reasoning. According to Ariely, "… we are always looking at the things around us in relation to others. We can't help it. This holds true not only for physical things—toasters, bicycles, puppies, restaurant entrees, and spouses—but also for experiences such as vacations and educational options, and for ephemeral things as well: emotions, attitudes, and point of view."[21] This is a frequent perceptual response because our brain is "wired" to do this.[22]

Depending upon the context of the comparison and the characteristics of the object upon which we are focusing our attention (e.g., a smell of perfume, a touch on the elbow, etc.), our perception of the object can be altered. A single, unattached woman who is by objective standards rather plain-looking can become transformed into a beauty queen in the eyes of 100 single men if, in part, there is no other woman within a 100 miles with which to compare her. Anecdotal evidence has also revealed that people under the influence of alcohol perceive others as more physically attractive than they otherwise would have rated those same people. Ariely found that when he manipulated people's photographs in an experiment, 75% of the subjects who were shown 2 pictures said they would prefer to date the "regular" person shown over both the distorted version of the same person and another regular person whose photograph was provided.[23] On this basis, the author suggested that people could increase their perceived attractiveness to other potential dating partners at a party by attending with a friend who has similar physical characteristics but is slightly less attractive. Without comparable people around (the relevance of a model, or schemata), people will have difficulty evaluating an individual's attractiveness. With a "decoy," a person would not only appear better looking than the decoy but in general look better than other people at the party. If you decide to try this, you probably do not want to tell your friend that you are using them as a decoy.

The subject of our perception, be it a person, object, or idea, can change in comparison to other elements around the subject. Thus, some subject can appear lighter or darker, smaller or bigger, generous or stingy, rich or poor, free or confined, sweet-smelling or fetid, and so on, depending upon the composition of the subject and even what it is paired. It is as if our eyes, ears, nose, skin, and tongue can be fooled.

As Zweig suggests, cognitive thinking is taxing so our brain tends to avoid it.[24] This affects our comparing, for as Ariely concludes, we tend to compare those "… things that are easily comparable—and avoid comparing things that cannot be compared easily."[25] While there are benefits for our brain functioning this way, the weakness is that people often compare two things that have few, if any, significant characteristics in common. This is why reasoning by analogy is often called the worst form of debate. By its very nature, a comparison focuses on a few characteristics and omits sufficient analysis of other characteristics the compared phenomena do not have in common that could be of even more significance.

The significance for perception is that the quality of our comparisons will influence the perceptual meanings we come to form. The mental outline or model we have stored in our memory may or may not be a close enough fit to the new experience to justify its use. How accurate or relevant are our comparisons? How far can we extend the similarities to still draw a meaningful conclusion about the unknown? The perceiver will have to satisfactorily answer these for him or herself to feel comfortable about the comparisons made.

The *object* of our comparisons also influences our perception. Different physical objects, attributes, and skills are important to different people, so people vary in the significance they place on the comparison of these objects and on the amount of these possessed by others and themselves. Our constant comparing of these can result in our feeling miserable.[26] People compare the size of their income to other's income, their bodies to other peoples' bodies, their voice to other peoples' voices, and so on. Inevitably, people find someone with whom to compare themselves (and their spouses and kids) who has more of what they wish they had or think they should have and they become envious. We could compare ourselves to Einstein's intellectual achievements or to Bill Gates' wealth and become jealous. Many of us can compare our speech making to the oratorical skills and themes of Martin Luther King, Jr. and become envious. Many married people compare other men or women to their own spouses and wish they were married to the other man or woman. The objects for comparison are endless. According to Zweig, "The roots of envy and social comparison run so deep that they are an instinctive part of our biological makeup."[27] We cannot help but compare. Depending upon what is compared, to whom we compare ourselves, and the extent to which we value what is being compared, we will be satisfied or dissatisfied, happy or sad.

Improving Our Comparing

What can we do to improve our comparing? In jest, from a wife's point of view, a husband should make sure he earns more than his wife's brother-in-law. On a more serious note:

- Evaluate the representativeness of the significant traits or criteria in your mental model.

- Consciously revise your conception of that model and remind yourself in the future of this.
- Make yourself articulate the significant similar traits between the known and the unknown.
- Mentally or on paper list the key similarities and attempt to discover glaring differences.
- Ask yourself if your given comparison is reasonable for you and your circumstances.
- Are you being fooled in any way by the context of comparison?

2. *Stereotyping*. This is another predisposition that influences our perceptions. A stereotype a term or phrase expressing a common, oversimplified understanding about a person, place, object, or concept. It is based upon incomplete information that may only consist of one or more pieces of information assumed to be true, yet these are presumed to provide sufficient understanding. Stereotypes overlook individuality and uniqueness, and they are frequently disparaging about those or that to which they refer.

Given the limited information we typically have, the stereotype mischaracterizes the person or thing being observed by omitting the unique qualities of the same; it *labels* or ascribes a generalized characteristic which purports to create knowing. On the basis of this understanding about stereotypes, a number of questions can be raised. How do we know which supposed stereotypes we hold or hear are oversimplifications? Are not all of them generalizations? Can the people that do not know you claim that your ideas have been fixed and unvarying? If fixed, how long is relevant? How much of the "whole group" does our generalization have to reflect to be acknowledged as a legitimate observation of the group and not a mere stereotype? Who is the expert to say that a given generalization of ours is accurate for a significant number of group members or is a stereotype? How legitimate is it to say that someone is stereotyping just because we do not like what he or she is saying, especially if there is obvious evidence of a certain behavior shown by many people in the designated group? Notice that this questioning of the definition of stereotyping shows it to be more than a little unclear. Using an inference, we could say that stereotyping is often subjectively applied.

Stereotypes are considered the bane of social interaction, falsely maligning an individual or a group of people of that the individual is presumed to be a member. They may lead to a conflict when the individual or group being stereotyped does not like what is perceived as demeaning and a mischaracterization. Individuals may be discriminated against by not getting a job or a position they were otherwise qualified for when they are associated with a negative group attribute.

Another real danger of stereotypes is that targeted people may hear and accept the stereotypes, and follow that by acting out counterproductive and/or anti-social behavior. According to Williams, this is what some of his friends did.[28] Rather than try to disprove an uncomplimentary stereotype about themselves, they came to enjoy acting it out. This, in turn, provided evidence and justification for those who believed and communicated the initial stereotype. They would be disinclined to hire or go out of their way to help the group members they had in fact prejudged. Even people who are not actually members of the group targeted by the stereotype but become associated with it may act out the stereotype.[29]

Stereotypes can also harm the person stereotyping. In writing and speaking, stereotypes are considered too vague to be insightful, and are representative of fallacious hasty generalizations. They fool the user of the stereotype into believing that he or she has touched the essence of something when they have actually only touched some of the form. According to Verderber, stereotypes may be "...the most commonly known barrier to our accurate judgment of others."[30] Those who act on a negative stereotype about an individual based on the individual's associated group may harm themselves by overlooking that prospective employee or group member's unique individual characteristics which could have benefited the stereotyping individual's personal or group endeavors. The person not selected may then join a competitor's team or company, putting the stereotyping person at a physical or financial disadvantage (a losing sports season, a financial loss, or a bankrupt company).

According to Thaler and Sunstein, our complicated lives do not allow us time to methodically examine everything we perceive. To compensate for this, it is suggested that we use mental "rules of thumb" to quickly process and interpret our mental inputs. One of these mental shortcuts is termed *reasoning by representativeness*. "... [W]hen asked to judge how likely it is that A belongs to category B, people (and especially their Automatic [reflexive] Systems) answer by asking themselves how similar A is to their image or stereotype of B."[31] If people conclude that A is representative of B, A is referred to as a member of B and is presumed to hold category B beliefs and act in category B ways. Just one or two perceived characteristics about "Bill" is enough to get him "pigeonholed," "labeled," categorized as a car mechanic, as generous, or whatever.

We continually form generalizations from all sorts of information we encounter during a day based upon our past experiences, our reflexive impulses and the extent we have conditioned those reflexes, and our reflective thoughts about a myriad number of phenomena and situations. The stimuli we process are compared with constructs or patterns that we have previously formed in our brain. Our brain sorts through these, seeking a close fit. When one is found, we experience the existing meaning established for that construct. Our brain not only forms mental patterns but also creates expectations about those patterns.[32] Our perception may register what is a trash collector before us, or a continued, sincere look in someone's eye-contact with us, or a stranger standing within our intimate zone, and then our expectations (stereotypes) of such people influence the perceptual meaning we come to have for people in these situations, as well as our resultant communication with them. These expectations give us a basis for predicting what might happen between ourselves and other people.

Our brain has to respond to people and other messages in our environment on the basis of generalized experience, or a generalized *other*. According to Ariely, "The brain cannot start from scratch at every new situation. It must build on what it has seen before."[33] An outline of past experiences provides a mental shortcut for understanding someone or some thing "... in our never-ending attempt to make sense of complicated surroundings."[34] Further, our brain does not process information in its raw form. It needs to compress the available data to effectively work with it. At this point, the incomplete details are interpreted and we have meaning while other details are blocked out.[35] The process that begins with selected stimuli ends with a selected generalization.

It is not as if we can avoid interpreting the stimuli around us. According to Taleb, "... brain functions often operate outside our awareness. [We] interpret pretty much as [we] perform other activities deemed automatic and outside [our] control, like breathing."[36] We chance upon a person, place, or object and our brain responds with an evaluation. Thus, stereotyping is natural and necessary.

As Taleb concludes, we are vulnerable "... to oversimplification and our predilection for compact stories over raw truths."[37] We seem to have a "... limited ability to look at sequences of facts without weaving an explanation into them [to] bind the facts together."[38] Stories, or narrations, about some person, group, or phenomenon not only make the recognition of the image created from the facts more easily remembered but they also provide a sense of understanding. With our stereotypes, we gain an impression of reality. We fool ourselves in thinking we know, thereby gaining a sense of certainty. Stereotypes provide us with something to refer to as well as ready-made explanations for why the person does what they do.[39]

Yet, when we reason by representativeness, we often misperceive patterns occurring in our everyday life. Chance events easily appear to be the real thing, so we either buy or sell stocks, blame our boss for picking on us, provide a large financial contract to someone we just saw make three, three-point shots on a basketball court, and so on. Thaler and Sunstein found that most people with strongly held beliefs about an existing pattern "... are unwilling even to consider the possibility that their strongly held beliefs might be wrong."[40] While we might term this a hardening of the categories, it cannot be overlooked that some of our stereotypes are accurate, which in turn reinforces in our communication and behavior the validity of the stereotype.[41]

Even when new information might naturally lead us to a new conclusion about some person or phenomenon, our opinions of these are not easily altered since there is pressure within us and from others to maintain a consistency of beliefs.[42] Coupled with this, that information we do attend to typically becomes noticed because it confirms our vision of reality. The function of our brain makes it very difficult for us to alter our stereotypes and to avoid viewing someone else in a non-stereotypical fashion. We do not constantly update our mental constructs.

While people generally have a negative conception of stereotypes, there is nothing inherently evil in them.[43] In fact, they provide us with a means for achieving the main purpose of communication, which is to predict and control our environment. Stereotypes fulfill a central need.[44] They give us a quick, albeit generalized, conception of someone or something. They represent a probability that the person or phenomenon under discussion or in our presence is likely to exhibit certain, limited characteristics, and this limited meaningful framework gives us a basis from which to communicate and act. Of course, we do not have to maintain a stereotype for we can formulate and reformulate our generalizations. Still, we expect that Catholics will have a certain belief about the morality of abortions. It is not wicked or injurious to say that Catholics think abortion is a sin. This is the position of the Catholic Church. No doubt some Catholics have had an abortion and some do not think it is a sin, so we cannot accurately say *all* Catholics believe the same thing.

While acknowledging that stereotypes are a simplification of reality, they may not necessarily be inaccurate for the group as a whole. They typically exist and continue to exist because a critical amount of some trait or behavior within a given group, activity, or place does exist. According to Williams, knowing the height of people can allow a prediction of which person is likely to be a better basketball player; a person's ethnicity can predict a higher amount of certain diseases; people of some ethnicities are more highly associated with criminal activity than are people of other ethnicities.[45] This should not surprise anyone. If someone's stereotype is an accurate reflection of a group, it provides the person with some information upon which to base a conversation and action.

Should it anger you if do not like the stereotype of some group you are associated with, be it your family, school, sports team, profession, church, or political party? If you do not like people stereotyping the way you or someone else in your identified group, for example, speak non-Standard American English and your group suffers job discrimination, who do you blame? Do you place primary responsibility on the person expressing and acting upon the stereotype, or do you chiefly condemn the people in your group or even yourself for doing enough of the behavior that created or maintained the disliked stereotype? Williams suggests, "The rightful recipients of [this] anger should be those [who made the group synonymous with the disliked behavior] and not the taxi driver or the policemen trying to do his job."[46] If a high school teacher previously had your two older brothers and those two brothers' classroom behavior stood out from their classmates in very obvious ways, and then you come along, what is the teacher to expect? Who do you blame if you do not like the teacher's expectations? Although it does not justify it, we may recall Zweig's finding that two in a row often leads people to form a pattern.[47]

It is easy to say, as many people do, that we should not stereotype, but who has enough time to investigate every person or even most people they perceive? How can people realistically "context" (sufficiently get to know) every person, food, activity (and so on) with which they come into contact, especially in emergency situations? It is probably fair to say that few people judge individuals *as* individuals. People have to depend upon their previously formed generalizations (not to imply that people should harbor inaccurate ones). Long, un-kept hair on people in a certain occupational context may well suggest a significant and legitimate meaning to other people in that context (such as to the military or an investment banker), in which case it would not be a "mere" stereotype. "Help wanted. No Irish need apply" signs were seen in nineteenth and early twentieth century America[48] because of their perceived excessive drunkenness and fighting.[49] Although not all Irish were that way, enough businesses considered it too expensive to attempt to discover which Irish job seekers were not. It is easy for people now to say that business owners then were prejudiced but might we now be the ones who are actually prejudging them? What is the origin of the "fighting Irish of Notre Dame?"

Thus, in the abstract, stereotypes may appear patently false but in the everyday experience of people who have first-hand knowledge of the behavior of the people in question, there may be sufficient support for using the stereotype.[50] After the fact, it is easy for people removed from the context, moment, and people in question to label a generalization about those people as prejudicial and stereotyping of the group. Booker T. Washington made generalizations about differing groups of black Americans.[51] Was he stereotyping, were his assessments inaccurate, and was he some sort of bad person for making those evaluations? Groups are not the same[52] nor do all people presumed to be members of a group exhibit all of the supposed group characteristics. To some degree, differences between groups are reflected in stereotypes.

As Berlo noted long ago, there are an infinite number of possible perceptions that can be made by someone of some other person or phenomenon occurring at any one time and place.[53] We cannot help but be limited in our perception for we cannot observe or register all the stimuli around us. From the information present we have to select some of it on which to focus and draw meaning. Thus, from the very start of the perception/meaning formation process, we process incomplete information. Further, since we seek to create meaning from what we do notice, this very meaning omits and even blocks our awareness of the other available stimuli and the meanings to be gained from them. Depending upon our awareness, we are left with a sketch of the present reality.

Avoiding Stereotypes

If you do not know you are stereotyping, how can you hope to recognize it? Even if you do notice it, what can be done about it? There are a few options.

Discriminate. Look for differences among different people, places, objects, events, and changes over time. Examine the available stimuli for clues that distinguish the one person from the other person, the one object from the next, and so on. Presumably, not all Democratic party members will vote for Democratic candidates in every election. If you like creamy ice cream, it is in your interest to discover which brand is creamier than the rest. Be specific and descriptive in your use of language about each person you refer to. Not all politicians are alike. Consciously think to yourself, when you hear yourself or someone else say "_____ are alike," *no they are not.* Create this mental habit.

While we typically refer to people and places as if they are unchanging (static), if we examine them we know this is not the case. Rectify this by adding a time (date) reference to your statements. George Washington High School may have excelled in Mock Trial in 1980 but was dismal in 2000. Its 2007 varsity football team ranked number four, unlike the championship 2003-2006 teams.

Use *Reflective Thinking.* Replace the method of reaching conclusions largely based on emotions and intuition with thinking that applies standards of logic. Test the legitimacy of your thinking. Use reasoned thoughts that you can monitor as you cognitively process them.

Our emotional and our rational responses can work together to help people reach legitimate and effective decisions. As Taleb concludes, most of our errors in thinking come from *quick and dirty* judgments when what we need it more introspection.[54] This takes mental energy and time, as well as a wide study of people, groups, and so on. We cannot expect to do this for every situation we face but we can occasionally hold our emotions in check as we seek out and listen to information that counters our stereotypes.

Taleb suggests that we be suspicious of the past and avoid the easy and apparently obvious stories explaining how and why things are the way they are.[55]

Curtail Media Information. Drastically reduce information, descriptions, and explanations provided by the media. Turn off the television and minimize your time spent reading printed media material.[56] Much of the information we encounter in our daily lives is more than mere information overload, it is toxic. It easily reinforces stereotypes. Sensational stories, not reality, are what sell news. According to Stossel, "… thirty-six years working in the media has left me much more skeptical of its product. … when it comes to science and economics, and putting life's risks in perspective, the media do a dismal job."[57] Taleb recommends that we practice spotting "… the difference between the sensational and the empirical."[58] This may require taking classes in logic and statistics. What is the probability that a given person will exhibit a characteristic that you ascribe to a larger, possibly fictitious group of which you presume they are a member?

Avoid Noise. Noise is *not* information. According to Berlo, noise is any *distortion* of one or more elements in the process of communication (source-encoder, receiver-decoder, message, channel, context) that reduces communication effectiveness.[59] Beware of creating or accepting a stereotype based on weak evidence, including anecdotal evidence. Contrary, subsequent information about a person, group, object, or event in question will be difficult to interpret and accept once a stereotype is established. Increase your chance of recognizing the noise about someone or a given group by entertaining more detailed, empirical knowledge (not more information) of them.

Disregard Stereotypes. Know that you do not have to accept stereotypes that others may ascribe to you. The stereotypes do not have to be a controlling element in your life. People will face stereotypes their entire lives. They can get angry about them but anger will not change the story. Responding like the stereotype will provide a self-fulfilling prophecy for the stereotyping person who has now found legitimacy in her his/her stereotype, and it can influence the person stereotyped to think they are the stereotype.

People can review both stereotypes others have of them as well as those they believe about themselves. The unjustified ones can be discounted, and if other ones have a basis in personal reality and are disliked, people can change their behavior.

Stereotype Summary

Our brain naturally categorizes and judges, reducing the totality of an experience. It has to do this to process the experiences we have. As Taleb concludes, "Categorization is necessary for humans, but it becomes pathological when the category is seen as definitive, preventing people from considering the fuzziness of boundaries, let alone revising their categories."[60] Stereotyping ignores individual differences and perpetuates inaccuracies. This is the weakness of stereotypes: they are fixed and unchanging group generalizations applied to a single individual, sometimes with harmful consequences. According to Taleb, this was shown on the part of U.S. political leaders who thought radical Islamic people were allies against Communism but were shocked when some of these same Islamists crashed airplanes into New York City's Twin Towers.[61]

Further, it is difficult to remove personal biases when thinking about the characteristics of a situation, and these biases contain inaccuracies about individuals, groups, places, or other phenomenon. It is possible, though, to withhold personal judgments and recognize facts as they are. We can use reasoning to learn and to avoid some of the harms of stereotypes.

Chamorros on Guam often say that they are polite, friendly and generous. Presumably not all of them are this way so this is just a stereotype. Still, they have created a yardstick by which they identity and thus, judge themselves, something to which they aspire, and they are proud of it. Here is a stereotype we can all enjoy.

3. Expectations and the Self-Fulfilling Prophecy. According to Zweig, people are aversive to randomness.[62] Originating in the reflexive part of our brain (and thus, largely automatic), people have a strong desire to know in advance how something will turn out.

In fact, people have such a strong desire that things turn out the way they want or expect them to turn out that their sensing of data can be altered to fit their expectations and they misperceive obvious objective data. By changing their expectations, Ariely found that his subjects' perception of taste could be altered (most chose vinegar beer over regular beer). He concludes that "...beliefs and expectations affect how we perceive and interpret sights, tastes, and other sensory phenomena, but also ... our expectations can affect us by altering our subjective and even objective expectations ...."[63] Of two friends watching a baseball game on TV or in person, the one favoring one team could objectively see the hit ball as being a foul ball while the other friend favoring the other team could objectively see the ball land in fair territory. We should not be surprised when we hear the infrequent story of a hunter shooting at a four-legged deer that had horns, only to later discover the deer was actually a two-legged human. Most people have heard that people can feel better after taking placebos that they believe to be real medicine. It is not simply that we mentally will ourselves better, but that our body inside releases various chemicals that begin the healing process.[64] Suggestions and our expectations based on them can be very powerful.

A *self-fulfilling prophecy* is a type of expectation. It occurs when a person's anticipation of an outcome increases the likelihood it will occur. We often behave in ways that are consistent with others' perceptions of us.[65]

For example, a person can think to him or herself the thought that he or she can successfully complete a task, which in turn subtly influences his or her subsequent behavior to pay more attention to the details of the task and perform them at a high level of quality, resulting in the desired outcome. Or, Person A can expect that Person B will not achieve an outcome desired by A, and then A communicates subtle or not-so-subtle messages to B that B is not expected to achieve what A supposedly really wants. In this event, Person B may "get the message" and tailor his or her subsequent work to provide the less-desired outcome, fulfilling A's expectation.

Notice that for there to be any self-fulfilling prophecy influence, it is insufficient for someone to merely have an expectation about him or herself or someone else. People have to communicate this message and the targeted person has to receive that message. These messages may be directly or indirectly stated through oral and/or nonverbal communication or implied by what is not stated. In brief, people communicate a prediction that is acted upon in a way to bring about that prediction.

Self-fulfilling prophecies are common in our everyday lives.

Bob tells another student, Jim, that he is nervous about the up-coming test. Bob not only keeps studying, but also keeps thinking about doing poorly. When the test day arrives, Bob takes the test but continues to think about his nervousness. He ends up getting a low grade. Your driving license instructor tells you that you are driving well and you should pass the driving test. You feel confident, you are observant, and you practice driving over and over so you can do everything right on the test. When you get behind the wheel for the test, you do not think of failure. When your high school coach is interviewed pre-season about how well he expects your team to do during the season, he tells the reporter that the team is in a rebuilding year, the message being that you and your teammates are not good enough to be champions. As a team, you become convinced you are not very good so you do not try very hard, and your team loses nearly every game.

As noted earlier, there are two general types of self-fulfilling prophecies. One type includes the expectations you have of yourself. We have all had expectations about some of our own outcomes, accompanied by behavior of ours that increased the chance the predicted outcome would occur. We may use self-talk, either a verbal utterance or a conscious thought, that we think such-and-such will happen. "I can do it. I know I can." Sometimes, people simply have a mental acknowledgement not put into words that they will do well (or not) in the completion of the task After the message to ourselves, we can take specific actions that culminate in the situation turning out the way we anticipated. Of course, many people on many occasions take little, no, or irrelevant actions after creating their expectation, so they do not experience the expected outcome.

The other type of self-fulfilling prophecy represents the expectations one person has of another person's outcome. People receive these prophecies from their parents, teachers, coaches, bosses, and others. We hear statements like "You're not living up to your potential," or "I always told you you'd end up no good," or "You can do it, I know you can," or "You've never let me down before." Some of the messages are more subtle, like an unconvincing, hesitant tone of voice from the coach when she says the team "… should go all the way," but leave out "… to the bottom," or, the serious look on your father's face as he looks steadily toward you and slowly nods his head up and down just as you step on the bus to leave for military training.

Ariely found that if you tell people in advance that something is not very good, such as some food or drink, they are likely to agree with you after they taste it because of the expectations you set for them.[66] Conversely, when you make the same food or drink presentation appear fancy and expensive, people report they like the taste better than when the exact same food or drink is served with plain kitchenware or foam plates and cups. Wine tastes better in good wine glasses made for the particular type of wine.[67] The physical reaction in the brain is different, and different parts of the brain are activated when there are different expectations.

The purpose of expectations is not simply to prime our senses for pain or pleasure or to be motivated to have some desire satisfied, but to communicate more effectively and efficiently. Ariely suggests that expectations "… enable us to make sense of a conversation in a noisy room, despite the loss of a word here and there, and likewise, to be able to read text messages on our cell phones, despite the fact that some of the words are scrambled."[68] The more we are familiar with other communicators (and vice versa), the better our language capability, and the more skilled we are at adjusting our communication to fit different contexts, the more likely we will experience effective communication.

A well-known study of self-fulfilling prophecy was completed by Rosenthal and Jacobson, who showed that teacher expectations influence student achievement.[69] The team got the student names and evaluations at the end of a school year of an elementary class before the next year's teacher got them, randomly assigning the student evaluations to the entire class roster. The new teacher received the "doctored" student evaluations. At the end of the next school year, a statistically significant number of student evaluations were different from the preceding year's. The researchers concluded that the second teacher had interacted with the students according to the altered evaluations, influencing the students to act according to the evaluations ascribed to them. This author noticed during his own grammar school experience that each succeeding teacher had a file on him from the preceding year's teacher. While this study may not be allowed again, this type of sharing of information behind the scenes before people actually meet is common throughout education and business. It will continue. Although they are just Hollywood films, viewers may see an element of self-fulfilling prophecy in *Hoosiers* (the coach's expectations of a small-town basketball team that goes on to win the state championship) and *Stand and Deliver* (poor, minority students at a run-down school succeed in math, influenced by a teacher expecting them to succeed).

Overall, when we expect that something will be good, it often will be. When we expect that something will not be good, it often turns out to be so. This suggests that we can influence in positive or negative ways the outcomes we end up experiences in our own lives in

4. Implicit Personality Theory. As suggested earlier in this chapter, people's perceptions of available information at a given time and place are limited and incomplete. Further, people need to fill in, provide *closure* for what is otherwise missing information so they can gain a more complete picture of the phenomenon, and with this picture generate an interpretation of the original stimuli. This very process also occurs when we perceive people's personalities. We think we notice a given trait of another person in their communication and/or behavior, and then assume that the individual has other personality traits, too, even though we have not observed them. In other words, we have in our mind what might be termed a laundry list of characteristics that we think go together. Once we perceive one trait being exhibited by another person (which we may, at the start, be wrong about), we assume this other person also has and will exhibit certain other traits.[70] This helps us predict and control our environment.

This amounts to stereotyping. On the basis of one or a few perceived characteristics, we presume to know the entire person, and people in general who we believe exhibit the minimal traits. We may observe someone as being a nervous type of person, then add to that perception that they are also insecure and lack emotional warmth. We may think of another person as generous, and then assume that they are also an extrovert and sensitive to others' feelings. We complete the "picture" of these people, and then we feel more assured in communicating with or about them. Still, since we are all different people with different experiences, knowledge, values, and beliefs, we will create and maintain differing sets of characteristics. Our conceptions of many people will be simplified and over-generalized, and in the end, we may easily be incorrect about them. Thus, we could end up hiring the wrong in-dividual for a job, mischaracterizing a player on the soccer team, or marrying the wrong person, all by giving too much credence to our initial perception of someone else and the accompanying personality traits we ascribe to them.

Both Beebe, Beebe and Redmond and DeVito propose that the qualities we assign to people tend to be dependent on whether we in general like or dislike the people in question.[71] For those we like or believe to have a certain good quality, we often attribute additional positive qualities to them. This is termed the *halo effect*. After initially determining that a person is loyal, we may infer, for example, that they are also dedicated, hard working, sensitive, modest, and sincere. If someone thinks well of people in a given profession, such as priests and preachers, we would expect them to hold positive per-sonality traits about the people in this profession. In the same manner, if we conclude that a stranger exhibits a negative characteristic, the *reverse halo effect* influences us to assume they also have other poor personality qualities. We rarely stop to think that we may be wrong, and given that first impressions can be very inaccurate, we incorrectly attribute additional negative traits to other people. This should remind us that who we are has a significant impact on our perceptual outcomes, including the meaning we derive from the other person as a person.

Consider a twist in our attributing positive qualities to other people. Once we assign our list, we expect the person to exhibit the added-on (positive) traits. If we later do not see the person exhibit these positive traits, we are likely to hold this failing against them and to think less of them for they have not fulfilled what we believe to be a justified composite of qualities. We over-look our own mistaken generalization and inaccurate composite of human qualities. Further, if we are initially wrong in our assignment of a quality to someone else, it is highly likely that the additional personality traits added on by us are also a misrepresentation of the individual.

5. Primacy-Recency. People's interpretation of someone or some phenom-ena is influenced by when the perception occurs. Our first or early impres-sions about someone, a place, an object, or concept have a greater influence on our estimation them than do later occurrences. This is the *primacy effect*. First impressions are most important in our overall perceptions, including those of people we meet. Subsequent (later) and more recent information are typically interpreted as refining the initial interpretation. This latter in-formation is typically interpreted in light of the first impression, and may be thought of as bolstering the first impressions.

This should not seem surprising, for strangers meeting for the first time make quick, first impressions and decide in a virtual instance whether or not to continue communication with the other person; a veritable do-or-die situation that most, if not all people, have experienced.

Research in persuasion[72] and marketing[73] has found that people's first impressions about all sorts of phenomena create an anchor that can have a long-term influence on their subsequent evaluations and decisions about these phenomena, including products, events, places, people, behaviors, and ideas. For example, some kids have heard their grandparents complain about the current price of candy, toys, and so on, while the price seems okay to the grandchildren. This stems from the grandparents being imprinted with perhaps 1960 prices. This also may act as a barrier or check on their spending (to the grandkids' dismay). When new products reach the market, people become anchored to the original prices if they consider buying them at that time, with subsequent lower prices seemingly a "deal" in comparison, which makes their purchase more likely. When people move to a new city they typically spend the same amount there as they did in their previous city, regardless whether the city is more expensive or cheaper. Their financial anchors travel with them. This should not imply that people do not change their first impression, or anchors, for they do, but that explanation will be omitted here for the sake of brevity. Suffice it to say that our initial decisions about someone or some thing can influence our future decisions about these.[74] This implies that we need to be careful with our initial decisions.

There are at least a few situations when it is better to be the last impression than the first one, and that includes job interviews and debates. Although few interviewees can know or schedule to be last, characteristics of the latter interviewees are more likely to be better remembered by the interviewers than the characteristics of the earlier interviewees. Debaters know that being last, not first, is the preferred position since they have the opportunity to rebut their opponent's positions and what they say will be the last thing heard, most likely to be remembered by their audience.

6. Consistency. Consciously or unconsciously, most people feel a need to appear consistent in their thoughts, speech, and action. If I think to myself that I am generous, then I will have to show some actual generosity to other people or I will feel uncomfortable with this conception I have formed about myself.. Still, if I am not always generous, no one but I will know about my inconsistency and I may be able to rationalize not always being generous. If I say to others that I am generous or if I know that other people publicly say I am and I accept that conclusion, I will have to clearly show generosity in various public situations to both maintain my public image and my private image (the self-reflective nature of communication). If I do not think of myself as generous but then I do something generous, I am likely to think of myself as generous and then pay more future attention to my and others people's generosity (or lack thereof).

Consistency theories as a whole suggest that we assume we are rational and that we seek (have a need for) logical coherence and compatibility among perceptions of our own attitudes and behaviors.[75] We attempt to create a balance in our attitudes, beliefs, and behaviors. If we notice inconsistencies within or between our belief system and our behavior, we will feel anxious and uncomfortable. If we tell everyone we are on a diet then we see them see us eating candy, desserts, and soda pop, we will recognize our inconsistency. To get rid of or decrease this mental tension, we will attempt to either alter some aspect of our own belief system and/or behavior or get someone else to change their conception of what we may have said or done. Being thought of as consistent gives us a feeling of harmony and consonance.

We also tend to seek consonance with the majority opinion or ideas of those around us. As noted earlier in this chapter, we compare some aspect of ourselves to other people and form a conclusion about the merits of that artifact and our self as a result of that comparison. There is a tendency to believe what the majority believes, to align our selves with what is termed *conventional wisdom*, the prevailing belief about a given issue. If our beliefs are not consistent with the crowd's, we are often considered an odd-ball, a weirdo, someone to be shunned. So there is social pressure to think like the rest, and if we do not, we probably keep our mouths shut.

Ironically, that which we often strive to be consistent with, the conventional wisdom, is almost always wrong. [76]

Barnlund provides a common example of people in a balanced relationship: Person A likes object X as well as Person B.[77] Person B likes Person A and object X, too. This should not be surprising since people know that most friends like many of the same things and they spend time together experiencing those things, be they a type of music, a certain sporting activity, the same religion, and so on. We also know that if Person A and Person B have very different thoughts and feelings about some object X and their individual position on the matter is central to their lives, there will be pressure toward reassessing their thoughts about each other, about the object X, and even behavioral changes toward each other. They are likely to avoid establishing a friendship in the first place or diminish it if this differing concern over the object arises after the friendship has begun. Most people have had elementary and high school experiences of Friend X of theirs trying to convince them to dislike some other kid in school so this Friend X could maintain a balanced state between the three of you. We also feel unbalanced when someone we dislike likes us.

The desire to be consistent may alter our evaluation of what is or is not consistent. We might easily view two disparate beliefs, attitudes, and/or behaviors of ours as consistent simply because we want to appear consistent, even if it is only in our mind. For example, assuming that most people are against cheating, that they teach their children not to cheat, that they do not like people cheating them, and given that the pressure toward consistency should limit people's cheating, we might assume that people would not cheat very much. Surprisingly, Ariely found quite of bit of cheating in his study on cheating, be it taking a pencil from work, a Coke, or whatever.[78] Most people are aware of their software theft. According to Ariely, if we do such things, "There's always a convenient rationale"[79] such as 'I work extra time I'm not paid for' or 'I always pay for the coffee at work.' The implication (not recommended) for many people is to avoid strict honesty criteria so they can cheat a little without considering themselves dishonest. This will allow them to view themselves as consistent, and being consistent, feel balanced about themselves. Of course, any expected guilt feelings about being dishonest exist to keep us "honest," and remorse after being dishonest may pressure us to avoid dishonesty thereafter.

People look for information that corroborates—is consistent with—their view of the world, as if they need to bolster their sense of who they are.[80] Both Ariely and Taleb conclude that two individuals or separate groups of people witnessing the same event can have two very different stories about what occurred.[81] Most people should have observed this in their own lives. Taleb suggests, "Once your mind is inhabited with a certain view of the world, you will tend to only consider incidences proving you to be right. Paradoxically, the more information you have, the more justified you will feel in your views."[82]

As noted above, there is a tendency for people to conform to other people's beliefs or behaviors, to hold ideas consistent with those around us.[83] This can lead us to change our conclusion, for example, after an initial visual perception reveals our answer is at odds with the rest of the group's. Moreover, Thaler and Sunstein report, "… recent brain-imaging work has suggested that when people conform in Asch-like settings, they actually see the situation as everyone else."[84] Individual subjects, when put in a room of strangers who all said that one line on the board was exactly like another of obviously different-length, ended up agreeing with the group about three-fourths of the time.

Thus, in our perception, we look for consistency in both our self and in others. We have a readiness to perceive consistency, even if it does not exist. People are respected for being consistent, even if they are wrong. Still, we are reminded of that old adage from 1841 by Emerson, "A foolish consistency is the hobgoblin of little minds …."[85] We may think that we would change our mind on a given issue or about a person if new information suggests the contrary, but many people do not. They maintain a *foolish consistency*. It is not easy for people to admit that earlier beliefs may be wrong.

It may be appropriate to recognize that no one is perfect. Further, there are numerous, complicated, and divergent issues that impinge upon our lives. Making choices in hope of maintaining a balanced state is difficult. Even friends may agree to disagree about some differences. People make compromises about all sorts of people and things in their lives.

OVERCOMING PERCEPTION BARRIERS

In addition to the suggestions previously offered in this chapter to increase our perceptual accuracy, DeVito offers a few additional recommendations for overcoming our perceptual limitations.[86]

1. *Analyze Your Perceptions.* This is not easy since much of the foundation for the existence and operation of our perceptions is a result of our physiology combined with our unique individuality and experience (influenced by our religious beliefs, assumptions about human nature, the existence (or not) of free will, and others). Can we be more mindful of our perceptions as well as analyze their legitimacy? Can we take the time to reflect upon them? Remember that who you are, what you bring to the communication moment, significantly determines your perception of the communication that occurs. Our illegitimate partiality for one person or thing over another person or something else prevents a clearer view and evaluation of these same people or phenomena, leading to weaker and potentially harmful results for us. In brief, can we be a little surer about our perceptions?

Further, we can attempt to withhold evaluations of people and phenomena until we believe we have justifiable information upon which to judge them. Avoid jumping to conclusions. Communication is a package of signals so there is much to evaluate in that, alone, in addition to all of the other circumstances and issues in life. You will rarely have unlimited time to gather information so you have to do the best you can under the circumstances. While you may find additional information that justifies your initial position, attempt to discover any existing contradictory information that would suggest you re-evaluate that position.

2. *Seek Perception Feedback* (check your perceptions). Get other people's interpretation of the person or phenomenon in question. This can add insight and provide a means of comparison to your own impressions. We can seek feedback by *describing* (in simple and direct terms) to the other person what we have seen and heard. Telling someone else your perception of them or what you have seen them do gives them an opportunity to correct what they

think are inaccuracies on your part. Ask them if you are correct. Avoid *mind reading*.[87] While it is normal and legitimate for our brains to make guesses about people's thoughts, feelings, and intentions, we can remind ourselves to be cautious in forming conclusions, be open to additional information, and avoid telling the person what they must be thinking or feeling. Ask them to share their position, their pleasure, or their intention.

3. *Reduce Uncertainty*. This recommendation encompasses the two listed above. The purpose of analysis and seeking feedback is to reduce uncertainty, which in turn increases our ability to predict and control our environment (a major purpose of communication). Perceptual uncertainty can also be decreased through additional observation, getting third-party input, and appropriately questioning the person in question (termed *cognitive* questions in Griffin) to determine what differentiates them from other people.[88]

CONCLUSION

Chapter 1 in this book stated that communication entails (among other processes) the sending and receiving of messages. Meaning is created within each individual as they decode (translate) the stimuli received. This chapter began with the idea that in the perception process that we create the meanings for the messages we receive, which in turn influence the messages of our response. As discussed herein, it can be suggested that perception not only influences which stimuli we process but how we process those stimuli to end up with the meaning we have in fact created. This is why who we are as individuals has a great influence on the reality of our individual perceptions and the meanings we draw (create) from the messages we receive and send. Perception is very subjective. As Ariely concluded, "…perception has more to do with our desires—with how we want to view ourselves—than with reality."[89] Since our brain responds with our reflexive part first, our predispositions are extremely influential. It is on the basis of our predispositions and the contextual stimuli that we make snap judgments.

Since people's perceptions can literally be all over the map, you might conclude that some portion of people's thinking are mentally *on Mars*. You are amazed by and wonder how someone else—or even yourself—can arrive at such disparate meanings to a given situation. Fortunately, people can have a significant overlap with each other's realities through their communication. Through careful analysis and practice, people do incorporate more logical (reflective) thinking into their own perception experiences. As can be imagined, perceptual errors can be the basis for human conflicts. This will be discussed further in the chapter on conflict.

CHAPTER 3 HOMEWORK

1. Stereotype. [Omit your name on the paper containing the stereotype so your work can be anonymous. A separate paper will be circulated in class so you can record that you submitted your homework.]
   a. Concisely write a stereotype you have of a place (village/city, territory/ state, country), a type of food, a religion, an organization, a career/ac- tivity, or a group of people (specific family (omit real name), ethnicity, height, age, intelligence, etc.).
   b. How accurate is this stereotype? Do you think it reflects 5% of the people or phenomenon in this group? 25%? 50%? 75%? 95% 100%? Write down a number, your best estimate.
   c. Do you think this stereotype is still legitimate for the group, as a whole?

2. Implicit Personality Theory
   [On a separate piece of paper, include your name for the following home- work submitted]
   List five different personality traits. For each word, add one additional characteristic that you commonly associate with that word. Do not use syn- onyms or antonyms. Each of the paired words should be at little different, but from your view, fit together in peoples' personality. Example: serious and conservative, arrogant and spoiled, friendly and conscientious, etc.

3. Changing a First Impression
   Describe a first impression you had of someone or some belief system (religious, political, ideological) that you later significantly altered.
   a. What was your first impression?
   b. What did it change to over time? (What did it later become?)
   c. Why did you change your first impression?

4. Inconsistency
   Give an example of an inconsistency exhibited by an individual, territory/ state/federal government, business, or religion. DO NOT use the real person's or organization's name but simply refer to them as Mr./Ms. "X," Senator/Governor/President/CEO "Y," or Religious Person "Z," etc. An actual public law can be specified. Briefly explain how the phenomenon is inconsistent.

5. Self-Fulfilling Prophecy
   Describe an example of a self-fulfilling prophecy you have experienced or witnessed. DO NOT use the actual names of the real people or organization.

a. Clearly state what was the implied expectation of which person X or group Y.
b. Give details of the communication (what was said, how it was said, what was not said, and any relevant behavior) that implied that expectation.
c. To what extent was the expectation achieved in the outcome.
d. Briefly explain whether you were surprised by the outcome

REFERENCES

1. J. Zweig, *Your Money and Your Brain* (New York: Simon & Schuster, 2007).
2. Ibid., p. 14.
3. Ibid.
4. D. Berlo, *The Process of Communication* (New York: Holt, Rinehart and Winston, 1960).
5. N. Taleb, *Fooled By Randomness: The Hidden Role of Chance in Life and in the Markets* (New York: Random House Trade Paperbacks, 2004).
6. Zweig, op cit., p. 58.
7. N. Taleb, *The Black Swan: The Impact of the Highly Improbable* (New York: Random House, 2007).
8. Ibid., p. 61.
9. J. DeVito, *Human Communication: The Basic Course* (10th ed.) (Boston: Pearson Education, Inc., 2006).
10. R. Buckhout, "Eyewitness Testimony." *Scientific American*, 231, No. 4 (December, 1974).
11. Taleb (2007), op cit., p. 21.
12. Taleb (2004), op cit.; Taleb (2007), op cit.; Zweig, op cit.
13. Taleb (2004), op cit.
14. R. Thaler and C. Sunstein, *Nudge: Improving Decisions About Health, Wealth, and Happiness* (New Haven: Yale University Press, 2008).
15. Taleb (2007), op cit., p.82.
16. Ibid., p. 203.
17. Pearson and Nelson, op cit., p.32.
18. Zweig, op cit.
19. Berlo, op cit.
20. Zweig, op cit.
21. D. Ariely, *predictably irrational: The Hidden Forces That Shape Our Decisions* (New York: HarperCollins Publishers, 2008), p. 7.
22. Ibid.
23. Ibid.
24. Zweig, op cit.
25. Ariely, op cit., p. 8.
26. Ibid.

27. Zweig, op cit., p. 243.
28. J. William, "The Visible Man." *The Discovery Channel* (February, 1990).
29. Ariely, op cit.
30. R. Verderber, *Communicate!* (7th ed.) (Belmont, CA: Wadsworth Publishing Company, 1993), p. 48.
31. Thaler and Sunstein, op cit., p. 26.
32. Zweig, op cit.
33. Ariely, op cit., p. 168.
34. Ibid.
35. Taleb (2007), op cit.
36. Ibid., p. 66.
37. Ibid., p. 63.
38. Ibid., p. 64.
39. Ibid.
40. Thaler and Sunstein, op cit., p. 30.
41. Ibid.
42. Taleb (2007), op cit.
43. Ariely, op cit.
44. Berlo, op cit.
45. W. Williams, "Racial profiling," in *Jewish World Review*. April 21, 2004.
46. Ibid., p. 2.
47. Zweig, op cit.
48. T. Sowell, *Black Rednecks and White Liberals* (San Francisco: Encounter Books, 2005).
49. T. Sowell, *The Economics and Politics of Race: An International Perspective* (New York: William Morrow and Company, Inc., 1983).
50. Sowell (2005), op cit.
51. B. Washington, *Up From Slavery: An Autobiography* (Garden City, New York: Doubleday & Company, Inc., 1900).
52. Sowell (2005), op cit.
53. Berlo, op cit.
54. Taleb (2007), op cit.
55. Ibid.
56. Ibid.
57. J. Stossel, *Myths, Lies, and Downright Stupidity. Get Out the Shovel—Why Everything You Know is Wrong* (New York: Hyperion, 2006), p. 1.
58. Taleb (2007), op cit., p. 133.
59. Berlo, op cit.
60. Taleb (2007), op cit., p. 15.
61. Taleb (2007), op cit.
62. Zweig, op cit.
63. Ariely, op cit., p. 176.
64. Ibid.
65. Pearson and Nelson, op cit.
66. Ariely, op cit.

67. Ibid.

68. Ibid., p. 171.

69. R. Rosenthal and L. Jacobson, *Pygmalion in the Classroom* (New York: Holt, Rinehart and Winston, 1992).

70. DeVito, op cit.

71. S. Beebe, S. Beebe, and M. Richmond, *Interpersonal Communication: Relating to Others* (Boston: Allyn and Bacon, 1999); DeVito, op cit.

72. E. Griffin, *A First Look at Communication Theory* (5th ed.) (Boston: McGraw Hill, 2003); D. Stacks, S. Hill, and M. Hickson, *An Introduction to Communication Theory* (Ft. Worth: Holt, Rinehart and Winston, Inc., 1991).

73. Ariely, op cit.

74. Ibid.

75. Griffin, op cit., Stacks, Hill, and Hickson, op cit.

76. R. Samuelson, UNTRUTH: Why the Conventional Wisdom Is (Almost Always) Wrong (New York: Random House, Inc., 2001).

77. D. Barnlund, *Interpersonal Communication: Survey and Studies* (Boston: Houghton Mifflin Company, 1968).

78. Ariely, op cit.

79. Ibid., p. 229.

80. Taleb (2007), op cit.

81. Ariely, op cit.; Taleb (2007), op cit.

82. Taleb, op cit., p. 59.

83. Thaler and Sunstein, op cit.

84. Ibid., p. 57.

85. R. Emerson, "Self-Reliance," in *Collected Essays, First Series* (Rockville, MD: Arc Manor, 2007), p. 23.

86. DeVito, op cit.

87. Ibid.

88. Griffin, op cit.

89. Ariely, op cit., p. 243.

CHAPTER FOUR

Self-Disclosure

"Do you want to know a secret? Do you promise not to tell anyone? Well, I just _____." "Oh, really? I feel _____ for you. That must have been _____. Thanks for sharing this." People want to know who we are. Many people just simply like to hear about other people's personal business, much of which is later the subject matter of gossip. We, too, seek to know who we are. To do so, we have to communicate (to some degree) the essence of our individuality. According to Barnlund, "Only by expressing what one feels or thinks can one gain a sense of one's own uniqueness."[1] In combination with our own reactions to ourselves, other people interpret our expressions and then communicate their impression of us to us.

Thus, it is through our communication about ourselves with others that we, to a great extent, inform and confirm to ourselves and to these others, and they in return with their response to us, both who we are as individuals and how we perceive the nature of our relationship with these others. Self-disclosure is the name given to this type of communication: our talking about and the revealing of ourselves to others.

THE *SELF* IN DISCLOSURE

The existence of the "self" part of self-disclosure needs some discussion. Jourard, who did much of the initial research and writing about self-disclosure, suggests that a real self exists in each of us yet we hide some of it behind a façade.[2] At a given moment, at least, it is our withheld thoughts, feelings, abilities, and behaviors that are at the heart of what he considered our *real* self. Wilmot concludes that there is no one self, but a complex and changing self that leaves a little bit different impression with each person we know.[3]

A combination of these two views provides for a person with some enduring qualities, beliefs, values, and behaviors who also exhibits aspects of a changing individual (self), with other beliefs, values, and behaviors added or dropped along the way. Further, the transactional nature of communication supports the idea that people are at least a little different *self* with each other person.

DEFINITION OF SELF-DISCLOSURE

While telling someone else *anything* about yourself, such as biographical information and general feelings or ideas can be considered disclosure and does aid the listener in knowing more about you (that you like the color red or prefer broccoli over green beans), such common personal information can be easily known and responded to. It is what we do not know about a person that can lead to misunderstandings and conflict, preventing us from more accurately predicting what they are likely to do or say. Moreover, it is the not knowing about the other person's more private self that prevents a closer relationship with them. It is this private self (or parts thereof) that is typically kept hidden from most, if not all, other people. It is the sharing of this private information that is the primary focus of people studying self-disclosure.

Self-disclosure is defined as someone (the speaker) intentionally telling someone else information about themselves (the speaker) that the listener does not know and would not otherwise find out. It is the revealing of personal information, often over time, about our thoughts, beliefs, and previous actions as a method for making our self known to others and to ourselves. The disclosed information could include some previous personal experiences, thoughts and/or feelings in a given moment about a current subject, person, or event, or future aspirations and goals.

Since communication is not a one-way street, the transactional view of communication (Chapters 1 and 2) suggests that the receiver of any disclosure has an influence on the context and individual making the disclosure[4] and is a source of messages occurring simultaneously with the verbal disclosure being made by the other person.

IMPORTANCE OF SELF-DISCLOSURE

Self-disclosure is important for a number of reasons. First, as noted above, it helps the discloser acquire increased information about him or her self. This knowledge can be used by individuals to make ongoing life decisions that they deem appropriate to their existence, including what type of people they enjoy being around, how they prefer to communicate and why, what job or family goals may or do satisfy them, what their strengths and weaknesses are across a range of activities, and so on. According to Barnlund, "Revealing past disappointments, current needs or confusions, and emerging fears or hopes is a way of clarifying them so they may be thought about and resolved."[5] The effect of saying something, and hearing ourselves say it, encourages us to reassess in a new and different way what is said. Further, since people are not a single, permanent self, they can (and many certainly do) consciously seek to alter their recognized values, beliefs, and behaviors. People even discover information about themselves in the moment as they disclose. While people may gain comfort from recognizing certain individual attributes, they may also discover some aspects of the less-revealed self that they do not like, such as jealousy, shyness, extreme pride, selfishness, an inconsistent work ethic, a perceived lack of sufficient intelligence, and so on. Some people make changes for the better in their lives based upon knowing their weaknesses.

Second, self-disclosure provides a means for establishing friendships and intimacy. If you know little about someone else, you will have little basis for feeling close to or even loving him or her. Gradually, but also occasionally with leaps and bounds, people forming friendships increase both the breadth and depth of disclosure.[6] Two people in a beginning friendship typically share general information about themselves such as interests, hobbies, and what they do for a living (or what their major is in school). If they like the image they have projected to the other person, feel comfortable with the other person, and if the other person has provided a similar level and amount of information, they may, for example, comment on some general family matters, what they think of their own abilities and what they expect to be doing in the near future. Added to this, they may discuss the friendships they currently have, and indirectly (at least) their availability for a closer relationship with the new person. If the two people want to be even closer, they may then share information about personal dreams, failures, sexual experiences, and possibly their money management. If communication is a transaction, as earlier suggested, then getting to know your self is connected with getting to know someone else.

Third, disclosure allows the receivers of the disclosure to more accurately anticipate what the discloser is likely to do and/or say in a given future situation, thereby aiding communication efficiency and effectiveness. Those who are most intimate with the discloser have the greatest amount of information upon which to act with that discloser. In one way, this is illustrated by the delight of someone who receives what otherwise appears to be an insignificant gift since the gift reveals that the gift giver knows the receiver well and the thought is an affirmation of the receiver of the gift. People often say that it is the "little things" that people do for and say to each other, without any apparent information shared about the given object, event or idea, that are so meaningful simply because these things show the giver knew idiosyncrasies of the receiver. They accurately predicted. Barnlund adds that knowing about someone else also allows us to help protect that person from others who could say or do something to hurt the individual.[7]

Some additional reasons that people disclose information include: an attempt to release emotional tension, influence the impression others have of themselves, influence other people's behavior, and the discloser can take some comfort in recognizing how he or she is similar to other people. It cannot be overlooked that, upon hearing someone else's disclosure, we may determine that the discloser's beliefs, moral standards, and behavior do not match our own,[8] so we can use the disclosure to help us decide not to spend time with some people—in this respect, an important message for us.

SUBJECT AREAS TYPICALLY NOT DISCLOSED

People disclose more about work (or school), attitudes, and individual tastes than they do about their money, body, and perceived personal and/or family flaws or failings. The following list reflects topics people tend not to talk about, even, in some cases, with family members and close friends. This list is not all-inclusive but does provide some sense of what is kept private.

Financial assets, income, spending habits	Career and/or social aspirations
Sexual experience, orientation, desire for/not	Credit card debt, credit report
Previous intimate relationships, affairs	Lack of a current, close relationship
Family secrets (may relate to topics listed)	Addictions to alcohol, drugs, food
Criminal or significant anti-social behavior	Incurable disease
Religious affiliation, commitment to	Political affiliation
	Body weight
	Age

FIGURE 4.1

People vary dramatically about the personal information they are comfortable and uncomfortable sharing with others, as well as in the perceived utility of self-disclosing as a method of knowing more about themselves or being intimate with others. People's individual wants, needs, character qualities, experiences, and behavior are quite diverse. Thus, there is no clear "normal" or "natural" amount of information that is kept private, but rather, what a given individual is content with sharing.

RISKS OF DISCLOSING

Certainly college students already know most of the risks. Common ones include: personal rejection by someone who negatively evaluates the disclosure provided, verbal attacks on the discloser and possibly humiliation over disclosures that reflect negatively upon the discloser, threats of blackmail about a significant failure, and material and/or financial loss (the theft of actual items or money or pressure to pay money). People can also lose their jobs over disclosure that reveals negative qualities for that job or for information that is inconsistent with information provided on the job application. In brief, people are vulnerable if they disclose, but if they do not, they will limit their intimacy with others.

Self-disclosure can be a threat to people's perceived self-worth and public image. Either the discloser or the receiver of the disclosure may think negatively of the discloser after the information is shared. The discloser may also think of him or herself as stupid for having made the disclosure. People may terminate a budding or existing friendship after hearing something that they (the listener) construe as particularly distasteful. After hearing something considered startling, the listener may wonder if they even know the discloser very well. A permanent ending of the friendship may result from disclosures made.

Although it cannot be quantified, there is certainly a risk of disclosing *too much* personal information. Even Jourard, who asserts the importance of disclosing, concludes that people also need to maintain secluded and confidential aspects of themselves or their own psychological and physical health would be at risk.[9] Moreover, we could put our individuality in jeopardy: "Where there is no privacy, there is no or little individuality."[10] According to Luft, "Disclosing too much creates at least as many problems as disclosing too little—but of a different kind."[11] Such disclosure can result in the listener feeling overwhelmed and stifled if he or she perceives the discloser as attempting to control him or her. On the other hand, excessive disclosure can be an effort on the discloser's part to persuade the listener to take some emotional or physical control over the discloser's personal life for which the listener is unable or unwilling.[12] An uncomfortable result for the listener could be feelings of sadness for the discloser or even guilt for not being a *crutch* for them.

There appears to be an ongoing dilemma in people between what to share about themselves to others and what to keep private. If there is something particularly troubling to a person, it may well feel better for them to "get it off their chest" (catharsis). There can also be a feeling of anticipation and elation when sharing goals and aspirations but also the danger that the listener will discount them and even deride the discloser. Many people like to tell of their accomplishments but often do not because they do not want to appear as boasting and egotistical.

RISKS OF NOT DISCLOSING

Ironically, people who disclose little or at least insufficiently in the view of those closest to them, may also suffer. According to Griffin and his explanation of Social Penetration Theory, people cannot become close to others if they do not make their own inner selves known to these other people.[13] Self-disclosure provides the means for getting to know someone. If a person does not disclose their inner self, there will be no closeness between that person and others with whom she or he has contact. The result will be loneliness, alienation from others, and some private anxiety from having a doubt about who he or she is. Further, the non-disclosure of harsh emotions such as anger can result in an increase of that anger within the non-discloser, increasing the possibility that he or she will later act in a physically or emotionally abusive manner with the subject of that anger.

Thus, there are negative outcomes of not disclosing, opposites of the reasons listed earlier in this chapter in favor of disclosing. Interpersonal relationships will not be closer. There will be little or no emotional release of personal feelings so people will likely let emotions create further emotional tensions: personal thoughts and feelings will continue to be mixed up and unresolved for the individual, there is likely to be little or a lesser amount of self-worth, and there will be little or no personal affirmation by other people of the individual as an individual if the other people are unfamiliar with the individual. It also takes extra mental effort and time to hide ourselves, which distracts us and decreases our concentration on other communication occurring at a given time. When other people sense that a person is withholding some pertinent thoughts and/or feelings, the people may conclude that the person is lying by omission which in turn may influence them to withhold some of their own pertinent information from the non-disclosing person. Now there are two barriers to intimacy and closer friendship.

In America, at least, it is accepted (noted in the previous chapter) that we are supposed to be consistent in and among our beliefs, values, and behaviors.

When there is inconsistency within or between these, we are thought to experience personal anxiety that puts pressure on us to change some aspects of our beliefs, values, and/or behaviors.[14] If our public persona—what we disclose publicly about ourselves—does not match what we perceive to be our private persona, then we are said to be living a lie and we will suppress both this recognition and the pertinent information. Jourard suggests that this will emotionally and physically harm us.[15]

GUIDELINES FOR DISCLOSING

People differ as individuals so they feel varying levels of comfort with and have different perceptions about the effectiveness of the who, what, where, when, why, and how's of self-disclosure. The larger question is, and this is somewhat intangible: when is it appropriate?

1. *The other person is important to y*ou. Disclose to those with whom you desire to create or maintain a closer friendship. Otherwise, it will be a waste of your time and effort. Both the act of becoming a friend or of maintaining a friendship coincide with knowing—disclosing with—the other person. Do you feel emotionally close enough to the person to reveal private information and can you trust the person with the information? Considering that self-disclosure is an intentional revelation about yourself, do you consciously want to disclose something personal to someone you accidentally met?

2. *Use positive disclosure when initially meeting people.* Listeners are likely to become defensive upon hearing negative evaluations about something from someone they just met. Consider a complementary comment about the weather, the food you are eating the activity occurring in your presence, and so on. People typically form a negative impression of strangers communicating a negative attitude. Consider stating something positive about the surrounding context in which you first meet someone, or perhaps give a subtle compliment to the other person to reduce their anxiety about you, a stranger. Withhold negative evaluations of yourself, what you are involved in, or even of the other person until your relationship has had some positive experiences to support an ongoing relationship.

3. *Continue disclosing only if it is reciprocated.* If one person discloses personal data and the other does not, then there is an imbalance in their relationship that will likely get weaker. If the two interacting people reveal a similar level of disclosure, it indicates that they perceive each other as mutually

involved with each other in some interdependent manner. They "connect" through their disclosure. As might be imagined, reciprocated self-disclosure has a more positive impact on a relationship than disclosure by only one of the persons.[16] If your disclosure is not reciprocated, it may mean that the listener is uncomfortable with it. In this event, reassess the content of your disclosure or the appropriateness of it. In general, consider disclosing the type of information that you desire from others.[17]

4. *The Amount and Intimacy Level Fits the Maturity of the Relationship.* In initial meeting, people often share and are comfortable revealing non-intimate information about themselves such as their names, occupation, place of residence. People who are perceived as *coming on too strong* (asking for or providing too intimate information) scare away listeners, who then seek to end the conversation and avoid future meetings. More disclosure is not better for new encounters. If the individuals find they have an affinity for each other, they tend to gradually increase the amount of personal and emotionally significant information about themselves. Given the idiosyncratic nature of relationships, Judd suggests that there cannot be a general prescription for the amount, degree of intimacy, timing, and percentage of positive and negative statements.[18] Over time, however, ongoing friendships tend to show an increase in the breadth and depth of disclosure.[19]

Adler and Rodman and Burgoon and Ruffner report that effective self-disclosure is both evenly matched between individuals and occurs in incremental steps over time.[20] There may also be random moments of very intimate disclosure, especially if the discloser is experiencing a personal crisis, and other periods of time when there is little or no disclosure.

It is recommended that we make careful distinctions about what or to whom we disclose. According to Scott and Brydon, "… self-disclosure is a gift because it suggests you trust someone to whom you've self-disclosed. To give this gift indiscriminately lessens its value."[21] Overall, see what impact your disclosure has on your listener and how they respond to it. Do they appear to think it was fitting for the association they have with you?

5. *The Disclosure Directly Relates to the Current Situation.* People often have a misconception that self-disclosure necessarily means revealing any and all of their "skeletons in the closet," which might include previous transgressions, weird thoughts, silent fears, and so forth. Although these may be significant to the individual, does the disclosure fit the behaviors and communication occurring at a given moment? Jourard's fundamental question about being known by others and being true to our self may be interpreted as emphasizing

the current situation: "A choice that confronts every one *at every moment* is this: Shall we permit our fellows to know us *as we are*, or shall we remain enigmas, wishing to be seen as persons *we are not?*"[22] (emphasis added). In short, should we disclose who we presently are and disclose what we are presently thinking and feeling, or should we disclose what we think will fit the image we have of ourselves and the image we would like others to have of us?

The following scenarios raise this dilemma. You are with your friends at the beach as the sun is close to setting. What are your topics of conversation? What meanings do you create from their nonverbal messages? Can you share the thoughts and feelings triggered in your mind from the then and there communication? During a fall, Saturday afternoon when there are no pressing activities, high school senior Diane is sitting with her parents in the living room; they ask her about her college plans. Is this the moment she should tell them about her yearning to go to a special art school in another state, or that she does not want to be a business major like her dad wants her to be, or possibly that she does not even want to attend college—at least, not yet? While watching someone steal second base at a baseball game, should you tell your friend you got fired once from a job for stealing? While attending a wedding, should you tell someone you are with that you are divorced? If your small group of non-intimate classmates is doing a project on physical abuse, should you tell them you were once abused? If you are with your colleagues at a fun, social function, should someone ask you why you are divorced, should you tell the entire group why, and should you tell them the painful details? What is the relevance of your disclosure to what is occurring in the here-and-now?

According to Burgoon and Ruffner, if the disclosure is constant and irrelevant, listeners will consider the discloser a bore.[23] A constant disclosure of feelings may interfere with the completion of a group task. Someone frequently telling you how difficult their personal or professional life is may result in an undo emotional strain on yourself as you worry about what might happen to them. To clear your mind of the person's problems, you may avoid them in the future.

There is so much focus by self-disclosers on the "history" of their lives, as if that largely defines who or what they are thinking and feeling presently. Many people change and even mature over time. What does the past have to do with the person you are with in the moment, in the present context, with whom you have constructed a unique relationship? Individuals are at least slightly different people with each different person with whom they interact. This reflects the transactional nature of communication. A focusing on past events can become a barrier to present moment self-disclosure and communication in general simply because it *is* history. Rather, history can be shared as it relates to the present experience individuals are sharing and the uniqueness that each other created by their transaction..

This does not mean that certain past behaviors and their effects are irrelevant, such as alcoholism, drug addiction, spousal infidelity, spouse or child abuse, inconsistent employment, not living within financial means, being materialistic, sterility, and others.

6. *The Potential Risks are Reasonable.* You have to determine if the potential rewards of disclosing sufficiently outweigh the potential risks. This may be easy to judge after the fact, but for a novice discloser, at least, may be difficult to determine at the moment. Expect that early, intimate friendships may exhibit some self-disclosure that, in retrospect (even a moment later), is embarrassing and/or ineffective. No one can anticipate all the outcomes. After some experience of what works and when, people can gain a sense what is prudent while largely avoiding personal rejection and other trouble. Over time, people get a sense of who they can trust to keep their disclosure confidential. Overall, is the listener expected to be discreet and nonjudgmental?

Interestingly, a similarly high level of reported self-disclosure occurs between strangers on public transportation as among close friends.[24] Disclosers can trust the situation to protect themselves from typical disclosure risks since the listener is unlikely to meet someone who knows the discloser.[25] Cozby suggests that the *stranger effect* occurs because strangers do not have current or future expectations of each other that could inhibit personal or social constraints to disclosing.[26] In sum, there is a reasonable risk to disclose with strangers in this situation.

7. *An Improvement Is Expected.* Can you expect the disclosure to help yourself and/or the listener in some way? Will the disclosure advance the relationship between the two of you? Is there a pressing need for the disclosure? This will require us to think through whether the likely effects will be constructive for the one or both of you.

A great deal of what people do know about other people's lives is actually none of their personal business so their disclosure of other's lives is generally disliked and not helpful. Also avoid knowingly revealing something that may be particularly difficult for the listener to effectively respond to, like a previously embarrassing or regretful act by you, the listener, or someone closely connected to the two of you. In short, avoid burdening the listener.[27] Maintain some personal privacy—of your own and/or of theirs. Jourard suggests that people have a part of themselves that should be kept private to maintain their individuality.[28] Barnlund concludes that we would lose our identity and the control over our self to other people if they knew all about us.[29] Scott and Brydon recommend that we create *privacy boundaries* even in our established relationships.[30] While someone else may guess that we are hiding something about the past, such self-disclosure may become an obstacle or hindrance for the current relationship.

As earlier noted, it can be difficult to know in advance whether your self-disclosure will aid the relationship between you and the listener. This means the self-disclosure improves the relationship or the subject's life; it does not mean that no one feels uncomfortable. Demeaning and hurtful comments cannot be expected to be constructive. Can you anticipate how you would feel if you were in the other person's position, be it as the discloser or as the listener? What if you were the subject in the disclosure? Would you want to know? Would it help to know?

Many disclosers overlook the possibility that they will later feel guilty for having disclosed with a third party something unbecoming about their selves. Knowing the otherwise innocent third-party listener knows the negative information, the discloser may feel uncomfortable being around them and attempt to avoid them; thereby, ending a previous friendship. Consider the chance this will happen.

8. *You Are Motivated to Improve the Relationship.*[31] To the extent that we are aware of them, and given that our motives are not always clear to ourselves, we can ask ourselves whether we want to self-disclose out of concern for the esteem and well-being of everyone involved. We can ask ourselves the results we hope for[32] as a way to assess our reason for disclosing.

DeVito cautions us against trying to use disclosure to punish others, make them feel guilty,

or even make ourselves feel guilty.[33] We should avoid disclosing just because it feels good to ourselves (gets it off our chest) without thinking of the negative impact it may have on our listeners. Scott and Brydon recommend that you "… don't make a disclosure unless you are willing to take responsibility for its consequences."[34]

9. *Disclose to a Professional if You Cannot Trust Anyone to Maintain Confidentiality.* It is a sad commentary on the state of everyday interpersonal affairs that many (even most) people do not have a listener who will maintain the speaker's privacy. Thankfully, there are plenty of professionals available who are trained to listen and maintain confidentiality, such as religious clergy, social workers, and counselors. We can avoid a lot of disclosure risks if we use them. One difficulty is that they are not as readily available to listen to us as are our friends when we feel the need or are in the mood to self-disclose.

GUIDELINES FOR INTERNET AND
SOCIAL MEDIA DISCLOSURE

With the advent and widespread use of social media and computer emails, a wider audience typically receives individual participant's disclosures about everything from everyday mundane topics to intimate, or at least what used to be considered intimate, disclosure. The following provide some considerations, particularly since they may affect current and/or future employment or a person's public image. What may have once been relatively harmless since only one person or a few friends heard or saw something intimate may easily be shared with a wider target audience, including from hacked emails and government spying. Some employers are using Internet searches in an attempt to discover more about potential and current employees than is apparent on job applications, in interviews, or seen and heard at work.

1. No Nude Pictures or Inappropriate Stages of Undress. Females, particularly, may want to avoid all such photos even if they are not intended for distribution. Even shirtless men posing at work can reflect poorly on the men and on the company for whom they work. A male boss photographed shirtless at home with a big beer belly while mowing his front lawn may appear a little less credible to the employees he oversees.

2. No Outlandish Behavior. While this is somewhat subjective, anything perceived as gross or particularly stupid can reflect negatively on someone's public image. Sharing an episode of being drunk or being photographed while being inebriated should be avoided. Since more companies and government agencies prohibit smoking at work, smokers may want to avoid disclosures of smoking at home. President Obama, like some other public and private officials, has kept his cigarette smoking pretty private. Avoid all references to or any pictures of you smoking marijuana.

3. Avoid Racial and Gender Jokes or Related Comments. These are easily taken out of context and it is difficult to determine how receivers, particularly unintended ones, will respond to jokes. While most of us are not in the public's eye, people have a way of finding and sharing what you said ten to twenty years ago, particularly if they think it may embarrass you.

4. Avoid Disparaging Comments about your Employer or your Boss, and do not use the Organization's Internet Accounts to send your Personal Messages. This could embarrass the company's external (public) image or the supervisor's internal company image and reveal poor judgment on your part. Company time and resources belong to the company so your personal use of them could be considered a form of theft.

It was formerly thought that what you did on your own time was your own business and few, if anyone, knew your business, but now if you disclose online you are making it many other peoples' business, for good or ill. While we may still have private moments with our family, friends, and associates, the technology that makes it so easy to record and transmit personal information means that more of our personal disclosures will be shared with a larger audience.

GUIDELINES FOR RESPONDING TO THE SELF-DISCLOSURE OF OTHERS

In the list below, DeVito offers a number of recommendations for us when responding to the self-disclosure of other people.[35]

1. *Be an Effective and Active Listener.* Listen, without interrupting. Initially (at least), withhold verbal evaluation. Consider potential meanings of the information. Try to sense his/her feelings. Consider the ramifications of the information for your relationship. Ask questions if the disclosure seems unclear, but avoid leading questions. Paraphrase for the discloser what you heard them say. Better yet, respond with active listening (see Chapter 5) in which you suggest what they seem to be feeling and combine that with a paraphrase of the content. In this situation, you are not evaluating them or advising them, but giving them a sense of emotional support.

2. *Be Willing to Reciprocate.* If the guidelines for disclosure noted in the previous section are accurately reflected in the speaker's disclosure to you, then it would be appropriate for you to respond in kind. This is an opportunity for the two of you to build a closer relationship with each other. Your reciprocating shows the other discloser that you understand them[36] and are mutually willing to both risk disclosure and trust their confidence. The reciprocation encourages more disclosure in the future.

Do not think that just because the other person disclosed, you have to? Maybe you determine that the other person just wants someone with whom to share their thoughts or feelings and nothing more, so you act as a good listener. There may be other times when you conclude that the discloser is using his or her disclosure as a ploy to get you to disclose, so you decide to avoid being manipulated. Further, there could be times that people ask you very personal questions that you think are inappropriate, so you change the subject, directly refuse to answer,

Or you leave their presence.

3. *Keep the Disclosures Confidential.* The narrow definition of self-disclosure refers to private information that other people do not know about an individual and otherwise would not know unless the individual told them. Disclosers normally assume and trust that the listener will keep their personal information will be kept private. Ironically, a cursory survey of any group of people you know will reveal that little disclosed information is kept private by listeners. Some respondents will say that listeners keep nothing private while others will say that only about 1%-10% of disclosure is kept private. Assuming this understanding is accurate, we might wonder why anyone discloses at all to normal receivers of disclosure. No answer for this is offered here.

The lack of confidentiality about disclosed information will probably raise a question in the discloser's mind about the closeness of the relationship and limit future disclosure to both the listener and others. The discloser will lose trust in and respect for the listener. The discloser can easily suffer all the harms of disclosure noted early in this chapter. It would not take very many broken confidences before a discloser has few, if any, people left to whom he or she might readily disclose. Overall, revealing what someone has said in confidence devalues that person's special meaning for what has been said and their perception of the relationship.[37]

Thus, it is recommended that receivers of self-disclosure keep the disclosed information secret. Be responsible. Use the opportunity to increase the trust between yourself and the disclosing person. It is recognized that maintaining confidentiality is not easy. Ask permission of the discloser if you wish to reveal any part of it.[38] If you feel burdened by the disclosure made to you, consider speaking with a professional.

4. *Do Not Use the Disclosures as a Weapon Against the Person.* To do so would be a betrayal of the discloser's trust in you, the listener, and could irreparably harm the relationship between the two of you. As noted earlier in the chapter, self-disclosure leaves us in a position to be helped (and loved) by they who know us, yet its big risk is that it will be used to harm us. This is a big dilemma. When people's anger is intense and their emotional state (System 1) is largely running their mental operations, it is difficult for them to be sufficiently rational to overcome normal desires to attack the discloser's weaknesses. Still, even the person who is tempted to harm someone else might consider that they could also hurt themselves in harming that other person.

CONCLUSION

Self-disclosure is considered an integral part of social relationships, especially in intimate friendships. How can we confirm our thoughts about who we are unless we communicate those to other people and receive feedback about our thoughts? Other than just observations of us, how can other people know us well enough to efficiently and effectively communicate with us and partially satisfy our needs if they do not have a fairly clear sense of who we are? Further, how can we have a close, personal, and satisfying association with someone else if the two of us do not self-disclose?

Probably the most significant criterion guiding the use of self-disclosure is, what is the *appropriate* disclosure to use at that moment, in that context, and for that relationship? Adler and Rodman provide an explication of this: "It's ludicrous to picture the self-disclosing person as someone who blurts out intimate details of every past experience. Instead, our model is someone who, when the time is appropriate, trusts us enough to share the hidden parts of himself that affect our relationship."[39] Even if this criterion is accepted, it is not easy to determine what is appropriate, given the breadth and depth of information and experience needed about the varied situations and people we experience and our own personal changes over time.

It is not recommended that people force their disclosures on others or disclose under pressure to other people. We should not disclose all now.[40] Everyone needs some *self* privacy. Stein offers a useful mental strategy that (with practice) can guide our disclosures in the moment: disciplined spontaneity.[41] This may seem like an oxymoron but it refers to using a balance of our brain's System 1 and System 2 responses. This method requires a keen observation of the other person and his or her expected response to the disclosure.

While some self-disclosure will help the listener know more about the discloser, much of what people would like to know about other people does not have to be disclosed but merely learned by observing the person in question. You can observe their communication and behavior across a variety of topics and in a variety of situations over a period of time.

CHAPTER 4 HOMEWORK

Specifically refer to the chapter information to help you explain and justify your responses to the homework.

1. Give one example of someone (not yourself or someone who could be identified locally) who publicly self-disclosed something (state it here) that you think should have been kept private, and explain why. Which risks did they take and which guidelines for disclosing did they overlook?

2. Which subjects typically not disclosed that are listed earlier in the chapter (fourth page) would you be willing to discuss (but NOT HERE) with the

media, and why? If none, explain why not. Which risks are you taking, and which guidelines for disclosing help explain your position?

3. Give 1 example of someone (be anonymous) who disclosed false information (what?) about themselves (possibly on the Internet) and later had their lie revealed. What was the outcome?
Your overall observation of this event?

DISCUSSION QUESTIONS

Your instructor may assign one or more of the following to the class.

Should you tell people that you previously lied to them?

Should you tell family or friends that they have a poor appearance?

Should you tell family or friends that they are gaining or losing weight?

Should adopted children be told of their adoption?

Should children be told who their biological parents are?

Should a child be told of any artificial means used for their birth?

Should spousal/friend disagreements be kept between the spouses/friends?

Should someone's ill health (physical or mental) be disclosed to a potential or actual partner?

Should the cause of someone's physical disability be explained to others?

Should a criminal past be disclosed?

Should you tell family, friends, or others about an unhappy relationship or marriage?

Should people tell others why they got divorced? Tell their own children?

Should people tell others why they are not married, when they will, or if they will not?

Should people tell others what they plan to do with their lives?

Should people's sexual orientation be revealed?

Should previous relationships be revealed? Previous affairs?

Should children or friends who discover a parent's or friend's infidelity reveal it? To whom?

Should parents be told of their children's sexual relationships?

Should biological parents be told of unknown off-spring? Even if 20, 30, 40, 50 years later?

Should anyone be told of a couple's sexual behaviors? Should best friends tell each other?

Should people tell a date or a prospective partner that they will not engage in premarital sex?

Should a friend or sibling tell a bride or groom that they do not support the wedding?

Should a friend who discovers that a friend's partner/prospective spouse is not who they pretend to be, tell the friend?

Should people be told of a person's private, family abusiveness?

Should people be told that someone is stealing from them?

Should people be told their gifts (given or received) are not high quality or inappropriate?

Should a couple's financial assets be revealed to each other before marriage? Amount of income within marriage? Significant purchases or spending during marriage?

Should family members tell non-members their family's financial status?

Should monetary gifts given to 1 spouse or partner be kept secret from the other?

Should people's body alterations be revealed?

Should people always disclose their true age?

Should people make death-bed confessions? Should some secrets be taken to the grave?

What significance should listeners place on death-bed confessions?

REFERENCES

1. D. Barnlund, *Communicative Styles of Japanese and Americans: Images and Realities* (Belmont, CA: Wadsworth Publishing Company, 1989).
2. S. Jourard, *The Transparent Self* (New York: Van Nostrand Reinhold, 1964).
3. W. Wilmot, *Dyadic Communication* (Menlo Park, CA: Addison-Wesley Publishing Company, 1975).
4. W. Pearce, and S. Sharp, "Self-disclosing communication." *Journal of Communication* 23 (1973): 409-425.
5. Barnlund, op cit., p. 103.
6. Ibid.
7. Ibid.
8. Jourard (1964), op cit.
9. Ibid.
10. Ibid., p. 70.

11. J. Luft, *Of Human Interaction*, (Palo Alto: Mayfield Publishing Company, 1969), p. 57.
12. Ibid.
13. E. Griffin, *A First Look At Communication Theory* (5th ed.) (Boston: McGraw Hill, 2003).
14. Ibid.
15. Jourard (1964), op cit.
16. M. Scott, and S. Brydon, *Dimensions of Communication: An Introduction* (Mountain View, CA: Mayfield Publishing Company, 1997).
17. R. Verderber, *Communicate!*,(7th ed.) (Belmont, CA: Wadsworth Publishing Company, 1993).
18. L. Judd, "Self-disclosure in speech communication pedagogy: a case against overemphasis." Paper presented at the International Communication Association Convention, Chicago, IL, 1978.
19. Barnlund, op cit.
20. R. Adler, and G. Rodman, *Understanding Human Communication* (10th ed.) (New York: Oxford University Press, 2009).; M. Burgoon, and M. Ruffner, *Human Communication* (New York: Holt, Rinehart and Winston, 1978).
21. Scott and Brydon, op cit., p. 200.
22. Jourard (1964), op cit., p. vii.
23. Burgoon and Ruffner, op cit.
24. Pearce and Sharp, op cit.
25. M. Griffin, Self-Disclosure: Theoretical, Research, and Pragmatic Implications. Unpublished Masters' Thesis, San Francisco State University, 1979.
26. P. Cozby, "Self-disclosure: a literature review." *Psychological Bulletin* 79 (1973): 73-91.
27. J. DeVito, *Human Communication: The Basic Course* (10th ed.) (Boston: Pearson Education, Inc., 2006).
28. Jourard (1964), op cit.
29. Barnlund, op cit.
30. Scott and Brydon, op cit.
31. DeVito, op cit.
32. Scott and Brydon, op cit.
33. DeVito, op cit.
34. Scott and Brydon, op cit., p. 200.
35. DeVito, op cit.
36. Ibid.
37. Ibid.
38. Adler and Rodman, op cit.
39. R. Adler, and N. Towne, *Looking Out/Looking In: Interpersonal Communication* (2nd ed.) (New York: Holt, Rinehart and Winston, 1978).
40. M. Griffin, op cit.
41. W. Stein, "The myth of the transparent self." *Journal of Humanistic Psychology* 15 (1975): 71-78.

CHAPTER FIVE

Listening

Many people lead busy lives. Adults must satisfy their job requirements and/or their home needs, which may include care of parents and/or children. There is always community work to be done. Most college students work part-time jobs and they may have children. Even high school students can be very involved in sports or other extra-curricular activities in addition to what amounts to a full-time job of class time and home studying. If they work at part-time jobs, there is not much time left in the average day. Further, people enjoy some private moments of peace and quiet at home after the physical and/or mental stress incurred in their daily activities. While not excusing it, it should not surprise us that after a long day of work, parents may initially be unreceptive to their children. It is easy to envision a college student trying to seek advice or a frank talk about a troubling situation to a pseudo-listening roommate or parent who is reading the newspaper or watching the six-o'clock news while drinking a favorite beverage, and the latter responds with a, "Whatever you think."

In general, people's performance as effective listeners suggests that listening is arguably their weakest communication skill. People feel much more of an urge to speak than to listen. We spend more time listening than speaking[1] yet there is little instruction in listening.[2] Speaking contests are common but when did we hear of someone winning a listening trophy? People who could be labeled as good listeners are so few that most other people would only need one hand to count the number of good listeners they know. Although verbal messages are constantly being sent and people presume to be in sync with each other, there is a frequent glitch in the decoding of and responses to the messages received.

Although not all communication has an aural (sound) component in the message, much of it does. For there to be a speaker, there has to be a listener.

While we normally think of the listener as separate from the speaker, the listener could just be the speaker speaking to him or herself. Listening is a regular component of the transactional nature of communication.

LISTENING DEFINED AND THE
LISTENING PROCESS

In Chapter 3, *perception* was defined as the process of assigning meaning to stimuli we become aware of through our senses. Listening, too, requires the receiving of stimuli but in this case, those with an aural component. Listening requires the physical registering of sound waves by our ears, typically spoken words, which are then interpreted as in the process of perception. Following this, a response is made to provide feedback for the speaker.

The preceding steps reveal that *listening* is a combined a physical and mental process which assigns meaning to aural stimuli while what is termed *hearing* is simply a physical act of detecting sounds. Someone could *hear* or notice that someone else said something but not physically hear it well enough to draw significant meaning from it. There could be some reasons for this: there was existing physical noise in the environment, the listener had sub-par listening acuity, the listener was preoccupied with something he or she deemed more important at that moment, the message topic was uninteresting to the listener, the listener did not like the speaker so he or she did not make sufficient effort to listen, and so on. Given these possible justifications for not listening, it can be difficult for either the speaker or an observer to evaluate the listener as wrong or label him or her as a poor listener.

Communication is self-reflective. When we speak we are sending messages to two main audiences: one to the listener and one to our self. We hear ourselves speak even as others do. We are influenced by our own communication even as we communicate with and influence others. At the same time, we, in turn, are also influenced by the interpretations of our observations of the listener's response. As Chapter One described the communication process, we are all both senders and receivers. While we speak we, too, listen. In fact, Johnson suggests that each of us is our own most enchanted listener. "[I]t is the responses we make as our own listeners that are undoubtedly the most fateful of all. For every speaker … is his own most affected eavesdropper."[3]

WHY WE NEED TO LISTEN: BENEFITS

1. *Confirmation.* People have a great desire to be heard and feel a sense of confirmation that they are some body, an individual, unique and special in their own

right. We, in our listening mode, provide that validation for others. To not be listened to engenders a sense of isolation, loneliness, and diminished self-worth. As suggested in the previous chapter on self-disclosure, we in part learn from other people about who we are based on their listening to (and observations of) us.

2. *Knowledge.* From listening to others, we learn a great deal about the content of life issues. Further, gaining a sense of knowing others from our listening to them, we reach conclusions about whether we would like to build or maintain a further relationship with them. Moreover, the more we know others, the better able we are to predict and control our communication with them (the fundamental purpose of communication). In this case, a listener has a greater potential to *persuade* a speaker about an issue, and a speaker is more willing to follow the suggestions of a listener who conveys the idea that they have carefully listened to the concerns of the speaker.[4]

Wolvin and DeVito report that high school and college students spend the greater majority of their time in class listening, by which they are expected to learn.[5] Organizational members have to listen to each other so they will know what to do. Businesses have to listen to their customers and tailor the business products and/or services to the customers if the business expects to stay in business. Granted that people can and do acquire knowledge from independent reading and studying, it could also be said that we cannot not listen if we expect to expand our understanding.

3. *Shared Existence of Reality.* In seeking to validate our perception of the world, we listen to other people's points of view. Through this, we discover who around us is of like-mind. We tend to associate with people who share our view of about what is meaningful in life and how we think the world operates. The existence and operations of different religions and political parties illustrate this. Listeners who provide a response reflective of a speaker's perspective will be more liked and accepted by the speaker.[6]

4. *Feelings.* Knowing the content of the speaker's message is useful but that is not all there is to know about the message. Just as important, and in some cases more so, is recognition of the speaker's emotional response accompanying the content message. It is the speaker's feeling and intensity accompanying the content that provides a personal message about the content. This is vital for us to recognize in our attempting to discern the more complete meaning from the message. Acknowledging people's feelings is a necessary part of knowing and confirming who they are, and sharing the existence of their reality.

5. *Helping.* With the knowledge that comes from listening to those around us, including the intensity of feeling they have about a given phenomenon, we

are in an informed position to help them in their daily lives. We may recognize that our friend really needs a favor, a family member is really sick, that our child is having difficulty in a certain class, and so on. In perceiving the distress in each case we may then decide whether and to what extent we will help them with their personal difficulty. Do not overlook the fact that many people do not want to directly say they need help so you as a listener will have to pay close attention to their messages.

⨯MISCONCEPTIONS ABOUT LISTENING

1. *The Meaning Is In The Message.* Speakers often assume that if the listener did not "get" the meaning they "sent" and had in mind, then something is wrong with the listener. We know from the definition of *communication* in Chapter One that we do not send meaning, only messages. Messages are open to interpretation and not everyone will interpret them in the same way. As the Perception chapter explained, there are many variables that affect the meanings we end up with, so the meanings decoded (created) by the listener are often in conflict with the meanings encoded by the speaker.

2. *Listening Means Agreement or Obedience.* A listener might well have created a similar meaning in his or her mind to the speaker's but disagreed with the validity of that meaning and/or decided not to do the behavior suggested by the meaning. In this case, the listener cannot be accused of merely *hearing* or *not listening* to the speaker. They know well what the speaker implied but chose not to agree with and/or follow it. It is common in political an religious debates that after an in-depth listening to and investigation of an opponents position, a listener still maintains the beliefs that he or she had before the speaking event occurred.

3. *It Is Easy To Listen.* As suggested in the definition of listening, we can *hear* with our ears but it takes our ears and mental cognition to create meaning. If listening was so easy we might presume we would have fewer listening mistakes, mistakes that are so common in everyday life. As Wolvin and Coakley suggest, it is common to think of listening to people as a passive exercise.[7] This is often the case when people listen to music, but to really listen to people speak, our body's metabolism has to speed up. We also have to put distractions aside and consciously concentrate on the message and the speaker. We often have to sit up straight if we are in a chair and position our body toward the speaker. Our head probably leans forward. We create short summaries in our mind as the speaker speaks and may also think about the implications of the message. Then we may formulate a question for the speaker. All told, this is not passive and

it is not easy, especially if we are tired, uncomfortable, bored with the subject, have little or no knowledge about the subject, and so on.

4. *Just Because Someone Speaks, You Have To Listen.* Yes, it is in our interest to carefully listen to authority figures be they teachers, preachers, parents, police officers, supervisors at work, and so on. Separate from these, what right do people have to command our attention? Where do people get the idea that just because they are speaking, the other person has to listen? Sure, we want to be polite but we do not have to allow ourselves to be unnecessarily controlled. Do you want to give them the message that they control you just by their speaking?

REASONS FOR INEFFECTIVE LISTENING

1. *Noise.* You may remember from the Communication Model in Chapter One that noise is anything that reduces the clarity of a message, anything that interferes with or prevents the listener from acquiring the complete message. There is noise in all communication. Five types of noise are described below.[8]

Physical (external) noise, such as other people talking, equipment noise, blaring music or television programs, and so on. This noise might drown out the entire message but most commonly it blocks or alters a part of it. This could be sufficient for the listener to create an entirely different meaning from the message than they would otherwise have.

Physical distractions can also act as noise when they draw our attention away from the speaker's messages. It is very common to be listening to a friend or co-worker and simultaneously see someone else you know in the distance and wave to them, or say "Hi" to another friend passing nearby, or turn your head a little to the side and make a face in response to the smell of something you particularly like or dislike, and so on.

Physiological noise, such as an aching back that distracts our attention as we sit and listen to someone, or other physical problems such as headaches or ear damage that alter our hearing.

Psychological noise, which creates a mental focus on a personal want or need that takes our attention away from the verbal message occurring at that moment. We may also feel very emotional, such as being either happy or upset about something. Mental stress blocks and/or distorts messages coming from someone else in our presence.

Semantic noise occurs when someone uses words that are unfamiliar to the listener. Further, a *distraction* can occur when the listener overemphasizes the speaker's use of a word (generally a word the listener does not like or thinks does not fit the situation). As a result, the listener does not hear everything the speaker says and may easily take the use of the word out of context. This is why you will hear some speaker's say when they see this reaction in the listener, "Hear me out," or "Let me finish before you respond" in hope of not being inaccurately misjudged.

2. *Speech Speed, Thought Speed.* People can listen to what someone else says and still have mental time to think about other things, and they frequently do. Wolvin and Coakley report that the regular rate of speech is between 125-150 words per minute while listeners can take in around 500 words per minute.[9] The additional thoughts listeners entertain distracts them from the current message and the lack of full attention greatly increases the likelihood that the listener will miss some key points made by the speaker. While it is easy to bemoan a listener not paying full attention, they do have some excess mental time to use and most people have an endless supply of important concerns that also need their attention (it is acknowledged, though, that people probably do this excessively).

3. *Little Familiarity with the Topic or the Vocabulary.* If listeners know little or nothing about the topic under discussion or the terms used for it, they will be able to hear the message but will have little basis for creating meaning. For example, most people know little about how an automobile runs or the terms for its parts. An uninformed car owner will hear a lot of noise, will not know what to listen for, and will not be able to discuss his car's condition. This lack of knowledge can cost such car owners a great deal of money as they make uninformed decisions to spend more than they need.

4. *Biases.* A bias in this application means prejudging something by forming an opinion about it before being adequately acquainted with it. If we have a bias about people in a certain religion, ethnic, or other groups, we will tend to hear only what fits our bias, not the more complete message of the speaker. Incomplete knowledge can lead to hasty generalizations about other people and concepts with which we probably form stereotypes. People do not reflect much on their biases, so what they hear is often interpreted and distorted according to the bias. It can be said that people often say that someone is biased simply because they do not like what the person has said. Can we be comfortable about what we know so we do not let prejudging alter the messages we receive? Taking a cue from the title of the General Semantics' journal, *ETC,* there is always more to be said—and listened to and learned.

INEFFECTIVE LISTENING BEHAVIORS

Most people commonly use one or more defective listening behaviors in their everyday communication. Some of these are listed below.

1. *Pseudolistening.* As the term indicates, the listener doing this only pretends to listen, and he or she may be a good pretender. In reality, the person is deceptive. He or she is really thinking about his or her own business and concerns. You can often catch this person in this façade by asking them pointed questions about what you have just said.

2. *Selective Listening.* We cannot be too hard on people in this situation since, as we know from the Perception chapter that perception (and therefore, listening) is selective. That being said, this type of listening focuses on just some parts of the speaker's message, giving an incomplete assessment of the speaker's implied meaning. There is some justification for being selective since there are many demands on our listening attention and we may have a good reason to also listen to something else (like an important phone call) or for a particular idea or speaker point of view. Further, since not all topics are interesting to everyone, we might remember that our friends and co-workers do not like everything we speak so we might indulge them, in turn.

3. *Defensive Listening.* Knowing that many people have experienced verbal attacks by others who are in some position of power over them, we can understand that they could be on guard to protect themselves to deter additional aggression. It is easy for third party observers to dismiss this, especially college professors who can observe aggression themselves occurring in some of their faculty meetings. Still, we also know that people in a defensive mode easily misperceive and misconstrue innocent remarks made by parents, bosses, neighbors, and others, incurring what in this case would be an unjustified aggressive verbal response by them towards the speaker and the likelihood of increased tension between the two parties. A defensive reaction by the listener impedes his or her getting the full message. Being defensive, the listener will spend his or her time thinking about what he or she wants to say to the speaker, not on what the speaker is actually saying. What often occurs is a form of bypassing in which the two respondents speak past each other, not realizing or acknowledging the other's perspective.

4. *Ambushing.* In this form, the listener listens just for information that they can use to attack the speaker. This strategy is sometimes used with defensive listening described above. Making a surprise attack on someone has its advantages, but those who use it could ask themselves if this method will help

them achieve their overall goal. On the other hand, there could easily be a few people you will have to interact with in your life who will have nothing but ill will toward you. There are authoritarian leaders out there who will abuse you. You have to protect yourself.

EFFECTIVE LISTENING RESPONSES

People can minimize or even avoid the barriers discussed in the previous sections by using the following listening behaviors. While at any one moment we may use only one of these, during the next moment we will probably switch to another, and then to another, and so on as our listening to someone else continues throughout an interaction. Different listening methods fit different situations and peoples. We need to determine which is most appropriate in a given moment.. This section lists and provides an explanation of effective listening styles, or skills as noted by DeVito[10] and Wolvin and Coakley.[11]

1. *Surface and Depth Listening.* Messages we receive vary in their complexity and in the speaker's internationality (to the extent we can determine it). A message may simply be a literal content message about an action the speaker would like to take or their point of view about some current issue. Yes, it can be difficult to determine someone's intentions and we know there are many manipulators out there, but certainly among most people you know you would expect to receive a fair amount of surface messages which you could safely interpret literally.

For the other type of messages, we have to "listen" between the "lines." Sometimes people think, for whatever reason, that they cannot be very direct with us so they give us incomplete or suggestive comments that requires us to consider the ramifications of what we just heard. The speaker might be conveying any one of a variety of messages, such as a quiet plea for help, a suggestion that they like us, or the conclusion that they dislike what we are doing. According to DeVito, "If you respond only to the surface-level communication (the literal meaning), you miss the opportunity to make meaningful contact with the other person's feelings and needs."[12]

To determine whether to give the surface meaning or an implied one more emphasis, examine both the verbal and nonverbal messages to see if any inconsistencies between the two give you a reason to assume the message is either surface or depth, and note any inconsistency between the content (words) and the relationship you have with this person. While both content and relationship messages will be present, determine which one appears the most significant.

2. *Empathic and Objective Listening.* People vary in their needs. Some people want listeners to pay more attention to their (the speaker's) feelings, and some people want more emphasis on listening to the objective information given. Some listeners are more feeling oriented and others are more objective oriented. If the speaker desires that someone focus on his or her feelings, they feel comforted when we respond to their feelings. We can provide a therapeutic moment for speakers if we can listen to them in a non-threatening, understanding manner. To achieve this, try to put your self in the speaker's situation as an aid to envision the feelings the speaker is experiencing. Give the speaker your full attention.

As an aside and not to belittle those people who seek more empathic listening from others than whatever the norm might be, consider the symbolic interaction involved. Assume Speaker A is sad and wants some empathy so he or she tells someone the sad story. Listener B hears Speaker A's message and if Listener B provides a message that Speaker A finds convincingly representative of the sad feeling, Speaker A feels relieved. If you are the empathetic listener, though, you could feel sad that the speaker felt sad, but now the speaker feels somewhat relieved that someone was empathetic. Is this possibly selfish? Now it must be said that people make many personal connections with others through the expression of their feelings and people do want and need to be heard. Further, empathic listening can certainly lead to two individuals becoming more intimate.

Listeners also need to occasionally give a great deal of attention to the information and the logic of the message. There is much we need to understand so we can operate effectively in our everyday life. For this we have to evaluate a speaker's message based upon its legitimate reasoning and evidence. This is virtually the polar opposite of listening for feeling in the empathic listening mode. Maybe the speaker is missing some key understanding of what he or she is going through and you could tell him or her. Maybe the speaker is proposing to do something that either makes a lot of sense or appears unsound and they need to know that from you, the listener. To accomplish this style of listening will be a test of your own logic and objectivity. Attempt to listen for key ideas.

3. *Nonjudgmental and Judgmental Listening.* Sometimes speakers, particularly those we are closest to, want someone who will just hear them out without evaluating them. If the speaker thinks he or she will not be judged, and while speaking is not overtly judged, then the speaker is much more likely to say more of what they have to say. Some people express more of a desire to talk out loud as a way of getting clear about their own thoughts. In this case, we as listeners can just hear what is said, nod our head to show we are

listening, and avoid making evaluative comments about their expressions being good or bad, right or wrong. We can take the position that if they want our critique or advice, they can ask for it. We will just try to understand.

Opposite from this are the obvious judgments that listeners communicate to speakers. Listeners may need to comprehend the speaker and provide him or her with an in-depth examination of what was heard. Hear the speaker out so you do not jump to conclusions. Consider whether it is in your place to judge the speaker, and if you think the speaker will be receptive to your judgments. When judgments are made, they should refer to the main message of the speaker, not simply to lesser ideas. Overall, try not to prematurely judge the message.

It is common after judging a speaker's misadventure or mistake to offer *advice*. While the giving of advice may be well-intentioned, advice columnists Mitchell and Sugar who write for Annie's Mailbox (*Dear Annie*) suggests that it is useless when unsolicited and frequently resented.[13] Adler and Rodman also provide us with advice about giving advice: it should be correct for the situation, the listener is receptive to it, the listener will take responsibility of any action taken, and the advice should be conveyed in a constructive manner.[14] Unfortunately, much advice given by listeners is unsolicited. We are so quick to judge and add our "two cents worth." Adler and Rodman report that advice is unhelpful about one-half the time.[15]

4. *Critical Listening*. Overlapping with the listening responses of listening for depth of content, objective listening, and judgmental listening, is what may be called *critical listening*. This is listening that focuses on comprehending and evaluating the message according to its sound logic and evidence, and then accepting or rejecting the message on that basis.

We face a multitude of daily persuasive messages so we have to be critical listeners if we are to maintain some control over our lives. We need to assess the speaker's believability, intentions toward us, and the validity of his or her message. We need to apply reasoned skepticism to the messages from politicians, salespeople, and advertisements, and so on to guard against being taken advantage of. We can analyze the content of the message both for inconsistencies with other parts of the message and with other sources of information.

While the goals of some persuasive attempts may be humane, such as seeking to get us to donate to a charity for typhoon victims, other persuaders will try to get us to purchase a product or service that solely benefits the persuader. There are a near-endless number of unsound or unnecessary ideas, products, services, and political office holders. People have to defend themselves against these, and they can do it with critical listening. Is the speaker's evidence and reasoning sound? Does the speaker refer to reliable sources of information?

Does the speaker seem impartial? Are the speaker's emotional appeals justified and consistent with the evidence presented? Overall, listeners need to determine the strength and weaknesses of a speaker's sales pitch. The implication of the message may benefit or harm the listener. Buyer (listener) beware.

5. *Active Listening*. Active listening is a paraphrase by the listener of the speaker's message, coupled with an educated guess of what the speaker feels. This message is conveyed back to the speaker in a questioning, tentative tone of voice. There is no evaluation of the content, no praise or blame of what has been said, no advice, and no leading questions. There cannot be statements like "you must feel (or think) ...." since they convey certainty, making it more difficult for the other speaker to disagree. The listener attempts to simply be a mirror for the content and feeling communicated by the speaker, using fewer words than did the speaker. This is not intended to manipulate the speaker or to make the speaker think the listener really cares about the speaker's topic or feeling (not that the listener does not care). It is an attempt to center the conversation on the speaker's message and his or her feeling about it. This requires a real effort by the listener.

> Consider the following situation. Don has just lost his department head supervisory position in the company after 18 years so he said to his friends: "I just got demoted to the Number 2 position. Man, I don't deserve this! I had no support from management or from the union. That's terrible! After all I've done for the firm. Can you believe it?"
>
> Duke: "Hey Don, guess what happened to me? I was out of work for over a year and only recently got another, similar job in the valley. Man! At least you've had a job."
>
> Red: "Don. What's the problem? At least you weren't fired like me. On the other hand, I got a better job. Things work out. Suck it up! Want to compare paychecks?"
>
> Cat: "Don, you seem angry about losing your position and surprised at the lack of help you've received after your years of dedication."

Notice the comments by Duke and Red that are trying to make Don feel better by comparing his experience with theirs. Still, they need to avoid evaluations if they want Don to more freely respond. Red gives Don the impression that Don is making too big a deal about his job situation. Then he advises Don to get tough about the situation, advice Don does not seek. Lastly, he thinks he is better than Don and wants to prove it by showing that he earns more. This is in stark contrast to Don's unhappy situation. Further, there is no reference to what Don is feeling.

Cat's statement is very different as she suggests, on the basis of a judgment, what Don is probably feeling under the circumstance and adds a paraphrase of the content. The word "seem" is tentative which make's it easier for Don to correct either the suggested feelings and/or the paraphrase if he thinks they are inaccurate. Cat could also have added a brief question such as, "Is that it" if she had omitted the word "seem."

Benefits. An active listening response is an attempt by the listener to allow the speaker to dwell upon what he or she has just said if he or she so chooses. It leaves the responsibility for the interpretation of the speaker's comments with the speaker. It also lets the speaker know if the listener understood what the speaker just said and acknowledges the speaker's feelings. If the listener does not accurately understand, the speaker can easily correct him or her.

Time after time in our daily lives we have people telling us what we should think and/or feel, what we should or should not do, and so on. So much of the time the listener directs the focus of communication to him or herself and then advises us, the speaker. When do we, as speakers, have a chance to think through some of our own thoughts and feelings about an issue? Occasionally, at least, it would be helpful for those to whom we listen to think for themselves—which they certainly can and should do. Our active listening allows the speaker to reach his or her own conclusion about the issue being discussed. In encouraging speakers to reach their own conclusion, they are likely to form a stronger and more personally relevant decision about it. Active listening also benefits the listener. Recognizing the speaker's feeling encourages listener empathy. Through the act of paraphrasing, the message becomes more obvious to the listener and they are likely to better understand it. They cannot simply deny the content since they heard themselves saying it, so the paraphrase also acts like a check on their own interpretation and behavioral response. Consider a mundane example. I, as a listener, might want to cook your hamburger well done but if I paraphrase your request that yours be cooked medium, it is more difficult for me to do it *my* way. Active listening is a technique that recognizes the self-reflective aspect of communication discussed earlier in this chapter. This listening encourages the speaker to put additional focus on the meaning of the message he or she received from his or her own response and compare it to the meaning he or she concludes the listener has created. If there is any discrepancy, the speaker can clarify his or her own thoughts and/or feelings or the listener's understanding.

Recommendations for use. When should we use active listening? If you think the topic is relatively important to the speaker, if the speaker seems to desire personal reflection, if you have a personal interest in the speaker, if you need clarification, if you can withhold evaluation and advice, and if both of you have sufficient time to do it. Since there are a variety of other effective listening responses to use, active listening might only be fitting 5-10% of the time. Further, the hamburger example above may seem too simplistic to bother with yet it is surprising how often people, as listeners, attempt to control other people's decisions and outcomes in both large and small ways.

If you attempt to put active listening into practice, you may discover that other people will think you are playing games and trying to manipulate them. In this event, you will have to explain what and why you are doing this.

FEELING WORDS

Since listeners have to consider the speaker's feelings, they will have to be familiar with words suggesting a feeling. We might think this is obvious but it is not. Notice how frequently even educated people will make statements such as, "I feel the decision is a good (or poor) one," or "I feel people on Guam (or in town X) are friendly (or hard working)." These are not feelings but statements of fact (logical conclusions) for which the speaker could presumably provide supporting evidence. Adler and Towne suggest that statements such as "I feel like going to a show"[16] are really intentions and not feelings at all.

Feelings are physical sensations and feeling words describe an emotional state or response. To *feel* something is often associated with touching it. When people experience a strong feeling there are detectable physiological changes in the body such as increased heart rate and blood pressure.[17] These changes are typically accompanied by nonverbal behaviors and verbal messages, such as a change in posture, gesture, or eye contact, or expressions like "I'm happy" or "I'm scared."

As a clue to what the speaker is feeling, ask yourself how you think you would feel if you were in his or her situation. Avoid statements like "I know how you feel" since this diminishes the feeling the speaker has and you, not being them, cannot know just how they feel. People feel slighted upon hearing a comment like this and they do not like it. These type of statements also shifts the focus of communication to you, the listener, rather than on the speaker, so it can be viewed as selfish and controlling.

The following words from Adler are an attempt to refer to emotional states.[18] With these and words like them the active listener can be clear and descriptive when referring to a speaker's feelings. It can be difficult to determine whether a given word refers primarily to a physical response or to a thought. If in doubt, search for another word such as those suggested in Table 5.1.

Table 5.1

afraid	disappointed	fearful	hurt	passionate	sexy
annoyed	enthusiastic	frustrated	intense	peaceful	shy
anxious	ecstatic	furious	irritable	pleased	silly
angry	disgusted	gleeful	joyful	relieved	tense
ashamed	eager	glum	lonely	resentful	terrified
bewildered	elated	happy	mean	restless	tired
calm	embarrassed	hostile	miserable	sad	uneasy
depressed	excited	humiliated	nervous	sentimental	worried

6. *Nonverbal Listening Behavior.* The following nonverbal behaviors[19] are consistent with effective listening: mostly direct eye contact, open and relaxed body posture, uncrossed arms and legs, appropriate hand gestures, reinforcing head nods, responsive facial expression, appropriate tone of voice, and appropriate loudness.

The listening styles listed in this section are useful at different times and places. One is not necessarily better than another. They even work in combinations to provide effective, appropriate, and satisfying communication interaction.

BEING LISTENED TO

People desire to be heard and many people complain that they are not listened to. The implication is that something is wrong with those other people, the listeners. This may well be accurate for this chapter has described some poor listening behaviors. On the other hand, we also know that some people talk too much, their conversation is boring, or they speak excessively about themselves. On these occasions, listeners usually tune out the speaker. According to Nemko, you can tell if listeners are uninterested in your talk if they fidget, do not look at you while you speak, interrupt you, or frequently vocalize "uh-huh" in an attempt to get you to finish.[20] This suggests that we as speakers need to examine our own conversation for these weaknesses and alter them accordingly if we desire to be heard.

Nemko recommends that we continually remind ourselves to be concise. Say what you have to say in about thirty seconds. One minute is too long. Then, during a pause, ask a question like "What do you think" or "Am I being clear—really?"[21] This makes it easy for the listener to comment on your communication or on his or her understanding. As a rule of thumb, avoid speaking over 50% of the time and attempt to limit it to 30-40% of the total interaction time.

The overall idea here is that effective listening requires a *listener-centered approach*. Speakers need to tailor their messages for the listener or audience. The same is true of public speeches as for casual, everyday conversation. Speak to the listeners where they are. What are their interests or in what topic could you encourage them to be interested? How relevant is your topic to the communication situation? Do you have sufficient time to speak and allow for their response? Do you want a response, and if so, will you accept the advice? Show the listener the same courtesies he or she provides for you. Be a listener for them, as well.

CONCLUSION

There are many benefits to listening yet there are also many barriers to overcome. It is frequently difficult to do so. The chapter offered a description of useful listening styles that most people already employ and supplemented these with the active listening technique. Barnlund provides an overview of what characterizes effective listening in a constructive relationship: "... listening without anticipating, without interfering, without competing, without refuting, and without forcing meaning into preconceived standards of interpretation. It involves a sensitive, total concentration on what is explicitly stated as well as what is implied by nuances of inflection, phrasing, and movement."[22]

The entire listening sequence starts with someone's unique world inside his or her brain. They want to communicate something. While exhaling air, they make their vocal cords vibrate with a certain tension as they shape sounds with their mouth, lips, and tongue, which in turn cause changes in the air pressure existing in their mouth and nose. Another person's eardrums vibrate according to the received changes in air pressure—something is "heard," which is then understood according to the world existing inside this second person's brain. This second person responds to their own interpretation with bodily movements that are probably coupled with vocalizations, which provide nonverbal and verbal feedback to the first speaker about the meaning they "got" from listening. A single listening sequence is complete. It is also complex. Another sequence begins with the first speaker's interpretations of the listening response. Bear in mind, though, that there is no real beginning or end to the communication.

People spend more time listening than in engaging in any other communication activity.[23] Further, our parents, teachers, preachers, bosses, and friends will not always be interesting. Not only do we have to listen in many of these circumstances, we may remind ourselves that we can do our part as listeners since we, too, want someone else to listen to us. We already listen to ourselves.

CHAPTER 5 EXERCISES

Chapter 5 Exercise #A. Active Listening Sentences (multiple choice, not graded, do not turn in)

Multiple-choice. For each of the set of statements below, identify the one that is an *active listening* response, a concise yet complete and accurate reflection of the speaker's thoughts and feelings. These responses should be a paraphrase of the message content, in the listener's own words, and include a feeling word conveying the first speaker's emotion/s. No advice, leading questions, evaluations of the message content, or what the listener feels.

Circle the letter next to the correct response:

1 [student to teacher] "Sir, sometimes I think I'd like to fight that kid but I don't want to get kicked out of school." [respond as the teacher, speaking to the student]

   a. "Maybe it would be helpful to cool off. You wouldn't want to get kicked out of school, would you?"
   b. "You can't fight anyone. You're too small. Anyway, why waste your time?"
   c. "I can really relate to what you're saying. I like to occasionally express my frustrations."
   d. "So you occasionally feel angry toward Ryan and think hitting him would be good and bad?"

2. [school teacher to administrator] "The kids are crazy, like animals. What can I do?" [respond as the administrator]

   a. "Well, you can always get out the duct tape. See the aide for more if you run out."
   b. "It's not your fault that parents send us kids who have no respect for legitimate authorities."
   c. "You seem frustrated with the students' poor discipline and manners, and seek answers."
   d. "I know what you mean. That's why I got out of the classroom after 20 years of headaches."

3. [school custodian to front office staff] "Geez, those so-and-so guys left this place dirty again. They know the rules. I'm tired of them!" [respond as the staff person to the custodian]

   a. "Hey, don't worry, they'll be gone by ... by next month ... maybe in 2 months ... or was it by Christmas? Possibly Easter ...for sure by summer ... oh, ... don't hold your breath."
   b. "You're upset about repeatedly cleaning after people who're supposed to be responsible."
   c. "Even the most patient people get irritated sometime."
   d. "Have you given any thought to dumping extra trash in their office so they'll get the idea?"

4. College student to parents: "I'm thinking of dropping out of school, but I don't want you to be mad at me." [give a parental response]

   a. "Maybe it would be useful to find out what you really want. No sense wasting our money."
   b. "You're afraid that you would be wasting our money getting low grades, is that it?"
   c. "I hear what you're saying. I wanted to drop out of school, too. I'd like to drop work, too."
   d. "You're considering quitting college but you're afraid we'll be upset if you do?"

5. [school aide to his/her supervisor] "Well nobody told me it was on the calendar. All the bell changes, student activities, student getting mad at me for checking their passes, and so on." [respond as the aides' supervisor to the aide]

   a. "You probably need to check the calendar before work begins. You'll get it."
   b. "You're feeling sorry for yourself."
   c. "Where do you think the problem is?"
   d. "You seem discouraged about daily student issues."

Chapter 5 Exercise #B. **Active Listening Sentences (class exercise, not graded, do not turn in)**

Directions: Assume that someone has made these verbal statements to you, the listener. Respond to them in an "active listening" manner.

Guidelines: Paraphrase the content (fewer number of words); use your own words; omit evaluations, judgment, and advice about the message content; avoid leading questions; omit your own feelings but do say what the speaker seems to feel; and respond in a tentative manner. Further, it is *not a feeling* to say, "I feel people on Guam are friendly." This is an objective evaluation so avoid it here. In brief, convey back to the speaker what he/she appears to both think and feel. Omit "You must feel…." or "I know how you feel." This is presumptive and suggests certainty. Review Exercise #A.

1. Maria, a friend of yours, just got a little raise but is depressed because she did not get the promotion and additional money she thought she deserved. Maria: "I know I'm more qualified than the person selected. I wanted that big salary, too. [respond to your friend]:

2. Your professor has just won the university teacher-of-the-year award and is speaking to you: "I didn't think anything about such an award, being so busy helping you students. I just tried to do my job. Kind of hard to believe. Very nice to be thought well of." [respond to the teacher]:

3. After six years, John has just graduated from college and says to you, "Man, that seemed like forever. All that work for Griffmeister's classes, being a poor student, and having a lousy social life. Boy, I'm glad it's over." [respond to John who has just said this to you]:

4. A class of students speaks to their teacher (you): "Why do we have to do this? This is Active Listening exercise is boring." [your response as the teacher, to your students]:

5. A female friend of yours has just gotten married: "No more 'Always a bridesmaid' and leaping for the bouquet for me. I finally did it!" [respond to your friend]:

Answers for Exercise A multiple choice Active Listening sentences: 1d, 2c, 3b, 4d, 5d.

Chapter 5 Exercise #C. **Small Group Listening[24] (not graded)**

Three people are to be in each group (a speaker, a listener, an observer)

Directions: Working in groups of three, Student A should briefly identify a recent problem or conflict he or she is having (not too personal) with another person. Student B should use questions, content paraphrasing, and emotion paraphrasing to explore the problem. Student C should observe the discussion and evaluate Student B's listening skills and ability to reflect upon Student A's situation, using the Observer Checklist (see Table 5.2). Make a check mark next to all of the skills that Student B uses effectively.

When Student B is finished speaking and Student C has scored the responses, Student C should report the results to Students A and B. If Students A's or B's experience differs from what Student C observed, they should attempt to clarify it.

Table 5.2

OBSERVER CHECKLIST OF STUDENT B

Nonverbal Skills		Verbal Skills	
Direct eye contact	_____	Effective and appropriate questions	_____
Open, relaxed body posture	_____	Accurate paraphrase of content	_____
Uncrossed arm	_____	Accurate paraphrase of emotion	_____
Appropriate hand gestures	_____	Timely paraphrase	_____
Reinforcing head nods	_____	Didn't interrupt the speaker	_____
Reinforcing facial expression	_____		
Appropriate tone of voice	_____		
Appropriate volume	_____		

Answers for Listening-Nonverbal exercise:

Distracting: 1, 6, 7, 8, 11, 12, 14, 15, 18, 21, 22, 24, 26, 28, 29, 31, 32, 33, 34, 35, 36

The remaining behaviors would motivate us to listen.

Chapter 5 Exercise #D. Listening-Nonverbal Communication Awareness[25] (not graded) *Directions*: Put an "M" by the nonverbal communication behaviors of one person (the sender) that you think would *motivate* another person in his or her presence (the receiver) to listen. Put a "D" by those behaviors conveyed by the sender that you think would *distract* the receiver from listening. (See Table 5.3)

Chapter 5 Exercise E. Provide one written description from your experience of someone suffering in some way because someone (either themselves or someone else) did not listen effectively.

Table 5.3

____1. Raising an eyebrow	___19. Letting head almost touch shoulders
____2. Smiling	___20. Looking delighted
____3. Nodding head	___21. Scowling
____4. Sitting forward in chair	___22. Rotating head from side to side
____5. Remaining silent	___23. Slumping in chair
____6. Frowning	___24. Folding arms across chest
____7. Looking away from listener	___25. Tilting head down
____8. Rolling eyes	___26. Narrowing eyes
____9. Opening and relaxing body	___27. Arching neck forward
___10. Touching	___28. Looking at listener sideways
___11. Closing and stiffening posture expression	___29. Having a critical facial
___12. Withdrawing	___30.Looking straight at listener
___13. Not moving	___31. Drumming fingers
___14. Behaving restlessly	___32. Shrugging shoulders
___15. Hanging head down	___33. Puffing cheeks
___16. Having eye contact	___34. Pulling back corners of mouth
___17. Sighing!	___35. Swishing foot
___18. Squinting eyes	___36. Bouncing leg

Answers for Active Listening Class Exercise #A on a prior page: 1d, 2c, 3b, 4d, 5d

CHAPTER 5 HOMEWORK
Active Listening Sentences

Directions: Assume that someone has made these verbal statements *to you*. You, as the listener, are to respond to them in an *active listening* manner. *Guidelines*: Paraphrase the content (fewer number of words); use your own words; omit evaluations, judgment, and advice about the message content; avoid leading questions; omit your own feelings but do state what the speaker seems to feel; and respond in a tentative manner. Further, it is *not a feeling* to say that "I feel people on Guam are friendly." This is an objective evaluation so avoid it here. Omit "You must feel...." or "I know how you feel." This is presumptive and suggests certainty. In brief, convey back to the speaker what he/she appears to both think and feel.

1. School teacher speaking to a school aide: "You're doing such a good job monitoring the students and clearing the hallways." [the aide's active listening response to the teacher]:

2. School teacher speaking to the Assistant Principal: " How can you expect us to teach without supplies? We don't even have books." [Asst. Principal's active listening response to the teacher]:

3. School teacher to a friend: "I wouldn't trade that hard-working custodian for anything. I never have to clean my room. Even the chalkboard is cleaned daily." [the friend's active listening response to the teacher]:

4. One teacher to another teacher, "Why can't I find an aide when I need one? What's going on around here? [the second teacher's active listening response to the first teacher]:

5. A new teacher in the community speaking to an old school counselor, "Oh, I just love the students here. They always say "Sir" and "Miss" They ask to do extra credit. They daily pick up all the trash on the school grounds. They put a shiny, fresh apple on my desk every day."[the school counselor's active listening response to the new teacher]:

REFERENCES

1. A. Wolvin and C. Coakley, *Listening* (5th ed.) (Boston: McGraw Hill, 1996).
2. D. Borisoff and M. Purdy, *Listening in Everyday Life: A Personal and Professional Approach* (Lanham, NY: University Press of America, 1991).
3. W. Johnson, *Your Most Enchanted Listener* (New York: Harper and Brothers, 1956), p. 66.
4. J. DeVito, *Human Communication: The Basic Course* (10th ed.) (Boston: Pearson Education, Inc., 2006).
5. Wolvin and Coakley, op cit.; DeVito, op cit
6. Ibid.
7. Ibid.
8. DeVito, op cit.
9. Wolvin and Coakley, op cit.
10. Ibid.
11. Wolvin and Coakley, op cit.
12. DeVito, op cit., p. 90.
13. K. Mitchell and M. Sugar, "Annie's Mailbox." *Pacific Daily News* (June 1, 2010).
14. R. Adler and G. Rodman, *Understanding Human Communication* (10th ed.) (New York: Oxford University Press, 2009).

15. Ibid.
16. R. Adler and N. Towne, *Looking Out/Looking In: Interpersonal Communication* (3rd ed.).(New York: Holt, Rinehart and Winston, 1981).
17. Adler and Towne, op cit.
18. Adler and Towne, op cit.
19. S. Beebe, S. Beebe, and M. Redmond, *Interpersonal Communication: Relating to Others.* (Boston: Allyn and Bacon, 1999).
20. M. Nemko, "Do you TALK too much?" *Kiplinger's Personal Finance* (April, 2007).
21. Ibid., p. 90.
22. D. Barnlund, *Interpersonal Communication: Surveys and Studies* (Boston: Houghton Mifflin Company, 1968).
23. Wolvin and Coakley, op cit.
24. Beebe et al., op cit.
25. C. Hamilton and C. Parker, *Communicating For Results* (Belmont, CA: Wadsworth Publishing Company, 1993).

CHAPTER SIX

Using Language In Verbal Messages

"Back at five." "Give me five!" "I'll take five." "Five in a row." "The top five." "Chapter Five." So many *fives* in our daily lives. With so many implied meanings, how do we know which one to choose? If we misunderstand, it might *cost* us five.

This chapter examines the functions of language in our verbal messages. The concepts and points of view largely represent General Semantics which, according to Berman, " … is the study of the relationship between language, thought, and human behavior. It is concerned with the ways in which our language and other symbols can lead us to make assumptions that influence our thinking and behavior."[1] It is also the study of our emotional, cognitive, and linguistic reactions to language. General Semantics examines the connection between the words we use, the meanings we create from that usage, and our behavior that results. This is different from what is termed *semantics*, which studies the meanings of words (as in dictionaries).

If the purpose of communication is to predict and control our environment, the promoting of clear speech as a method for describing and interacting with our world provides us a measure of control. General Semantics can help us avoid being fooled by either our own or other people's use of language and being manipulated by what might be described as a misuse of language. Effective communication increases the control we have over what occurs in our lives for it minimizes, goes around, or logically overcomes existing personal, social, or legal barriers to our reaching our goals.

LANGUAGE AND MEANING

Language is an organized system of symbols used to express our thoughts and feelings in some message form, in an attempt to communicate (share our

meaning). In short, we use language to verbally communicate. As Chapter
One explained, we encode (translate) our thoughts (meaning) into some sort
of message such as language that is then transmitted orally to some receiver/
sender who then decodes (translates) the language message into some meaning in his or her mind. Given communication variables and the uniqueness of
individuals, the thoughts or meaning in each communicator's minds are not
exactly the same.

It is the intent of this chapter to illuminate some of the important reasons
communicator's meanings differ and what they can do to gain a clearer idea
of what each other's meanings appear to be. The following language characteristics will provide some understanding of this.

1. *Words are symbols.*   A symbol is something that stands for or represents
something else, such as the American flag symbolizing America, the color
and word *red* represents a certain color in the spectrum of colors we recognize, and your name referencing you. According to Condon, "The ability to
symbolize means the ability to call up internal experience using only the symbols."[2] To think about and discuss the world in or about us, we need a means
of referencing it. This is the purpose of symbols. They are not the actual
"thing" but, in the case of words, they are shorthand for a tangible person or
substance, or for an intangible concept or idea to which is being referred.

One way to visualize the connection between words (symbols) and what
they represent is to imagine a triangle with three equal length sides.[3] At one
angle or point of the triangle, we could place the object of our perception,
such as an actual American flag (the referent) or your memory of one. At
another point, we could place our symbol, the word for it, *American flag*. At
the third and last point, we could place our thought or reference about this
flag, what meaning you think the flag represents or symbolizes to you, such
as freedom.

What is the point of this language/symbol-thought-referent connection?
Symbols (words) allow us to think and speak about things in our physical
environment whether they are visually present or not. Symbols also permit
us to discuss abstract ideas like "freedom," "America," and "generosity." Unfortunately, people may respond to symbols (words) as if they, the symbols
(words), are the tangible reality. On one hand, someone may feel elation and
joy when receiving an "I love you" (or expensive engagement ring) and believe
that the words (or ring) means the speaker loves him or her. On the other
hand, what is the tangible reality of the speaker's love? Experience has shown
there is often a large disparity between, for example, this symbol (words) of
love and behavior purporting to be love. With this disparity, there has been
much anguish. We have to remind ourselves that a word (symbol) may have
little or no connection with what is referred to. We can be fooled in accepting

words and what they purport to symbolize (a thought) when the object or tangible reality is not present. We may vote for a politician who says he or she will do things for the middle class, and after elected the politician keeps saying it and the voters keep thinking positively about it. In reality, though, middle class taxes go up, public schools continue to degenerate, and various laws and regulations further restrict middle class lives. Our looking for the referent, the object of our expectation, provides us with evidence about the extent to which we have achieved or grasped our thought, or reference.

What is a symbol of *wealth*? To a high school graduate, is it a $100,000/ year salary? To a middle class family, is it a $500,000 worth of blue-chip (large, stable companies) stocks? Could the reality be gone tomorrow and take the symbol with it? What about *financial independence*, and how would we know we have it? Would we want other people to know we have it?

Thus, General Semantics tells us that since words, being symbols, are only maps of reality and maps omit many features, any words in our mind about some "territory" or what we perceive to be reality have to be recognized as only a partial representation of that territory. Hayakawa succinctly states this, "The symbol is not the thing symbolized. The map is not the territory. The word is not the thing."[4] If you are primarily reacting to words and other symbols that occur in a given moment and there is a disconnect with the more tangible reality that exists, then you are likely to be unhappy with the outcome of that difference, costing you money, time, emotions, and so on.

2. Meanings are in people. If words are symbols, how do we know the meaning of that to which they refer? You may recall the idea presented in Chapter One that we send messages, not meaning, when we communicate, for the meaning is in us. The meaning for our symbol usage is in us.

We are typically told to look up the meanings of words in a dictionary, yet in most instances, we cannot find in them the way people actually use words. Further, Hayakawa suggests that it would be more accurate to call dictionary editors historians for they merely record what words have meant to authors in the past.[5] Dictionaries contain words about words, which should caution us that dictionaries only give us a semblance about some idea, event, or person. This does not mean that dictionaries are not useful or necessary, but we need to recognize their limitations. Many meanings from the past do carry over to the present in people's minds and words do allow us to gain a sense of what someone meant as they used a word in a certain way. Dictionaries give us with a place to start when we think about word usage and associated meanings.

Still, words do not simply suggest *any* meaning and it is presumptuous for politicians and judges to say that a given word or phrase in the U.S. Constitution (for example) means what *they* say it means, as if any or all original textual meanings are *after-the-fact* open to personal interpretation in the present moment and we can blithely disregard for our own personal agenda the explicit words and their implied meanings used by the writers at the time, even when there are existing documents elaborating the writer's or speaker's use of the word/s (e.g., *The Federalist Papers* elaborate on the *Constitution*). Overall, the words people use in speech and writing are crucial to the meanings listeners and readers gain (create) from the speech or written text, particularly regarding legal interpretations. We need the historical meanings associated with words, including knowledge about the context in which they were (are) used.

The following are just a few of the words used over the last fifty-plus years that can have multiple and quite varied suggested meanings (definitions), depending upon who is using them: equality (before the law, of opportunity, or of outcomes?), no access (prohibited by law or someone not attaining something as a result of their personal choices and actions?), public use (the general public will have use of the former private property in the altered form of a highway, etc., or another private individual or corporation will exclusively use the property? Public use is identical to public purpose?), fair/fairness (impartial, an absence of favoritism/bias, or everyone ends up with the same outcome regardless of their work effort or merit?), economic stimulus (a catalyst for creating increased overall economic assets and wealth or spending money on any project whatsoever, regardless of its economic costs?), income distribution (just the seemingly unbiased act of spreading money around) or the taking (stealing, really) of an individual's private wealth (usually earned income) and giving it to other people the government thinks are entitled to it—including illegal aliens), government jobs bill/creating jobs (a private company using its profits to pay someone to do a job, or the government taking private citizens' money to pay someone else to do a job that is economically unsustainable), poverty, living wage, rights, social responsibility, society, greed, stereotype, racism, freedom, achievement, education, and truth.

Occasionally there may be a change in terms for what basically is the same concept and meaning—at least for the believers in the underlying concept. According to Sowell, over the last one hundred years in America, those believing that government that should largely control the economy and society (a collective approach of central planning and the redistribution of income/wealth; in short, run our lives) have expediently varied the labels they attached to themselves.[6] From at least the 1890's such people referred to themselves as *Progressives* and in 1912, Teddy Roosevelt was the nominee of the *Progressive* Party.[7] In the 1920's, the public went against the idea of big government so Progressives changed their name for themselves to *Liberals*, co-opting the term which Sowell reports had meant "the freedom of individuals to attain their fullest development"[8] without government intrusion into their lives.

Classical liberalism had held that people had natural rights and self-owner-ship. Goldberg suggests that *liberal*, as was used and applied by Progressives, came to mean just about the exact opposite of its original meaning.[9] Some *like-minded* people in England called themselves Socialists, others in Italy called themselves Fascists, others in Germany started the Nazi Party (National Socialist German Workers' Party), and still others called themselves Communists.[10] *Liberal* stayed in vogue until after President Johnson's Great Society programs of the 1960's revealed their weaknesses. When then-Vice President Bush ran against Gov. Dukakis in 1988 for the presidency, the "L-word" tag on Dukakis suggested a negative connotation. *Liberalism* came to mean the failure of big government intervention in the economy and people's everyday lives. By 2008, Senator Obama referred to himself as a *Progressive* seeking *change*, suggesting that *progressive* and its connection with *liberal* no longer had a negative connotation in peoples' minds. The use of this word has come full-circle while the underlying meaning associated with it has remained basically the same.

While knowing words and their associated meanings are crucial for know-ing people's intentions, to merely understand a word at its "face" value over-looks the meaning a person has for it. It is more useful to ask someone using a word what it means to them, for meanings are in people and their responses, not in words. You also have to know something about the person using the word—his or her values, beliefs, experiences, education, and so on—to get a sense of what he or she might have meant. For example, if one of your friends who is modest and emotionally "low key" happens to mention that they are "in a little trouble," you might well interpret that to mean that they think they are in serious trouble about something and might even need your help. Words do not mean. We do.

3. *Meanings depend on context.* According to Hayakawa, we come to learn word meanings by hearing them used in real-life situations.[11] We hear the same word used in varying situations so we learn that the context is key in gaining a sense of what a speaker is implying. "Give me some sugar" could mean: pass the white, granulated, sweet substance to your sister seated nearby, or put a teaspoon of sugar into a boss's cup of coffee, or kiss your aunt on the cheek. "Sugar" is also a term signifying that the speaker feels affection-ate towards someone. Even if you are familiar with the context there may be some misunderstanding. A friendly-sounding "Hi" from someone at work may simply be a surface-level message of open courtesy and friendliness. If the listener pursues an intimate relationship on the basis of this, they could easily be rebuffed. We do know, though, that many people meet and marry other people they work with so a fair number of those "Hi's" at work are "I might be interested in knowing you better."

4. *Words have denotative and/or connotative meanings.* Some confusion about the implied meanings associated with words is due to a misunderstanding about their basis or disagreement about which type of meaning is more important. For example, politicians may rail against "the rich" earning a lot of money but not paying enough taxes, but this implies a personal, subjective, connotative meaning use of "rich," while "rich" in its denotative meaning means having great wealth (property, art work, stocks, and/or money in the bank). Politicians thinking "the rich" should pay more in taxes raise the income tax rates, which really wealthy people like Warren Buffet are not affected by since they receive no salary (they do get interest and dividends—taxed at a significantly lower tax rate). The (confused?) politicians do not achieve their stated goal.

Denotative meanings refer to objects in our physical world that can be pointed to (like a wealthy person's assets). Even if most people cannot always (or easily) point to everything (such as the parts of an atom or a geographical place half way around the world), we have dictionary definitions and scientific explanations that can point to a factual basis. These meanings are more agreed upon and supposed to be more objective. We would expect little disagreement about the descriptions and implied meanings from these sources. Another category of meanings are termed *connotative meanings.* As noted above, these are individual or personalized meanings that may be emotionally laden. When a girl or woman says a boy or man is "cute," we cannot be sure that the male would be rated handsome or attractive by a majority of girls or women surveyed about the male. There is probably a connotative meaning in the girl or woman's mind.

According to Johnson, our observations of the world around us are to a lesser degree descriptions (as in denotative meanings) and to a greater degree "… our feelings about it or our judgments of it."[12] Thus, "… we more commonly *evaluate* [things] as beautiful or good, wise or stupid, ugly or bad. Such words, of course, describe nothing. They express our personal standards and reflect our feelings about whatever we may be responding to."[13] Thus, we are using connotative meanings much of the time, potentially fooling our self and others about the reality we think we are observing.

Confusion, disagreement, and sometimes emotions are raised when people disagree about the basis of their meanings for the same object. Someone is likely to have implied that their subjective, connotative meanings have the denotative status of objectivity. Hayakawa labels our use of connotative judgments masquerading as denotative ones "snarl-words" and "purr-words."[14] For example, my first car may have sentimental value to me so I may refer to "her" as "Betsy" and speak about "her" in the most laudatory language to you, a perspective buyer. You are looking at the car in terms of what you tangibly see: a little rust in a few places, faded paint, bald tires, mushy feeling shocks, torn up dash and upholstery, and so on. You offer me $500 dollars less than I asked for. I am upset since my sentimental value tells me the car is worth much more. I am "purring" about my car. I do not realize it but my highly positive "purr-words" only really convey the idea that I like the car. They say nothing about the objective condition of it. What can the perspective buyer and I agree upon as the car's condition? On the other hand, I might use the subjective and highly negative "snarl-words" to refer to a neighbor as a "witch" and a "scum-bag," thinking I am being objective and the people in authority should do something to this identified neighbor. My statements really only tell the authority that I dislike the person so how can they justifiably take action against the neighbor on that non-factual basis? I, then, get upset when they do not. As suggested earlier, we might ask people what they meant by their use of the word/words, ask the "snarling" or "purring" person why they feel the way they do. This would tell us something about them, the speaker.

5. *Words are abstract and vary in their degree of abstraction.* As previously discussed, words are symbols. As such, they do not have a concrete existence. This explains why words are not the "thing." Still, some words are more specific and descriptive of the phenomenon to which they refer than are other, related words. In total, these words can be placed on a continuum, from those that suggest a meaning closest to the object of discussion to those words that make a vague, general, and abstract reference to the same object. We cannot avoid using abstractions since no two objects, ideas, or events are exactly alike. To speak about them, we have to find some more general (abstract) characteristics that each has in common.

Hayakawa suggests that varying levels of abstraction can be illustrated with what he terms an *Abstraction Ladder* to show how abstraction can lead to misunderstanding.[15] Imagine four people are speaking with each other about homes. One of them could be thinking about acquiring and/or using basic building materials needed to construct a typical family residence. Another could be thinking about homes being where the heart is, some kind of shelter such as a tree house, a car, an RV, or a mansion. Another speaker could be thinking about homes in terms of their economic value, being merely one financial asset among many that a financially independent person would want to acquire, and the last speaker could be thinking of homes in terms of their symbolizing wealth and his or her personal success. The first speaker mentions the specific materials needed to build a home while the second speaker notes that various shelters that can serve as a home. The third speaker says that the assessed value of the house could be borrowed against to invest in a second home or some business that could also be a financial asset. The last speaker interjects that it would be nice to have a grand house on the hill, a "McMansion" everyone would look up to and "ooh" and "aah" about.

Notice that each speaker was envisioning and speaking about homes with different criteria and a understanding, from the "nuts and bolts" of homes to their symbolization of wealth. This is illustrated by the abstraction ladder below:

Table 6.1

‖ wealth (most abstract)
‖ financial assets
‖ home
‖ construction wood, sheet rock, cement, nails, screws, door hinges, asphalt roof shingles, galvanized heating/cooling ducts, door locks and knobs. (least abstract)

With each succeeding ladder rung and term from the bottom up, the implied meanings that can easily be formed in the minds for two or more conversing people can become increasingly ambiguous and abstract, leaving out an increasing amount of characteristics of the basic elements of the subject under discussion (what materials residential homes are commonly built with). With each succeeding loss of detail, there is increased overgeneralization. At some point as the words become more abstract, we can expect that the people using the terms would have dissimilar mental images. People's thoughts vary in terms of what they think a "home" is, vary even more about whether a home is a financial asset and what might constitute a financial asset, and the uppermost term on the ladder, wealth, can include an even greater number and quality of ideas as to what it constitutes. In a discussion about homes, a listener may never actually know what was originally being referred to since a husband envisions an unstated workshop and his wife envisions an unstated large kitchen with an island in the middle. The term *financial asset* could itself be any number of phenomenon including a person's human capital and work ethic, old baseball cards, various bank and investment accounts (amongst others), and a *vacation condo* in reference to a home. *Wealth* is even broader and more encompassing in its suggested meanings. People in America and around the rest of the world define wealth in markedly different ways and amounts, from owning 12 pigs on a Micronesian island in the Pacific Ocean to owning a Greek island in the Aegean, to the biggest yacht at the dock, to being a physically healthy 63 year old male in Napa, California, to a 12 year-old boy with a Schwinn Typhoon bicycle in Berkeley with which he can deliver newspapers and go most places his heart desires.

The point of all this is that the higher up the ladder we go in using increasingly abstract terms, the greater likelihood of misunderstanding. Do we know what the speaker is referring to when he or she is using more abstract terms?

While all the terms are useful in their appropriate contexts, the more abstract ones will need further clarification and examples to increase understanding, and thus, communication. We can attempt to use specific words that will increase the likelihood that the listener will have a meaning in his or her mind that is similar to the meaning that we have in our mind.

6. *Language varies in directness.* Similar to the discussion about least abstract to very abstract words in the previous section, language can differ widely in its explicitness. Your words can be unambiguous in their meaning or you can be circumspect while attempting to convey your meaning. Most, if not all people, alter their degree of directness depending on the context, especially if there is an authority figure in their presence. A mother who is direct with her son about his chores may be slightly indirect with her boss, with whom she is careful not to be seen as challenging the boss's intelligence or integrity. When this same parent goes shopping she probably mixes together some direct and indirect statements about the price levels and the quality of the merchandise she observes.

Not only do contexts influence the appropriateness of directness/indirectness, but there are individual preferences and habits, as well. People differ in their comfort level with the degree of directness. They have grown up around a variety of people and circumstances so they have come to think that a particular place on the continuum suits them and is effective for them. Some people want to be known as being direct while others cultivate the perception of being "sensitive."

As you may already have noticed, there are both advantages and disadvantages for the two separate positions. Direct speech is more concise so it is quicker to state, it is more to the point so it is both quicker and more accurately understood by the listener, its explicitness reduces the possibility of a large, unstated speaker strategy, and it may be considered appropriate by both the speaker and listener when listeners know that there is little time to communicate or orders are expected. On the other hand, direct speech is often considered impolite and insulting, particularly to those who are not used to it, and the tone of voice often used with the direct message may imply the speaker is upset with the listener or even dislikes the listener. If you tend to use more direct speech, you are probably comfortable with it and dislike indirect speech

With indirect language, the speaker avoids explicitly stating his or her point of view or intention so there is nothing about which the listener can clearly be upset. There is no direct challenge to the listener's character, actions, or public image so the listener finds this much less offensive and possibly non-insulting. You call up your friend on a holiday to see how he's feeling. After telling you his medical situation, he says, "I'm at a family gathering right now," indirectly meaning that he should not spend any more time on the phone, away from his family. You respond, "Okay, I'll talk to you later." You never got a chance to also ask him to get together with you and your other friends but you were updated about his medical condition, you found out he was not in a position to speak any further, and you appreciate his politeness. If his wife overheard the conversation she could understand the medical update being given and that he then cut off the conversation. The weakness of indirect speech is that the listener may not create a meaning similar to the speaker's or understand the speaker's intention, and the indirect speaker may resent this. The person using the indirect speech may also be evaluated as manipulative and indecisive ("wishy-washy) since they do not directly state their point. They also waste time.

7. *The power of words.* Words are symbols so they have no inherent meaning or power over people, but certainly people come to associate certain words with certain beliefs and/or actions so the emotional and/or behavioral response of the listener can become dramatic from someone else's or even their own use of certain words. In this sense, words can be powerful. Symbolic Interaction Theory[16] holds that through the use of language (symbols) we learn to associate certain meanings with certain words (the interaction). Throughout the world and over time, "freedom" has been a powerful word. Some people have died for that concept so that other people might become or stay free. Some voters have a positive reaction to such words as (and presumably political candidates who promise) "affordable health care," "affordable housing," "a living wage,"[17] or "_____ for our children" legislation. Ironically, in America of all places, few people get a positive, emotional reaction to "the rule of law," "private property," "the Constitution," and "self-defense" while a surprising number of citizens have a strong, negative response to "U.S. military," "U.S. history," "the American flag," and "high income/wealth."

In addition, Russell suggests that the words *make* and *made* as in, "Joe made me mad" blames other people for our feelings, as if they control our lives.[18] It is as if we make ourselves into victims by saying the words *make* and *made* for an outcome we are not happy with. If we say to someone else, "You make me happy," it relieves us as individuals of the responsibility for our own feelings and projects this power over our feelings to someone else. Alternately, in grammar school it used to be common for a child who was teased to reply, "Sticks and stones may break my bones but words will never hurt me." People are not powerless when it comes to accepting or not others' words that supposedly symbolize some reality about the people.

LANGUAGE USAGE OBSTACLES
AND IMPROVEMENT

In the previous pages of this chapter, there was an attempt to investigate and report on important language characteristics. This current section will reveal some of the more obvious barriers to our communication created by our language usage and provide recommendations for overcoming these barriers.

1. *Meanings are in people.* This idea was discussed earlier in this chapter and in Chapter One. It becomes an obstacle when someone assumes that words carry a meaning that the listener should get from knowing word meanings, and when the listener does not, the speaker is likely to get upset and presume something is wrong with the listener. Words do not merely mean what we think they mean. As noted earlier, we need to check on the meaning the listener forms. A mother could tell her teenage boy who is cooking dinner to "cook the meat well done," who then does so to the point of dryness. The mother tastes the meat and is unhappy with its dryness. The boy blames the parent, saying, "You told me to cook it well done." The parent responds, "I said well done. I did not say overdone and dry." Here, the meaning in each other's mind *bypassed*, did not meet, the other person's meaning. Bypassing occurs much more than we realize, with two interacting people using the same word but not realizing that they have at least slightly different mean-ings in their minds, and often significantly different meanings that become the basis for a misunderstanding and conflict. It is very easy to assume that others know what we mean and use words the way we mean them to be used since most, if not all of us, are raised with the idea that meanings are in words. A common language expression that has been the basis of a great deal of by-passing and subsequent sadness is, "I love you." People can have a markedly different sense of what this means and frequently show *love* in different ways. We hear people imply bypassing s when they say, with angst, "But I thought you said you loved me."

Recommendation. First, try to be clear about what the other person said, what it means to you, and what it might mean for the other person from his or her perspective and the context in which he or she used the word. Sometimes people interpret someone else's words out of context. Second, ask the other speaker (sender) what the word or words mean to them. Third, paraphrase what you think was the speaker's basic idea for the speaker to check on your interpretation. Fourth, if you are the speaker, ask the listener if they think you need to rephrase what you said.

2. *Language symbolizes reality only partially.* Symbols, such as words, being symbols, are representational and thus limited in what they represent of any reality referred to.

An *intensional orientation* is one way we convey a partial reflection of reality with our words. Given the language-meaning associations we have, when we hear a word like the label "lazy" attached to someone, we are likely to think of the person in that way, in terms of the label. If the label is considered positive, the person may be treated with respect, if negative, with disrespect. Relevant facts of the person might be discussed later, if at all. Given Implicit Personality Theory discussed in Chapter Three, we are likely to add a few more descriptors to "lazy." Now we have words on top of words about someone. How close does this bring us to the reality of the person's behavior?

We also know that some product brands are held in high regard and become sought after by consumers who then pay more attention to the names of these products than the quality or use of the product, and frequently try to impress other people that they have the *name* brand. In this case, they are buying the meaning associated with the name, not the reality of the product.

Hayakawa explains that when the focus of our meaning for some phenomenon is on a word (such as the label) rather than in the physical world of the phenomenon, then this is an *intensional orientation*.[19] While words are necessary and useful, and it is a major theme of this chapter that we use words that help us create and share meanings that is as close as possible to the reality that exists in our environment, an emphasis on words to the exclusion of actual and additional characteristics of the person, place, event, or concept limits our understanding of these. Imagine two people who, like most non-professionals, know little or nothing about real estate but are engaged in a conversation about what they think some homes are worth, how to successfully sell homes, what is going to happen near-term in the housing market, and so on. As a bystander, we would hear a lot of blah, blah, blah, words about words about words that symbolize little, if any, of the reality, but the two communicators think they know since they are using some real estate terms.

Could we imagine what people think about when some unknown person is labeled "rich"?

As opposed to an intentional orientation, an *extensional orientation* uses words that point to something in the physical world. These words stress the denotation of that which is referenced.[20] An *extensional orientation* stresses the need to look first for existing facts before we draw a conclusion about people, events, or things existing in our environment. Afterwards, we can evaluate how representative the generalizations and labels are about these so we would not be fooled by words and preconceived ideas they might suggest. Look at what people actually say and do.

One way to extensionalize meanings is to use fewer definitions and more examples that refer to the concept or phenomenon in question.[21] Another method is to use *operational definitions* that describe physical actions necessary to experience the phenomenon. Provide the facts and details about what to observe and what to do in order to experience the phenomenon in question. For example, describe loving behavior as opposed to "love is kind." Give detailed instructions for eating an ice cream cone, and so forth.

Another benefit of using language that emphasizes statements of fact is that communicators have a much-increased chance of reaching some agreement about the reality of a situation. When we use language with nebulous references, discussions are pretty abstract and cannot reach a definite conclusion.

The concept of *allness* suggests that we overstate our knowledge and end up making generalizations based upon insufficient data, and thereby fool ourselves and other people into thinking we really know all about which we speak. We overlook that we only partially symbolize reality, which is all that our language can do. Further, we rarely say all we do know about a given person or other phenomenon, and we do not know all there is to know about those subjects. All we know is what we know so it is easy to assume or actually think that we do know about the subjects we discuss.

Recognizing this, it makes our decision making problematic. We have to make them on the basis of limited information. Still, we may avoid making some decisions until we think we know enough. As listeners, we need to remind ourselves that we are not hearing all, or probably even close to all there is to know.

Recommendations. To avoid or overcome our tendency to think that language represents reality, we use what are termed *extensional devices* to overcome some of the language usage barriers discussed above.

First, create a mental habit of thinking about and speaking to someone based on their individuality, not their titles or the labels attached to them. For example, think of the medical doctor as a person, not as a medical authority, so you can easily ask questions about the tests, your health, and justifications for the prescribed remedies. Attempt to analyze the reasoning and evidence existing for your boss's decision, not merely accept it since it is "the boss's idea." Avoid first impressions highly influenced by emotional, stimulating or colorful words. Symbols other than words also deserve our scrutiny. Wall St., in New York, has the symbol of a bull in front of the Stock Exchange. Investors can ask themselves what the Wall St. "bulls," purportedly representing strength and knowledge, have actually done with investors' money. Have investors earned a return on investment commensurate with the risk? Did those who invested with the major Wall Street firms have more or less money in December 2008 than they had in December 2007? Have the "bulls" pay off over 20-30-40 years?

Second, to avoid the allness trap of making unqualified and unsupported generalizations, remind yourself to think "*et cetera*," meaning that there is more to say on the topic, and then attempt to discover a sufficient amount or quality of information that would allow you to make an informed opinion about the topic. Look for individual differences within the general area you are examining. Some grocery stores devote sections of the store to products for certain groups of customers. Many such stores cannot afford to practice an allness orientation. Auto insurers avoid the allness trap to a certain extent by charging young, single male drivers under age twenty-five more money for insurance than they do women of similar characteristics since there is more reckless driving among such males. Not all males under twenty-five are reckless but the auto insurers do provide discounts to those with good school grades and to non-smokers as a further way to distinguish among them.

3. *Language is relatively static.* When we speak about people, objects, and events, the language we use tends to stay the same over time, yet people, objects, and events are in constant flux. The boy we knew in first grade is not the same boy that is now in twelfth grade, but we probably think about and speak about him in a similar way. A house we lived in for ten years is not now the same house we moved into. Local political races have changed but we might speak about them like we did in years past. These are examples of *static evaluations*, having a fixed and unchangeable judgment about a person, idea, place, object, or event. Everything is always changing, often in ways we cannot easily observe in our daily life (such as objects or events requiring scientific measurement). If we maintain the negative descriptions we have for some people, foods, places, or activities, for example, we prevent ourselves from enjoying or benefiting from them later on when either they change for the better or we change in a way that these people or phenomena now appear attractive. Does the language we use for assessing ourselves over time change

to reflect the changed self? If not, the language can be a barrier to personal change. Haney termed this a "hardening of the categories."[22]

Recommendation: dating. The extensional device for preventing a *static evaluation* is to use either verbally state an actual date or think of one. Avoid stating that something is always a given way. If the speaker does not make a reference *when* something was observed, then ask him or her. Maybe the date will suggest that there is likely to have been a change over time. A sports player may have been outstanding three years ago but his performance could easily be much less now. If there is an evaluation about your mom, remember to think that your mom age 30 is not your mom age 40. Speak to her about who she is now, at age 40. She is very likely to have different concerns and interests at this time than at an earlier age, and she is much more like now to view you as an adult (presuming you are of age). The current "map" of the territory of your mom should be a different "map" than you previously had of her. If your mom views *you* with a different map, as an adult, she might expect you to be more responsible for your own room, board, and laundry. In summary, make a brief reference to a period of time that your observations and evaluations are applicable: "Last year, the house ...."

4. *Language can obscure distinctions.* The use of language terms that refer to either general or extreme qualities can overlook details of a given phenomena from being observed and accurately evaluated. We already recognize that this occurs with generalizations. There are two main ways the use of some words can blur distinctions between phenomena.

Indiscrimination is one way our language obscures distinction. Sometimes our words illustrate that we do not sufficiently discrimination among differing phenomenon, we do make sufficient distinctions between members of a group, be they people, objects, smells, places, events, or other phenomenon. A common form of this was discussed in the Perception chapter: stereotyping, in which one or a few peoples' characteristics are presumed to exist in other members of some group. Although stereotyping is natural and can be expedient, we do not have to let it control our thinking and speaking.

Recommendation: indexing. This is not a new technique, as people have used index cards to sort all manner of information such as recipes, and librarians have indexed books so the books can be placed on the shelves in a systematic order and easily retrieved. When we or someone else generalize about a group of people, we ask our self or the speaker, *which* police officer? If "Politicians vote on laws to please lobbyists, not the public interest," we should ask *which* politicians, *which* lobbyists, and *which* public interest? Another way to distinguish among separate entities in a group to show that they are not the same is to label them, for example, student$_1$, student$_2$, and so on. In summary, we need to discriminate, like the chef that has a discriminating palate.

Polarization is another way our words do not show a clear distinction between the realities of varying stimuli. This occurs when our descriptions or evaluations of something includes terms referencing extreme characteristics of that phenomenon, overlooking degrees or gradations that exist between the extremes or polar opposites. While something in our experience may accurately represent an extreme case, such as being very cold one summer evening in San Francisco or very hot one summer day in Palm Springs, California, there is a continuum between these opposites. Yet it is common to hear people overstate a situation as they speak about something being either very good or very bad, which does not accurately reflect reality.

We might label a product as "fabulous" and spend more money than we can afford on it only to discover upon using or eating it that it is mediocre. We are then disappointed and may feel regretful about "wasting" our money. Thus, with polarizing statements we can delude both ourselves and other people about things. While you may rate the food at one Mexican restaurant a #2 (low) and another one a #10 (best), you may rate some others a #5 and a #8.

Recommendation. With terms representing opposite and opposing statements, you can first verify whether there is a middle ground to describe or evaluate. For example, there is no middle ground with pregnancy, for someone either is or is not pregnant. People are either dead or alive. If there is a middle ground, we can make a reference to that specific area. Instead of, or in addition to, saying someone is *tall* or *short*, specify the exact height (e.g., 5'8"). Instead of saying someone is *rich* or *poor*, give the exact amount of his or her assets (e.g., $200,000). If something cannot be quantified, use some descriptive adjectives that suggest gradations or degrees along the continuum (such as on the "beautiful/ugly" continuum). Further, qualifying terms such as "rarely," "significantly," "typically," etc., do add a little specificity.

We might notice that using demeaning, polarizing statements about other people is likely to lead to a conflict with them. "Always" and "never" statements frequently spark arguments. A conflict may be been avoided if you say, for example, "You are late about one-half the time" instead of "You are always late."

5. *Language expresses both facts and inferences.* When we communicate, we create statements reporting either what we have observed or what we have concluded based upon a limited amount of information. Misevaluations about

the person, place, object, or concept under discussion can easily arise from the latter situation.

According to Berman, "... a factual statement can only be made after you have observed something,"[23] it reflects only what is observed, it is closer to the certain end of the certain/uncertain continuum, and it provides a basis that can lead to agreement. For example, a statement of fact may be that "Mary had on seven gold bracelets, a one carrot diamond ring, a bright red silk cocktail dress, and drove a brand-new white, Lexus sedan." A statement of fact is not necessarily factual or accurate but it can be verified, by scientific investigation if necessary.

An inference is a conclusion based upon some fact or evidence. It is an implication of the available data. Hayakawa suggests that an inference "... is a statement about the unknown made on the basis of the known."[24] Inferences are not factual so we cannot be sure about their degree of legitimacy, and that being the case, they often lead to disagreements that cannot be resolved. Given the above statement about Mary, we might *infer* that she is rich and try to befriend her but we do not really know if she is. She may be using someone else's artifacts or even charged some of them on credit because she did not have the cash to pay for them. Maybe she borrowed someone's car.

Notice that inferences are assumptions, possibly educated guesses, and people do create such conclusion about virtually anyone or anything. We make inferences all day long about such things as how the day's weather will be by taking one look out the kitchen window at 7:00 AM, or about how good a painter someone is by how much paint we see on his or her clothes, and so on. We cannot get away from making inferences for we cannot get all the facts about a given situation before making every decision or taking every action.

Recommendation. Just because we have to make assumptions, that does not mean we have to be careless about making them. First, we can consciously remind ourselves that we are making an assumption and that we have to maintain our awareness for additional information that might lead to a different conclusion. Second, we can analyze the existing evidence to see whether it is sufficient to act upon. Third, we can tell other people that our conclusions are a guess, as a way to remind ourselves and be clear to them. Fourth, we can be tentative about our conclusions and continually reassess them over time. Fifth, we can be mindful of accepting other people's inferences.

6. *Language confusion: doublespeak.* It could probably be said that everyone has unintentionally used language in ways that has led to confusion among

listeners. A previous section noted earlier about abstract language use is one example of our words suggesting a lack of clarity. In this section, the emphasis will be on the use of a type of language, *doublespeak*, that intends to confuse listeners.

According to Lutz, in *Doublespeak*, "Doublespeak is language that pretends to communicate but really doesn't." " [It] is language that avoids or shifts responsibility, language that is at variance with its real or purported meaning. It is language that conceals or prevents thought ...."[25] In general, there is an incongruity or disconnect between the general understanding of the meaning people would form for a word (the symbol) and the reality being referenced. The person using doublespeak hopes that people do not notice the word/reality gap. The outcome of doublespeak, in fact, the purpose of doublespeak, is to "... mislead, distort, deceive, inflate, circumvent, obfuscate."[26] Larson suggests that doublespeak "... is the opposite of straightforward language. It tries to miscommunicate; it tries to conceal the truth and to confuse." [It is an attempt] to shift meanings for words and concepts to confuse the citizenry."[27] The result of doublespeak makes the underlying subject of discussion difficult to understand.

Doublespeak suggests that the speaker does not think he or she can be successful in achieving his or her goals by being honest and explanatory about the goals, so he or she has to manipulate people (often the general public) to get what he or she wants. Doublespeak also assumes that the target audience is too stupid to know what is best for itself, or too stupid to figure out the speaker's doublespeak and challenge the speaker's proposed or actual actions.

The *dangers of doublespeak* are related to one another. In brief, the purpose of doublespeak is to fool people. Why fool people? To control them. To get the target audience members to do something against their free will and informed self-interest. Doublespeak is used to convince people of the legitimacy of an idea or action, but provide them another, possibly opposite outcome that invariably suits the self-interest of the doublespeak provider and hurts the target audience..

We can be fooled by the government about the quality of education our kids receive and get something less, what is healthy to eat or drink and get sick, whether we are financially able to purchase a house and, if so, which one suits our circumstances and end up losing the house and our equity in it, whether the city, county, state, or federal government is financially stable and can be expected to be so long-term but then not receive an earned or promised pension and other paid-into benefits, what the politicians in Washington we are voting say they are for and will do but then once they get there we often get more taxes, regulations, and ineptness, why we pay all those taxes and what they are actually used for, whether the varied government programs actually succeed in reaching the goals stated at inception that justified their creation, and about what the Constitution actually says versus various

Table 6.2

Euphemism	*The more unpleasant reality*
Federal and Guam budgets	works of fiction about government spending
entitlement	legalized government theft of working people's income
low-income	poor, possibly lazy and against society's success norms
inner city	slum, likely inhabited by poor people
correctional facility	prison (how many "clients" are being "corrected"?)
equal opportunity	discrimination in favor of women and some minorities
unequal access	not taking advantage of opportunities to participate
guest worker	illegal alien, law breaker
economic stimulus 2009-10	increased unemployment and future U.S. debt obligation
nonpublic data accumulation	spying on private, personal data of U.S. citizens, data that is clearly protected by the 4th Amendment
fair share	government taking the most productive citizens' legally earned money, and little or nothing from the rest
shared sacrifice	earners of $154,000+, paying 70% of taxes, do not pay enough so should pay more while 47% of workers, paying 0% of federal taxes, have sacrificed enough

politicians and judges rulings that take and have taken so much of our liberties in just over the last one-hundred years, and so on.

Spotting doublespeak is challenging. According to Lutz, there are at least four kinds of doublespeak.[28]

First, *euphemisms*. These are inoffensive or positive words or phrases that attempt to avoid n unpleasant reality. It is not doublespeak when a euphemism is used out of concern for someone's feelings, such as saying someone "passed on" instead of "died." While no one is misled when someone says "Jose is having an *affair* with Maria," it seems less harsh than *fornication*. It is doublespeak when a word is used to mislead or deceive. Hybels and Weaver add: "Sometimes [organizations] create euphemisms to either cover up the truth or make the truth more palatable."[29] The table below contains examples of attempts to cover up something distasteful, to change peoples' perception of reality, from Lutz,[30] Sowell,[31] and this author.

Second, *jargon*. This is the specialized language used by professions or trade groups that is, according to Lutz "... pretentious, obscure, and esoteric terminology used to give an air of profundity, authority, and prestige to speakers and their subject matter. Jargon, as doublespeak, often makes the simple appear complex, the ordinary profound, the obvious insightful. In this sense it is used not to express but impress."[32]

This does not mean that all jargon is doublespeak. Jargon is appropriately used between professionals since they know of what they are speaking, and it is quick and efficient for them. Yet, when jargon is used with people outside the group who cannot be expected to know it, it is doublespeak. The table below contains some examples of doublespeak jargon from Lutz and this author, followed by more realistic description.[33]

Third, *gobbledygook*. This is the purposeful adding of more and "bigger" words to our sentences to make them longer and more impressive appearing. It is actually more confusing. It includes the needlessly complex language of government bureaucrats, the writing of some laws, a fair amount of academic writing, and even what some public relations professionals create. With the length and confusing words, the speaker or writer may seem profound, but upon further reflection the text may not make sense. In our confusion, we may even think that our intelligence is somehow lacking for our not clarifying the key point or ideas.

The Federal tax code can be considered *confusing*, and *needlessly* complex. Brinkley provides an example of tax code instructions: "Subparagraph B in section 1 G 7, relating to income included on parents' returns, is amended (1) by striking $1,000 in clause i and inserting twice the amount described in 4 A ii I and (2) by amending subclause (capital II) of clause small ii to read as follows...."[34]

Table 6.3

Jargon	Plain language
hematophagous arthropod vectors	fleas
service the car's distributor	grease the cam lobes, put a oil drop in the shaft
involuntary conversion of property	a house burned down or a car was stolen
fused silicate	glass
cardiac infarction	heart attack
greed, selfish	political jargon for productive income earners who wrongly believe the fruit of their labor— their income—is rightly theirs' to keep
social justice	politicians' jargon for reducing successful people's freedom and property in an attempt to give equal financial outcomes to all
compassion	political jargon for the government's taking of self-reliant people's money to give to those deemed more deserving (poor/er people)

There are obvious negative outcomes of such language. First, many people have to pay tax experts to do their taxes, costing them money. Second, there is the bureaucratic cost of maintaining such a confusing system, so the taxpayer pays again, in increased taxes. Third, individuals and tax experts can make mistakes, costing the taxpayer and/or expert fines. Congressional members benefit from this confusion and complexity since it allows them to create tax benefits for constituents without being noticed. This leads to a fourth outcome, that given the length and confusion of the code, taxpayers do not know who benefits and who does not by it so they cannot protest and seek changes (such as rich people not paying taxes for the two weeks of renting their homes astride the Augusta, Georgia, Masters Golf Course during the tournament). Fifth, as reported by Brinkley, "... for 90% of the smaller American corporations it costs more to comply with the hideous complexities of the tax code than it costs to pay the taxes," [35] $390 for every $100 due in taxes. These costs have to be paid by the consumer in increased prices, so taxpayers who are consumers have to pay again. According to Brinkley, we should not be misled into thinking that the writing and purpose of the tax code is primarily about the government or individuals getting rich. Overall, the sinister purpose of doublespeak is when it comes to the IRS, at least, "... greed for power."[36]

Fourth, *inflated language*. According to Lutz, this type of language "... is designed to make the ordinary seem extraordinary; to make everyday things seem impressive; to give an air of importance to people, situations, or things that would not normally be considered important; to make the simple seem complex."[37] Examples from Sowell[38] and this author can be found in the table below.

Table 6.4

Inflated language	More descriptive reality
for mature audiences	for those who want to watch sex and violence
public interest law firms	lawyers who oppose policies the public has voted for
in-depth report	TV news story which adds superficial editorializing to superficial information
victims	anyone feeling unhappy, even if caused by themselves
ocular inspection	a university administrator plans to look at something
certified pre-owned cars	used cars that the car dealer says are used
fragile	a Guam coral reef with numerous, huge holes caused by WWII U.S. Navy bombing that cannot now survive underwater tourist sightseeing from inside a cylinder
food transportation engineer	waiter, waitress, server
director of development	university fund raiser

DOUBLESPEAK SUMMARY

As you might imagine, people regularly use doublespeak in persuasion, so it is pervasive in advertising, politics, sales, and from bureaucracies. Such deceptive language will be used as long as people try to control other people or have something to "sell" to someone else. To defend yourself, you need to recognize it for what it is.

Recommendation. In our own language usage we need to be descriptive and concrete. Strive for clarity. When people use doublespeak with you, ask "What do you mean?," "Give me an example of what the people are doing or what goes on," and "What is the outcome, the end result?" When you have the answers to these you will have a much clearer idea about the speaker's intention and about the meaning of the content.

7. *Unconventional language.* This refers to language that does not meet the accepted standards or norms. It includes a variety of language that is not ordinarily taught or used in public schools, courts, government laws, and so on since it deviates from established customs. A few types of such language are discussed below.

First, *clichés* are words or phrases that have been so overused over the years that their expression does not lead to some unique and distinct meaning in people that fits the referenced phenomenon. Clichés lack clarity and uniqueness so they are often ineffective in evoking more than a simplistic response in the listener. They are a lazy way to describe something. They are fall-back expressions to use if we cannot come up with something more insightful to say. A few you have probably heard include "Here's to you," "There's no magic bullet," "Bite the bullet," "Make my day," and "Love is __(like a rose, etc.)."

*Recommendation*s. As mentioned earlier in this chapter, go "down" the Abstraction Ladder to the extensional reality, attempt to report the facts that can be observed, and use concrete terms. Describe the uniqueness of the circumstance.

Second, *slang* are the casual and even playful words and expressions used in lieu of standard ones by a particular group of people in a given area and time period. Slang terms provide a connection to other group members. Some originate from popular songs or movies. Some people use it in an attempt to fit into a group while others' use of it is motivated by anti-establishment thoughts.

People "date" themselves with the slang they use. Illustrating the changing nature of slang, in the 1960's there was "bad," "grass," "pigs," and "trip," in the early 1970's there was "far out," "right on," "solid," and some more recent examples after the year 2000 include "crib," "bling," and "shoot." For some people, slang seems to fit the nature of the times. At a later date, using it can be fun and it can also elicit fond memories of bygone days when we had used the language.

Recommendation. There is nothing inherently wrong with slang or regionalisms (terms used in a certain region). People can use conventional speech at school or work and then use slang at home with their "dawgs." If slang is what they primarily know and use, then a great deal of conventional communication will just be *noise* to them. In this event, we could expect their formal education to suffer and create barriers to achieving careers in education, law, medicine, the media, and so on. Furthermore, people judge us according to the language we use, for better or worse (the cliché) or somewhere in between. If, in a formal speaking interaction, the speaker is using slang or what is deemed to be excessive slang in the listener's mind, the listener is likely to think the speaker is uneducated. If a goal of communication is to be understood and slang, by definition, is non-standard and specialized for a group of people or specific region, we could not expect widespread understanding arising from its use. In short, use slang in its appropriate place.

Third, *profanity* is a form of non-standard language used to express anger, disrespect, and/or contempt toward someone, an object, an event, or idea. Words associated with our more bodily functions are typically used. Before the latter part of the twentieth century, it was generally thought in America to be impolite for men to swear in the company of women. Now an occasional cuss word may be heard on the major news networks and anecdotal evidence suggests that even most high school girls at least occasionally cuss.

Babcock's World War II experience suggests that blithely cussing can be counterproductive for "… during serious weapons instruction, I discovered that the men paid closer attention to the message if I avoided the ___-word and swearing in general. They took me more seriously, knowing instinctively that empty expletives lack substance and credibility."[39]

Recommendation. While profanity has come into increasing use, most people can recognize its inappropriateness in job interviews and public-speaking events. Further, given harassment and sexual harassment suits, people have to be careful what they say at work, especially anything of a sexual nature. As with slang, people judge us by how we speak. We can ask ourselves what image we want other people to have of us, and to what extent profanity is linked with that image.

Fourth, *racist language* refers to language expressing the idea that one race is superior to another race, the latter of which is obviously inferior in comparison. Racism is "judging by genes," the belief that biology or genes provide a legitimate basis for evaluating someone's character or ability, that we can know a person by knowing about some of his or her ancestors from the past. This can be illustrated by the statement, "_____(insert a racial or ethnic group of your choice) people are _____" (insert characteristics of your choice: smart, stupid, lazy, brave, and so on, usually of a disparaging nature). Racism is not the same as discrimination, which is the creating and enforcing of artificial and/or unconstitutional barriers preventing someone from voting, getting a job or promotion, gaining school admission, and so on. Discrimination could stem from racism.

After the 1960's there have been some newer ideas about what is or is not racism, and thus, racist language. One idea suggests that words that can be interpreted as an unfavorable group judgment, and thereby insulting someone's ethnicity, are racist language.[40] Another definition suggests that only opposing and derogatory remarks about *some* ethnic minority groups is racism, while such remarks made by minority group members about white people, and possibly Jews, is not racism. It may even be considered racist if a white person disagrees with a black person, which was the expressed message by former president Carter in 2009 about some white people's dislike of President Obama's political positions.[41] Lastly, comparisons between groups that reveal one group to be deficient or inadequate in some way might be considered racist.

Notice that *insulting* and saying that *an ethnic group is not as good as* (does not, as a group, perform as well on a given task) some other group *as a group* are quite different from references to genetic characteristics. People saying that they are insulted, that they do not like something, is a very individual and subjective conclusion, not an external, objective one. People claiming that that there are more individuals of one or another ethnic group performing well in a given activity in a given time and place, or the opposite, that members of one or another ethnic group are not performing much, or as well, in some other activity, does not mean that group differences are a reflection of genes and that members of any disparaged group could not successfully compete in the activity if they so chose.

Anyone with a longer view of employment numbers could point out, for example, that there were less of one ethnic group or another involved in a particular profession at a certain point in time, and then point out that there were more of these group members in the profession at another point in time, clearly showing that the identified group members could successfully do the task. Even for those groups revealing few members engaged in a given profession, it is no proof that the members could not be successful in that area for there are many variables influencing employment, certainly apart from any genetic evaluations for those who wish to make a racial argument.

Even in other areas, it is not necessarily racist to acknowledge group differences. According to Sowell, it has been well documented that "Rates of [alcoholism,] crime, disease and other adverse conditions have ... varied widely among various groups [in the United States and] in countries around the world."[42] This is not a matter of prejudgment (prejudice) or racism to acknowledge such group differences. On what basis can we legitimately denigrate the messenger for stating the differences?

There is also a great deal of hypocrisy in the public use of racist language.
One particular group that has been the butt of many statements and jokes
from about 1990 to the present is the loosely identified group of white people
referred to as *rednecks*. For example, there was a television show about redneck wedding ceremonies and one particular comedian provided a litany of
behaviors that fit in his phrase, "If you ever ...., you might be a redneck.". If
these jokes and shows were about another socio-economic group of people
within a larger ethnic group, would these latter people have evaluated both
the word and the program as racist and demanded that the show be removed
from television? About 1990 there was a well-known movie entitled *White
Men Can't Jump*. Did non-white people get upset about this movie title? If we
substituted another skin color word for *white* and another descriptor in place
of *jump*, would members of *this* identified group have been upset and cried
racism? If members of one ethnic, career, or other grouping do not want or
like the derogatory statements made about their own group members, how
can they tolerate the saying of the very such statements about members in
other groups?

Recommendation. It seems so obvious to say so, but people have to mentally recognize racist language and remind themselves (if they have not
done so already) that such thoughts are baseless and to avoid verbalizing
such statements. Even if someone has a racist thought, they can keep it to
themselves. Since people can be biased when claiming that racism does or
does not exist, they need a simple strategy to help them determine this.
You can mentally change the skin color/ethnicity of the person who made
the statement and of the person or group of people being referred to, to
see if you would then evaluate the statement any differently. Goldberg
cautions us about inaccurately "crying wolf" too many times since people
will stop listening and we will have diluted the more traditional meaning
of racism.[43]

If members of one group do not like a certain potentially (at least) racist
word used by members of other groups in reference to it, does it increase or
decrease the use of this word (as well as concomitant thoughts that may arise)
by everyone if members of the referenced group also use this word toward
their own group members, and possibly in much greater quantity? Presumably most black Americans do not like the word *nigger* and do not want other
people to think disparaging things about them that might be associated with
this word's use. Still, what is the impact of some (many?) black people saying
this word and using it in song lyrics in reference to other black people? Does
this help or hinder the cause against racist language? Does it help or hurt if

people of Italian heritage in America say *dago* or *wop* in reference to other Italians?

Fifth, *sexist language* is defined as words "… assign[ing] characteristics to others based on their sex."[44] "Sexism is manifested by [speaking of] women as genetically inferior, supporting discriminatory practices against women, engaging in hostility toward women who do not fulfill traditional sex roles, … using derogatory names to refer to women or negatively stereotyping women, and treating women as sex objects."[45] This definition coincides with the one of racism about judging others on the basis of their genes. *The American Heritage College Dictionary* provides a similar yet different definition, explaining that sexism is *discrimination* against someone because of their gender, based upon the idea that one gender group is superior to the other.[46] This suggests that sexism is not simply an expressed mental attitude but also an outward act creating an artificial barrier to someone's career or other aspirations (similar to *discrimination* used in the racist language section).

While statements such as "All _____(men, women) are alike," "Men are dogs," "Women have PMS," and "Can't live with them, can't live without them" suggest both a genetic reflection and denigration, some statements about male and female differences are not a denigration and some statements purported to either reveal exclusion or discrimination are not factually incorrect. These groups do have some variances.

We might think that proving sex discrimination and thus, sexism, is easy but that has not been the case. Even verbal references suggesting that one gender or the other has not shown itself equally capable of doing something cannot be so easily characterized as sexist. Men are physically stronger and run faster as each Olympics competition reveals. Gender differences also exist in cognition. Functional magnetic resonance imaging (fMRI) scans have shown that male and female subjects differ in their use of brain hemispheres when responding to some language tasks (males may tend to use one hemisphere while females use both hemispheres).[47] This suggests that biological (innate) brain differences exist between the sexes. If a woman reports research showing that girls perform better on verbal tests and that is not sexist language, then how is it sexist language if a man reports research showing large ratios of boys outnumbering girls with top math and science scores? If males and females are genetically different, we should expect some differences in outcomes when comparing the two. According to Sowell, we may have to keep silent about this for Harvard University's President Summers was demonized and lost his job when he offered some existing data about why there were fewer women in top science positions. This includes: women who are mothers have difficulty working the requisite long hours required by the jobs, women are outnumbered by men at the highest (and lowest) IQ levels, as well as possible socialization and discrimination factors. Apparently, discrimination was the only acceptable answer.[48] Verbalizing any existing behavioral and genetic differences and showing one group to have achieved less in some areas (and, coincidentally, achieved more in others) is somehow denigrating for the group and individual members so it can be terms sexism. Assuming the data Summers referred to was accurate, it did not represent or imply *mere* stereotypes. Sowell concludes that "Neither truth nor standards matter when it comes to one of the ideological raw nerves like race [and gender]."[49] Was someone *excluded* from teaching at Harvard? We are sexist to speak about IQ data? This situation illustrates what communicators face when speaking about gender differences.

Thus, sorting out what is or might be sexism so we can know if we are using sexist language is not so clear. Simple group comparisons between males and females in terms of money earned, college admissions, college graduation rates, academic fields of degrees earned, career field employment, and so on, on the surface indicate differences but gross differences do not in and of themselves prove discrimination. If they did, then for example we could say that colleges are sexist since as of 2006 women comprised 57% of college students.[50] Are colleges actively preventing more qualified men from attending college? For those who believe in Affirmative Action, should we now actively limit female admissions in colleges to one-half the total population (and provide special financial scholarships for men only)? According to Kingsbury, some colleges are essentially doing just this or something close to it, as they are rejecting women at a higher rate.[51] This is sexist if we apply Pearson and Nelson's and Gudykunst and Kim's definitions.[52] This means it was also sexist immediately after the early 1970's when Affirmative Action came into being *if* more qualified men were excluded in favor of women.

Sowell offers further data about purported sexism.[53] College-educated men and women in America differ in academic disciplines and in postgraduate work completed. These factors make significant differences in subsequent occupations and earned income. Still, some people think that all college graduates are somehow the same and should be earning the same money, and if they do not then it is presumed after-the-fact that discrimination (sexism) must have occurred.

Sowell also reports that while American women's incomes as a whole do not equal men's incomes as a whole, "[a]mong college faculty members, American women who had never married earned slightly *higher* incomes than men who had never married, as far back as 1969."[54] Further, "… as early as 1971, women in their thirties who had never married and who had worked continuously since school earned slightly *higher* incomes than men of the same description."[55] If women do not work as many longer hours as do men or as continuously as do men, then how could their income be the same?

Sowell's evidence is consistent with data from the Census Bureau, Internal Revenue Service, and the Bureau of Labor Statistics cited by Farrell[56] as well as data from a report by the American Association of University Women.[57] It is illegitimate to make broad statements about sexism being the reason that women, as a group, earn less than men. Further, it is hardly sexist language to verbalize the data noted above.

Overall, without terms that point to an *extensional* reality, there will be continued disagreements about what is or is not sexist language. Similarly, Sowell suggests that there has been difficulty in resolving different points of view of discrimination since "… so many of the words used have ambiguous and shifting meanings."[58] These words include, but are not limited to: discrimination, prejudice, bias, sexism, exclusion, denigrates, access, and opportunity. Without an agreed-upon vocabulary that references observable actions, questions about the existence of discrimination or how much discrimination exists will be difficult to determine.

One common example purportedly illustrating sexist language has been the longstanding use of male references in written and spoken language (he, man, mankind, fireman, policeman, etc.). Since at least the 1970's, gender-neutral terms have become commonly used in their place (he or she, people, police officer, firefighter, etc.). Hughes argues that this approach is misguided.

> Anyone who knows the history of our language knows that, in Old English and Anglo-Saxon, the suffix -man was gender-neutral, it had and retains, the same meaning, as 'person' today, referring to all people equally, To denote gender, it had to be qualified: a male was called a *waepman*, a female *wifman*. This gender-free use of -man gives us forms like chairman, fisherman, craftsman, meaning simply a person of either sex who engages a denoted work or profession. The ancient sexist wrong supposed to be enshrined in the word since the time of Beowulf turns out not to exist.[59]

Even if Hughes has a legitimate point, the use of gender-free terms has been so commonplace since the 1970's that anyone not using them will probably be considered an uneducated, sexist boor.[60]

Inconsistency is common among those labeling language or deeds as sexist. As with people incorrectly crying racism when it is a non- or insignificant factor for some outcome, there are inconsistencies in crying sexism. The following examples reveal some of the hypocrisy surrounding this issue. First, it is supposedly okay and non-sexist if at a certain point in time, all three college deans at a particular university in America are females, but if two or all three of them at a later date are replaced by males, then it must be due to sex discrimination. Second, it is supposedly okay for a female, U.S. Federal District Court judge in a commencement address to laud women for being in so many professional positions and shout "Girl Power!" but it would be sexist for a man to say exactly the same thing in reference to men. Third, it was supposedly sexist that all 21 tenured, secondary education professors at a large west coast university were males, but it was not sexist that all 23 tenured professors in elementary education at the same university at the same time and in the same building were females. If "the old boys' network" was sexist, what about the "oldgirls" (cannot say "old"—that is derogatory, cannot say "girls"—that is sexist; say "women") network? These examples do not prove there is no sexism, simply that there are inconsistent applications.

Recommendation. Pearson and Nelson suggest that we avoid stereo-types.[61] As the Perception chapter notes, our mind generalizes as a matter of course. This does not mean that we should *not* develop a mental habit to review our generalizations and stereotypes for legitimacy and limitations before verbalizing them. At the same time, is it really a gross error to think of or refer to high school varsity football teams as being *boys* teams since they have been almost exclusively male since their inception? This is different than the person who crassly argues that one gender cannot do much of what the other gender does, and especially overlooks the extreme range of employment contributions made by women during World War II. Another recommendation is for people to develop in their own mind their own aspirations and a plan of action to achieve those goals so as to make someone else's stereotypical reference of them irrelevant and inconsequential.

CONCLUSION

This chapter explored the functions of language in our verbal messages. General Semantics provided most of the concepts with which to analyze language usage. Its key ideas are that words are symbols; meanings are in people, meanings depend upon context, words imply denotative and connotative meanings, words are abstract and vary in their abstractness, language varies in directness, and words can evoke emotional and/or behavioral responses in people. Further, various language obstacles were described and accompanied with recommendations for overcoming the barriers. Additional space and discussion were given to the topics of racism and sexism since they continue to be highly controversial subjects in America. The language and purposes of *doublespeak* were also explained. We can think of it as mixed messages and usage that attempts to evade the extensional, tangible reality of the subject, place, person, or phenomenon being referred to.

Doublespeak attempts to distort our understanding and control our reaction to the reality around us.

Overall, this chapter recommends that we be as specific and as descriptive as possible of our thoughts and in our language usage so as to increase the likelihood the receiver will create a meaning in his or her mind that is similar to the meaning in our mind. Clear speech increases the chance the listener will reach a closer understanding of what we have communicated. Effective communication increases the control we have over what occurs in our lives for it minimizes, goes around, or logically overcomes existing personal, social, or legal barriers to our reaching our goals.

CHAPTER 6 EXERCISES

Chapter 6 Exercise #A: Abstractions (class exercise, not graded)

1. *Levels of Abstraction*[62]
   Directions: Starting with the sentence that is most clear and descriptive (#1, least abstract), number the following sentences in order of their increasing abstraction (the sentence considered most abstract in its meaning should be given a #5). Review Hayakawa's Abstraction Ladder in this chapter.
   _____ a. All of our students will get an adequate education.
   _____ b. Students are just no good.
   _____ c. Students are required by law to attend school until age 16.
   _____ d. Marvin is a great student.
   _____ e. The population of this school will increase 25% .

2. *Abstractions* (generalities)[63]
   Directions: Quickly write down your response to each of the next 5 incomplete sentences.
   a. College women are _____
   b. Teenage boys are _____
   c. Politicians are: _____

   Now reduce the subject of each sentence above to a less abstract word or phrase.

   a. College women are _____
   b. Teenage boys are _____
   c. Politicians are: _____

Chapter 6 Exercise #B: Overcoming Generalizations: Dating and Indexing[64]

1. *Dating* generalizations means to include a specific time reference in your statements that specifies when a given fact was true so the listener will not so easily assume that people, places, events or other things stay the same and thereby reach an unsupported conclusion.

   Directions: Date the following statement by Juan to help Brian avoid a mistaken impression. Brian says, "I'm going to Angel's restaurant to-night." Juan replies, "Angel's restaurant? For real? The last time I ate there the food was very tasty!" On the basis of what Juan has said, Brian is likely to think that he will really enjoy the restaurant since he assumes that restaurants stay the same over time (they do not). Rewrite Juan's statement to include a date reference.

   Juan: "_____."

2. *Indexing* is a verbal response that accounts for individual differences among groups of people, objects, or places (similar to *Dating* which accounts for differences over time). *Indexing* is an effort to overcome the effect of over-generalizing (such as stereotyping)

   Directions: Rewrite the statements below, indicating with just a few added key words, that the original generalization is not necessarily true.
   a. "Since banks are bigger than credit unions, banks are safer places to put your money."

   _____

   b. "You know those Belgum kids are known for being smart, so Cindy Belgum should be, too."

   _____

Chapter 6 Exercise #C: Inference Test

Directions: Carefully read the story that follows, assuming that all of the information is accurate. Next, read the statements about the story, answering them in numerical order. Do not go back to change any previous answers. After you read each statement, circle *T* if the statement is true on the basis of the information presented in the story, *F* if the statement is false, and *?* if you cannot be certain whether the statement is true or false.

A person wearing a hospital uniform was shopping in a grocery story. A store clerk was about to ring up some items at the check stand when there was a loud "pop" sound, like gunfire. A hooded man with a hand in a coat pocket ran by the check stand and out the door. The store clerk and a shopper ran toward the origination of the noise and found someone lying on an aisle floor with dark red stains on their leg and a red-colored pool forming on the floor around it. "Someone's been shot!" screamed the clerk. Moaning was heard. "Doc, help."

T / F / ?   1.   A shopper was waiting at the check stand to have groceries rung up.

T / F / ?   2.   A store clerk was ringing up the cost of some groceries.

T / F / ?   3.   There was a loud noise in the store, like a gun firing.

T / F / ?   4.   There was a shooter with a hood on who ran out the door.

T / F / ?   5.   The customer on the floor was moaning.

T / F / ?   6.   The shopper from the hospital went with the clerk toward the noise.

T / F / ?   7.   The man on the floor had a leg wound, with blood leaking out, although the story did not say which leg had a wound.

T / F / ?   8.   The clerk asked the doctor to help.

T / F / ?   9.   There are four people referred to in this story.

* This test is modeled on *The Story* by W. Haney.[65]

Answer for Exercise A.1. Levels of Abstraction
4a, 5b, 1c, 3d, 2e

Chapter 6 Exercise D. Doublespeak ** (Hybels, statements #1-9[66]; Shearer, statements #10-15[67]; author #16-20)

Directions: Match the more descriptive (extensional) statements on the right column with the euphemisms on the left (see next page).

Complete this in three groups (A-C): #1-9 with #a-i, #10-15 with #j-o; and #16-20 with #p-t.

Group   __ 1. sufferer from fictional disorder
                syndrome   a. stolen goods
        __ 2. sub-optimal   b. junkyard
        __ 3. temporarily displaced inventory   c. plastic
        __ 4. negative gain in test scores   d. bag of ice cubes
        __ 5. synthetic glass   e. bribe
        __ 6. normal gratitude   f. death
        __ 7. thermal therapy kit   g. liar
        __ 8. substantive negative outcome   h. failed
        __ 9. reutilization marketing yard   i. lower test score

Group B
        __10. safety-related occurrence   j. bum
        __11. incomplete success   k. grocery-store
                                                       checkout clerk
        __12. fiscal underachievers   l. accident
        __13. non-goal oriented member   m. bank robbery
                of society
        __14. career associate scanning   n. failure
                professional
        __15. unauthorized withdrawal   o. the poor

Group C
        __16. free 99   p. prostitute
        __17. public use   q. government
        __18. investment   enforced giveaway
                                                       to 1 group while
                                                       charging another
        __19. free   r. Guam/Chamorro
                                                       phrase for stealing
        __20. lady of the night   s. anything the
                                                       government wants
                                                       to justify spending
                                                       money on
                                                   t. government taking
                                                       one person's
                                                       property to sell to
                                                       another person

Answers for Exercise C: Inference Test
False: 2; True: 3; rest are ?.

CHAPTER 6 HOMEWORK
Language

A. *Levels of Abstraction.*[68]

An *abstract* word is one that does not reflect a concrete idea in our mind about what is being referenced. In General Semantics, *abstraction* refers to the use of words/symbols that are removed (and remove our thinking) from the *extensional* (physical) *reality* around us. *Directions*: Starting with the sentence at the lowest level of abstraction (the most specific, clear, concrete), renumber the following statements in order of increasing abstraction. The lowest, least abstract statement should be numbered as #1, on up to the most abstract statement as #5. Refer to the sample abstraction provided in the Exercise section to help you do this. Submit your homework of these sentences in this exact order.

    ____ a.   Dave ensures all of our cars are safe to drive on the road.
    ____ b.   Dave is some kind of an automotive guru.
    ____ c.   Dave knows what to do with his car tools.
    ____ d.   Dave is a good old boy.
    ____ e.   Today, Dave installed a new Volkswagen engine in Tom's dune buggy.

B. *Euphemisms and Inflated Language.*

A *euphemism* is an inoffensive or positive word or phrase that attempts to avoid an unpleasant reality, while *inflated language* attempts to make something ordinary seem impressive. *Directions*: In the exercise below, list the euphemisms you have heard or could be used to make the listed behaviors (or objects) seem better than they more accurately are. Consider thinking of a creative way to make these negative phenomena sound acceptable or even good. For words implying an ordinary job, think of terms to make the jobs seem impressive.

Euphemism/Inflated Language

1. Physical beating (spouse, child, etc.)

_____

2. Cheating on in-class school exams

_____

3. Stealing

_____

4. Loud, heated argument

_____

5. Mean tempered

_____

6. Secretary

_____

7. Plumber

_____

For 8-10, you choose three disdainful or even ordinary situations or objects, and provide a coinciding euphemism or inflated term for them.

8. _____   _____

9. _____   _____

10. _____   _____

C. *Connotative Meanings.*[69]

These are the subjective, personal meanings we have for phenomena. This exercise is designed to illustrate how we are subjective with our descriptions and have a bias towards favoring what we do over what others do, even when they do the same or a similar thing.

Directions: Demonstrate how the connotative meanings of the expressions below can be changed by choosing alternate words. Note the shift in degrees of meaning as you provide a positive sounding word for the first level, to a neutral word in the middle level, to a negative sounding word for the third or last (bottom) level. Put words on the blank lines that relate to the italicized words/concepts provided to you in each case.

Example:

a. I'm __(prudent)__. (give a positive word relating to spending money in a conscious way)
b. You're *mindful of your money.*(a neutral word, given here, relating to the spending of money)
c. He's __(stingy, cheap)__. (give a negative meaning for the conscious spending of money)

   1. a. I'm *respectful.*
      b. You're _____
      c. He's _____
   2. a. I'm _____
      b. You're _____
      c. She's *mean.*
   3. a. I'm *modest*
      b. You're _____
      c. He's _____
   4. a. I watch _____
      b. You watch *sensual movies.*
      c. He watches _____
   5. a. I'm_____
      b. You're *under the influence of alcohol.*
      c. She's_____

Answers for Exercise D: Doublespeak (on a previous page)
Group A, 1-9: g,h,a,i,c,e,d,f,b
Group B, 10-15: l,n,o,j,k,m
Group C, 16-20: r,t,s,q,p

REFERENCES

1. S. Berman, *Understanding and Being Understood* (San Francisco: International Society for General Semantics, 1969), p .2.
2. J. Condon, Jr., *Semantics and Communication* (3rd ed.) (New York: Macmillan Publishing Company, 1985), p. 16.
3. C. Ogden and I. Richards, *The Meaning of Meaning: A Study of the Influence of Language Upon Thought and of the Science of Symbolism* (New York: Harcourt, Brace and World, 1923).
4. Ibid., p. 27.

5. Ibid.
6. T. Sowell, *Intellectuals and Society* (New York: Basic Books, 2009).
7. J. Goldberg, *Liberal Fascism: The Secret History of the American Left, from Mussolini to the Politics of Change* (New York: Broadway Books, 2009).
8. Sowell, op cit., p. 142.
9. Goldberg, op cit.
10. Ibid.
11. Hayakawa, op cit.
12. W. Johnson, *Your Most Enchanted Listener* (New York: Harper & Brothers, 1956), p. 75.
13. Ibid.
14. Hayakawa, op cit.
15. Ibid.
16. E. Griffin, *A First Look at Communication Theory* (5th ed.) (New York: McGraw Hill, 2003).
17. T. Sowell, "A War of Words." *Jewish World Review* (May 29, 2007).
18. C. Russell and J. White, "Who Controls Your Life?" *ETC: A Review of General Semantics* 50, 1 (Spring, 1993): 17-19.
19. Hayakawa, op cit.
20. Hayakawa, op cit.
21. Hayakawa, op cit.
22. Haney, op cit., p. 101.
23. Berman, op cit., p. 35.
24. Hayakawa, op cit., p. 36.
25. W. Lutz, *Doublespeak* (New York: Harper Perennial, 1989), p. 1.
26. Ibid., p. 2.
27. C. Larson, *Persuasion: Reception and Responsibility* (United States: Wadsworth/Thomson Learning, 2001).
28. Lutz, op cit.
29. S. Hybels and R. Weaver, II, *Communicating Effectively* (6th ed.) (New York: McGraw-Hill: New York, 2001), p. 105.
30. Lutz, op cit.
31. T. Sowell, "Fighting words." *The San Francisco Chronicle* (November 20, 1985).
32. Lutz, op cit., p. 4.
33. Ibid.
34. D. Brinkley, *11 Presidents, 4 Wars, 22 Political Conventions, 1 Moon Landing, 3 Assassinations, 2,000 Weeks of News and Other Stuff on Television and 18 years of Growing Up in North Carolina* (New York: Ballantine Books, 1995), p. 226.
35. Ibid., p. 268.
36. Ibid., p. 266.
37. Lutz, op cit., p.6.
38. T. Sowell, "With-it lexicon." *The San Francisco Chronicle* (April 24, 1987).
39. J. Babcock, *Taught To Kill: An American Boy's War From the Ardennes to Berlin* (Washington, D.C.: Potomac Books, Inc., 2007), p. 10.
40. Ibid.

41. W. Williams, "Is disagreement with Obama Racism?" in *Jewish World Report*, September 30, 2009.
42. T. Sowell, *Applied Economics: Thinking Beyond Stage One* (2nd ed.) (New York: Basic Books, 2009), p. 208.
43. Ibid.
44. W. Gudykunst and Y. Kim, *Communicating With Strangers: An Approach To Intercultural Communication* (3rd ed.) (Boston: McGraw-Hill, 1997).
45. Ibid., p. 131.
46. *The American Heritage College Dictionary*, op cit.
47. B. Shaywitz, S. Shaywitz, K. Pugh, R. Constable, P. Skudiarski, R. Fulbright, R. Bronen, J. Fletcher, D. Shankweller, L. Katz, and J. Gore, J. "Sex differences in the functional organization of the brain for language." *Nature* 373, 6515 (February 16, 1995).
48. T. Sowell, "Another academic casualty." *Jewish World Review* (February 23, 2006), pp. 2-3.
49. Sowell, 2006, op cit., p. 2.
50. A Kingsbury, "Admittedly Unequal." *U.S.News & World Report* (June 25, 2007).
51. Ibid.
52. Pearson and Nelson, op cit.; Gudykunst and Kim, op cit.
53. T. Sowell, *Applied Economics. Thinking Beyond Stage One* (2nd ed.) (New York: Basic Books, 2009).
54. Ibid., p. 226.
55. Ibid.
56. J. Leo, "A wage gap? It's men who get paid less." *Jewish World Review* (March 14, 2005); S. Swoboda, "Facts dispute assertions on gender bias," *Pacific Daily News* (September 9, 2001).
57. S. Chapman, "The truth about the pay gap," Reasononline (April 30, 2007).
58. Sowell, op cit., p. 236.
59. R. Hughes, *Culture of Complaint: The Fraying of America* (New York: Oxford University Press, 1993), p. 22.
60. Ibid.
61. Pearson and Nelson, op cit.
62. R. Adler and N. Towne, *Instructor's Manual for Looking Out/Looking In: Interpersonal Communication* (3rd ed.) (New York: Holt, Rinehart and Winston, 1981).
63. Ibid.
64. R. Verderber and C. Berryman-Fink, *Instructor's Manual For Communicate!* (5th ed.) (Belmont, CA: Wadsworth Publishing Company, 1987).
65. Haney, op cit.
66. Hybels and Weaver, op cit.
67. L. Shearer, "Stamp Out 'Doublespeak'." *Parade Magazine* (January 10, 1988).
68. Adler and Towne, op cit.
69. Ibid.

CHAPTER SEVEN

Nonverbal Communication

Nonverbal Communication refers to all the messages we send to and receive from people other than verbal content words, including: the look on people's faces, their tone of voice, their gestures and other movements, the distance they stand from us, and so on. An exception would be communication like the American Sign Language that does lack verbal words but is not included as nonverbal communication.

With accurate observations and a clear understanding of people's nonverbal messages, we could read people's nonverbal messages more so like a book. We could then directly respond to them and this would make for effective communication. Still, communication is a package of signals, with so many inter-relating and even contradicting nonverbal and verbal messages that it is difficult to make sense of a complete communication event. We typically cannot interpret one nonverbal message in isolation since there is a package of nonverbal messages, and these are often combined with verbal words to inform our interpretation. Further, we often need to know something about the person to form an accurate conclusion about a given nonverbal message.

DISTINCT FEATURES OF
NONVERBAL COMMUNICATION

Although people are certainly able to gain understanding from their use of words, the previous chapter suggested that there are limits to our language and its usage. Words are abstractions and representations of that to which they refer. Thus, they are separated from the stimuli in our perception from which we draw meaning. Words typically refer to something in the past which is limited by our memory and/or by the persona we want accepted, or to what we intend to do in the future (many intentions are not fulfilled). These and other characteristics are in contrast to nonverbal communication.

The following are a number of nonverbal communication characteristics that differ from those of verbal communication.

1. *Nonverbal Communication is Ambiguous.* Multiple interpretations can be drawn from a given message. This makes it very difficult to say with certainty that a given interpretation is correct. Imagine trying to decide whether certain eye behavior is a leer or a stare, whether a sincere tone of voice covered up a lie or conveyed the truth, if you could trust the person who just gave you a firm handshake, or if a friendly smile and eye contact is simple friendliness or reveals an interest to start a social relationship. This list can go on. Since so many messages are conveyed nonverbally, it is critical for the success of our social and business relationships that we accurately interpret many such messages provided by both others and by ourselves.

2. *Nonverbal Communication is Continuous.* We know from Chapter Two that communication is inevitable. We cannot not communicate because nonverbal communication is ever-present and ongoing. We may speak one or a few words and then stop our verbal communication, yet multiple nonverbal messages preceded the verbal content, multiple accompany the verbal content, and other ones occur after we stop talking. The color of our clothes, our changing posture, the directing of our eyes here and there, our body odor, and so on, continue to provide messages to people who detect them.

3. *Most Nonverbal Communication is Spontaneous.* We recognize that people monitor some of their nonverbal communication and may be able to convince others with an expected or appropriate facial expression, tone of voice, and so on. Good actors and politicians are so convincing because their nonverbal behavior is so fitting to the roles they are fulfilling. Still, much of our nonverbal communication is unintentional so it just comes out, ready to be seen, heard, smelled, tasted, or even touched by all. It is as if we are naked. People may like us for our spontaneity that they think reveals our "true" selves. Overall, while we intend to send or provide some messages, many of our continuous messages are unintentional.

4. *Nonverbal Communication Messages Occur Simultaneously.* While we can speak only one word at a time, and follow those words with other, discreet words, at any given moment there are multiple nonverbal messages that occur with one another. Our forehead, eyebrows, eyelids, and/or our mouth work in concert to form a smile or frown, Added to this, we may lean toward the person to whom we are speaking, have an open body posture, use our voice

to make a m-m-m-m-m sound, and so on. The simultaneous messages make it difficult to notice all of them and accurately evaluate the combinations of them. Receivers have to look at a cluster of gestures to get a clearer sense of what the message is.

5. *When A Verbal Message Is Inconsistent With A Nonverbal One, the Nonverbal One Is Usually More Meaningful.* In this situation, people tend to believe the nonverbal message rather than the verbal words because the nonverbal messages seem to be more spontaneous and thus, a more accurate depiction of the communicator's emotions and thoughts. As Barnlund explains, nonverbal communication "… seems less subject to conscious control and hence more revealing of the true inner state of the person."[1] A half-hearted stated "yes" without an accompanying smile is likely to be viewed as a "no" by the listener. Most people seem to agree that actions speak louder than words.

6. *Nonverbal Communication is Conveyed Through Multiple Senses.* Remember the channels of communication noted in Chapter One? As listeners, we hear the explicit words people use, but as nonverbal receivers, we hear the speaker's tone of voice, see his posture and facial expression, smell his sweat-soaked clothes, feel the coarse skin on his hand as we shake it, and possibly taste some chocolate cake they just ate if we kiss them. These are the basic channels of nonverbal communication we can examine for meaning.

7. *Nonverbal Messages Communicate Feelings and Attitudes.*[2] A majority of the emotional meaning of a message is communicated nonverbally. We do not need people's explicit words for us to recognize many of their feelings and attitudes. We can acquire implicit information about people's feelings and attitudes by examining what they self-disclose through their face, eye movement, body positioning, touch, smell, distance from us, their vocal expressions, and so on.

Mehrabian suggests "… implicit [nonverbal] communication deals primarily with the transmission of information about feelings and like-dislike or attitudes."[3] These emotions and our readiness to respond favorably or unfavorably toward a person, place, or thing can be categorized as pleasure-displeasure (liking-disliking), arousal-nonarousal (responsiveness), or dominance-submissiveness (power, status). In other words, we use nonverbal messages to express three different sets of feelings or attitudes about someone or something. The following are some nonverbal signs or clues to look for that can indicate how we or other people feel about someone or something.

a. Liking/Disliking. We indicate our liking or interest in someone by leaning toward them, by standing close or closer to them, by facing our body toward them, by having an open and relaxed posture toward them, by favorable facial expressions such as smiling and increased eye contact, and by more touching of them. Disliking is shown by the opposite of these, including increased physical distance and avoid contact with the person, little or no eye contact with them, lack of touching, closed or crossed arms, frowning expressions, and looking away from them. Similar (but not exact) liking/disliking is shown toward favorable and unfavorable objects.

b. Responsiveness. This is indicated by the intensity and amount of our nonverbal reaction, showing either a positive or negative regard for the person or thing. An expressive voice reveals a strong regard while a hesitant one suggests the person has little regard for the phenomenon. Arousal is also revealed by how quickly people respond, their loudness, and how fast they speak.

c. *Domi*nance/Submissiveness. People who either believe or want to pretend they have social, political, or financial power (higher status) adopt a more relaxed posture around others, they use more expansive gestures, and they look at others less often. More powerful family, group, or organizational members show their power through the larger space they are given or take, the location and use of space to prevent others from easily entering or navigating their space, and their asserting themselves in someone else's space. Bosses can lean back and to the side in their chair. They can speak to the floor, wall, or windows rather than to the subordinate before them. They can use a neutral sounding tone of voice. Lower status and less powerful people need to be more alert, tense with an upright body posture, and more strictly eye their boss. Overall, they act submissive in the presence of a perceived higher-status person. Whatever the degree of power used, it silently reinforces in both communicator's minds their power status vis-à-vis each other. People in the lower status position can subtly convey their own self-worth and independence by sitting in a more relaxed manner in their boss's office, speak firmly at a moderate rate of speech, stare off into space once in awhile as they speak, and lean forward with their elbows resting on a desk and their chin cradled in their hands. This is not about challenging the legitimate authority of the boss but to influence the boss to respect them as an individual.

NONVERBAL INTERACTION
WITH VERBAL MESSAGES

Nonverbal and verbal messages invariably occur together and typically operate in unison to provide a package of signals, each form referencing and/or responding to the others' features. Given the principle that communication is a package of signals, nonverbal communication is not an inseparable entity from verbal content so it has to be studied as part of the total communication process. This section lists uses of nonverbal communication taken from Knapp and describes how they interrelate with and support verbal messages.[4]

1. *Repeating*. Nonverbal message can restate or say again the verbal message. Pointing in the particular direction is an action people often do after telling someone to "go up the left-hand stairs," using a raised arm and forefinger sticking out in a leftward direction. Another example could be a basketball coach telling the players what to do, then using chalk to create circles, x's, and arrowed directions on the gym floor. Repeating reinforces the verbal message.

2. *Contradicting*. When people have multiple and opposing thoughts and/or feelings about something or are attempting to convey what they think they should "say" rather than what they more completely think or feel about something, they are likely to provide a nonverbal message that suggests a meaning opposite or logically inconsistent to that of the verbal message. For example, your sister asks you for a ride to the mall and you reply "Alright" with your voice pitch up on "al" and your pitch down on "right," accompanied by a quieter voice, your eye-contact on the floor or to one side of your sister, and with an unhappy tone of voice. You do not want to take her to the mall but you will do it if you must. She might recognize you do not really want to do it but accept the contradiction because she is more concerned about getting to the mall. On the other hand, she might get upset and say, "I willingly help you do your homework and chores but now you only grudgingly agree to do me a favor? Forget it!"

There are a number of statements people make that are frequently accompanied by contradictory nonverbal messages, such as "Yes, I love you," "The check's in the mail," "I promise not to do it," "I like it," "It's OK," "I'm happy," "I'm not nervous," "I'm ready," "I'll be there," "I support you," "I'll call you," "I'll pay you on payday," "I'm not busy," "We can talk later," and "It's not out of my way." There may be legitimate, non-selfish reasons for people to make such statements. People such as parents and bosses and teachers face competing demands on their time and resources so they cannot satisfy everyone else as much as they try or would like to, and sometimes they over-extend themselves with their promises. Sometimes they do not want to give someone a direct, harsh evaluation. Sometimes they want to save face for themselves and the other person, and so on. They also have their individual likes, dislikes, beliefs, values, and goals. People such as parents and bosses and teachers are under pressure to be this way and that way in their relations with people. For most people, meeting life's demands is a juggling act.

Contradictory messages even provide a blessing in disguise since it is impolite to say some things, especially in public, and for those who can notice them, they are a less-confrontational way to say "no," or "I don't like it," or "I don't believe you," or "I don't want to hurt your feelings." We rarely make these verbal statements to our boss or family members but we may not mind showing them nonverbally, even unintentionally. With these messages, the receiver is usually less upset with the sender. This fits the purpose of communication.

Since some nonverbal messages are harder to fake and most nonverbal messages are presumed to be more spontaneous than verbal ones, people tend to believe the meaning gained from the nonverbal message rather than the verbal meaning implied.[5] In a contradiction among nonverbal messages, people will tend to believe the one that is more difficult to feign or stage.

3. *Substituting*. Nonverbal messages can take the place of verbal ones. We use the variety of nonverbal communication elements, such as gestures, facial expressions, eye contact, and so on to take the place of a verbal message. If happy, or wanting to project happiness, people often show a vibrant, smiling face, substituting for "I'm happy" or "I just had a great experience." People can, if they are perceptive, "get it" by looking at the person. If you are sad and do not want to talk about it with your family or friends, you can show a glum face with your face turned partially away from them when you pass them, and keep your distance. Instead of saying "Thanks," some people give a hug, a pat on the shoulder, or a handshake, instead of saying "I love you," you can give the other person a warm, loving look, and so on. While these nonverbal messages are substitutes, they are not equal to the verbal message. Nonverbal messages have more intensity to them, so they are a stronger message. As with the contradictory messages, nonverbal messages offer an easy to accept message than what can seem to be stark direct, verbal one. A clenched-lip, lowered brow, tilted head, slow left-to-right head nod "No" is not as harsh a "No" as often verbalized. A nonverbal grudging "Yes" shows you have mixed feelings, a yes-with-reservations. This is an excellent substitute for the verbal message.

4. *Complementing*. The basic idea of complement is that something completes something else. The nonverbal messages that accompany verbal ones can add to and complete the verbal message and meaning created. Nonverbal messages may reinforce and elaborate on the verbal content message, even add subtle distinctions of potential meaning. Someone says "Glad to see you" and they give you a firm, vigorous handshake. "I'm so happy to see you" and they jump into your arms. "I'm so sorry" and they bury their face in your

shoulder and grasp you tightly around your back. These reflect what Knapp states as the reason for complementary, nonverbal messages: to "... serve to signal one's attitudes and intentions toward another person."[6]

5. *Regulating*. Given the presence of nonverbal communication, two communicators provide ongoing messages for each other even if only one of them is temporarily speaking. To signal the speaker that you wish them to continue speaking or that you would like to interject something, you can loudly interrupt them and say so. Or, you can use some nonverbal indicators that the speaker can see that you either wish them to continue their train of thought accordingly or finish their thought and let you speak. A slight head nod up and down and an occasional "uh-uh" can tell the speaker you are following them and they should continue. To signal that you want to speak, you can lean forward, raise your eyebrows, open your mouth and even start to silently form a word or raise your hand. Students raise their hands in class to indicate their desire to speak. You may even try to interrupt by quietly saying "but ...." with your chin stuck out one-half inch, or lightly touch the speaker's hand.

In summary of this section, nonverbal and verbal behaviors cannot be separated. They operate in tandem, each influencing the message choices as well as the subtle and not so subtle meanings of messages provided by the other forms.

NONVERBAL COMMUNICATION
SYSTEM COMPONENTS

There are a number of nonverbal elements that work together to provide us with messages. As a system of mutually dependent parts, a change in any one of these forms results in changing the others.[7] They also operate as a transaction with ourselves, influencing us to feel something as a result of enacting the nonverbal behavior (creating a smiley face when sad can lead you to feel better[8] or standing erect with shoulders squared can influence you to feel determined.[9]

The use and interpretation of these elements can vary from culture to culture. This chapter generally applies them to America while a later chapter on Intercultural Communication will provide examples and interpretations of some of these from other cultures' perspectives.

1. *The Body and Body Movements*. These include our posture, various gestures, facial movements, and eye activity. Seven categories of body movements are described below, along with sub-elements.

First, posture. Posture is the position of a person's body, typically while standing, sitting, or kneeling. Someone standing up straight suggests confidence while an erect posture with chin out and hands behind the back suggests authority. Sitting upright in a chair in someone else's presence conveys the idea of lower status and attention while leaning back in a chair suggests superiority and relaxation. Someone standing up after having a conversation sitting down can indicate that the person is finished and wants to leave.

Second, gestures. These are the movement of our arms, legs, and/or body to express or reinforce a thought. They are difficult to understand apart from other gestures and outside the context in which they occur. We need to observe whether there are gestures that are congruent (fit) with each other, thereby revealing a particular attitude about something. The following are common classification of gestures, posture, body movements, and facial expressions (the study of which is termed *kinesics*) that are combined with everyday verbal messages.

Emblems are those gestures that directly translate into no more than a few words, and they can be a substitute for words. For example, the thumbs-up gesture means "I did it" or "good job." On he other hand, if a baseball umpire has a raised arm, the thumb up and a four finger fist, it signals to the player "you're out."

Illustrators are gestures that accompany verbal messages, complementing or enhancing them. We often point with a finger to accompany the direction we have given someone, nod our head "yes" while we say the word, shake our head from side to side when we say "no," and so forth.

Third, affect displays are those body movements that show emotion, especially the movement of our face, but also through our vocalizations, gestures, and posture. These are usually communicated unintentionally and spontaneously so people tend to think these accurately display emotions: a gleeful, smiling face on the child that just won the spelling bee competition and a sad face on a bowed head of the last competitor.

Fourth, regulators are the behaviors we use to attempt to influence the ongoing verbal communication. As noted in the discussion on the previous page under *Regulating*, leaning forward, raising your eyebrows, or raising your hand slightly can signal your desire to talk.

Fifth, self-adaptors are those movements, often using touch, that we make to satisfy some uncomfortable body situation. We may scratch an itch, rub our hands together if cold, move our hair out of our eyes, or even use our hand to fan our face. However, given social graces, in public we are not as free to perform some adaptors as we are in private.

Sixth, face and facial expressions. Americans tend to look at peoples face (and eyes) more so than at other body parts so messages gained from these places carry more significance. Facial expressions are the primary indicator of our thoughts, feelings, and attitudes[10] as well as of the intensity of our feelings. At least six different emotions (*affect displays*) are conveyed by the face, similarly by people around the world.[11] These are: surprise, happiness, sadness, anger, fear, and disgust. In addition, Ekman suggests our face reveals our "... mood, attitudes, character, intelligence, attractiveness, age, sex, [and] race ...."[12] The following is a description of how the face appears when the six identified emotions are portrayed.

- *surprise.* Eyebrows are lifted high (like an eyebrow flash), the eyes are opened wide so the whites of the eye above the iris can be seen, the jaw drops with the mouth slightly to widely open.
- *happiness.* The corners of the lips are pulled back and up into an obvious smile the bottom of the cheeks are raised, and "crows-feet" wrinkling appears around the corners of the eyes, as people become older.
- *sadness.* The corners of the lips may be down or the lips may appear straight across as if they are about to tremble, the inner corners of the eyebrows are raised; there are some uneven lines on the forehead, the inner corners of the upper eyelid may be raised, and the lower eyelid may be raised which suggests increased sadness.
- *anger.* The eyebrows are lowered and pulled toward each other, the eyelids cover part of the iris and there is a sense of the person staring at you, and the lips are either pressed tightly together or open.
- *fear.* The forehead usually has horizontal wrinkles, the eyebrows and upper eyelids are raised, and the mouth is open with tense lips possibly having the corners pulled back.
- *disgust.* The upper lip is raised with either a raised or lowered lower lip, there is a wrinkled nose, the eyebrow is lowered, the cheeks may be raised along with the lower eyelid, and the upper eyelid is lowered.

Even though Americans tend to look at other people's faces when they communicate, they still miss some emotional messages because these messages can be so brief. Some *micromomentary* expressions last no longer than one-fifth to one-eighth of a second.[13] Still, even though you might not consciously notice something, your vision and your brain may register some meaning at a low level of awareness that simply gives you a general "sense" or "feeling" about the person. Some people label this type of observation as intuition.

Since we know that people tend to believe the nonverbal message over the verbal message when these are in conflict, people consider our face's emotional displays as more believable than our words. Learning at a young age that people are looking at our faces and that we may have to look back at them, we learn to *monitor* (*self-monitor*) our facial expressions so we can adjust them to project what we think is an appropriate expression for the moment. We block the expression of some emotions and put on display other emotions, particularly happiness,[14] so there is some dishonesty with our facial expressions. Unfortunately, or fortunately, depending how you evaluate it, we are not as practiced projecting lying faces as we are lying with words so facial expressions are potentially more accurate indications of what someone is feeling.

Seventh (and last), the eyes. The eyes have it. They are said to be the window to a person's soul. We may like those pretty blue or bedroom eyes but not those cold, beady ones. Of course, our eyes are not solely looked at but are viewed in combination with other facial movements.

Our eye movement provides a number of communication purposes.

- *personal connection*. With our eyes, we feel linked to people when we see them, particularly when there is a mutual gaze. For example, "Sue and I saw each other while passing on the road and smiled toward each other." We avoid eye contact, particularly in public settings, when we do not want a personal connection, such as those with whom we may be riding on public transportation.
- *expressive*. Our eye behavior indicates our involvement and possibly feelings of arousal with the person at whom we are looking.[15] As might be noticed, people look more at other people and objects they like and less at those which are disliked. The eyes (and accompanying facial features) express our feelings about the person with whom we are communicating, the context of communication, or the topic of discussion. If someone in your presence purposely does not look at you, they are probably anxious about something that they wish to hide. On the other hand, when a listener conclude that the speaker is communicating something private and sensitive, the listener may practice *civil inattention* by looking away from the speaker's eyes as if to give them some privacy.
- *monitoring and seeking feedback*. We particularly look at each other people's reactions and attentiveness when we seek feedback. We can see the effect of the other speaker's communication within his or her own nonverbal communication, as well as the impact of our spoken and/or nonverbal communication upon the other speaker. This allows us to make an assessment of our communication and alter it as we think appropriate.
- *regulate the conversation*. When one person speaking to another person is about to finish, he or she looks at the listener to let them know that now it is the listener's turn to speak. While speaking, speakers look at the listener

about 40 percent of the time.[16] If the speaker reaches the end of a phrase or thought and wants to continue speaking, he or she will look away from the listener to avoid seeing any listener message showing a desire to speak. If a listener does not want to speak when the speaker is at finished, the listener may look away.

In general, people's individual body movements are identifiable. According to Barnlund, "The way we walk, the way we stand or sit, the way we smile and gesture are even more easily recognized than the topics we like to discuss or the opinions we hold."[17] That is how at a distance we have a clue whether or not we think we see someone we know.

2. *Appearance.* We place a great deal of emphasis on how people look, acknowledging there can be wide differences among people. We know that other people, as well as ourselves, judge us in part based upon our appearance.

Physical appearance includes the elements of body type (thin, medium, large), height, the quality and color of the skin, hair color and style, clothing, and artifacts. First impressions, largely based upon people's appearance, are a significant factor in people's decision to interact with a stranger since that is the only information available. Many people feel compelled to interact with people they consider to be physically attractive.

Attractive women have been found to have a number of advantages over unattractive women, such as receiving higher college grades, having more dates, are more persuasive with men,[18] and are more self-confident.[19] Still, this is a two-edged sword for attractive women are often put under a lot of suspicion and scrutiny by their co-workers about whether they can perform as well as they look.

Perception, as discussed in Chapter Three, provides some implications for attractiveness. Since we are all different people with different sense abilities, needs, values, and beliefs, our actual visual perceptions of whether someone else is attractive do differ and these impact our subsequent perceptions. For example, assume that you value intelligence or kindness. Then you meet someone who does not initially "catch your eye" but over time you discover that they have one of these qualities you value. You are likely to come to see them as physically more attractive than you earlier judged them to be. Otherwise mundane and often overlooked behaviors such as having an erect posture, being polite, speaking in a sincere and friendly voice, having someone else be seated or served first, sharing a sandwich or apple at lunch, offering to do a small favor, showing a look of sympathy for someone's misfortune, exhibiting at least a minimum amount of physical fitness, and so on, can all make us appear more physically attractive and desirable. Beauty is created in the eye of the beholder and this is a process. On a lighter note, we might agree that beauty is only skin deep, but how far can you see? Anyway, ugly goes all the way to the bone and may last four generations.

Clothing and artifacts are also part of our appearance package. People know what clothes are, but *artifacts* may be an unfamiliar term. These are the material objects we attach to ourselves or the alterations we make to our body, including such things as jewelry, glasses, cosmetics, hairstyles, tattoos, body piercing, and the like. They are adornments created to increase our attractiveness (sexual and other) and they display or suggest (along with our clothes) our socioeconomic status, personality, group membership, and gender. Besides protection from the weather, they provide for personal expression and give clues about what we think about our self. Cars and houses may also be thought of as artifacts since they provide information about our image.

We have heard that old story that clothes make the man/woman. There are two effects in this. One, in the initial *appearance* discussions above, it was noted that first impressions are largely based upon appearance. Clothes are a significant part of this. People form ideas in their mind about who we are based upon the clothes they see us wear. College students think that informally dressed instructors are "…friendly, fair, enthusiastic, and flexible" [while] "… the same instructors dressed formally [are perceived] as prepared, knowledgeable, and organized."[20] Women place a great deal of significance on clothing for, as Barnlund notes, when women first meet a male stranger they notice, in order, the man's dress (clothes and artifacts), figure, and then face.[21] When women meet female strangers they also notice each other's dress first, followed in order, by their hair—an artifact, then their face. People whose physical appearance would otherwise be judged as plain can have their appearance evaluated as being much more attractive if they wear clothes that emphasize (complement) their positive physical attributes. Look at the people who get a clothes (and possibly hair) makeover on the television shows. Their friends and family are amazed at how much more attractive they look.

The second effect of *the clothes making us* is the impact the clothes we wear have upon us. They *make us*, in our own eyes. We reflect upon and respond to our own clothes. Notice the change in peoples' behavior to the wearing of Halloween or other costumes—both from their own reactions and others' to them. It is as if they have a license to act differently. Do not women feel sexier in sexy clothes, and do they not both feel and exude more confidence about themselves while in their power suits, as men feel in their own suits? Look at some teenage boys and young men stick out their chest when they wear a suit. So a company's dress code is partially for its clients or the public view and partially to get the employees imbued with the company's persona and professional work ethic as symbolized by the clothes.

Anyone growing up in America before the late 1960's may remember that they could form a fairly accurate idea about a kid's family income by the clothes the kid wore. Even First Graders could notice who were well off, average, and poor. If you were from a poorer family, you knew the non-poor knew and that there was no way to hide it. Using a materialistic yardstick, the poor kids were often thought of as being of less worth than were the kids from higher income families, in both their sets of minds. Since then, with the huge amount of government aid given to poorer families, the use of credit cards by people living beyond their means, and with clothes becoming relatively cheaper (among other factors), it has become much more difficult to determine a person's demographic information by his or her clothes and artifacts. Barnlund confirms this trend, adding, "It is relatively easy to mask one's status by conforming to current standards of taste, obscuring one's identity behind a standardized uniform. Even such obvious characteristics as age, race, and sex have become less predictable from appearance alone."[22]

Since people to a large degree evaluate and base their initial attraction to other people by the latter's clothes and artifacts and what these symbolize, it is ironic to consider that most people who look like they are doing well financially are not. This is clearly shown in *The Millionaire Next Door*[23] and *Smart Couples Finish Rich*[24] which describe how much money Americans save and have in assets, how so few are saving even 10% of their income for retirement, how so few have even three months of emergency money in the bank, and so on. In fact, you could easily reach the conclusion that people who look rich are not rich. According to Bach,

> I know plenty of people who seem to be very well off, who live in nice homes and drive nice cars, wear nice clothes and belong to country clubs ... and none of them are saving ten percent of their income. As I said before, this is true of many Americans. Well, guess what? Many Americans, when they reach retirement age, won't have enough money to maintain their comfortable lifestyles.... This is because most people who look rich really aren't. In fact, they are working their tails off, and once you peel back the façade, what you find isn't wealth and security but stress and debt.[25]

Thus, we have to be very skeptical about our ability to judge a person by his or her jacket. It would appear to be just as accurate (if not more so) to make the opposite inference than the one people traditionally hold when they see someone with better quality and styling of clothes, accessories, and cars. Imagine that so many people have it wrong when they are impressed with or initially seek to establish relationships based on their perceptions of another person's material wealth and stability. In *The Millionaire Next Door*,[26] a Mr. Friend has a vacation condo he pays a mortgage on, six cars (for two drivers, leased or purchased with credit), two boats, one jet ski, wears expensive clothes and a $5,000+ watch, and belongs to two country clubs. His clothes and artifacts have quite an allure for many people. However, the authors Stanley and Danko calculated that Mr. Friend was not even close to being wealthy since his net assets were about $250,000 (on a $221,000 income). Rather, they concluded, "Mr. Friend is possessed by possessions. He works for things. His motivation and his thoughts are focused on the symbols of economic success." "Unhappily, he has never convinced himself. In essence, he works, he earns, and he sacrificed to impress others,"[27] motivated by a fear of default. This statement is consistent with the quote by Bach above about the "seeming well off" living a life of debt and stress.[28] Clothes and other artifacts can certainly be deceiving.

3. *The Voice. How* we say something, including our use of pitch, degree of loudness, rate of speech, and vocal qualities (harsh, hoarse, strident, breathy, nasal) is known as *paralanguage*, the nonverbal, oral messages we send (and hear). Added to these are the vocal signals of articulation (forming individual sounds), pronunciation (combining individual sounds into words), and use of silence during a vocal interaction. Our voice conveys important messages for both ourselves and others in interpreting the verbal content that accompany them.

Our individual voices are unique and can be linked directly to us, like a fingerprint. Further, "[Y]our speech ... reveals you as you are at this moment. It is the product of your inheritance, environment, and learning experiences."[29] Our speaking ability also influences our self-image and our self-image influences our manner of speaking. In addition, our speaking also influences other people's perception of us. Whether we like or dislike the evaluations others form about us based on our manner of speaking, the stereotypes people form about us based upon our voice will influence their response to us.[30]

On the basis of the vocal cues provided, listeners in the different paralanguage studies cited by Beebe formed fairly accurate judgments about people's age, gender, level of education, region of accent, social class, and emotional state.[31] The expression of some emotions, such as anger and joy, can be more readily identified than others, such as shame and love.

People may pay more attention to our paralanguage than to the words they accompany when our voice seems to be more revealing of significant meaning. For example, how someone says "I *love* you" can indicate their love or not (in your estimation), their degree or depth of such an emotion, and their unique conceptualization of this subject. Further, when the meaning suggested by the paralanguage is inconsistent with (does not fit) the verbal content message, people tend to believe the paralanguage message. Notice in the following repeated sentence how the implied meaning can be changed by changing the vocal emphasis given to a single word in the sentence. This is adapted from Knapp.[32]

- *Give* it to the man. [put it into the man's hand]
- Give *it* to the man. [give the specific item being referred to, not something else]
- Give it *to* the man. [ensure you give it directly to him, not to someone else]
- Give it to *the* man. [place in that specific, significant man's hand]
- Give it to the *man*. [do not give it to a woman but to that specific man]

Not only does our paralanguage emphasize *how* something is said, but it also can suggest something about the speaker's intent. Most kids know when their parents are *really* mad at them by how their parents express their verbal content.

Our speaking skills have a large impact upon our career success, beginning with our job interviews through advancement in organizations for which we work. We need to be clearly understood. Long-time NBC and ABC broadcaster, David Brinkley, was thankful that at his first serious college girlfriend was a speech and drama major who taught him how to speak standard English. His North Carolina southern style of speech would not have gotten him his first radio job.[33] People do not have to give up any present accent they use but to broaden their career possibilities and public receptivity; they need to speak what is termed Standard American English when it is appropriate to do so. To gain broad, community understanding and even support on an issue, people can use the standard dialect. People with a non-standard accent can speak that accent at home, in the park with their friends, when not working, and so on. How many parents really want their kids to be schooled in non-standard English and thereby decrease their children's future educational and career possibilities?

In public speaking, our voice can create and/or increase our credibility, and thereby persuasiveness, as a speaker, depending on whether we sound sincere, assertive, aesthetically pleasing, having appropriate pauses, varying our vocal characteristics (loudness, pitch, rate, and emphasis), avoiding hesitations and filler words or sounds, and using correct pronunciations. Three of the more recent American Presidents who effectively used or continue to use dynamic and persuasive voices were Presidents Ronald Reagan, Bill Clinton, and Barrack Obama.

The *rate* of speech can also influence persuasion in one-way communication. DeVito reports that people who speak faster than normal (up to 50% faster) are perceived as being more intelligent, objective, and persuasive.[34] One hundred words/minute is considered slow, 200 words/minute is very fast, 125-150 words/minute is normal, and 135-185 words/minutes is most favorable for speaking.[35] While 200-250/minute may seem fast, Wolvin reports that listeners can process about 500 words/minute and that studies on compressed speech have shown listeners suffer little comprehension loss when rates get up to 275 words/minute.[36] On a lighter note, this may suggests that students who do not have to take classroom notes but complain about instructors speaking too fast may actually dislike that they cannot daydream as much in class.

4. *Silence.* Even silence communicates messages. We cannot *not* communicate (see Chapter Two). Not speaking during an interaction is as inherently powerful a form of conveying messages as is speaking. Barnlund lists some recognizable *silent* occasions: an unanswered question, an uncompleted sentence, during (or after) an overwhelming occurrence, an indescribable experience, and the occasions when we lack words for what we are feeling.[37] There are also extremely varied times when speaking would ruin the moment by interruption, redundancy, and/or minimizing it with limited description. For example, you could be listening to the lively background sounds at a party and daydreaming, you could be with a friend watching a dramatic sunrise or sunset over a scenic landscape or seascape, or you could be mutually gazing at a loved one while also using your face, eyes, posture, and/or touch to suggest the depth of that love. Most people enjoy someone else's silent presence.

Beebe provides some additional reasons for people's occasional silent times[38]: someone about to tell a lie may need more time to formulate a legitimate-sounding answer, someone may want to avoid being grouped together with those who are saying something the person disagrees with, someone may need more time to reflect on what to add to the conversation, someone may want to convey a desire not to communicate with others nearby, someone may need to be silent while an authority figure is giving orders, directions, or explanations, and silence may be a polite form of communication whereby the individual is waiting to be spoken to. Silence could also indicate a person's shyness.

Silence is occasionally used as a weapon (the silent treatment) or to belittle someone else. For instance, someone could be upset about something and want to speak with someone involved in the conflict, but the second person may refuse to talk about it to further spite or anger the first person. People who think they are somehow socially, financially, or politically better than others may avoid speaking with those "beneath" them, recognized as a personal rejection.

5. *Touch.* Tactile communication (hptics) is one of our first operational senses and we can recognize that it predates speech and sight, at least. Further, as Barnlund reports, our skin "… is the largest and most sensitive of all

our receptors."[39] If the feelings and level of perceived relationship between two people are not similar, consistent, and agreed upon, and if the touch is not considered appropriate to the relationship, then the person touched is likely to become angry.

Just how "sensitive" people can be to touch is demonstrated by people's reaction to a stranger touching them, particularly in an intimate part of the body.

Touch in public can be a ritual form of greeting, as when people shake hands or give someone a hug. Touching is only allowed in certain contexts and only in certain areas on the body: professional baseball players may slap each other on the butt while most of us are limited to a handshake, a gentle hug with a friend of the opposite sex, or a friendly slap on the shoulder or a tap on the elbow or forearm. Some people dislike even their boyfriend/girlfriend/spouse touching their butt in public so people need to be careful. Ironically, the touching occurring between young adults bodies while dancing in some nightclubs leaves little to the imagination. Sometimes by accident and occasionally by design, intimate touch between relative strangers can mislead one or both of them to think they are as emotionally close as they are (were) physically. While an inordinately high amount and degree of initial touch may "jump start" a relationship, it cannot create instant emotional intimacy.

For nearly all parents with at least their younger children and for most friends, touch is a silent means to show personal warmth, trust, interest, and love, and increases as intimacy increases. Touching provides a sense of closeness that mere words cannot attain. Touch can also comfort those touched.

Touching may also be task related, as when used to position someone in a certain way to have a picture taken or help someone get onto public transportation, and people working in close quarters will occasionally, at least, bump into each other. Employment policies generally forbid touching. Still, higher status people can and do more readily initiate touch than do lower-status people who do not always reciprocate.[40]

Overall, there appears to be a strong relationship between the amount of touch given and the level of verbal disclosure, the degree of communication apprehension, the age of communicators, and the relationship stage. Barnlund suggests that the amount of self-disclosure and touch between people tends to be raised or lowered in unison.[41]

6. *Space.* Stand 12" from strangers in America when there is space for you to be farther away and you can be pretty assured there will be some nonverbal responses from them, such as a quizzical or angry look on their face, an arm turned sideways at mid-waist, a leaning back at the waist and possibly a step back backwards, and so on. Depending on the relationship we have with those people in our immediate vicinity, the activity we are engaged in, the

existing physical context, and individual preferences, we feel comfortable being at a certain physical distance from each other. It is as if we carry different sizes of invisible bubbles around with us, using one or the other to keep what we think is an appropriate distance from each other. The study of our treatment of and response to personal space is termed *proxemics*.

Informal Space

Hall proposes that people (differing by culture) have a sense of personal space, such that there should be a certain space between themselves and others, depending on whom they are with, what they are doing, and other factors.[42] In addition to fixed physical features like walls and room sizes that define space, or semi-fixed objects like furniture that alters our use of and reaction to the space, we also have informal space. Hall describes four generalized categories of informal space that we attempt to manage as we communicate. These are noted below.

a. intimate distance. This encompasses contact out to about 18". People in this zone can readily smell, touch, hear, and see one another. Excluding the times when public crowding forces physical closeness, people sharing an intimate distance feel emotionally close and a sense of trust with each other. Thus, our most personal conversations occur within this space as do the varied instances of touch and close proximity we share with family and friends, doctors and other professionals, sports members, military personnel, and so forth. Sometimes, as when with doctors, we have no choice but to trust them to do us no harm. Some restaurants and bars create certain fixed spaces that put customers into this personal space to encourage intimate conversation.

b. personal distance. This is the area from about 18" to 4' within which non-intimate, personal conversation occurs. For example, many friends and family members, but only some co-workers and fellow students, can be seen standing, sitting, and speaking together within this range. Topics of discussion include such matters as non-intimate personal or family experiences, goals, and concerns, job-related issues, and school affairs. The implied messages in this zone vary from friendliness to compatibility to a "strictly work" relationship and can include hostile remarks from a boss, family member, and so on. If a stranger or disliked person enters this zone without permission, particularly while you are chatting with your friends, you might think to yourself "Who invited you?" People who go to public places in hope of meeting new people allow others to enter their personal zone or they themselves enter someone else's outer limit of this zone so interpersonal conversations can occur. Subjects such as their names, what they do (school, work, other), recreational activities, hobbies, travel, are commonly discussed.

c. social distance. This encompasses 4' to 12', fitting our more impersonal encounters such a business communication and group interaction. Conversations between co-workers and between salespeople and customers usually occur in the lower end of this range. Management offices are typically arranged to provide distance from employees, which gives an aura of power and leadership.

d. public distance. This space goes from 12' to 25' and more. Government agencies and large businesses have meetings within this zone, and public performances are at this distance. Many students in classrooms are more than twelve feet away from the teacher so two-way communication is difficult unless the teacher walks to where the students are seated. Given the sizes of audiences and the construction of available facilities, most public speaking audiences are more than twenty-five feet away so both the speaker and the audience feel the distance. If at all possible, speakers should move closer to the audience to establish a personal rapport. Adler reports that students have an increased liking for teachers and courses when the teachers physically reduce the distance between them, and the students also more readily follow teacher instructions (given those who are more interested in dong the coursework may make a point to sit closest to the teacher).[43]

Overall, people stand and sit closer to those people they like or are from a similar age or ethnic group. People with perceived higher status or authority are often granted more space. Men take and use more space than do women.[44] As Barnlund concludes, "... physical distance reflects psychological distance."[45]

Territory

When people believe that they own a given space, they respond to people in it differently than when they do not own it. In families, someone has a favorite living room chair or their specific seat at the dining room table so if they find a brother or sister sitting there, they probably tell them to move. At work, employees rarely enter a boss's office territory without permission, and when they do they use a lower-status posture and voice. When bosses go to an employee's work space, the bosses they do not always need permission and we would not expect them to act subservient. Parents occasionally tell their children when the kids visit their friends' or relatives' houses that the kids should be on their "best" behavior (respect their territory). People often do not like being in someone else's territory since they are not as free to do what they want and when they want to do it. Further, any negotiation occurring in one person's territory gives him or her a psychological advantage so always request a neutral meeting place.

Rank (status) hath its privileges when it comes to territory, for higher-status or ranking people are often provided *prime* territory, if not larger space. They may be given parking slots immediately in front of the main entrance, keys to the "executive" washroom, and entrée to the faculty or officer's dining room or club. Teachers at many public schools have their "teacher's lounge" where, in a bygone era, cigarette smoke could be seen wafting out the windows.

Ironically, people commonly get the idea that they "own" a public space (like a bench in a park) or a private space (such as a booth in a restaurant) they temporarily occupy. This can also be seen in classrooms where many students sit at the same desk each day and come to think of that desk as *their* desk, getting miffed if they find someone else sitting there later in the semester. Even classmates seated nearby will think the newcomer is sitting in "Bill's" seat. This occurs despite their knowing the rule of "first come, first served."

Territorial invasion generally results in defensive behaviors. The two long-standing responses have been flight (leaving the place for a presumably safer one) or fight. Fight has meant physically attempting to force an uninvited and/or unwanted person off your property. Another method used as a defense against intruders is insulation. At work, people may use personal artifacts, equipment, or partition boards to at least visually separate themselves from disliked co-workers and reduce prevent potential interpersonal communication. If two or more people speak a second language, they can exclude others from the conversation.

7. *Time.* Chronemics is the study of how people use their time, and people in America tend to highly value their time. Our use of time can be described in one or three general ways.

a. personal time. Time can be explained in a number of ways. One method is to think about it in terms of personal time, social time, and formal time. *Personal time* is an individual's structuring of their own time and attempting to live according to their own body clock. People come to form their own individual ideas about when they think certain activities are best done or best suit themselves. Some students dislike and avoid 8:00 AM classes, preferring to start later and work later through the day, while others like an early start. For some individuals, their personal time is very organized while other individuals act more spontaneously and do things when they get around to it (if at all). Most people know someone who is unaware of or not bothered by their own use of personal time that impinges upon and decreases other people's use of *their* own time while these latter people wait for the late person. Still, the world does not conform to an individual's structured time so the individual has to adjust at least some of his or her individual time orientation to fit the public's or nature's schedule. A person's communication during their personal time is most idiosyncratic and topics are widely varied.

b. social time. This refers to the occasions we interact with people for the purpose of enjoying their company, often in the completion of an activity, and possibly seeking further knowledge on a given topic or commitment to a religious belief. There is a greater recognition that the group interaction will be more influenced by time constraints than someone's personal time at home. Such group time is often characterized as being fun, and could range from listening to music with friends to playing baseball with some co-workers. Activities usually have a stated time they will begin but individuals arriving after that either cannot be punished or only slightly so. It is expected for social occasions such as parties that people will typically arrive after the stated starting time and drift in over the ensuing hours. We manage our social interactions in part through the medium of time so each of our relationships can be evaluated based on the amount of time we spend with each person.[46] Making time to spend with someone suggests you have high regard for him or her. Occasionally we "show our face" at a social event that we do not want to commit much time to, so the host or the key person at the event will know we thought of them, and then we sneak out quickly, hoping they do not see us leave. The social context encourages communication about the social occasion, personal relationships, and group interaction.

c. formal time. This is structured, having a clear beginning and end (a strict observance of time). Events are expected to follow the clock at definite intervals, *on time,* according to stated minutes and hours, and there are clear deadlines. Almost all government and private businesses and employment in America follow formal time. This creates more efficient use of time, and with this a greater production of goods and services and a higher standard of living. If a person is not on time or does not finish their work on time, they can expect to be punished. The U.S. military's strict observance of time has helped many young men and women members become more time conscious. On the other hand, some people chaff at being a slave to the clock and seek employment in careers that allow for more flexible application of their time.

In countries like America or contexts in which time is highly valued, a person's *status* influences the interacting people's structuring of time. People in high-status positions know they do not have to try so hard to be on time so some of them do not. They can even be supercilious about it. In recent memory, a U.S. president's desire for a haircut at a particular moment on Air Force One while it sat on the ground at one of the largest commercial airports in America forced the airport to delay all landings for twenty minutes. Many people had to wait, and some at a big expense. According to Adler, "[W]aiting can be an indicator of status. 'Important' people (whose time is supposedly more valuable than that of others) may be seen by appointment only, whereas it is acceptable [for them] to intrude without notice on lesser beings."[47] While higher-status people like teachers can be late to a meeting or to class plus not have their own work (e.g., student tests) completed for the following meeting (class), they will not have to apologize or have their lateness questioned by those waiting. Since the managing of time in America is so valued, people will evaluate others on the basis of their punctuality.

People's time orientation toward the future has a significant impact on their future financial well-being and general freedom. According to Banfield, those who are present-oriented are likely to make time-life decisions on an ad-hoc, day-to-day basis, focusing on present circumstances rather than planning for and act toward achieving future goals.[48] In general, this is indicative of lower-class behavior. At the other end of the spectrum, upper-class time behavior reflects the greatest amount of planning for the future, with working class and middle class falling in between. Most middle-class parents want their kids to get a college degree that will help them financially in the future.[49] To achieve this, students have to sacrifice present-day fun time for future enjoyment and security. Most college students know that the majority of them are financially poor but time is money when it comes to time spent on education. This is borne out in part by unemployment figures that continue to show that people with B.A. degrees and higher are unemployed at about one-half the national rate. Additionally, lifetime earnings of college graduates are much higher (about 90% more) than that of high school graduates and over twice as much as those who drop out of high school.[50] Banfield suggests that a person cannot expect to achieve upward mobility (a future gratification) without sacrificing some current gratification.[51]

8. *Smell*. Along with our other senses that initially perceive stimuli, our nose can pick up the odor of something and our body react with a motion even before we are consciously aware of the smell. People vary in their ability to smell, they have their own "smelling" experience, and they form their own ideas and intensity about which smells they like and which they dislike. Some important messages are communicated through scent.[52]

a. attraction messages. We know that people use scents to get other people's attention and make ourselves appear alluring. As with other nonverbal stimuli, the positive evaluation of one of them (in this case, smell) leads to a positive evaluation of others (such as appearance). If the amount of money spent on scents is an affirmation of the importance Americans place on them, then it is huge. In 2005, we spent $663 million on perfume and cologne and $90.6 million on other fragrant items such as lotions, creams, soaps, and bath gels, for an approximate total of $750 million just to smell good.[53] While many people scoff at the effectiveness of love potions, promoted in part by the song from about 1960, there are Micronesians from the Caroline Islands in the western Pacific Ocean who think they work. We do not have to be conscious of a nonverbal message for it to influence us. Are love potions so different from the advertisements over the years showing either women or men to be incomprehensibly irresistible to the opposite sex when wearing this perfume or that after-shave? In one commercial, for example, a man had to use karate to fight off all the women who could not resist his allure. As with other nonverbal elements, we, also, receive the message we are providing to others and we generate a separate response to our smell, influenced by the evaluation other people have to it. In brief, we can feel sexier or more handsome and act that way when using that special perfume or aftershave lotion.

Furthermore, some scents create physiological changes in men (and possibly women). In a study reported by *Gannett News Service* of men wearing dust masks scented with various odors such as cheese pizza, popcorn, pumpkin pie, roses, and so forth, the men showed increased sexual arousal as evidenced by their sexual blood flow.[54] The smell of pumpkin pie and lavender was the most stimulating, revealing a forty percent increase. Does this imply that women should bake and apply some pumpkin pie rather then use that expensive perfume? Libby's, instead of Channel #5, Barfumes Belong, Lovely, or Miami Glow?

b. taste messages. While we can distinguish some flavors on our tongue, our noses pick up a significant amount of food scents. The old strategy for women who wanted to catch a man, "The way to a man's heart is through his stomach" might more accurately be rephrased as "... through his nose." People have wagered that if you pinch your nose shut and close your eyes, you can drink different soda pop but cannot tell the difference in their taste. People's appetite is whetted when smelling cooked food they like. Those who have camped in a forest can probably attest to how good is the smell and taste of fried bacon or brewed coffee.

c. memory messages. Perceiving a scent now that we have not smelled in awhile will sometimes remind us of what occurred in the past when we smelled that same scent. As reported by Dreifus in an interview with the 2004 Nobel Prize co-winner in medicine, Linda Buck, Ms. Buck stated: "There is a precise map of odorant receptor signals in the cortex. That map is maintained throughout a lifetime, which is how you can recognize odors you haven't smelled in years."[55] Just smelling some eucalyptus, for example, can lead you to not only visualize playing with Joe one day in a public park filled with eucalyptus trees when you were seven years old, " … but [also] how you felt at the time. This is why the smell of a baking apple pie can immediately bring back memories of a childhood Thanksgiving at grandmother's house. Why this is so is yet to be understood."[56] Thus, smell can recreate in your mind exactly you were doing and how you felt about doing it many years in the past. Some businesses use this to their advantage. Real estate sales people want the house they are trying to sell look good and also smell like new. They know fresh paint can cover up lots of tobacco, fried food, and mold smells. Some also use the strategy of baking a loaf of bread in the oven before showing the house so the unconsciously noticed favorable smell will help seal the deal. The notion that smell can incite the memory was also illustrated in a 1980's movie (*Apocalypse Now*) in which one of the characters said something to the effect that he "loved the smell of napalm in the morning," presumably because he previously had some successful morning attacks using napalm. For a short time after the movie was first released, movie goers created a litany of humorous phrases about smells, following the same pattern, "I love the smell of _____ in the morning."

9. *Temperature, Lighting, Color*. We also have control over and provide messages through these three elements combined here. *Temperature* extremes, given the ensuing physical discomfort, distract our attention away from verbal interaction, curtailing our concentration and listening. Provide a more moderate temperature if you desire increased verbal interaction and less talk about the weather. When it is extremely cold, people invariably huddle closer together (proxemics) for warmth. *Lighting* provides its practical purpose of allowing people to comfortably see in what would otherwise be some measure of darkness and it influences the ambiance of a setting. According to Verderber, "[B]right light is expected [in lecture halls and reading rooms]—it encourages good listening and comfortable reading."[57] Most work settings have bright lights. In other settings, particularly social settings where there is a desire for more private talking, dimmed light is conducive for this, making facial expressions, eye contact, and gestures more hidden from others' view. Family restaurants seem bright and encourage loud conversation while many bars are dark and discourage it. *Color* is another nonverbal variable we make choices about that influences our own communication and that of

others interacting with us. While the Gothic look is not just about color, the prevalent use of black is foreboding. White used to represent purity and virginity in America until the sexual revolution in the latter one-third of the 20th Century altered that. Now it is not a faux pas for a female non-virgin to wear a white wedding dress on her wedding day. Red is supposed to be stimulating and represent a desire to draw attention to yourself. Blues are supposed to encourage a comforting atmosphere while yellow conveys cheerfulness,[58] encouraging up-beat talk.

As this section on nonverbal communication elements has described, there are various channels of nonverbal communication that are used to convey messages. Since they are used in combination, there are so many elements to evaluate at any one moment that it can be difficult for an observer to accurately do so. As the principle in Chapter Two notes, communication is a package of signals. This further includes verbal messages, making a communication analysis even more challenging.

CONCLUSION

An individual's nonverbal physical behaviors over time tend to be consistent. People rarely make sudden changes in their physical style such as being animated or not, mode of gesturing, posture, walk, eye behavior, touch, and use of space.[59] We practice self-monitoring to gain an idea how we are appearing to others, and make changes in our nonverbal behavior if we deem it important. Nonverbal messages provide a huge source of meaning for our interaction with each other. Knapp reports that a majority of the relationship (social) meaning we acquire is gained through nonverbal messages; a lesser extent through verbal messages.[60] Can you read people like a book? That depends upon whether you have read *the book* on interpreting nonverbal behavior.

CHAPTER 7 HOMEWORK
Nonverbal Communication[61]

Directions: Provide an answer for each of the six sections below.

1. What would a stranger think about you, as a person, based upon the clothes you typically wear here to school? In short, what do your (school) clothes suggest about the type of person you are? Provide four different and distinct characteristics (e.g., moody, outgoing, nerd, and so on).

2. What is the image a stranger might have of you as a person based upon the car you normally drive (or the car you'd like to own). State the make, model, and year. Provide 4 different personal characteristics suggested about you.

3. Violate "civil inattention" behavior in one communication experiment. Rather than glancing at an approaching stranger and then looking away until the two of you have passed one another, keep looking at the stranger until he/she has passed. Observe and detail the stranger's nonverbal reactions. [62]

4. Describe exactly what you did and how the other people reacted, both verbally and nonverbally, to your nonverbal behavior. Be sure to describe how the event ended. Be concise. *Perform only 1 of the following*, one that you feel comfortable with.
   a. Sit directly next to a stranger at an empty table in the library, a restaurant, a bar, a near-empty theater, etc.
   b. Face the people in an elevator (rather than face the elevator door).
   c. Stand closer than normal to another person in an otherwise empty elevator, in front of a store about to open its door, etc.
   d. Take someone else's chair in a restaurant/cafeteria/library.
   e. Invade the space of the same person (a stranger) for several successive days.
   f. For one to two days, maintain a greater than normal physical distance from a close friend.
   g. Provide your own suggestion of a proxemic (informal space/distance) norm to break and *do it*.

5. Give a descriptive example from your own communication experience of someone else being inconsistent between his or her verbal and nonverbal behavior. In short, describe a situation when someone's verbal (content) message does not agree with that person's nonverbal message. Which message did you believe, and why? Did you let them know of this contradiction?

6. Describe one of the most embarrassing experiences involving human touching that has occurred to you. What did that experience reveal about the touch norms or values for touching that are important to you? [if you cannot remember your own inc ident, you can refer to an incident that happened to someone else]

REFERENCES

1.   D. Barnlund, *Communication Styles of Japanese and Americans* (Belmont, CA: Wadsworth Publishing Company, 1989), p. 126.

2. A. Mehrabian, *Silent Messages: Implicit Communication of Emotions and Attitudes* (2nd ed.) (Belmont, CA: Wadsworth Publishing Company, 1981).
3. Ibid., p. 3.
4. M. Knapp, *Nonverbal Communication in Human Interaction* (New York: Holt, Rinehart and Winston, Inc., 1972).
5. Ibid.
6. Ibid., p. 11.
7. M. Scott and S. Brydon, *Dimensions of Communication: An Introduction* (Mountain View, CA: Mayfield Publishing Company, 1997).
8. J. Stossel, Myths, *Lies, & Downright Stupidity* (New York: Hyperion, 2006).
9. G. Nierenberg and H. Calero, *How to Read a Person Like a Book* (New York: Barnes and Noble, Inc., 1993).
10. Knapp, op cit.
11. P. Ekman and W. Friesen, *Unmasking The Face: A Guide to Recognizing Emotions From Facial Clues* (Englewood Cliffs, NJ: Prentice-Hall, Inc., 1975), p. 27.
12. Ibid., p. 11.
13. Mehrabian, op cit.
14. Ekman, op cit.
15. Knapp, op cit.
16. R. Verderber, *Communicate!* (7th ed.) (Belmont, CA: Wadsworth Publishing Company, 1993).
17. Barnlund, op cit., p. 126.
18. R. Adler and B. Rodman, Understanding Human Communication (10th ed.) (New York: Oxford University Press, 2009).
19. Scott and Brydon, op cit.
20. J. DeVito, *Human Communication: The Basic Course* (10th ed.) (Boston: Pearson Education, Inc., 2006), p. 144.
21. Barnlund, op cit.
22. Barnlund, op cit., p. 59.
23. T. Stanley and W. Danko, *The Millionaire Next Door* (New York: Pocket Books, 1996).
24. D. Bach, *Smart Couples Finish Rich. 9 Steps to Creating A Rich Future for You And Your Partner* (New York: Broadway Books, 2001).
25. Ibid., p. 105.
26. Stanley and Danko, op cit.
27. Ibid., p. 51.
28. Bach, op cit.
29. N. Modisett and J. Luter, *Speaking Clearly* (5th ed.) (Boston: Pearson Custom Publishing, 2006), p. xi.
30. Knapp, op cit.
31. S. Beebe, S. Beebe and M. Redman, *Interpersonal Communication: Relating to Others* (Boston: Allyn and Bacon, 1999).
32. Knapp, op cit.
33. D. Brinkley, *11 Presidents, 4 Wars, 22 Political Conventions, 1 Moon Landing, 3 Assassinations, 2,000 Weeks of News and Other Stuff on Television and 18 years of Growing Up in North Carolina* (New York: Ballantine Books, 1995).

34. DeVito, *Human Communication: The Basic Course (*11th ed.) (Boston: Pearson Education, Inc., 2009).
35. A. Wolvin and C. Coakley, *Listening* (5th ed.) (Boston: McGraw Hill, 1996).
36. Ibid.
37. Barnlund, op cit.
38. Beebe, op cit.
39. Barnlund, p. 139.
40. J. Pearson and P. Nelson, *An Introduction to Human Communication* (8th ed.) (Boston: The McGraw-Hill Companies, Inc., 2000).
41. Barnlund, op cit.
42. E.T. Hall, *The Hidden Dimension* (New York: Doubleday, 1969).
43. Adler and Rodman, op cit.
44. Pearson and Nelson, op cit.
45. Barnlund, op cit., p. 138.
46. Ibid.
47. Adler and Rodman, op cit., p. 155.
48. E. Banfield, *The Un-heavenly City Revisited* (Boston: Little, Brown and Company, 1974).
49. Ibid.
50. B. Stein, and P. DeMuth, *Yes, You Can Get a Financial Life! Your Lifetime Guide To Financial Planning.* (Carlsbad, CA: New Beginnings Press, 2007).
51. Banfield, op cit
52. DeVito (2009), op cit.
53. "Americans Spend on Scents," *Pacific Daily News* (October 31, 2005).
54. "Smell of Pie Arouses Men Most," *Gannet News Service* (March 2, 1995)
55. C. Dreifus, "The Sweet Success of Smell," *AARP Bulletin* (October, 2005), p. 26.
56. Ibid, p. 27.
57. Verderber, op cit., p. 108.
58. Ibid.
59. Barnlund, op cit.
60. Knapp, op cit.
61. J. DeVito, *Human Communication: The Baisc Course* (5th ed.) (New York: HarperCollins Publishers Inc., 1991).
62. Wolvin and Coakley, op cit.

CHAPTER EIGHT

Relationship Communication

Person-to-person. Who you have been and *are*, who you are *becoming* as you discover who they *are*, and their *becoming* to you alters who they *are* to both you and them: trying yourself on, so to speak, one suit per moment; trying them on even as they are trying you on; the connection—a transactional and self-reflective process.

Interpersonal communication is simply the communication between two persons. At this point in the textbook, this is not a new concept. There has been a discussion about perceptions of other people and the meaning outcomes of those. Self-disclosure between two people has been described, as has the listening between individuals. Verbal and nonverbal messages between a variety of people have been explored. This chapter encompasses all of these elements of communication and focuses on the one-to-one relationships we have with other people.

Chapter One suggested that one of the purposes of communication is to establish relationships with other people. Most people usually want to interact with some other people. In Chapter Two, one of the principles of communication stated that communication is relational: our communication with other people reveals the type of relationship we have with them. Combined, these concepts provide a foundation for this chapter.

FORMING AND MAINTAINING RELATIONSHIPS

There are some basic assumptions and systematic explanations for why people form and how they maintain particular relationships. A key variable in this process is who or what is attractive to us. People we find pleasing invariably have some redeeming qualities.

Attraction

1. *Physical appearance*, as noted in the previous chapter, is a highly influential nonverbal message. We pay a great deal of attention to our own and other people's physical appearance, as well as to their physical attractiveness. It should be no surprise to anyone that the main reason we seek interaction with others is due to their attractiveness.[1] What we see is what first gets our attention. As Barnlund similarly suggests, Americans value individual attractiveness and "[p]reliminary visual appraisal may supply enough information about such attributes [of physical appearance, attitude similarity, and lifestyle compatibility] to prompt an American to talk to or avoid a stranger."[2] As noted in the previous chapter on Nonverbal Communication, our clothes and personal artifacts also influence our perceived physical attractiveness.

2. *Reward* is a second factor of attraction. According to Thibaut and Kelley in *Social Exchange Theory*, people anticipate (predict) the result of socially interacting (or continuing to do so) with someone by determining the future ratio of rewards versus costs for doing so.[3] The more likely a favorable ratio of rewards is expected, the more attractive the person will become, so the increased probability we will initiate an interaction. As suggested in the Perception chapter, people are attracted to other people and relationship outcomes that they expect to be satisfying. We do not know if someone is as good as he or she "looks" but first impressions are sometimes all we have to go on. Some people highly value humor in their lives, or their particular religious beliefs, or food, or financial independence, or someone that listens to them, and so on, so discovering these in other people will be rewarding and encourage an ongoing relationship. Many (most?) men and women think it would be rewarding to have an attractive boy/girlfriend/spouse. Many man and women find it rewarding to have find and be with people who are loyal, honest, and generous. You like "Randy" because he is handsome, funny, polite, and buys you nice gifts (rewards, all, for you). Notice that communication itself can be rewarding or used as an instrument to achieve rewards.[4]

People also try to avoid or minimize their interactions with people or relationship outcomes that they think will be harmful or costly. If a mental or physical act requires a great deal of effort or if an activity is or is expected to be stressful, then people are likely to avoid it. If we find it unpleasant (costly) to be around someone who continually speaks about his or her own personal troubles, is conceited or too materialistic, is too judgmental or demanding, and other features which are or we would expect to be too unpleasant (costly) for us, we will avoid or minimize interacting with that someone.

From this, people may seem too self-interested, yet why would they not be interested in achieving rewarding relationships? This economic description does not sound romantic about intimate or prospective intimate relationships but is there a cost/benefits aspect to them?

We not only compare the rewards and costs we actually receive or expect to receive, but we compare our outcomes with the outcomes of those with whom we have a relationship. As long as we are getting, in our estimation, a similar amount of rewards and bearing a similar level of costs, we are likely to continue in the relationship. On the other hand, if we think the other person is getting more benefits than we are, or if it is costing us more than it is to them, then we will be unhappy and are likely to end the relationship.[5] You have heard people comment, after ending a relationship, something to the effect of, "It was a one-way street" or "I did favors for them but they did few (if any) for me, and they were not there for me when I needed them."

Thibaut and Kelley also suggest that people compare the overall ratio of rewards and costs with what they think they ought to receive from the relationship.[6] If you do not expect much, you will be easy to please, but if you expect a great deal of self-disclosure privacy and trust in your relationships then you will not be satisfied or attracted to relationships with others that do not provide these elements.

In addition, we compare the rewards we are currently getting from a given relationship with the rewards we think we could get from being in some other relationship.[7] Sometimes the grass does look greener on the other side of the fence. If our *comparison level of alternatives* suggests we would gain more rewards by being with someone else, we are likely to leave the current relationship and develop what is perceived to be the more profitable relationship. Advice columnists receive many queries from people thinking about changing relationships and after-action reports from many of those who have.

Social Exchange communication guidelines are suggested by DeVito to overcome the inevitable costs that exist in relationships.[8]

First, exchange rewards. Do additional favors for your friends, family, and co-workers. These do not have to be expensive or outlandish. A simple, homemade "Thank You" card, a little pat on his or her back, provide them a particular food or drink they like, meeting them for lunch, tell them something funny you heard that day, do one of their household or workplace chores, and otherwise do whatever is a reward for that person.

Second, bear your share of the costs. Alter what is a cost from your partner's point of view, the idea being that your partner will feel better about you if he has fewer costs associated with you, and his or her comparison level of costs will be smaller or lower if you are bearing one or more additional costs. For instance, maybe you will be civil with his obnoxious brother, or not complain about his mothers poor cooking or his snoring, or maybe you will wash the dishes for him at 10 PM when he is too tired. Cutting his or her costs enlarges his or her reward/cost gap.

Third, intensify the exchange of rewards in times of rising costs. When there are angry and/or unhappy thoughts, feelings, and/or actions between two people, there is inertia for this to continue unless someone does something to turn the situation around. Thus, despite the acrimony between the two of you, provide an increased amount of rewards for your partner as a method for diminishing what are costs for him or her. DeVito suggests that we be empathetic and proactive, and use increased touching and holding [to silently and gently get across the idea that we care.[9]

Fourth, increase rewards to reduce the attractiveness of alternatives. Recognize that a person will feel like ending the relationship with you if it gets too costly for him or herself, or if, in comparison, someone else begins to look more enticing to your partner. This leads many people to believe the grass is greener on the other side of the fence. Assuming you want your relationship to continue, you have got to make yourself more rewarding for your partner and keep them on your turf. Can you make yourself more attractive physically and/or with your temperament? Get a makeover? Do some favors for your mother-in-law? Can you find new ways to please him or her that remove some of the drudgery in their life, such as take out the garbage, clean the house, pay the bills, or wash the laundry? Find some jokes to tell him/her? Sincerely tell him/her you appreciate all the love and/or friendship shown to you.

Overall, Social Exchange Theory suggests that people build and maintain relationships on the basis of rewards and costs engendered. Still, some limits may exist for this theory. Roloff suggests that people only calculate their rewards when a situation requires it (e.g., choosing between A or B to marry), that people differ in the extent to which they make calculations, that people often make inaccurate appraisals of current profits, that the increase or decrease in rewards or costs may be so slight and gradual that it is not noticed until a future time, and some reward/cost calculations may occur after-the-fact as a way for a person to explain what has already occurred (e.g., "I was happy/unhappy then due to the rewards/costs I received.").[10]

Social Penetration Theory[11] also proposes that individuals' communication is effected by perceived rewards and costs of interacting. Altman suggests that our relationships with other people develop gradually in a step-by-step fashion as our self-disclosure is determined to be rewarding, and if this increasingly intimate disclosure is reciprocated, the individuals will become further committed to each other.[12] The breadth of topics and depth of disclosure will be influenced by the individual's satisfaction or dissatisfaction gained from the interaction and his or her forecast of rewards and costs expected in the future (as with Social Exchange Theory).

Rewarding communication experiences are expected to motivate individuals to reveal increasingly personal information about themselves, which allows the listener to "penetrate" or come to know their more complete uniqueness. Depending on how personal each person is willing to be, the interpersonal communication reveals the desired point of intimacy. An implication of this is that by knowing the breadth and depth of messages exchanged, an observer or even the two involved people can gain a sense of the closeness of the relationship.

If an interpersonal relationship deteriorates (when the costs outweigh the rewards), the individuals reverse the penetration process by increasing the barriers between their more private, inner self and the other person.[13] During this degeneration, two individuals would be expected to speak about fewer topics and at less depth. Occasionally, a person in this circumstance will say something very revealing that they previously held back, afraid that it would be unrewarding for the relationship. We cannot know for sure, but some of these very revealing, end game statements could have been just the type of honesty the relationship may have needed to maintain itself, before the decision was made to end it. Further, such disclosures during problem discussions occurring in this degeneration stage may ironically result in a feeling closeness between the individuals and an increased in liking for each other.[14]

3. *Friendship rules* are a third influence on sustaining relationships. Argyl found that close friendships maintained certain communication rules that less-close friendships did not.[15] These include: sharing news of success with the other person, showing emotional support for them, volunteering to help them in a time of need, trying to make them happy when with them, trusting and confiding in them, and speaking up for them if someone derides them in their absence. The relationship may even become closer as a result of following these rules. On the other hand, an indication that the friendship is about to be dissolved is when one or both people make verbal statements in public about the disdain and contempt they have for their partner, which Cole finds is the most accurate sign that a couple will get divorced.[16]

Many people have life-long friends and intimate relationships that span the years. Everyone has also had relationships that have diminished in closeness over time. Attractions of certain physical features, personality variables, behaviors, values and beliefs, and ways of communicating may increase or decrease in importance to us over time in our relationship with and about another person.

FURTHER IMPROVEMENTS FOR
INTERPERSONAL RELATIONSHIPS

Chapters 3-7 and the earlier part of this chapter have provided suggestions for improving communication. The following section adds some additional knowledge and skills.

1. *Language Nurturing Personal Success and Interpersonal Bonds: Gibbs Climate Language.* In general, nearly everyone tries to cultivate some friendships, maintain effective work relationships, create and/or be part of a family, and to overall satisfy their individual needs and achieve their personal goals. Language usage influences the attainment of these. According to Gibb, the language we use in our interactions can fit into two broad categories: language that encourages a defensive response from the other person or language that encourages a supportive response from the other person. [17]

When people become defensive, they listen to us in a defensive state of mind, usually creating a distorted understanding of our messages. Typically, they respond to us in a verbally and nonverbally defensive manner to which we are likely to react defensively, and so the interaction continues. Language that typically leads to a sense of ill will creates a *defensive climate* or feeling between two people, characterized by such terms as cold, insensitive, vengeful, blaming, indifferent, and even hateful. It often leads to wariness and a proclivity for people to verbally battle with each other. Overall, defensiveness reduces communication accuracy and efficiency.

In place of a climate of defensiveness, we can use language that suggests a feeling of well-being, that suggests a respectful and helping attitude toward the other person, and that suggests a personal sense of honesty and self-respect. Overall, the language climate is supportive of each person's individual needs and aspirations.

If supportive communication is supposed to be so effective, how can we account for the common defensiveness illustrated by the phrase, "The squeaky wheel gets the grease"? We know of many occasions when a relatively few people loudly yell and picket outside a government office or private company headquarters and a policy is altered to suit them, often accompanied by money. For example, from the mid-1960's into the 1970's at dozens of colleges and universities in America, a relatively small number of students picketed, yelled and cursed, physically took over administration buildings, and either threatened or used violence and these comparatively few people achieved many changes they desired. Consider all the times that consumers complain to a business about the product or service they receive, and they are rewarded. We cannot say that defensive-arousing communication does not work, or at least, does not achieve short-term goals, for it has and can.

Further, do not assume that language foretelling a supportive working climate among people should always be used. There are times when defensive-arousing communication increases the receiver's attention to a current issue and this receiver learns important information that can lead them to change their behavior for their own good—from their own point of view (probably after-the-fact). Defensive climate language has been occasionally effective for bosses, parents, and/or teachers. Further, there are some people in life who are mean, aggressive, self-centered, and/or very controlling and who will stop at nothing to get their own way to your (and even others') detriment. They may need to know by the strongest possible defensive-arousing language (and possibly legal action) that you will not comply with their attempts and that you will aggressively confront them if they attempt to (further) harm you.

That being said, you may give people the benefit of the doubt by using supportive-arousing language until you think you have sufficient reason to use defensive language. Be mindful about using defensive-arousing language for long-term effectiveness is certainly debatable. As a few other old sayings go, "You attract more flies with honey than with vinegar," and "A kind word tames the hardest heart."

Gibb identified six types of language usage that produced a defensive-arousing climate between individuals and six types of language usage that produced a supportive climate.[18] These are listed on the following page and explained over the following two pages.

Table 8.1

Defensive Climates		Supportive Climates
Evaluation	- versus -	Description
Control	- versus -	Problem orientation
Strategy	- versus -	Spontaneity
Neutrality	- versus -	Empathy
Superiority	- versus -	Equality
Certainty	- versus -	Provisionalism

Description rather than Evaluation. Give an account of your perceptions—a record of your thoughts and/or feelings of the situation at hand. Focus on the apparent facts of the case rather than being judgmental about the other person's supposed weakness of character, skill, and/or behavior. Avoid blaming or telling the other person how they should be. Although the details you describe may suggest an oversight by the other person about which they may feel unhappy, people typically appreciate the avoidance of personal attacks. "I sense that you are upset with getting a low grade" rather than "You have a poor attitude about school." Be cautions with questions for they invariably imply an answer that suits the speaker's point of view, meaning that the listener's is wrong. As Gibb suggests, our tone of voice, physical expression, and verbal content can communicate that we are evaluating the listener.[19]

Problem Orientation rather than Control. People frequently attempt to influence and direct other people. This is not always harmful for the receiver. Still, someone's attempt at controlling someone else implies that the receiver is ignorant, immature, possesses the wrong skills, cannot act independently, and so on. Methods of control include insistence on detail (which can be good), restrictive regulations, and conformity to behaviors. Problem orientation does not offer a solution but conveys a desire to collaborate, to seek a mutual understanding of a problem, or even allow others to work through their own problems. "Would you like my ideas about your lack of cash flow" rather than "If you want money from me, you'll have to do what I say." "What do you think is wrong with the financial aid office?" rather than "I already told you what is wrong with the financial aid department. Now go fix it." We cannot overlook the ubiquitous controlling statement: "It's my way or the highway!"

Spontaneity rather than Strategy. People who seem sincere and *honest* (which might be more descriptive than *spontaneity*) in expressing their thoughts and/or feelings of the moment, even if these reflect negatively on the listener, are more likely to be acknowledged and respected by the listener than comments by speakers who imply that they have a self-serving, hidden plan that takes advantage of or manipulates the listener. This does not mean that we simply blurt out whatever thought comes to our mind. We can choose among our more credible thoughts. On the other hand, most people are offended at the thought of being used for someone else's purposes or that someone is "playing games" with them. A spontaneous response could be "I don't like your opposition to my idea" rather than a strategy one like "I know how to make you do this."

Empathy rather than Neutrality. People more readily respond to and feel good about someone who identifies with their problems, accepts and shares their feelings, and expresses understanding of their motives than they do when someone conveys a lack of concern or an uncaring indifference to their welfare. "It is understandable why you missed class," rather than "I don't care about your situation. It's none of my business." Empathy requires us to know something about the person and attempting to understand the situation from his or her experience before expressing concern for him or her. Our nonverbal behavior can reveal empathy through a look of concern on our face, focused eye contact, a sincere tone of voice, and if in the person's presence, physical closeness and possibly touching. Avoid saying, "I know how you feel."

Equality rather than Superiority. Equality means speaking to the other individual on a person-to-person level without implying or referring to your higher rank or authority. People are never equal in all respects, but rather than sounding arrogant or haughty, you can use words that imply your having the same status or rights. "We respect your judgment" or "You can do this" as opposed to "I'll decide what to do and let you know" or "You're not experienced enough to figure it out." Superiority expresses an attitude of being better than others. It encourages the receiver to feel inadequate, and thus upset at the speaker for giving this message.

Provisionalism rather than Certainty. Provisionalism implies that there may be more than one possible answer. This encourages the listener to give their point of view. For Speaker A to say something different than Speaker B is harder when Speaker B sounds definite and final about the subject. Then for Speaker A to respond to Speaker B with a different answer may be taken as a challenge to Speaker B's authority or intelligence, which is likely to further increase the defensive climate. To sound provisional, we have to seem tentative and open to hearing opposing ideas rather than being so sure and dogmatic as to cut off the debate. "If/then" phrases suggest there are provisions or aspects that are likely to exist or occur in some situation. Consider saying "Can we explore what we think are the pros and cons of this idea?" or "If we go shopping now then we might be late for dinner." This is not to say that some things are not certain or cannot be said with certainty. As a group, men do run faster than women and can carry more weight, and sometimes a parent can legitimately say that a child needs to do his or her homework right now. Circumstances may dictate that certain actions have to be done and according to some timetable. An authority figure, such as a boss, may legitimately tell you that you have to do something but may leave it up to you to decide how to do it. If there is certainty phrased in a tentative way, it also encourages people to ponder it more. Many things in life that have seemed so certain have not, upon further reflection, turn out to be so.

Climate Language Summary

In summary, our communication can encourage listeners to clarify their own thoughts, feelings, and proposed actions, as well as feel satisfied about their relationship with us. Conversely, our communication can be interpreted as provoking a personal attack against the listener, creating an antagonistic context between the two of us. People work more effectively with each other and enjoy it more when there is communication producing a supportive climate between them.

   2. *Encouraging Personal Openness, Awareness, Responsibility, and Control: I Messages.* One of the main purposes of communication is to predict and control our environment. The more open we are with our thoughts and feelings, the more we can know each other and adapt to each other. Knowing more about each other, we can potentially be more empathetic and establish an intimate relationship. Sharing our thoughts and feelings about everyday situations we face, as well as about people we interact with, provides an opportunity for ourselves to increase our own awareness of our experience. Further, openness is both a necessary quality and communication skill for productive interpersonal relationships.

   Ellis[20] and Dyer[21] provide a communication tool termed *I-Messages* that promotes openness, personal awareness, personal responsibility, personal control over our communication, and to a degree, personal control over our lives.

Basic Assumptions[22]

First, people are largely in control of their thinking and their actions. Apart from religious beliefs about God or other deities putting thoughts into your mind, if you are not in control of your thoughts, who is? This idea about personal control of thinking and behavior is in opposition to those who give primacy to external forces of control over people. External forces like a persuasive speech may influence someone to believe or act in some way, but people themselves ultimately create the meaning from the message and accept, or not, the meaning.

   Second, much of our emotions originate from our thoughts. Emotions may also be stimulated by, among others, biological functions (e.g., hunger) or sensory stimulation (e.g., drugs), but these tend to exist briefly and tend not to be sustained without coinciding thoughts. Further, there is not always a clear line between emotions and thought. According to Ellis, "… a large part of what we call emotion is nothing more or less than a certain kind of thinking—biased, prejudiced, or strongly evaluative."[23] In brief, thinking and emotion are closely interrelated.

Lastly, since people are largely in control of their thoughts and much of their feelings come from their thoughts, then people, in effect, control their feelings. This means that people have a choice about their feelings in response to adversities they face in their lives. Dyer provides further explanation: "Feelings are not just emotions that happen to you. Feelings are reactions you choose to have. If you are in charge of your own emotions, you do not have to choose self-defeating reactions."[24]

The three assumptions can be briefly written as follows:

Major premise: I can control my thoughts.
Minor premise: My feelings come from my thoughts.
Conclusion: I can control my feelings.

As previously discussed, the first claim is supported. Within a very large boundary, we choose our thoughts and those we dwell upon. Still, how do we know our feelings come from our thoughts? According to Dyer, "If you cry, or blush, or increase your heartbeat, or any of an interminable list of potential emotional reactions, you have first had a signal from your thinking center. Once your thinking center is damaged or short-circuited, you cannot experience emotional reactions"[25] For example, you cried because you interpreted an event as sad, you blushed because you interpreted your appearance as inappropriate in public, or your heart beat faster because you thought you were in danger. We even have thoughts without thinking out each specific word. The thoughts come first, then the feelings, so this minor premise is supported.

The conclusion logically follows from the first two claims. Feeling do not just happen to us and we can change them by changing the basis for them—our thoughts. Maybe there is a legitimate way to think about the situation that does not lead to anger, if you think the anger is self-defeating. Maybe your clothes were not as expensive as everyone else's but that does not mean you are less of a person than they, so you do not have to blush. Maybe your brother said you were stupid so you might feel angry, yet on the other hand you do not have to agree with him and can laugh it off. Maybe the situation you were in was physically dangerous but thinking about bad outcomes that might happen to you can take your focus and physical effort from what to do to become safe.

This does not mean that we can blithely disregard and make light of a drug addict in the family, a friend who is a dangerous driver, or a typhoon having 150 mph winds and driving rain. Still, we can ask ourselves, "Why should I choose embarrassment, anger, or fear? Will my feelings help me successfully resolve the situation I am in?

In Dyer's professional experience, it was people's illogical (erroneous) thoughts that led to their counterproductive feelings and self-defeating behaviors, as well as the lost control over their individual lives.

Implications and Benefits

First, if people are largely in control of their thoughts and feelings, then they are responsible for them so they cannot justifiably attribute these to others. Further, they cannot hide behind their feelings and their use of their feelings as an excuse for feeling (and thereby thinking) whatever suits them in the moment, or action stemming from feelings. The basis of their feelings is not inviolate territory off limits to evaluation since thoughts are not off limit. The thoughts may easily be illogical and therefore erroneous.

Second, if people recognize and accept the idea that they are in control of their thoughts and feelings, they can investigate their thoughts for legitimacy, changing those that are erroneous. This, in turn, will prevent the associated feelings from arising. With a minimization of erroneous thoughts and feelings, there should also be a minimization of counterproductive behavior.

Third, those who assume more control over their thoughts and feelings will engage in less blaming communication since they know they are the responsible party for their own thoughts, feelings, and behaviors.

Fourth, those who refuse to recognize and assume control over their own thoughts and feelings (internal locus of control) are at the mercy and control of others (an external locus of control). They will continue the mindset of blaming disliked outcomes on others whom they have allowed some control over themselves. People exhibit this orientation by using words like *make* and *made*, as in "She made me upset." According to Russell, *make* and *made* are linguistic cop-outs since they give people the idea that they do not have control over the causes of their feelings and interpretation of their experiences.[26] These words also allow the speaker to avoid responsibility for his/her feelings. Although people may allow others to control them, this recognizes the individual's original control, and this control illustrates the individual's choices made.

Fifth, approval-seeking will diminish for those who desire more responsibility for themselves. They will be clearer about the legitimate basis of their feelings so external affirmation can be seen as superfluous.

Application: I-messages

To help us achieve this partial control and thereby responsibility in our communication and its outcomes, Ellis and Dyer provide a communication technique that also conveys openness and creates personal awareness: I-messages.[27] This parallels Gibb's supportive language technique of description and emphasizes honesty in the expression of the individual's thoughts and feelings.[28] Below is a brief list of phrases from Dyer that most people have heard or used over and over, revealing an external locus of control and non- responsibility for personal reactions.[29] This author's rewritten I-message phrases follow each statement. The following are some typical Non-I-messages, rewritten as I-messages:

"You hurt my feelings."

> "I feel ashamed that you told people I was an incompetent cook because I might be and I don't like having this public image."

"Heights scare me."

> "I am scared when I am in high places since I keep thinking that I will fall and die."

"I can't help the way I feel."

> "I can help the way I feel and I feel giddy about winning the $500,000 bingo prize since I have $25,000 in bills I thought I'd never pay off, and now I'll never be poor again."

"That makes me sick."

> "I make myself sick—nauseated—by thinking that okra is slimy like snot and believing that okra really is like eating snot."

"She/he really turns me on."

> "I am excited and breathless whenever I get a glimpse of her/him since I keep thinking she/he is so-o-o sexy."

I-Message Summary

I-message create openness, a sharing of the speaker's thoughts and feelings. They help the speaker clarify the thought basis of his or her feelings, and provide an opportunity to reject the feelings if the thought basis is determined to be unjustified. With a logical basis, speakers avoid an overly emotional response that can be self-defeating. This technique does not tell the listener how he or she should think or feel about the phenomenon in question, so it is respectful of the listener's point of view. I-messages also reinforce to both communicators that the control over each speaker's thoughts and feelings lie with the individual.

We cannot change much of the world outside ourselves nor can we avoid occasional catastrophes (e.g., sickness), but we do have the choice and the opportunity to avoid illogical thinking and impractical behavior. We can change the way we respond to people's communication and behavior. As Ellis reminds us, when people are responsible about and take control of their thoughts, they work harder toward and are more successful at achieving their goals in life.[30]

3. *Honesty in Relationships.* Honesty has long been considered a reflection of a person's character and character is an important component of credibility. With little or no credibility, people will not believe what you say. In this event, what comes out of your mouth is simply noise (and noisy noise, at that) to the people for whom you have little credibility.

Self-disclosure is promoted in communication textbooks as a good thing, but if it is not honest (accurate) then it is delusional for the speaker and listener. If people are generally dishonest about their thoughts and feelings, it is counterproductive to interpersonal relationships since someone will eventually find out and shun or feel distant from the dishonest person. This section will discuss honesty in relationships.

Is honesty the best policy? It is common in everyday life for your family, friends, co-workers, supervisors, students, and acquaintances to ask you "How do you like my (haircut/car/ dress/fried_chicken/idea, etc.)_?" What if you do not like their object, service, or concept? On other occasions they may ask to borrow something or for a favor from you. What if you do not want to loan them something or do the favor? Should you "be honest" and directly tell them? "It looks/ tastes/sounds terrible/weak/stupid." "I do not want to loan you X since you may not pay me back and it puts me at financial risk." "I do not want to do X since it is illegal/it takes advantage of my time/I do not think you deserve it/I doubt you will return the favor." What if your child, on return from kindergarten, asks you in an excited voice, "Mommy/ Daddy, how do you like my finger painting?" What if you are the teacher? What do you say to twenty-five kids about the quality of their finger painting? These are tough choices. What message are you giving people when you give them an "honest" versus a "non-honest" response? What influence do these different answers and responses have on the other person and on your relationships?

We also may consider that even if we think we are honest, we are not as honest as we think we are. We are not aware of our thoughts and feelings in a given situation, and sometimes we have mixed thoughts and mixed feelings about some one or a particular subject. Overall, we do not say all that we think and/or feel so most of us are dishonest much of the time.

HONESTY CRITERIA FOR DECISIONS

Self-esteem[31] concern is commonly used as a criterion for helping us decide whether or not to be completely honest with someone else. If we think the person's self-esteem will be diminished by a "negative (yet accurate) comment," then we may not be honest, or at least not completely honest to them. Thus, we might say, "Not bad," "I like the color/crunchiness/etc.," "It seems to suit you," and "A lot of people will like it." The idea is to give them an indirect, general compliment so they do not think there is a personal attack against their persona.

Discretion is another criterion or rule that we can use to guide the nature of our relationship honesty. What would be prudent? Should we be cautious about what we say? McCabe, a long-time columnist for the *San Francisco Chronicle*, in an article entitled "Honesty, Ugh!" claims that "Honesty has ruined more marriages and love affairs than infidelity."[32] This is based upon his experience that people are often hypocrites about honesty and use it as a weapon to hurt other people. People may not even realize that their honesty is subjective and hurtful to the listener. Telling your life partner that he or she is fat, thin, or balding, or has a parent who was an addict or a brother who is a bum may be honest (accurate). Yet it can also be viewed as demoralizing for the listener's weight-loss progress, a depressing idea that the listener is growing older, and a disheartening reminder about a parent or a brother. McCabe's answer to this is *good manners*. This criterion is consistent with those of self-esteem, diplomacy, and appropriateness. For an application of good manners, McCabe quotes a D. Fellows (no citation given) communication guideline for marriage and love affairs: "Never say anything to the other person when you are together that you would not say if there were guests in the room." McCabe adds: "Apart from love-making, of course."[33] Thus, we should disclose to our intimate partners few, if any, uncomplimentary comments about themselves or about their family. We should not be "brutally honest. Maybe the old injunction fits, "If you don't have anything nice to say, then don't say anything."

State everything honestly is the last criterion offered here for how or to what extent to be honest in your relationships with people. Keen suggests that truth-telling is necessary for developing healthy, intimate relationships.[34] He does not mean that we should tell someone who invited us to their home that the food tasted bad or tell the little kid their painting was poor. As Chapter Four cautioned, we should not disclose information for individual relief when others become burdened by what they hear. On the other hand, Keen found that "white lies are rarely as harmless as they seem, and that the untruths we offer in order to spare feelings can end up hurting others in the long run—because of their possible repercussions, because of the wall that they erect between two people in a relationship, because the 'deceived' often sense the truth anyway."[35] Adler reports that relationships are at least threatened, if not harmed, by deception.[36] Reflecting on his experience, Keen thought that the "white lies" (altruistic lies) he told his dad as a young adult seemed good at that time for his dad.[37] Since his dad's authority was not directly challenged, his dad's feelings were not hurt because he did not know his son was disobedient, and so there was general peace. Later, as an adult, the author concludes that,

> Our family would have been healthier .... Our love would have grown had we dared to speak our individual truths, risked more overt conflict, not been so afraid of hurting one another's feelings. The part of ourselves that we hid from one another by our polite lies ... went underground and emerged years later as rebellious emotions when we were grown and had kids of our own.[38]

Adler found that "If preserving a relationship is important, honesty—at least about important matters—really does appear to be the best policy."[39] Keen believes that people in relationships can tell the truth to each other if they treat each other as equals and create a supportive climate that allows truth to be easily told.[40]

Feynman[41], the scientist who discovered why the space shuttle *Challenger* burned and blew up shortly after its 1986 launch, shares his experience about a girl named Arlene who he dated in high school. Arleen had been raised in a very polite family that believed people should be tactful about what they say to others and that "white lies" were okay. Feynman believed that he should state all of his thoughts and feelings *honestly*. Why should he care what other people think? Sure, he should be polite and allow everyone to express their ideas but if what they say is nonsensical, then he should say so. Arlene accepted the idea that the two of them should be direct and frank about everything with each other. It worked very well in practice between them as they fell in love and later became engaged.

Feynman went away to college but visited Arlene during vacations. At a certain point, she became ill and doctors could not discover what was wrong. Feynman researched possibilities and came to the conclusion that Arlene had an incurable disease so when he next saw her, he told her this. The doctors later confirmed to him that she had one of the fatal diseases he had discussed with Arlene, and that she only had a few years to live. He then told one of the doctors that he would tell her the diagnosis, but the doctor said he should not since it would be upsetting to Arlene, and besides, her parents did not want her to know the troubling news. At home, his entire family thought it would be foolish for him to tell Arlene the truth, that she had a fatal disease. After further discussion, Feynman agreed to go along with the "white lie." Knowing that this would be diametrically opposite to the agreement he and Arlene had with each other and the trust in each other that was built upon that, he concluded that their relationship would be over if she later discovered the truth. Thus, he wrote her a goodbye letter that he kept with himself. When he next saw Arlene in the hospital, with her parents, she was initially in despair.

> When she sees me, her face lights up and she says, "Now I know how valuable it is that we tell each other the truth!" Nodding at her parents, she continues, "They're telling me I have glandular fever, and I'm not sure whether I believe them or not. Tell me, Richard, do I have Hodgkin's disease or glandular fever?"
>
> "You have glandular fever," I said, and I died inside. It was terrible—just terrible!
>
> Her reaction was completely simple, "Oh! Fine! Then I believe them." Because we had built up so much trust in each other, she was completely relieved. Everything was solved, and all was very nice.
>
> She got a little bit better, and went home for a while. About a week later, I got a telephone call. "Richard," she says, "I want to talk to you. Come on over."
>
> "Okay." I made sure I still had the letter with me. I could tell something was the matter.
>
> I go upstairs to her room, and she says, "Sit down." I sit down on the end of her bed.
>
> "All right, now tell me," she says, "do I have glandular fever or Hodgkin's disease?"
>
> "You have Hodgkin's disease." And I reached for the letter.
>
> "God!" she says, "They must have put you through hell!"
>
> I had just told her she has a fatal disease, and was admitting that I had lied to her as well, and what does she think of? She's worried about *me*! I was terrible ashamed of myself. I gave Arlene the letter.
>
> "You should have stuck by it. We know what we're doing, we are right!"
>
> "I'm sorry. I feel awful."
>
> "I understand, Richard. Just don't do it again."[42]

Feynman's experience illustrates the beauty and importance of more complete and direct honesty in relationships—even when the message is tragic—and Keen's conclusion that it can exist in a supportive climate.[43] Feynman's experience also illustrates the pitfalls of "white lies." We cannot count on the "white lying" people to be there for us in a crisis, just when we need them the most. Acknowledging our human frailties, it is sad when someone cannot trust his or her own parents during a critical situation, the result of a presumably well-intentioned family practice of "white lies."

The reader may wonder about the outcome of the "honesty at all costs" relationship between Feynman and Arlene. Since he loved her and was engaged to her, he expected to marry her despite her incurable disease and shortened life span. He did not care what the near-entirety of his family thought about it (they opposed it). He borrowed a station wagon, put a mattress in the back for her, picked her up at one hospital, drove to a city hall, carefully walked her inside, had a bookkeeper and an accountant as witnesses to the marriage ceremony, and drove Arlene to another hospital closer to Princeton where he finished his classes. Later, he had her transferred to a hospital in Albuquerque where he worked nearby on the World War II atom bomb project, seeing her on weekends. She passed away before the war ended.

This is a reminder that communication is a transaction and self-reflective, that each person influences both the other person and themselves with their communication. Feynman shows that people can establish a relationship within which they can speak so honestly. He and Arlene were the better for it. People can create the "climate of trust" that Keen says is a requirement for honesty.[44] Keen did not say it would be easy, and no one is perfect in their communication.

Concern For Those Pressured For White Lies

In the section above about honesty in relationships, criteria were offered to help readers make their own decision about how "honest" they desire to be. It was suggested that "white (altruistic) lies" were okay in a limited (but seemingly pervasive) sense. Still, what if you do not want to use them, as exemplified by Feynman? This is a question that can be raised for the receiver of requested evaluations or favors who wants to be honest and responsible in his or her behavior and not be put under pressure or manipulated by a sender to be dishonest just to "go along and get along." What if you do not think you should be put on the spot? What if the receiver of the requested evaluation thinks the dress/food/etc. is not good so they say so if questioned? Then the sender is likely to get upset. Communication experts might think such a receiver a boor. Is that the receiver's fault? Do not some people say, "Well, you shouldn't have asked me if you were not willing to accept my answer."? Why put the burden on the receiver and say that they have to be the diplomatic one, that they have to give the white lies? Cannot the requesting person know (predict and control) who is likely to give them an inaccurate, incomplete, and bolstering evaluation and ask that person/s? Why is it not their fault if they ask "the wrong person," someone who says their product or service is lousy? If you believe that we have to use white lies for self-esteem purposes, how long in life do we have to do it for them? To age 5? 10? 20? 50? When are they supposed to "get the message?" When is it counterproductive? Are people so fragile? How can people improve their work when they get the white lies? Is there any connection between people who frequently ask other people for their opinions of the asking person's hair/car/etc, and having an external locus of control as discussed by Dyer?[45] Do those people who have a largely internal locus of control seek so many compliments for what they have or do, as do the external locus of control individuals? No answers are provided for the questions here. Maybe the reader has some.

In a sense, our communication would be much easier if we just "called 'um as we see 'um" since we would not have to mentally strategize how to say something to make it sound pleasing to the other person. What under girds some of the honesty debate is, what is the person comfortable with or used to? Former President Truman is reputed to have said, "If you can't stand the heat, get out of the kitchen." Someone who would say this sounds like someone who likes to give and receive direct, frank, "honest" communication. Other people are comfortable with and used to being "nice" and "sensitive."

MONEY TALK IN INTIMATE RELATIONSHIPS: BEFORE A LONG-TERM COMMITMENT IS MADE[46]

This is a highly unusual section to find in a communication text. It is offered here since communication about money plays a significant part in people's relationships. Talking about money, especially between friends or family members, is fraught with difficulties. Many college students have had, are having, or will have in the years immediately after graduation an intimate relationship. Thus, communication up to the point of making a life-long commitment is relevant to the college years and shortly thereafter. This section of the chapter describes the impact of money on relationships and explores some effective ways that people becoming a couple can discuss their important, everyday money matters. This examination of money in relationships also integrates communication information and skills provided earlier in this chapter and from the preceding chapters.

Money Talk Is Problematic

While differences about any area of life may lead to conflicts between people, money is particularly troublesome. It is just not easy for people to talk about money with their friends and partners. It is more difficult for couples to talk about money than it is for them to discuss their sexual behavior.[47] Our sense of self-worth, our public image, our security, our independence, and our fears of failure and inadequacy are typically connected in some way to the amount of money we have so it is an emotionally-charged subject.[48] How much money we have and how we spend it reflects the relationships we have with people.[49] People may not like the relationship messages signaled by how money is handled, but money messages cannot be avoided since money is used to pay for necessities and desires in life. Given the communication principle that we cannot not communicate, so couples cannot not communicate about money.

Unfortunately, communication about money is all too often unsuccessful. For most students looking ahead, it is commonly reported that disagreements and fights about money are the number one cited cause of divorce in America,[50] up to as much as seventy percent of the cases.[51] Even in what otherwise appear to be strong relationships, money can short-circuit feelings of love.[52] Rich suggests that spouses who argue about money are more likely to be spending more than they can legitimately afford on extras, which in turn leads to more arguments about money.[53] Are college students bothered by how their previous or current partners spend money? Do they look forward to "marrying" their partner's debt after college? Do they expect someone to "marry" their own debt?

In an extensive survey conducted for her book, Chatzky finds that "... money can be a bigger cause of unhappiness [in life].than many other factors." "It is the factor we worry most about ...."[54] The continued worry about money drains people both physically and mentally. The stress can easily carry over into defensive-arousing language used between two people, leading to additional conflict. According to Hayden, money is the number one reason for frustration and discouragement, anger and accusations, and fussing and feuding.[55] The ongoing stress from couples not overcoming their debt leads to conflicts and a feeling of hopelessness.

Fortunately, couples who are able to communicate and work on their finances together increase the likelihood they will stay together, they increase their chances of being financially successful, and they are likely to be happy as a couple.[56]

Some Misconceptions about Money Talk

First, that people will not fight about money if they love each other. Bach suggests that this common assumption[57] is based on the idea that money equals loves. It does not. In fact, "Money has very little to do with love ... and a lot to do with how much you fight."[58] Liberman adds that love has to do with the romantic elements in the relationship, while marriage is actually a civil institution defined by financial and social obligations.[59]

Second, that ff you love someone you are likely to have a similar perception of money.[60] This misconception is explained by consistency theories as expecting certain perceptions to go together, and the halo effect that people tend to attribute positive characteristics to people they have previously perceived in some positive fashion. Unfortunately, Dubin finds that couples typically are at polar opposites when it comes to perceptions of money.[61]

Communication in the Early Encounters

To initially meet people, particularly to set up a potential romantic encounter, young adults have to notice and be noticed (noted earlier in this chapter) in the dating marketplace. To do so can entail spending money on (among others) their appearance and/or their cars. From these bodily features and artifacts, people can form initial physical and financial impressions of the person they are observing. We can recognize that people are attracted to success looking people so many people pretend to be more financially successful than they are in reality. Thus, in the initial and mostly nonverbal encounter, many people are providing inaccurate messages that they hope will lead to a false impression about themselves. We can sympathize with such messages, as Stein notes, "Let's be frank: The young man who pulls up in a BMW is more likely to get a second look from a table of ladies than the one arriving in a beat-up Geo. And the gal with the exaggerated physique will certainly attract more stares from men. So they start out with the clear advantage that they're more likely to be noticed.[62]

If people do notice each other and like or at least are comfortable with what they perceive financially (in part) about the other person, they may establish a date. In the big picture, people are "… looking for the best provider …"[63], in other words, financial security.

Initial Guidelines for Learning the Other Person's Orientation toward Money

1. *Observe Basic Money Decisions.* Who wants to go where, how much it costs, what items will be purchased on location, who will pay for it, and how will it be paid (e.g., cash).[64] Is a male who treats a female to Hilton Hotel's Friday night seafood buffet financially comfortable and generous? What if he uses a 2-for-1 dinner coupon and a credit card? The entertainment options for traditional college students are financially limited for they have little cash flow, yet the important money messages are still there.

2. *Avoid Seeking and/or Disclosing Intimate Financial Information.* As suggested in Chapter Four, the receiver will consider this type of inquiry inappropriate, especially if the information is negative. Avoid statements such as "I love going to the Outback Steakhouse" or "You must have a good income with the nice car you drive." Effective disclosure tends to occur little by little as people share a wider range of topics and depth of personal information.

3. *Begin With a Compliment.* Draw attention to something relatively innocuous the other person has, such as, "That's a nice shirt you're wearing," allowing the receiver to say something about how they got it, how long they have had it, and so on, providing you with some small pieces of financial insight.

4. *Ask About a Recent Financial News Story.*[65] On that same or next occasion with the person, ask them what they think of one or more money issues that have come up recently in the news. These could range from "What do you think about that guy who donated all that money to the local community center?" to "Did you notice that Bank of Xyz, which has overcharged credit card interest rates, is going to have to refund some money to customers?" to "I was surprised that Congress is against the President's desire to allow people to control the investment of some of the Social Security contributions from their paychecks." Such questions are likely to be responded to spontaneously, providing more background information about what the other person knows and feels about a range of money issues. If you rate an answer very negatively, you can avoid seeing the person again.

5. *Avoid a False Financial Image.* Your relationship will be easier in many respects if you have or are able to do this. People who establish a certain persona that is inconsistent with the reality of their financial assets create pressure on themselves to maintain this inconsistency. This typically means living beyond their means and being in debt. Moreover, the discrepancy is likely to eventually be noticed by their partner, who will begin to question the other person's credibility and financial fitness. At this stage, Stein provides some advice for us:

> In the long run, the guy who drives the car he can afford and the girl who lives with the [body] she already has may have an edge—the advantage of being real. They might have a harder time getting noticed, but once they've sorted each other out from the pack, they should find that the relationship is smooth sailing. Meanwhile, the guy with the BMW he can't afford will probably end up with the girl with the plastic [body parts].[66]

On the other hand, if your observations of your romantic interest suggest that he or she has created and maintained a significantly false financial image, you have a reason to have second thoughts about further involvement with the person. Another person's irresponsibility with money can spell trouble in the future.[67] According to Orman, "The way someone handles money is a personal character trait. A lack of respect for money is a powerful signal that can't be ignored. It's amazing how we try to rationalize and compartmentalize when we are dating. We are so eager to focus on the positives that we gloss over the problems."[68] Orman's evaluation for those who become aware of their romantic partner's debt, bounced checks, and senseless spending is, "… if you are dating someone who has absolutely no respect for money…[then] that's someone who isn't going to respect you, either."[69]

In essence, money tells a story, an intimate story about who the other person is, as well as who we are. At this point, we will have to decide whether to continue the relationship or not. Considering a future relationship with the other person, Rick found that the complementary relationship of spendthrifts (spenders) marrying tightwads experience financial conflicts and diminished marital health,[70] as we might have guessed. Tightwads marrying tightwads experience more desirable financial status and healthier marriages. The choice is yours.

All is not lost, though, if one or both individuals are spendthrifts, for with supportive climate language and descriptive, non-blaming questions, along with the financially irresponsible person's desire to change, there can be reformation. Financial counseling may be needed to acquire financial knowledge and methods.

The Ongoing Relationship

If a couple reaches the point where at least one of them thinks of the other one as someone with whom they would like to establish a long-term relationship, and the one thinks the other is of like mind, then the time has come for at least the one person to be very clear about the couple's money orientation. Dubin suggests that couples considering an engagement discuss their views of money and their own personal financial state before any wedding occurs.[71] It is better to be safe than sorry, it is better to know before any verbalized commitment their financial compatibility and any significant financial differences that could lead one or both of the individuals to forsake a long-term commitment. Ideally, each person's personal financial state should be shared before the actual engagement since someone cannot expect to make an informed engagement choice if both of their finances are a mystery to each other. Further, once an engagement occurs with a ring given and verbal affirmation of this life-altering decision shared with family, close friends, and acquaintances, and possibly a picture in the local paper, it becomes difficult to alter the earlier decision (Behavioral Commitment Theory[72]). As a wedding date approaches, it becomes even more difficult for the couple to reverse their decision since many people will have worked toward and paid for services to be provided, even up to a year in advance. To back out of a wedding at the last minute is very embarrassing and costly, which makes it difficult to do. For those who reject the idea of a couple being familiar and comfortable with each other's financial status, Lloyd asks "… how romantic is it to squabble over money after you're married? Besides, isn't it better to have these discussions before you've started amassing joint property?"[73]

Dreams and Goals before a Commitment

At this point, those couples anticipating an engagement or those who are already engaged, can begin to discover more personal information about each other's financial status and expectations. According to Hayden, all couples have unspoken hopes and dreams.[74] When these remain unspoken, problems arise. Bach recommends that couples clarify their financial dreams and goals to enable themselves to determine their individual compatibility and to recognize their differences as a basis for integrating them.[75] To do this, consider the following recommendations:

1. *Create a Supportive Atmosphere.* Find a neutral yet comfortable place where the both of you can easily sit next to each other and have the opportunity to face each other or look away as you desire. A bench in a park could be suitable, as would a living room sofa with nothing other than some background music playing.

The larger question they have to answer is, what does the couple, individually and collectively, want from their money? According to Chatzky, "Most people … have absolutely no idea what their financial goals are."[76] These goals could relate to such topics as having a family, the size of the family, where to live and what to live in, how much to spend in the present versus how much to save toward retirement, how to live in retirement, and whether and/or to what extent to take care of an aging parent.

2. *Start with Yourself.* To get the conversation going, consider an opening line such as, "Growing up, I don't remember my parents ever talking about money. How was it in your house?" or "These student loans are driving me nuts. Do you have them, too?"[77]

3. *Let Them Respond.* After they do, you can state the goals you have for yourself and presumably, the two of you. You can ask your partner if the two of you can share your financial goals. Presuming the answer is "Yes," you can begin by verbalizing your own goals that should have been privately clarified in advance. These should be as specific as possible and relate to specific events arising in different stages in life. These could include such things as: paying off a student loan, buying a car, going on a dream vacation to Italy, buying a house in a certain location, raising a few kids, giving money to a preferred charity, golfing daily in retirement in Arizona, and so on.

4. *Ask for Their Financial Goals.* Having just raised this idea earlier in the conversation, your friend probably will not have a well-formulated response. If your friend struggles to articulate some goals, tell them you understand and that this talk can be continued at a later time.

5. *Emphasize What Is In Common.* If your partner is able to share his or her goals, highlight the ones you share. Any personal evaluations and negative critiques of the goals should be withheld until the direction of the relationship is later determined to be favorable.

The overall strategy here is to invite a dialogue and through it help each person clarify his or her aspirations, and then see where or how these may fit together. The information revealed by this goals discussion gives an overview, a big picture of what each party expects to achieve with money. Based on the totality of the responses, you should have a go/no go answer to the question of seeking a permanent relationship with the other person, all without revealing any personal financial data.

Intimate Financial Information for a Commitment

If both parties still feel positive about each other and expect to draw closer together, they can carry their financial discussion to the next level. This recommendation raises the risks of self-disclosure noted in Chapter Four: risk of personal rejection, risk of being taken advantage of (the receiver may use this information in an attempt to actually steal the other person's money, or give that information to someone else who may), and risk of social rejection (others who learn about the disclosure may ignore the person).

1. *Set a Time and Place to Engage.* Create a favorable background for asking your partner to share this additional information. Use a neutral location and make sure there is a warm and comfortable feeling to the setting.

2. *Sound Provisional.* Use a tentative-sounding voice as a way of encouraging a supportive response, along with a provisional statement (Gibb's supportive climate language[78]). For example, you might say, "[Mary], do you think it might be useful for us to share the specifics of our personal finances?" or "I'd like to share some of my financial information so you can know me better. If you'd like, you could do the same."

3. *Watch Nonverbal Responses.* Close attention will have to be paid to your partner's nonverbal behavior accompanying any "yes" to determine if the verbal and nonverbal responses are consistent with each other. A frown and/or hesitant voice, for example, as someone says "yes" implies that the "yes" is not whole-hearted. In this case, your friend can be further questioned about his or her hesitation. "Would it be OK to tell me why you're unsure about speaking further about your personal finances?" or "Do you think we ought to talk about this later, maybe in the near future?" The issue should not be forced since your partner will get defensive both about money discussions and about your inquiring, and they may presume that you have some strategy to manipulate him or her in some unseen way (and may even be manipulative about money in the future). That being said, if your friend maintains his or her hesitancy over a period of time, you will have to question his or her commitment to you. On the other hand, if your intimate friend provides a positive response to your request, you can further engage his or her.

4. *Set a Date.* "How about we gather our papers over the next few weeks and go over them on a Saturday afternoon? Maybe at the park nearby which isn't windy?" This will achieve two purposes: it will give each of you more time to verify that you actually want to do this activity, as well as provide time (possibly a few weeks) to gather the necessary papers. You will again have to arrange to meet in a neutral place where you can feel comfortable and not be interrupted. Since papers will be examined and handed back and forth, a picnic table could be useful after having a picnic lunch date, creating a light-hearted mood to offset the stark reality of the presented numbers.

5. *Key Questions to Answer.* Overall, Rapacon suggests that four broad money questions have to be asked and answered by couples before they get married to enable them to determine their compatibility.[79] These are: how much is there, from where does it come, where is it kept, and where is it going? As a typical college student or if one or both of you have recently graduated from college, the two of you probably will not have very many financial statements to share. Still, there could be savings and checking accounts, credit

card accounts, a car loan, a student loan, a recent pay stub, and a credit report. There should be an advance agreement about what will be shared before the date arrives.

6. *The Money Date*. There is no assurance that the discloser will convince the listener to form what the discloser thinks is a legitimate interpretation of the discloser's financial status and general orientation to money. In addition, there are people who prey on others' money so those who do disclose personal financial information must know the other person pretty well. Still, people will have to mutually share their records if they are seriously contemplating an intimate, long-term relationship. Personal account numbers and social security numbers can be kept private at this point, even blacked out.

When the discussion time arrives and the two of you begin speaking, you can speak first and then ask your partner to summarize what you have said. After moments of hearing what your partner has said, practice active listening (see Chapter Five), supportive and reinforcing comments about the other's value as a person (supportive talk is discussed earlier in this chapter), and provide a verbal commitment to keep the information confidential (see Chapter 4 for this and other self-disclosure guidelines).

Following these suggestions will build trust and affection between the two of you and an increase in personal integrity for having respected the privacy of the other's disclosure. Thus, what begins as a somewhat objective exercise to discover information to help determine financial compatibility can easily create greater emotional closeness by the very process of sharing the objective information.

7. *Follow Up*. In later discussions about money, couples can consider revealing even more of their personal financial records and any refined assessment of their financial goals. By this time, the sharing of personal money information will likely to have either brought them closer together as a couple or already driven them apart. They should have experienced each other's handling of money over a period of time and circumstances, they should have revealed their financial goals, and they should have shared evidence of their financial affairs. Now couples have to be willing to create and entertain pointed money questions of each other to clarify their understanding of what has been revealed. The directness of these questions is appropriate given the information already revealed and conveys a trust on the questioner's part that the relationship is strong enough that they can ask such questions. After knowing what they know about each other's finances and financial goals (among other things), couples can make an informed

decision to get engaged or commit to some other type of long-term affair. This idea is reinforced by Liberman, who states, "We learned that once you understand how you both think about money you can work things out later on when you get hitched."[80]

At this point, those adult couples that desire an intimate, long-term commitment to each other should have a sound financial understanding about themselves and each other.

Commitment Postscript: Financial Honesty in Marriage

Open and ongoing financial discussions among committed partners are obviously encouraged. For those individuals who later think they can safely pretend to be honest yet become secretive and lie about their handling of money, Chatzki cautions them: they are likely to lose self-respect and they are likely to have diminished respect and love for their partner.[81] Medintz[82] reports on Money Magazine's survey of 1,001 adults (50% males, 50% females) who had household incomes of $50,000 or more at the time of the survey and finds that 71% revealed that they kept money secrets from their spouses. Forty-six percent of those surveyed said they lied to their partner about what they paid for their purchases or simply hid the objects.

To the question "I consider _____ a sensitive issue in my household," 53% of the spouses checked "sex" while 51% checked "money," a very close second. Respondents (43%) justified their money secrets as a method for avoiding household conflicts. Men and women (30%) said they hid purchases from their spouse to avoid a spousal lecture. Of those surveyed, 29% reported that they misled their families and friends about their overall financial situation. In a separate study reported by McGregor, approximately one-third of men and women reported that they had lied about the cost of some of their purchases to their spouses.[83] According to Medintz, "Nearly a quarter [of the spouses surveyed] worry that keeping secrets hurts their relationships."[84] Given the money and divorce connection, it seems plausible that financial troubles are a significant part of everyday marriages (and divorces) in America.

Money Talk Summary

Communication is a tool, not a product. It can be used by couples to determine their similarities and differences about money. Chatzky finds that marriages have reduced conflict if the spouses share their money thoughts and actions.[85] While discussing money is difficult, effective communication will increase the chances of a happy marriage.[86] Couples that learn about and take control of their personal finances will feel less stressed about money and happier about life.[87] Those couples who are happier with their finances also report being happier with their jobs, relationships, and life in general.

The purpose of all the money talk is to build a closer relationship and achieve financial independence. The process of all the money talk is likely to lead to the unexpected payoffs of increased couple communication about life in general, a deeper understanding of themselves and of each other, and a closer relationship with each other. Chatzky concludes, "If you can talk about your money, then you can talk about your dreams, your goals, your hopes, your fears. Your entire life comes more clearly into focus."[88] Effective money talk can help people control money and its impact on their relationship rather than money controlling them.

CONCLUSION

Most of our communication, most of the time, in most situations, for most people, is interpersonal communication. It is an interaction between two people. It begins when Person A senses Person B. Most of the time people are aware of each other as they use their communication to establish, maintain, or end a relationship. This chapter revisited the content and communication skills from the earlier chapters on self-disclosure, listening, verbal messages, and nonverbal communication. Supportive climate language and I-messages were offered as techniques to maintain effective interactions. Both honest and tactful communication were described and evaluated. Communication about money in our interpersonal affairs was included here since the topic has significant influence on the communication between couples and their subsequent interactions with each other. This discussion about money also illustrated the communication content and skills provided earlier in this chapter and in the preceding ones. [89]

CH.8 HOMEWORK #1
Defensive and Supportive Climate Language

Directions: For each of the following situations, create both a Defensive-arousing statement and a Supportive-arousing statement as if you are speaking to the other person. Then list the type(s) of either defensive or supportive language you have used.

Table 8.2

Defensive Climates		Supportive Climates
Evaluation	- versus -	Description
Control	- versus -	Problem orientation
Strategy	- versus -	Spontaneity
Neutrality	- versus -	Empathy
Superiority	- versus -	Equality
Certainty	- versus -	Provisionalism

Example (situation): Your brother is always coming over to your house to "borrow" some spam and rice to feed his family. [Create some likely responses.]

    a. *Defensive-arousing statement*: "Hey bro, get a life. You always bum food off me?"
    b. Type/s of defensive language used: evaluation, certainty.
    c. *Supportive-arousing statement*: "Jose, I feel frustrated with your continual living off me."
    d. Type/s of supportive language used: descriptive

1. Your spouse frequently buys raffle tickets (or beer) with his/her paycheck before arriving home with the balance.
    a. Defensive-arousing statement to your spouse:
       "_____
       _____."
    b. Type/s of defensive language used:
       _____."
    c. Supportive-arousing statement to your spouse:
       "_____
       _____."
    d. Type/s of supportive language used:
       _____."

2. One friend of yours continually comes to your parties without bringing anything—no snacks, barbeque, or drinks.
    a. Defensive-arousing statement to your friend:
       "_____
       _____."
    b. Type/s of defensive language used:
       _____."

   c. Supportive-arousing statement to your friend:

"_____

_____."

   d. Type/s of supportive language used:

_____."

3. Your child requests more than the agreed-upon allowance money you give him/her.

   a. Defensive-arousing statement to your child:

"_____

_____."

   b. Type/s of defensive language used:

_____."

   c. Supportive-arousing statement to your child:

"_____

_____."

   d. Type/s of supportive language used:

_____."

4. You and your spouse previously agreed to make joint household purchases, but now he/she solely bought furniture

   a. Defensive-arousing statement to your spouse:

"_____

_____."

   b. Type/s of defensive language used:

_____."

   c. Supportive-arousing statement to your spouse:

"_____

_____."

   d. Type/s of supportive language used:

_____."

5. You are very rich, and a certain other person clearly wants to spend a lot of time with you.

   a. Defensive-arousing statement to this other person:

"_____

_____."

   b. Type/s of defensive language used:

_____."

  c. Supportive-arousing statement to this other person:

"_____

_____."

  d. Type/s of supportive language used:

_____."

CH.8 HOMEWORK #2
Practicing I-messages.

Directions: Replace the following statements with I-messages. To do so, determine a feeling someone is likely to have had to make each individual statements, a simple, everyday situation in which each of the statements may have been said, and then give the basis, standard, or criteron a person could believe in that is the basis of the feeling experienced. These rewritten I-Messages should not blame or praise the other person (or yourself) for you feeling the way you do. Your I-message topic situations should be consistent with the subjects provided or implied by the given statements. The hypothetical examples to which you refer should be specific as to the subject, person, amounts, sizes, places and actions: *$100, 2 hours*, the *park, yelled and screamed*, and *jumping up/down*. There are 4 basic parts to an I-message: "I"—feel [a specific feeling] about [a specific individual action and situation occurring] since I …" [provide *your* basis/criterion/underlying reason for your feeling about the situation the way you say you do].

Example: You may be inclined to say to someone else: "Talking with you is a waste of time."

Changed to an "I" message (4 parts): "I'm—frustrated—explaining to you how to cook 3-minute scrambled eggs —since I think you're not listening which is wasting my time, and I don't like wasting time."

Part A: **Class Exercise (Part B below is homework)**

  1. "You always just think of yourself!"

    "I_____

_____."

  2. "Don't ever buy things without my consent."

    "I_____

_____."

3. "You're awfully sloppy with our finances."

   "I_____

   _____."

4. "We get along so well."

   "I_____

   _____."

5. "You've been very thoughtful about this."

   "I_____

   _____."

Part B: Homework.

6. "I wish you'd try to save some money."

   "_____

   _____."

7. "Some parent you are."

   "_____

   _____."

8. "You only want to be friends with me for my money."

   "_____

   _____."

9. "Don't be so excited."

   "_____

   _____."

10. "You should think about what you're spending money on before buying things like that."

   "_____

   _____."

Examples of Poor I-message Homework statements. Do not copy the content ideas of these.

6. "I upset myself when I find out you don't save money because you know we should."

Errors: Shorter to say "I'm upset when you", state money amount, avoid focus on them in "because you"—use a "because I …." plus give your basis/criteria for feeling upset.

7. "I get so angry when I see you fail as a parent because parents should never fail their kids."

Errors: Give an example of a specific parent failure of theirs, show your basis with "because I think parents should not [do such-and-such—referring to the specific failure of action].

8. "I don't like when I think people are with me for my money because I believe people are not that shallow."

Errors: poor grammar—missing "like *it*", lacks a feeling word, wordy—omit "I think," lacks a specific money situation and possibly an amount, nonsensical about people being with the speaker yet says they are not that way—which means there is no clear basis.

9. "I don't appreciate your enthusiasm because I am a pessimistic person."

Errors: lacks a feeling word (*appreciate* seems like an evaluation), lacks a specific enthusiastic action, and the "pessimistic" basis does not make sense or connect to the weak "appreciate."

10. "I get dumbfounded when I see useless spending. People should only buy what they need."

Errors: lacks a feeling word (*dumbfounded* a cognition), "useless spending" is vague—lacks a specific instance and amount, lacks a specific "I" basis—as in "… because I think people …."

Other examples of poorly written I-messages, errors therein, and correctly rewritten I-messages

1. "Why don't you ever come home on time?"

I-message: "I think you blew it again, keeping us in limbo. What is so difficult?"

Errors: The speaker provides no word reflecting a feeling, no specific content about the situation, and no reference to his or her own criteria/thoughts about the situation that would lead to a feeling.

Improved: " I am [feeling] frustrated [specific situation] when you arrive 30 minutes after our agreed upon departure time for dinner at Bill's since [criteria, basis for the feeling] I do not like waiting and I do not like keeping other people waiting for us."

2. "Your room is a mess, a real pig sty!"

I-message: "You are lazy, unorganized, and apparently like this filth."

Errors: No use of "I,", no speaker feeling word, no specific description about what exists, and no reference to the speaker's criteria or standards that would be a basis for having a feeling.

Improved: "I am [feeling] angry that [situation] you have not followed my 10 years of instructions and requests to either hang your clothes in the closet or put them in the dirty clothes basket, since [criteria/basis for feeling] I like an organized house and I think you need to learn tidiness, too.

3. "You are the light of my life."

I-message: "I think you are so wonderful and so good to me."

Errors: The speaker provides no feeling word, is not specific about something the person has done, and provides no set of criteria or standards by which they are judging the person's actions.

Poorly rewritten: "I like it when you are so generous since it shows you love me."

Errors: Still no speaker feeling word, no exact details revealing generosity, no criteria or standards shown to know how the speaker judges generosity, and it focuses on the other person.

Improved: "I am [feeling] elated that [specific situation] you surprised me with a single yellow rose in class since [criteria/basis] I think giving such a romantic symbol reveals your love for me."

CH.8 HOMEWORK #3
Relationship Questions Homework

1. Initiating relationships: the 1st encounter. Write down what you have said, directly heard, or heard of someone else saying when first meeting another person.

   a. Best opening phrase/pick-up line? (example: "Hi, can I buy/get you something to drink?")

_____

_____

   b. Worst opening phrase/pick-up line? (example: "What's your sign?")

_____

_____

2. Write a question about some specific aspect of *communication* occurring in relationships, to give you the chance to reflect upon a communication issue you have wondered about. Focus on *how* people communicate, not simply on *why* they communicate the way they do.

Example: *How* can you convince your boy/girlfriend that you're sorry?

_____

Frequently Told Lies[90]

"I was only following orders. I was only doing what I was told."

"I was only kidding. Can't you take a joke?"

"I was only trying to help."

"I'm sorry."

"I don't know what my serve will be like, that old football injury is acting up."

"Not tonight, I have a headache."

"Better late than never."

"I had to work late."

"I didn't want to hurt your feelings."

"I'll get right on it."

"I'll do it tomorrow."

"We must have lunch sometime."

"I don't expect anything in return."

"Of course, I care about you, it's just that …."

"I never lie."

Other Common Lies

"I'm from the government and I'm here to help you."

"I promise to pay you back on payday."

"Your hair looks fine."

"Your baby is beautiful."

"A guy's looks and money don't attract me. I want a sensitive guy who will listen to me."

REFERENCES

1. M. Burgoon and M. Ruffner, *Human Communication* (New York: Holt, Rinehart and Winston, 1978).
2. D. Barnlund, *Communication Styles of Japanese and Americans* (Belmont, CA: Wadsworth Publishing Company, 1989), p. 40.
3. Thibaut and Kelley, op cit.
4. M. Roloff, *Interpersonal Communication: The Social Exchange Approach* (Beverly Hills, CA: Sage Publications, Inc., 1981).
5. Thibaut and Kelley, op cit.
6. Ibid..
7. Ibid.
8. J. DeVito, *Human Communication: The Basic Course* (5th ed.) (New York: HarperCollins Publishers Inc., 1991).
9. Ibid.
10. Roloff, op cit.
11. I. Altman and D. Taylor, *Social Penetration: The Development of Interpersonal Relationships* (New York: Holt, Rinehart and Winston, Inc., 1973); D. Taylor and I. Altman, "Communication in Interpersonal Relationships: Social Penetration Process," in M. Roloff and G. Miller, eds., *Interpersonal Processes: New Directions in Communication Research* (Newbury Park, CA: Sage Publications 1987).
12. Altman and Taylor, op cit.
13. Ibid.
14. J. DeVito, *Human Communication: The Basic Course* (10th ed.) (Boston: Pearson Education, Inc., 2006).
15. M. Argyle and M. Henderson, "The rules of friendship." *Journal of Social and Personal Relationships*, 1, 2 (June), 211-237.
16. D. Cole, "Divorceproof Your Marriage." *U.S. News & World Report* (December 25, 2006/January 1, 2007), p. 72.
17. J. Gibb, "Defensive Communication." *Journal of Communication, 11* (1961): 141-148.
18. Ibid.
19. Ibid.
20. A. Ellis, *The Albert Ellis Reader: A Guide to Well-Being Using Rational Emotive Behavior Therapy* (Secaucus, NJ: Carol Publishing Group, 1998).
21. W. Dyer, *Your Erroneous Zones* (New York: Avon Books, 1976).
22. Ibid.
23. Ellis, op cit., p. 106.
24. Dyer, op cit., p. 20.

25. Ibid, p. 22.
26. C. Russell and J.White, "Who Controls Your Life." *ETC: A Review of General Semantics*, 50, 1 (Spring 1993): 17-19.
27. Ellis, op cit.; Dyer, op cit.
28. Gibb, op cit.
29. Dyer, op cit.
30. Ellis, op cit.
31. R. Adler and G. Rodman, *Understanding Human Communication* (10th ed.) (New York: Oxford University Press, 2009)
32. C. McCabe, "Honesty, Ugh!" *The San Francisco Chronicle* (July 24, 1983).
33. Ibid..
34. S. Keen, "Why Americans Love To Lie." *Family Weekly (*December 5, 1982).
35. Ibid., p. 7.
36. Adler and Rodman, op cit.
37. Keen, op cit.
38. Ibid p. 8.
39. Adler and Rodman, op cit, p. 192.
40. Keen, op cit.
41. R. Feynman, *"What Do You Care What Other People Think?" Further Adventures of a Curious Character (*New York: Bantam Books, 1988).
42. Ibid., p. 23-24.
43. Keen, op cit.
44. Ibid.
45. Dyer, op cit.
46. M. Griffin, "Talking About Money: What Couples Can Do To Be More Effective," unpublished paper presented at the University of Guam's CLASS 25th Annual Research Conference, March 8-9, 2004.
47. A. Dubin, *Prenups for Lovers: A Romantic Guide to Prenuptial Agreements* (New York: Villard Books, 2001).
48. C. Schwab-Pomerantz and C. Schwab, *It Pays to Talk: How to Have Essential Conversations With Your Family About Money and Investing* (New York: Crown Business, 2002).
49. D. Bach, *Smart Couples Finish Rich* (New York: Broadway Books, 2001).
50. T. Savage, *The Savage Truth on Money* (New York: John Wiley & Sons, Inc., 1999).
51. Dubin, op cit.
52. V. Collins, *Couples and Money: A Couples' Guide Updated for the New Millennium* (Encino, CA: Gabriel Publications, 1997).
53. J. Rich, *The Couples Guide to Love & Money* (Oakland: New Harbinger Publications, Inc., 2003).
54. J. Chatzky, *You Don't Have to Be Rich* (New York: Penguin Group, 2003), p. 7.
55. R. Hayden, *For Richer. Not Poorer: The Money Book for Couples* (Deerfield Beach, FL: Health Communications, Inc., 1999).
56. Bach opt cit.

57. Ibid.
58. Ibid., p. 18.
59. G. Liberman and A. Lavine, *Love, Marriage & Money: Understanding and Achieving Financial Compatibility Before and After You Say "I Do"* (Chicago: Dearborn Financial Publishing, Inc., 1998).
60. Ibid.
61. Dubin, op cit.
62. B. Stein and P. DeMuth, *Yes, You Can Get A Financial Life* (Carlsbad, CA: New Beginnings Press, 2007), p. 31.
63. Ibid., p. 30.
64. Liberman and Lavine, op cit.
65. Dubin, op cit.
66. Stein and DeMuth, op cit., p. 31.
67. Collins, op cit.
68. S. Orman, *The Money Book for the Young, Fabulous, & Broke* (New York: Riverhead Books, 2005).
69. Ibid., p. 333.
70. S. Rick, D. Small, and E. Finkel, "Fatal (Fiscal) Attraction: Spendthrifts and Tightwads in Marriage," *Journal of Marketing Research*, January 22, 2010.
71. Dubin, opt cit.
72. A. Infante, A. Rancer and D. Womack, *Building Communication Theory* (Prospect Heights, IL: Waveland Press, Inc., 1990).
73. N. Lloyd, *Simple Money Solutions: 10 Ways You Can Stop Feeling Overwhelmed by Money and Start Making It Work for You* (New York: Times Books, 2000), p. 106.
74. Hayden, opt cit.
75. Bach opt cit.
76. J. Chatzky, *Talking Money: Everything You Need to Know about Your Finances and Your Future* (New York: Warner Books, 2001), p. 4.
77. Ibid.
78. Gibb, opt cit.
79. S. Rapacon, "4 Critical Money Questions to Ask Before You Get Married." *Kiplinger Personal Finance* (December, 2009).
80. Liberman and Lavine, op cit., p. 4.
81. Chatzky (2003), op cit.
82. S. Medintz, "Secrets, Lies and Money." *Money Magazine* (April, 2005), p. 123.
83. J. McGregor, "Love & Money," smartmoney.com (February 9, 2004).
84. Medintz, op cit., p.128.
85. Chatzky (2003), op cit.
86. Dubin opt cit.
87. Chatzky (2003), op cit.
88. Chatzky (2001), op cit., p. xxii.
89. Dyer opt cit.
90. J. Jellison in S. Keen, "Why Americans Love To Lie." *Family Weekly* (December 5, 1982).

interpersonal conflict
online
workplace/formal
intrapersonal

CHAPTER NINE

Conflict Communication

M ost people do not like the experience of conflicts. Tension builds up inside our bodies, many times there is the feeling of anger, verbal attacks between the participants are common, and frustration increases when differences are not resolved. There is a feeling as if you need to take a shower to clean off.

NATURE OF CONFLICT

People are different and so they have different ideas about what they want at a given time and what they hope to gain at some point in the future. People also differ in their methods of satisfying their needs. Given these differences, people will naturally be in disagreement about what is individually important in life. This is not a matter of simple selfishness. If individuals do not speak up and work to satisfy what is meaningful to them in their lives, who will do it and how successful can we expect that to be?

At its base, conflict is the mental state of at least one person perceiving that he or she is experiencing disagreement and disharmony with another person over some issue that involves both of them. The conflict becomes a communication issue when one person expresses to another, mutually dependent person his or her displeasure about their use of limited resources or some behavior that prevents the one or both of them from satisfying an individual need or achieving an individual or combined goal.

MISCONCEPTIONS ABOUT
INTERPERSONAL CONFLICT

One of the reasons people have difficulty in resolving conflicts in their lives is due to their misunderstanding about the nature, impact, implications, and mismanagement of interpersonal conflict. Acting like one or more of the following common misconceptions are a truth can encourage a conflict to continue, to become larger, or even create a conflict separate from the original conflict. Still, it is acknowledged that the conflict issues *as stated* can also, at least occasionally and to some extent, be accurate. It is worthwhile to know when these apparent misconceptions are, in fact, a reality.

1. *Conflict is Abnormal.* Similar ideas are, conflict can be avoided and conflict indicates a poor relationship. These statements are largely inaccurate simply because everyone is a different person with at least slightly different needs, values, beliefs, goals, and both the means and plans for satisfying or bolstering these factors when compared to other people. To say that conflict is abnormal is to say that people are abnormal. This does not mean that there cannot be some atypical or deviant conflict, such murder or suicide, or psychological conflicts that require professional help. Although we generally do not go looking for conflicts, they are a natural part of interpersonal life. They cannot be avoided.

Given that conflict is a natural part of everyday existence and that no two people are alike, we would expect that any relationship would reveal some differences. If we can assume that conflicts in general cannot be avoided, then it can be assumed that they do not necessarily illustrate a poor relationship. Further, two people who can honestly disagree with each other in a respectful manner indicate that they have a strong, healthy relationship. On the other hand, those relationships that mask their disagreements with indirect, inoffensive, and diplomatic talk reveal a lack of honesty and closeness. Further, continued dismissive comments by one or both people in an interpersonal relationship may be indicative of a hidden problem between the two.

2. *Conflict is Bad.* Conflicts usually do lead to varied suffering and they can result in embattled and ruined relationships. Around the world and throughout history, horrible things have resulted from human conflicts. There have been evil rulers and immoral affairs of a wide variety.

On the other hand, does conflict produce nothing but harmful outcomes in relationships? When do people reflect upon those relationships? When *things* are going fine? No, two friends, relatives, co-workers, neighbors, and others usually only think about *how* they communicate and interact with another person when one of them is experiencing a conflict with the other person (if then). Through introspection, productive communication, and possibly one or both people saying they are sorry, the individuals have an opportunity to mature as individuals and become more intimate with each other. A generalization of marriage is that newlyweds face numerous family, career, and financial conflicts. Working through these as a team draws them closer together. People find out a little about themselves and their partners when they have conflicts. In this situation, conflict provides the means through which you can build your character and create closer relationships—a good outcome. Of course, they may discover something unfathomable and irreconcilable, but they also may find patience, understanding, loyalty, teamwork, commitment, and love (among others).

   3. *Conflict Does Not Reveal our Psychologically Weaker Side.* This idea may be an attempt to give people the benefit of the doubt. Still, who creates the meaning and actions of a given moment that can be justifiably interpreted by others as a basis for a conflict? Who is perceiving something as a conflict and what is it about themselves that they do? Who is using the attacking or other counterproductive conflict styles? Assuming there are psychological weakness, whose weakness is it, and can an individual say that they do not bring the entirety of themselves to a moment of perception and meaning creation? Whose conflict response communication and action is it? What a conflict may certainly reveal is a person's lack of knowing or using a productive conflict strategy.

   4. *The Content of the Conflict is Not as Problematic as the Conflict Response.* Yes, *how* we treat a conflict situation can enlarge the conflict and even become a larger issue than the content of the original conflict. How we respond to conflicts is crucial to resolving them. However, the original issue may be significant and urgent on its own merit. The existence of an alcoholic, drug addict, thief, adulterer, physical abuser, and so on in an interpersonal relationship can be so significant and devastating that the non-perpetrator may end the relationship without even attempting to resolve these behaviors. In brief, some content is *the big* problem outcome.

   5. *Conflict Occurs Due to a Misunderstanding.* There are many *honest* misunderstandings. We also know from Chapter 3 that our biases and other variables can influence our interpretations without a conscious effort to misperceive a message. Sill, readers should recognize that there are examples of kids and employees who clearly heard what their parents or bosses told them to do but these listeners chose to do something else. There is no misunderstanding

in these cases. Honest misinterpretation should not be a blanket excuse for someone doing whatever they want that differs from the desires of a legitimate authority.

6. *Conflict Can be Resolved.* Try as we might (and we might), some key differences continue to vex and exist between some people. First impressions are difficult to change. Religious and political beliefs and behaviors, sexual practices, and cultural habits can be difficult to change even if the individual desires it. There may be fundamental differences between people that cannot be resolved. Sowell, in *A Conflict of Visions*, explains that people's deep-seated visions of how the world should or does operate may not have any common ground.[1] Sometimes people are left with having to agree to disagree.

7. *Conflicts Should be Resolved Quickly.* This would be useful for it would prevent further emotional trauma, time, possibly money, and other undesired outcomes. Still, each conflict is unique, including the uniqueness of each individual and their unique relationship. Attempts to force interpersonal resolutions will probably backfire. Sure, some minor conflicts could be quickly solved, but underlying or more important ones usually take some time for the participants to reflect on what happened, why, who may have been at fault, what are possible solutions, and so on.

8. *It Takes Two to Fight so Each Person is Blameworthy.* This notion may first be heard in elementary school but in life, a verbal, physical, legal, or political interpersonal attack may be one-sided. One person may wage the entire verbal or physical attack on someone else who, at most, attempts to defend him or herself. One person can do the yelling and fallacious blaming of the other person who, in turn, responds with a moderate voice and rebuttals of the allegations. This is not *two* people "fighting." Blaming someone simply because they are present and the recipient of a verbal attack removes a significant amount of responsibility from the attacker and falsely maligns the receiver. How is such a receiver wrong to defend him or her self and how is that blameworthy?

9. *A Conflict's Direction and Outcome Can be Controlled.* It is likely that people think their position is correct when they become engaged in a conflict and that their point of view should prevail. It is a surprise to many people when it does not. There are inevitable twists and turns in the process of a conflict with people saying and doing a variety of things that cannot be predicted or controlled. This means there will be a lot of wasted time and ineffective effort, as well as the prospect of being on the losing end. Conflict resolution

strategies exist to replace attempts at personal control with teamwork to resolve the situation.

10. *There is a Legitimate Basis for the Conflict.* We may recognize that each person who thinks he or she has been wronged or is in some disagreement with another person might well believe that he or she has a valid conception of the situation. Certainly many people have had legitimate assessments about their differences with others or about their being wronged by someone We also know, though, that individual perceptions can be based on very limited stimuli and information, and people frequently form either weak or inaccurate inferences. Individual meanings can be very biased and self-serving. The basis of many conflicts may even be loosely characterized as originating in "never-never land." Who knows or can figure out why some people are unhappy, selfish, and so on about some state of affairs? Even the "conflicted" may be unclear about it and be unable to formulate a legitimate basis for their perceived suffering.

A variation of this misunderstanding is when one person concludes that another person is making a *mountain out of a molehill.* In effect, the observer is saying that there is a small sized difference, disagreement, or actual conflict issue that does not warrant the wronged person's large size and/or intensity of response. This is easy to say and possibly an excuse or cop-out for an observer but observers do not have the same goals, values, believes, behaviors, and so on of the observed person. Furthermore, if we do not "sweat the small stuff" in our lives, people may take advantage of us. For example, they can continually keep us waiting, wasting our time and costing us money. If they are not made aware of their behavior, how can they expect to change it and improve their own opportunities in life? In addition, is not the paying attention to details at least a partial reason why some students gets an A and others get a B or C letter grade, or why some people are promoted at a faster rate on the job than others? A small water leak can result in a flooded house requiring major repairs. Little things can make a difference.

11. *Any Ongoing, Slighting Remarks are Inconsequential.* What does a little put-down statement hurt? They are common enough between married couples, parents and children, siblings, co-workers, teammates, and so on, sometimes to the extent that the receivers of such statements attempt to tune them out. For the speaker, these may seem inconsequential but to the person these are directed—the receiver—these messages are perceived as a personal attack. The receiver typically responds defensively (as noted by Gibb[2] in the previous chapter) as well as by exhibiting one or more of the counterproductive conflict styles described a few pages later in this chapter (accommodating,

compromising, avoidance, and competing). People may not realize the gradual, *corrosive* impact of such statements upon a child or a friendship. There is some figurative "residue" in the receiver's memory. A cutting remark once a week with an accompanying tone of voice projecting superiority, disdain, or anger could be sufficient. The receiver may wonder where *that* came from— the content and the relationship message. Boy, maybe the relationship is not what they thought it was. The receiver of the "barbs" is likely to begin emotionally distancing him or herself from the speaker by building an emotional *wall* between him or herself and the speaker. Figuratively, another brick and mortar is added with each comment. Given the self-reflective (transactional) nature of communication, the speaker responds similarly with emotional distancing (how can they feel closeness with someone they continually disparage?). They keep adding bricks and mortar to their own wall. In effect, we have two walls going up simultaneously. Given what is recognized about perception (selective exposure and attention, subjectivity and bias, operating by rules, expectations, and consistency), the speaker will find some justification, even if they (have to) make it up (possibly unbeknownst to themselves). Personal bolstering (convincing) of the self is common. If these attacking statements are not ended soon after their inception, a significant rift in the relationship can be anticipated and possibly result in a dissolution of the relationship. It is as if you can see (hear) the end coming.

NEGATIVES AND POSITIVES OF CONFLICT

While the previous section discussed good and bad aspects of conflicts, this section will categorize and expand the extent of these outcomes. At least some of these will be familiar to the reader.

Negatives

1. *Terminated Relationship*. Friendships can be lost. While this may be for the better for at least one person, there is often an emotional and social loss. Divorce and its attendant distress and pain may occur. Personal loneliness may result. One or both people may seek intimacy elsewhere, possibly resulting in a sense of resentment by one person. In the process of ending the relationship, there could easily be physical and/or emotional trauma. Mean-spirited communication can result in listener sorrow and a poor self-image.

2. *Escalating Conflict*. This is when a conflict gets progressively worse, with wider and more painful ramifications. What may start out as a relatively small

conflict could result in abusive behavior and/or a terminated relationship. As noted previously, defensive communication usually engenders defensive communication, and the conflict can snowball from there.

3. *Counterproductive, Destructive Behavior is Reinforced.* This can include winning at the other person's expense. People may come to believe that destructive behavior is the only option so they continue such practices. Other people may figure that if they have to suffer, then everyone should, too. To some people, revenge is sweet but it can also escalate the conflict. Particularly destructive fighting can ensue. The person/s using destructive behavior does not go unharmed for the self-reflective nature of communication ensures that they will suffer some of the residue of their behaviors.

4. *Group Dissension May Result and Decreased Group Success.* A conflict between two group members could become a source of contention, distrust, and suspicion with other group members and people could take sides. Some information may be distorted on purpose to give an inaccurate impression of the conflict content. The dissension could easily reduce group time directed toward achieving group goals.

5. *People Become Less Communicative.* This could be a simple defensive reaction as people feel hurt and think that it would be worse to challenge the other person. Better let sleeping dogs lie. As a result, information tends to be withheld from each other that might otherwise help the individuals resolve the conflict.

Positives

1. *Individual and Interpersonal Growth and Intimacy.* As suggested in one of the misconceptions noted earlier, if individuals who experience conflict can communicate about it in a productive manner, they mature as individuals and grow closer to their companions. Also previously noted, people tend to pay more attention to the effect of their own communication on other people when a conflict arises from that communication. Finding and altering weak communication behaviors lead to individual growth, from which our friendships benefit, as well. In this sense, conflict can be a catalyst for self-improvement. According to Beebe, an individual may establish new patterns of communication and behavior as a result of airing differences with another partner.[3]

2. *Revitalized Relationship and Recommitment.* Many readers of this book should be able to cite some examples from their own lives. Self-disclosure is

a likely addition to constructive communication as one or both people share their changing needs and goals, giving the listener a chance to think of the speaker and their relationship in a different and fresh way. The discussion during a conflict can clarify points of agreement and disagreement, and cooperative communication can reinforce their bond.

3. *Reinforced Positive Aspects of a Person's Character.* An outcome that makes the best of a bad situation and benefits both people involved can lead the constructive communicator to feel good about how he or she communicated and behaved with the other person, thereby having the latter reinforced and more likely used in the future. Both the other party to the conflict and observers present are likely to judge the constructive individual as a desired companion (even laying the groundwork for the two conflicted individuals to restart their relationship at a later date if it is terminated in the present). In a particularly troubling situation, such as when a relationship is terminated, if an individual is able to provide cooperative communication such as active listening, supportive climate language, I-messages, and refrain from petty verbal attacks (among others), they can "hold their head high" to their personal arbiter—themselves.

4. *A Communicated Conflict Prevents Increased Resentment.* Talking about it to resolve it should prevent increased conflict. Rather than allow some annoyance or grudge about someone to become a bigger issue, an individual can air his or her unhappiness and have a chance to resolve it.

5. *Tolerating Relationship Conflict Suggests Relationship Value.* Attempts to resolve conflicts suggest that the individual thinks enough about the other person to make the effort to seek closure of the conflict. They could just say, "To heck with them," and let the conflict stay unresolved. According to Burgoon and Ruffner, "There is no greater sense of contentment than when two people struggle, find their relationship worthy of the test, and enjoy the security of mutual concern and affection."[4] Tolerating a relationship suggests that someone thinks it is more rewarding than costly.

While few people seek conflicts, the process of working through the conflict in a constructive manner can help the participants triumph over adversity, which will reinforce for both of them the value of each other and the relationship.

COMMUNICATION AND CONFLICT STYLES

While people are not always the same about everything, they do exhibit some repeated patterns of behavior and you may see people you know primarily use one or two of the following common styles as they react to, manage, and/or express communication when facing a conflict.

1. *Accommodating.* This sounds favorable about people helping others, making statements such as, "What can I do for you?" "No problem." "Anything you want." Unfortunately, this ends up being a nonassertive act of giving in to or going along with the wishes of someone else rather than satisfying his or her own needs or desires. It is a one-way street that attempts to preserve the harmony between two people by satisfying only one person, often to the detriment of the other person who invariably has less personal, social, legal, or organizational power and who is doing the accommodating. Accommodating can be a sensible and productive response when we realize, that we are mainly to blame for the conflict, when the other person is important to us, or when we might suffer the loss of our job (this does not mean we should accede to known, illegal acts). Ironically, some people may use accommodation as favors, to be returned in the future when they need something done.

2. *Compromising.* Like the previous style, this sounds favorable, giving a little to get a little, so to speak: "I'll give up this if you give up that." "Okay, you choose this week and I'll choose next week." Still, making concessions to reach an agreement has both benefits and side-effects. On one hand, it appears that both sides give up some goal they want while being allowed to achieve some other goal. On the other hand, what is given up is rarely equal and may even be insignificant to the one side. Further, there is often some continuing dissatisfaction with the agreement, especially when one individual "compromises" one or more of their values.

3. *Avoidance.* This is a very common style since people figuratively simply turn their back on it. They exert no energy to confront the person and the issue involved. Confrontation can be unpleasant, and people cannot predict which way a discussion may turn out. People may curse and embarrass the other person. Emotions may be so charged between two individuals that they cannot constructively discuss the conflict or clearly see their part in it. Confrontation may turn into a public spectacle, so people often dodge or escape from having to settle the dispute. There is usually no talking about the dispute and people may physically walk away from someone so they can duck the

issue. As most people know, this simply postpones resolving the dispute. The person doing the avoiding may hope a third party resolves the other people's needs but their own needs may go unresolved, too. Avoiding some issue too long can lead to an extreme emotional reaction when the person holding the tension within releases it. On the other hand, temporarily avoiding an issue can let people emotionally cool off a bit and give them time to reflect upon the situation, possibly gaining a different interpretation. Do not be surprised that it takes someone a year or two to come to a conclusion about the affair and then approach the other person.

4. *Competing.* Competing is fine in the classroom and at work so people can push themselves to increase their output. On the other hand, the common "What's mine is mine, and yours' is mine—if I can get it." And "Here's to you, and here's to me, and may we never disagree. But if by chance we do, then here's to me and to heck with you." Nearly everyone, if not everyone, wants to have their needs satisfied. We cannot fault people for that. Yet on occasion, many people act selfishly and few people are "team players." A concern for individual needs and little or no concern for other people's needs create a lot of tension between interacting people. Many people also have the idea that any gain by another person means a loss to them of the available resources. With competition, there are going to be winners and losers so there is a scramble to get whatever is to be gotten.

5. *Attacking.* This can be the outgrowth of the competing style. With conflicts, the discord can easily escalate and take on the elements of a war emanating from one or both people. Verbal hostility and/or violent force are responses. Competition is fine on the sports field and beneficial in the economic marketplace but when someone goes beyond trying to satisfy some legitimate human needs just to hurt someone else on purpose, they are in the attacking mode. When someone becomes so angry, shouting invectives, threats, and statements of blame, they are attacking by sneering, slighting, the dismissive remark, the serious teasing, the comparing of the other person to a five year-old, and so on. Those who are unhappy about something may even attack other people who have little or nothing to do with the attacker's unhappiness. The discussion of *I-messages* in Chapter 8 suggests that people commonly experience unjustifiable unhappiness and blame (attack) others. Some people even have a temper so they readily attack other people. The old phrase about people being their own worst enemy may fit the attacker. Rather than being so quick to blame others, people can examine their own thoughts and behaviors for personal weaknesses and oversights.

"I win, you win"

6. *Collaborating*. Communicating in a cooperative way seems so different than the other communication conflict styles. The is the only purely redeeming style. It requires a lot of communication time so each person can know and understand the other person's needs and limitations in fulfilling those needs. Illustrations include, "What do you need to get this done?" "Do you want to hear my ideas about what you might do?" As DeVito notes, this will require good listening on each individual's part so they can discover what each other's needs and goals are and then figure out a solution together that can help them reach those goals.[5] An added plus of the collaborative style is that interpersonal relationships report higher satisfaction.[6] A weakness of this approach to conflict is that each party has to commit to find solutions that satisfy both people. Not everyone has or wants to dedicate the time or even has the wherewithal to find solutions that can satisfy both individuals.

CONFLICT MANAGEMENT STRATEGIES

There is no one set method to use in response to a conflict. People may have to use a combination of them. The selection of an appropriate strategy will hinge on the individual's relationship with the person in the conflict, the context of the conflict, how important the issue is to the individual, the probability of success depending on the strategy used, the time the individual has available to communicate about the issue, the individual's long-term and short-term goals, and how flexible and competent they are in using the different strategies. This is not easy. In general, you can never be too smart when it comes to resolving conflicts.

Some of the previously discussed conflict styles are incorporated here as strategies. DeVito provides a number of contrasting action strategies people use in attempting to implement an effective solution.[7] Only one of each pair is the most productive, long-term strategy.

1. *Avoidance Versus Active Fighting*. As discussed earlier, an *avoidance* strategy tries to prevent a solution from occurring by staying away from people and discussions that attempt to fix some problem, or directly refusing to discuss the situation. Nothing is solved. On the other hand, *active fighting* means to be actively engaged in the conflict communication as both a sender and a receiver. Attempt to logically understand the conflict situation and generate possible solutions for resolving the conflict. "What's going on in this situation?" "How is someone or something being harmed?" "Is there sufficient justification for someone to be upset?" "How do both of us view he situation?" "What options exist for minimizing or preventing future harms?"

2. *Force Versus Talk.* Force means to be verbally forceful or using the threat of physical punishment to coerce someone into doing something desired by the speaker. An employer can force someone, on the threat of losing their job, to do something the employer wants done. "Don't come to work on Monday if you don't wave for the Governors' re-election rally on Saturday." A parent could physically spank their children or use the threat of "...or Daddy's going to whip you when he gets home." A police officer could threaten to arrest a citizen if the officer's orders are not followed. While the behavior sought may be legitimate and appropriate, the speaker in these situations wants to quickly and easily gain compliance. One weakness of using the threat of force is that the threatening person has to actually follow through and discipline the person not complying or the people present will not readily believe what the speaker says in the future. This puts pressure on the threatening person to be sure that he or she will act decisively if his or her directions are not followed, and has a legitimate and effective punishment. Another weakness of threats or actual force is that people will often only comply when the threatening person is around. This gives rise to the saying, "When the rat's away, the mice will play." On the other hand, an employer, police officer, or other legitimate authority might give a friendly warning (a "heads up") to people they are in contact with about existing regulations or laws that will force them, the authority figure, to fine, fire, or arrest people if certain behavior ensues. Any actual physical force used in interpersonal relationships should lead the receiver to question his or her continued relationship with the abuser.

As the *active fighting* idea above suggests, people in conflict need to talk. This is time consuming, it may well be frustrating, some of what the other person says may not make sense, and you cannot be sure what the outcome will be. Consider the benefits of using spontaneity, honesty, self-disclosure, I-messages, listening, and other supportive statements.

3. *Blame Versus Empathy.* Blaming, as indicated by the evaluation and certainty categories of defensive climate language (Chapter Eight) often results in defensiveness, such as verbal counter-attacks against the blamer. Another weakness of blaming is that it is often erroneous. Further, even if the person did state the message in question or enact the behavior, there could have been other communication or contextual variables that influenced the outcome (other people could have made statements that confused the issue, there could have been a lot of noise, the mood of the other communicator may have been influenced by something which occurred earlier, and so on). As most people have probably experienced, blaming does not encourage people to want to fix the apparent harm that occurred. On the other hand, the person or persons who were significantly involved with the communication or situation which

turned out badly may need to be identified since they could have the most intimate knowledge of it. They could provide the best chance of repairing the situation (another reason to avoid getting them defensive).

Empathy, as was previously discussed in Chapters Five and Eight, is an attempt to recognize and understand another person's feelings and the situation they are in, and provides a bridge, or connection between people. As a speaker, with a small amount of emotional burden removed, you may be better able to mentally describe and analyze more accurately what you had previously said and done. Possible solutions "pop into your head." You begin to think you can fix the situation.

Empathy is not easy to do and it holds risks for the person in a conflict. First, the listener has to be able to create a sense of the reality that his or her partner experienced. This requires a well-rounded sense of life and knowledge about the other person. If shared personal experiences are limited then there will be a limited perception of what the other person experienced or is experiencing.[8] Further, if the listener is able to get a sense of the speaker's experience, then the listener might change his or her mind in favor of the speaker's justification for what he or she had done. Moreover, it can be sufficiently difficult for a listener to hear and understand something that they consider to be offensive because their own emotions can get in the way of clear thinking about the situation.[9] Thus, we cannot blame or entirely blame the listener for not being able to empathize with the speaker if the speaker has not shared enough of him or herself with the listener. Empathy is a two-way street.

4. *Gunnysacking Versus Present Focus*. Gunnysacks are bags of coarsely woven plant fiber. Crop pickers used to and may still use these to put crops in as they pick their way through fields. *Gunnysacking* is the mental practice of storing or making a point of remembering grievances you have had with someone else. At a particular moment of frustration or anger over something that has just occurred between two people, the upset person verbally attacks the other person, complaining about an element in the present situation as well as numerous incidences in the past (last week, last month, last year, and so on). The first person figuratively hits the second person over the head with a number of uncomplimentary accusations. Is this an effective strategy for gaining sympathy, compliance, and forgiveness from the other person? Not likely. In fact, there is a good chance that the second person will get out *their* gunnysack and "smack" the first person with accusations of failures from the past (given how our mind works, this may bring up memories from the past when you had pillow fights with your siblings and/or friends).

From a self-centered point of view, this strategy rarely works. First, we have two people blaming each other for a number of previous failings, using a veritable "I can top that" list. They are very defensive so little listening occurs. Second, among the accusations heard, one or a few of them will have little or no evidence to back them up. Each hearer will likely focus his or her rebuttal on these weak or baseless claims, saying things like: "Yes, I did show up on time to pick up your mother last week. You can ask Bill," "I loaned your brother $20. How can you say I'm not nice to him?" and "I did empty the shower strainer cup when I finished my shower this morning. Go look in the bathroom waste basket." Whatever was important enough for the one person to talk about at the moment before the first gunnysack was used is now lost in all the verbiage that follows. Not only are such exchanges unproductive for solving a conflict but the participants incur some ill feelings about each other.

As an alternate strategy, we can speak about the issues and items of unhappiness when they occur and then be done with them. Left alone, they may grow and change into forms that barely resemble the original substance. What is difficult to determine is just which complaints we have are of significant size, relevance, and importance to speak about. If your spouse leaves a dirty sock on the living room floor for the first time in his or her life, are you going to say something? If your child leaves his or her fork in the sink after breakfast without scrubbing off the egg between the tines, will you make an issue of it? How many times should someone do something that you do not like before you say or do something? Some people are afraid a pattern might develop so they want to "nip it in the bud," the first time or two it occurs, yet for other people this is making a mountain out of a molehill. You may find that if the annoyance is not spoken about and it continues over a period of time, you lose the impact of saying something about it. It is not easy to determine the moment, but do not miss it.

5. *Manipulation Versus Spontaneity.* These two methods of response are also on Gibb's list,[10] manipulation, representing strategy on the defensive climate side, and spontaneity is listed on the supportive climate side, so the reader has already been introduced to these. Most people want to "win" the conflicts they are in so acting shrewdly or deviously are common enough practices. A speaker may lie by making up a piece of evidence or lie by omitting some evidence sought by the other person. The manipulator may pretend to be a "dumb hick" and like a sly fox get you to agree to his or her demands. Some people ingratiate themselves to others so they can later ask the other people to reciprocate when it is particularly advantageous to the manipulator. Some manipulators act charming to others so it is harder for these people to later say no to the manipulator's self-serving request. For these reasons,

readers are cautioned about accepting small gifts and favors from people they hardly or do not know, including salespeople.

In addition to the manipulations mentioned above, another strategy is to threatening people:: "If you don't do ____ ...." or "If you keep doing ____, I'm going to ____." (threats such as: "going to get you," "leave you," "cut you out of my will," and so on. The listener is likely to become defensive and respond defensively. They may comply or pretend to comply with the demands of the threatening person, but they will probably resent the speaker for using this tactic. If the person making the threat is primarily concerned with controlling the other person, then the absence of building or maintaining an emotionally close, friendly, and collaborative relationship with the listener is not so important.

Spontaneous responses, having the aura or truth, have a way of "cutting through" and shedding light on peoples' strategies and machinations, as well as the other counterproductive conflict strategies. People may well not like a comment that puts something of theirs in a negative light but if they believe the speaker is genuine and not trying to "game" the situation, they will appreciate the honesty over the evaluation. In fact, some political and military leaders have valued having staff members who have told the leader what they, the staff member thinks, not what the staff member thinks the leader wants to hear. When there is a conflict between people, a productive outcome is much more likely if the participants speak their mind as opposed to "playing games" for perceived personal advantage. People can "bank" more on the truth from someone they generally disdain than strategies from people on their own side.

6. *Personal Rejection Versus Acceptance.* A spectrum exists that represents those people on one end who have more personal affirmation and self belief (an internal locus of control) and those on the other end who seek and need more affirmation from others that they are a good and valued person (external locus of control). While no one enjoys statements about themselves that question their character or their being overlooked as if they are not present, some people are more readily bullied emotionally than others and these people can be "walked over" as others get their way. Harsh words, including references to a person's minimal intelligence, work ethic, and skills, can be very unsettling. The person rejected is likely to question their own worth.

In an effort to make everyone feel equal and respected, it is recommended that we give everyone an opportunity to speak, and practice active listening. If there is continued dissension, both parties will at least know that their point of view was heard, even if not adopted.

7. *Fighting Below Versus Above the Belt.* Over time, people forget many experiences but they rarely forget traumatic ones. Saying something to someone else about a particularly embarrassing moment, characteristic, or failure tends to stand out and incur defensiveness on the listener's part. The listener may say they forgive the speaker for this but they will probably never forget what is said since it seems to emphasize a core weakness or disability. After hearing something particularly troubling, the receiver is unlikely to trust and work constructively with the other person to resolve the conflict. They will likely feel bitter and believe they have been rejected. Those people who do make below-the-belt comments may need to anticipate the receiver of those comments trying to seek revenge for what they consider to be an insulting, personal attack.

Rather than get off track and incur the enmity of the person with whom you have a conflict, consider focusing on the conflict issue, not on the person (although in politics and leadership, personal character can count). This is the productive implication of Gibb's categories.[11] There are times, of course, when the person is the problem. Most people in their lives will work with someone who is simply problematic for clients and for co-workers. Personal evaluations of them will necessarily be troubling.

8. *Face-Detracting Versus Face-Enhancing.* Readers may have experienced a classmate's parent coming to the schoolyard or park, berating the child in front of everyone. It was an embarrassing moment for all the kids, particularly the child being admonished in public. This reaction does not change with age. If an authority figure like a parent, boss, or teacher scolds someone in public, especially with known people around, it is an attack against that person's public image. This makes it embarrassing. If your boss scolds you behind closed doors, no one else knows about it so you do not feel nearly as bad about the event. Thus, we are recommended to save our "dressing down" of others for a private place. Imagine the impact of doing this in public to someone with whom you are in conflict with? This could lead them to be an enemy of yours for life. Some women and at least a few men have avoided going to court to sue for what have appeared to be clear cases of sexual harassment because they wanted to avoid the negative publicity, the expected negative assault on their public image even if they won the case. Face-detracting comments in public are similar to the counterproductive strategies of fighting below the belt and personal rejection.

Helping (or at least not deliberately hurting) the person with whom we are in conflict to maintain a positive public image is actually in our own self-interest. Think about it on most people's everyday level. If you are having a disagreement with a sibling, parent, teacher, or boss, do they react favorably towards you when they hear "third hand" a depreciating comment you have said about them? Will they then negotiate in good faith with you? You do not like your conflicts to be made public by these same people, who may also add fictional information about you just to hurt you and make you look bad. It goes both ways, so you do not have to do it. In a quite unusual case, in the early 1990's in Massachusetts or Connecticut, neither of the two political candidates running against each other for the same office would say anything negative about the other candidate. It was "nice versus nicer."

9. *Nonassertiveness Versus Assertiveness.* If you do not speak up for your needs, goals, feelings, thoughts, and possible solutions, the person you are having a conflict with will simply speak up for themselves and presume to get what they want since your passive activity gives them tacit approval to do so. Unless we are mind readers, we cannot know what to do to help satisfy you. People will think you are unsure of yourself, do not know what you want, and are clueless about what is going on around you.

Assertiveness is speaking up for your self on behalf of your own actions and interests. It is stating with assurance what is legitimate about your position. Description, spontaneity, and equality climate language should be particularly useful in putting assertiveness into practice, as will I-messages. A simplified piece of history may be illustrative: "Speak for yourself, John Alden" [to Priscilla Mullens].. So John said, "Will thee marry me?" And she did (sorry, Miles).

10. *Aggressiveness Versus Argumentativeness.* There is a spectrum of behavior when it comes to arguing. For the sake of providing two simple extremes, some people are used to and comfortable with speaking in a moderate voice, calmly discussing the merits of some idea or the other, and being polite in their conversation. Other people are used to and comfortable being more aggressive, arguing their points with force and fervor, and even interrupting the other speaker. Simply put, to the first speaker, the second one is too aggressive and even uncivilized. To the second speaker, the first one is passive and lacking in conviction. Fortunately, both speakers can stop themselves from stepping over the line into aggressiveness by avoiding personal, verbal attacks and name-calling of the person with whom they are having a conflict.

Argumentativeness is reflected in the age-old application of logic and rhetoric to personal conflicts. Avoid fallacious reasoning, use good evidence, use an effective delivery, and seek to speak to the listener where he or she is located on the issue in question. Be mature in dealing with disagreements. The argumentative person has a large overlap with the assertive person.

11. *Win-Lose, Lose-Lose, and Win-Win*[12] Three separate strategies are described in the following.

First, *Win-Lose*, which is a method used by one or more individuals to get what they want that prevents the other person from achieving his or her goals. Participants in this conflict process typically view the conflict as an either/or situation: I either win or lose. If this means to win at the other person's expense, well, that is the existing situation. In interpersonal conflicts, the desire to win can be so powerful that it can lead one or both individuals to actively work against the other individual, to trip them up, as opposed to merely strengthening his or her own participation or ideas. When this occurs, it is particularly galling to the losing person for they believe the unfair process undercut their effort.

According to Adler, power is most often the decisive factor for winning, and can take the form of physical power, authority power, or intellectual power.[13]

Physical power is either the threatened or actual use of physical force. The implied justification is that might makes right.

A*uthority* power is used when someone who has a legitimate or recognized position expects or demands that his or her wishes be followed. This person may unilaterally determine what is to be done. Police, teachers, parents, and others have some authority power over some people in certain contexts. Organizational management people or business owners can hire and fire individuals. The conflict resolution strategy of the authoritative figure can be one-sided: my way or the highway. The figure may use the power of his or her office to *win* over you and you may have to do the authority's bidding or suffer further consequences.

Intellectual power can be seen in someone using their superior intellect, their intimate knowledge of a given subject, or their cleverness to outwit and overcome another person. This does not mean that you should not use your intelligence to secure the job you want, to help your team win the championship, to win the business contract, to convince a court to rule in your favor, and so on. You should use your intelligence to satisfy your needs and reach your personal goals. Yet, should you cleverly word an idea (weasel words) to your co-worker with whom you are having a conflict so you can fool them into thinking that you agree with them when you really do not? After a discussion with your spouse about what your family financial goals are, should you use your knowledge of math to trick your spouse into thinking that you are putting your *fair share* of money into the family budget, and then if they ever figure it out, claim a calculation mistake? This is knowingly taking advantage of the other person with one-sided, self-serving uses of intellectual power.

It is a fact of life that sometimes only one person will win, get the available job, and so on. In democratic decision making as it exists in legislatures, the majority vote normally wins. There is a winning side and a losing side. Majority rule voting by three siblings could have a similar outcome.

Second is the *Lose-Lose* strategy. Sometimes, both participants act in ways that lead to both of them losing. When neither side wins, both are obviously dissatisfied with the outcome. Two individuals trying to get the one job promotion could say derisive things about each other to management, which then decides not to promote either one because of their discordant communication. A married couple experiencing some differences could, not knowing about supportive communication (and the win-win steps to be covered) might well use defensive climate language, making both of their lives miserable, which in turn could lead to a divorce putting both of them in debt, and traumatizing their kids. Everyone loses.

Some win-lose situations become lose-lose, such as when the losing individual does things to undermine the winner. A losing associate could surreptitiously damage the winner's property, costing the winner money. An employee upset about not getting the managerial position could do something to undermine the success of the winning candidate. A disgruntled neighbor or spiteful ex-spouse could call up the IRS to say Bill or Maria has been cheating on income taxes (this may be the most common way the IRS catches tax cheats). In brief, losers may be successful in making apparent winners into losers, too.

Compromising is a common strategy in conflict resolutions and decision making, and often leads to a lose-lose outcome. Individuals may have good intentions and think that if both people give up some of their basic needs and if each achieves some of their goals, then it is even-Steven. Further, this strategy can speed up the negotiation phase and temporarily paper over some of the losses. People may figure that something is better than nothing (as if nothing was a real possibility). Still, if both people forgo satisfying some basic needs, then there are two losers.

Sometimes compromises may be the best available option. In these circumstances, according to Drucker, it is very important to begin with the "right" objectives. What conditions need be to met? What needs to be accomplished? "One has to start out with what is right rather than what is acceptable precisely because one always has to compromise in the end. But if one does not know what is right to satisfy the … conditions, one cannot distinguish between the right compromise and the wrong compromise—and will end up by making the wrong compromise."[14]

Notice that this strategy downplays people and personalities in an attempt to focus on goals.

Be cautious with people who say they will "compromise." This could easily be a one-sided, win-lose strategy for they could give up non-essential items while you give up essential ones. If some basic conditions cannot be met, ensure that both people have given up a similar amount of needs and both will have a similar quality and amount of needs satisfied.

Third is the *Win-Win* strategy. In this process, both or all people try to have each person's basic needs satisfied. Since everyone is different, conflict is bound to occur in all interpersonal relationships. With a win-win orientation, both work to see that each is satisfied. They do not try to win at the other's expense. We would expect to hear supportive communication, including provisionalism and problem orientation. Win-win does not mean that one or both people have to get everything they want (many people are confused about the difference between wants and needs) but they do have to be satisfied about the overall outcome. Two brothers might both want to use the computer at 3:30 PM but they obviously cannot. One uses it at 3:30 and the other at 4:30. The next conflicting time, the second brother uses the computer at 3:30 and the first brother at 4:30. They each got to use it an hour each day, but not always at the preferred time. Overall, they should be satisfied.

All problems, contexts, and people are unique so they need to be treated that way. When conflicts arise, the following communication guide gives those involved a method for resolving their differences. While the steps may seem mechanical, the interacting people will need a willingness to cooperate to increase the chance their minds will create more insights.

Win-Win Steps (adaptation from Adler and Rodman[15])

1. Clarify first to yourself how you are being harmed and reassess your needs and goals.
2. Make a date with the involved person/s to discuss it. Agree on an opportune time.
3. Describe to the other person how the situation is harming you and identify your unmet needs and goals. Ask them to summarize what you have said to confirm they understood.
4. Solicit the other person's view of the situation and their unmet needs/goals. Verify to the other person your understanding of their perception and needs. Use active listening.
5. Negotiate a solution. Both people should offer alternatives. Analyze their probability of satisfying each of your needs and goals. Agree on a solution within your capabilities.
6. After putting the solution into effect, verify that it resolves the problematic situation. Are the critical needs and goals of both of you being met? Adjust the solution if necessary.

Application of Win-Win Communication
Steps for Resolving Conflicts

To provide an application of these steps to a conflict, consider the following situation. Mary gets involved in a stamping group and ends up buying $1000 worth of stamps that are used to make personalized greeting cards. John notices on the IRA retirement statement that Mary has not been making her monthly contribution.

1. John mentally clarifies to himself what is occurring: "Mary is funding a hobby instead of her retirement account, which will later affect both of us. I have been making my contribution and did curtail purchasing high performance parts for my car. I want to feel secure about our retirement and know that each of us is doing our part."
2. John asks Mary, "Can we talk about our retirement accounts after dinner on Friday night?" Mary replies "Yes." On Friday night, he helps her make a nice dinner.
3. After Friday dinner, John says, "I'm upset and frustrated about you spending money on so many stamps rather than funding your retirement account that both of us will live on during retirement. Could you summarize what I've said?" Mary replies: "You're angry and disappointed that I've spent my retirement money on my stamps."
4. John asks Mary, "What is your perception of the situation?". She replies: "I'd gotten so involved in stamping that I didn't notice I'd overspent, leaving me with insufficient money to keep funding the IRA account. I'm sorry for doing this." John responds with active listening: "You regret spending so much on your stamping that you didn't have enough to put in your IRA account."
5. John and Mary both suggest solutions. Mary says: "I will temporarily stop buying stamps and going to the beauty parlor until I get caught up on my IRA account." John replies: "What if I help you color your roots since it's hard for you to do the rear of your head." They agree to this.
6. Four months later when Mary's IRA statement comes, she says, "This has worked out great. I'm all caught up." John replies, "I'll be glad to keep helping you with your hair." Mary: "Why don't I just borrow or trade for a few stamps with my friends and not buy any more. This way I can save the extra money for something special for both of us." "That's sweet," replies John.

There is no one right answer that will come from using these steps. Each person has to be clear about how they view the situation, communicate that to their partner, and then work with them to generate a solution that resolves the situation. If one or both people are reticent to discuss their finances, or if financial discussions tend to lead to unresolved conflicts, then a financial counselor can be used to help the couple talk about their money situation—both the communication part and the financial part. Couples having a disagreement are more spontaneous in this situation.

Adler offers a short list of criteria to help people in conflicts decide which type of conflict resolution response best fits which circumstance.[16]

1. Consider deferring to the other person:
   a. When you discover you are wrong.
   b. When the issue is more important to the other person than it is to you.
   c. To let others learn by making their own mistakes.
   d. When the long-term cost of winning may not be worth the short-term gain.
2. Consider compromising:
   a. When there is not enough time to seek a win-win outcome.
   b. When the issue is not important enough to negotiate at length.
   c. When the other person is not willing to seek a win-win outcome.
3. Consider competing:
   When the issue is important and the other person will take advantage of you.
4. Consider cooperating:
   a. When the issue is too important for a compromise.
   b. When a long-term relationship between you and the other person is important.
   c. When the other person is willing to co-operate.

CONCLUSION

In most interpersonal conflicts, people are dependent in some way on the other person. It is this interdependency that leads to conflict because each individual needs something at least a little bit different from the relationship than does the other individual, and existing resources for satisfying those desired needs and goals are probably limited. Thus, it is natural for any two people to have conflicts. This chapter listed some of the common misconceptions about conflicts, including that they are not necessarily counterproductive nor do they necessarily reveal a poor relationship. There are pluses and minuses to having a conflict with someone else. This chapter listed some common conflict styles and paired sets of conflict strategies. One strategy, Win-Win, was offered as an effective conflict resolution guideline. The chapter ended with some criteria for determining which conflict strategy may be most productive for a given situation.

CHAPTER 9 HOMEWORK #1
Analyzing A Conflict (adapted from Beebe, Beebe and Redmond[17])

Directions: Choose a recent conflict you had with someone and fill in the spaces below so you can trace its development and possible escalation. If this conflict is not yet resolved, create some possible solutions for it. Please do not reveal a conflict that would be considered *personal*, or very personal. Please create a fictitious name for the person with whom you are having a conflict, and omit references to Mom or Dad if your description of the conflict makes them look inept or ill-intentioned in any way (again, maintain personal privacy).

1. The existing conditions before the conflict arose: What is the source of the conflict?

   _____

   _____

2. Frustration awareness: When did you become aware of the conflict?

   _____

   _____

3. Active conflict: When and why did the conflict become an active conflict?

   _____

   _____

4. Resolution: Is there a resolution? If so, what is it? If not, what are some ways the conflict could be managed?

   _____

   _____

5. Follow-up: Is the conflict over? Do you still harbor some resentment? If so, what are strategies to help you manage the resentment?

   _____

   _____

CHAPTER 9 HOMEWORK #2
Conflict Content Areas

Directions: the following is a short list of content areas from which conflicts commonly arise. Add 5 other common but different content areas.

People try to control other people's lives or tell them how to live; people think they have a right to and attempt to get other people's money; they act as if they have a right to your property; they think their spouse's or partner's desire for sexual intimacy or acts thereof should match their own; they have ideas about who will perform the household chores; and people assume that other people should clean up after them.

Your list (5)

_____

_____

CHAPTER 9 HOMEWORK #3
Win-Win Steps (adapted from Adler and Rodman[18])

Directions: Apply the Win-Sine steps to one of the nine conflict situations provided on the following page (or a conflict assigned by your instructor) to the Win-Win steps below. You should use respectful and realistic dialogue between yourself and this other imaginary person. Be concise and ensure that statements made fit the appropriate steps. Use and follow exactly the numbers and letters of each step. Where possible, use *Supportive Climate* language or *I-messages* (see Chapter 8), as well as *Active Listening* (Chapter 5). All of the below is dialog.

1. In a dialogue with yourself, describe how someone/something is bothering you, how you are being harmed, and what your needs are. You are to "think out loud" here.

    _____

    _____

2. Make a date with the involved person/s to discuss it. Agree on a time suitable to each of you.
    a. You: _____
    b. Them: _____
    c. Agree: _____

3. Describe to the other person how the situation is harming you, and identify your unmet needs.

   Then ask the other person to summarize what you have said and have them do it.

   a. You:

   _____

   _____

   b. Them:

   _____

   _____

4. olicit the other person's view of the situation and their unmet needs. Then you use *Active Listening* to let them know you understand the other's feeling, perception, and needs.

   a. Them:

   _____

   _____

   b. You:

   _____

   _____

5. Negotiate a solution. First, each of you suggest personal, *specific actions* that have a high probability of meeting both of your needs. Next, agree on a solution. .

   a. Them:

   _____

   _____

   b. You:

   _____

   _____

   c. Agree on:

   _____

   _____

6. After putting the actions into effect, verbally verify later on that they resolve the situation.

   Are the critical needs of both of you being met? Adjust the solution as necessary.

   a. You:

_____

_____

b. Them:

_____

_____

Ch.9 Win-Win Homework Conflict Scenarios: **may be assigned for the Win-Win Homework.**

Directions: your instructor may assign one of the following conflict situations for you to use in completing the *Win-Win* Homework located on the previous page.

1. My boy/girlfriend has terrible eating manners. He/she eats with his/her mouth open, puts two successive bites of food into his/her mouth before chewing and swallowing and even adds more while chewing, he/she eats like a racehorse, licks his/her fingers and smacks his/her lips, he/she wipes his/her face with the back of his/her hand, his/her elbows are on the table, he/she leaves food pieces on glasses from which he/she drinks, and so on. Otherwise, he/she is very nice.
2. I am happily engaged. Unfortunately, my future mother-in-law presumes to tell us what to do for our wedding and expects us to go along with her. Incidentally, we are paying for everything. Both my fiancé and I are upset about this and want our wedding to be ours.
3. I have a barber/hairdresser/hair-cutting friend who does a great job at a reasonable price (even free). Still, he/she smokes when doing my hair. I do not like breathing the smoke or having my hair and clothes stink like cigarettes. I do not want to switch to another barber/hairdresser.
4. My sibling/roommate/boyfriend/girlfriend/spouse leaves our bedroom a mess, with dirty clothes on the floor, half-eaten food and food wrappers in the trashcan, and multiple piles of magazines and newspapers strewn about. I like a neat, clean, and organized living space, and I do not like picking or cleaning up after someone else.
5. I am a newlywed and am enjoying being married except for one small thing. Our bed is too hot for me so I like the electric blanket off. My spouse says it is too cold and wants the blanket control set high. One of us is always unhappy, and I am also unhappy when my spouse is.
6. My spouse and I have worked hard and scrimped to save enough money for a cabin on a lake that we occasionally use on weekends and every summer. My siblings and in-laws expect to use it whenever they desire, too. Sometimes my spouse and kids and I want to be alone at the cabin and we want to use it when it fits our schedule, not when it fits our family's schedule.

7. I am going to be married soon and just inherited $75,000 from a grand-parent. My spouse-to-be is a recent college graduate with $25,000 in school loans to repay. I love my spouse and do not want our money situations to create a rift between us (or why get married?), but I also think we should each act responsibly about our finances and not take advantage of the other.

8. My boy/girlfriend is invariably late when we go places, even on dates to a movie so we miss the opening scenes. I show up at his/her house on time but he/she is rarely ready. I hate for this to continue but he/she is otherwise a fine person, really seems to love me, and treats me nice.

9. My boyfriend/girlfriend/spouse is continually looking at, texting, or speaking on his/her cell phone (going with me down the street, in the car, during dinner, watching TV, and in bed). It is as if we have no peace, quiet, or privacy, and his/her attention is elsewhere.

REFERENCES

1. T. Sowell, *A Conflict of Visions: Ideological Origins of Political Struggles* (New York: Basic Books, 2002).
2. J. Gibb, "Defensive Communication." *Journal of Communication*, 11 (September, 1961).
3. S. Beebe, S. Beebe and M. Redmond, *Interpersonal Communication: Relating to Others* (2nd ed.) (Boston: Allyn and Bacon, 1999).
4. M. Burgoon M. Ruffner, *Human Communication* (New York: Holt, Rinehart and Winston, 1978), p. 498.
5. J. DeVito, *Human Communication: The Basic Course* (10th ed.) (Boston: Pearson Education, Inc., 2006).
6. M. Scott and S. Brydon, *Dimensions of Communication: An Introduction* (Mountain View, CA: Mayfield Publishing Company, 1997).
7. DeVito, op cit.
8. A. Wolvin and C. Coakley, *Listening* (5th ed.) (Boston: McGraw Hill, 1996).
9. Ibid.
10. Gibb, op cit.
11. Gibb, op cit.
12. R. Adler and G. Rodman, *Understanding Human Communication* (10th ed.) (New York: Oxford University Press, 2009).
13. Ibid.
14. P. Drucker with J. Meciariello, *The Daily Drucker* (New York: HarperBusiness, 2004), p. 303.
15. Adler and Rodman, op cit.
16. Ibid, p. 220.
17. Beebe et al., op cit.
18. Adler and Rodman, op cit.

CHAPTER TEN

Small Group and Organizational Communication

Inevitably, people have to interact and work with people as members of a group or even as part of a larger organization. Most people are or have been part of a family, a sports team, a school study group, a neighborhood association, a community or church group, and a work group, among others. It is around and through these groups that we live much of our lives. They enable us to achieve both individual and community goals. The group processes and the outcomes provide us with the means of and reasons for living. On one hand, group experiences can be very frustrating, but on the other hand, they be can be highly satisfying and enervating.

SMALL GROUP

A small group varies in size from three to about 13 interdependent members who know each other and share goals, patterns of behavior, and communicate, usually face-to-face, over time.

Group communication activities can be separated into two broad categories: those that primarily exist to satisfy our desire for social interaction and those that exist primarily to achieve some task.

People are largely social beings so many want to join groups to satisfy a basic desire for human bonds and a sense of belonging.. With relationships comes assistance and affection. People enjoy the company of the members of the groups to which they belong.. Most people have informal groups of friends and some even join community or religious social groups.

People also join groups to achieve some task apart from the personal interaction of group members. They have more clearly defined structures and rules to follow than do relationship groups. They usually get paid for their tasks, such as brewing and selling coffee, assembling computers, selling telephones, teaching elementary school students, and so on. They seek to solve an immediate problem or accomplish a long-term goal. A community group may organize itself to build a park. A telecommunications company may exist to make a profit by selling telephone and Internet connections and time. A government agency may exist to ensure the local environment is not polluted.

Certainly there is some overlap between the two broad groups for many people develop friendship groups at work, socializing together on the company basketball team on their time off, and many relationship groups accomplish tasks such as painting a house together or participating in a charity fundraiser. Since these two groups exist primarily for different purposes, the communication occurring in them exhibits some differences. More directions and commands are given and accepted in task groups such as private businesses while more requests are made of people in relationship groups. While commands are common in families, at some point many members will leave a family for personal independence. If someone in a social group tells someone else what to do, the receiver may readily refuse and, if necessary, quit the group. Overall, most of us are or have been members in both types of groups and participated in the communication peculiar to those groups.

FUNCTIONAL COMMUNICATION ROLES IN GROUPS

Benne suggests that the enacting of certain group member roles help groups accomplish their goals.[1] The author identified three general, informal (non-assigned) categories of roles common in group communication. Individual group member's activities within each of the three categories can be identified by the communication that he or she performs, as indicated by the role label. The three general functions and groupings of roles are as follows.

A. Group Task Roles

These emphasize communication that helps the group members define the problem facing the group and reaching a solution for that problem. While some group members may do none of the tasks, the leader and other members may carry out more than one. They may vary what they do in different meetings and in the different groups to which they belong.

1. *Initiator-Contributor.* This person contributes ideas to the group discussion or gives a new point of view to pre-existing ideas. He or she may propose an explanation of the problem facing the group, offer a solution, suggest a

new group goal, or propose a new procedure for the group to follow. "I think the public will like our proposed service," or "What if we contact the Student Government Association to find out if it would back our proposal?"

2. *Information Seeker.* This person asks others for information or for an explanation of facts provided. He or she may specify what information the group lacks so it can make an informed decision. "Joe, did you find out whether the property transfer was completed?" or "We need to know how many students are coming before we can place an order with the caterer."

3. *Opinion seeker.* This individual asks other members for their unsubstantiated conclusions, to explain their opinions, or to express how they feel about some aspect of the group activity. "Suze, what direction do you think the U.S. stock market is headed in the short term?"

4. *Information Giver.* This individual provides the group with data. "The Student Government Association requested that the school charge an internet fee to every student and thereby provide the service at a significantly reduced rate to each student.'

5. *Opinion Giver.* This person states their assessment about the topic under discussion and may even tell the group what its orientation to the task should be. "I think we ought to offer the students a choice of tuition payment plans."

6. *Elaborator.* This individual clarifies the comments and ideas being presented so members can have a similar understanding, and may suggest the ramifications of proposed solutions. "If we shorten the payment plan to three months from five months, the indications are that 10-20% of the students will be unable to meet the payment guideline and drop out of school."

7. *Coordinator.* This person organizes and integrates the group members' stated facts, opinions, and suggested solutions, and may arrange the group's activities. "The administration says that two hundred students will receive diplomas. Diana thinks we only need 170 seats at commencement since 15% of the graduates do not attend the ceremony. Joan thinks we should have a contingency plan to add another row of chairs just before the ceremony begins. Americorps students could be asked to stand by the entrance door with fifteen chairs and put them out on Julie's instruction."

8. *Orienter.* This person summarizes the group proceedings and keeps track of the group progress toward its goals. He or she tells the group the

direction it is headed and attempts to keep it on track toward its goals. "At this point, we are still less than one-half way toward our goal of adding one hundred new customers and we only have one week left. Can we alter our strategy to increase our sales?"

9. *Evaluator-Critic.* This individual critiques the strengths and weaknesses of the group's proposed solutions and possibly the logic for the decisions. Sometimes called "the devil's advocate," this person may question the practicality of the proposed actions. The evaluator-critic is often disliked since people do not like to have their ideas criticized. Many people are afraid to question a superior's ideas for fear of being demoted or fired. On the other hand, if a group does not analyze the strengths and weaknesses of its ideas, it is very likely to agree to unsupported decisions that lead to poor results. "On one hand, the new product is only *projected* to earn the company fifteen million dollars the first year. On the other, if the product fails, the company will go bankrupt. We are in a recession so the hoped-for results are very suspect."

10. *Energizer.* This is someone who encourages the group to keep on working and complete what they are doing. "We only have a little time left but we can do it. Let us all pull together."

11. *Procedural Technician.* This individual suggests to the group that they follow the procedures given to them, or that they use a specific procedure if it will help the group progress toward a solution. This person also may perform routine tasks, such as ensure that everyone has a seat and the necessary materials. "Mary, do you want to table that decision until we know what Bob will do?" or "You have the set of earning projections I copied for you."

12. *Recorder.* This person records the minutes of the meeting, keeping track of the group's activities, major ideas suggested, and decisions made. This is important later if someone needs to clarify a misunderstanding, and it keeps track of the group progress toward achieving its goals. "At this point, four of you are for the decision, three are against it, and one is undecided."

B. Group Building and Maintenance Roles

These communication activities help keep the group working together (maintenance). They are the means by which people build interpersonal companionship and a group-centered attitude. If this maintenance communication occurs, people are not so defensive and they are more willing to work together as a team.

1. *Encourager.* This individual commends and expresses gratitude for member contributions even if the encourager does not agree with what is said. The encourager uses positive reinforcement. "Good point, Sasha. We overlooked the need for faculty support."

2. *Harmonizer.* This member resolves conflict when it occurs, getting members to agree and work together in peace. In brief, settling differences between members to reduce tension. "Each of you have a different plan of action but each of you do agree that the Student Center should get priority. Is there some way to integrate your plans?"

3. *Compromiser.* This person tries to settle differences by offering concessions when his or her ideas are at odds with someone else; trying to get along to help keep the group together. "I'll agree to meet you halfway by working late every other day. Is that okay?"

4. *Gate-Keeper.* This individual attempts to keep the "gates" open between people. They have control over information coming to them and this is shared with the group. They also encourage other members to share with the group the information they have. While the content of the information is necessary, everyone needs to feel like they are part of the group so they have to share the information they have to enable the group to make the best decision. "I want everyone to know what I found out today ...." "Shasta, could you share with everyone what you know about this situation?"

5. *Standard Setter.* This person asks the group to abide by certain guidelines, either previously created or formed by the present group. This includes deciding what time and place meetings will be held, how the group will make its decisions, what to do when people are late or miss a meeting, and so on. This person is not making the standard, but asking that the group follow pre-existing ones or create ones that suit it. "Is everyone supposed to get a chance to speak? If so, Bill has not had an opportunity." "Are decisions going to be made by majority rule? If so, how few members need to be here for a quorum so the decisions made can count?"

6. *Group Observer and Commentator.* This member watches the group proceeding and then shares his or her perceptions of what is going on in the group. This provides an assessment of how the group is operating so the group can decide if it wants to continue doing what it has done or change some of its actions. "It appears that the group is unsure about how to fund the project. There are both pro and con statements of doing it. Further, only

one-half of the group is talking so we do not even know what the rest are thinking."

7. *Follower*. Groups have to have people who will go along with the decisions the groups reach. The downside is that passive followers simply accept what the group decides rather than being a critical listener and speaker. While passive responses do *maintain* the group, they do not reveal strong, committed agreement. "If that is what you guys want to do, that is fine with me."

C. Individual (counterproductive) Roles

We might presume that not every communication role enacted is productive. There are a number of communication activities that satisfy the individual person's needs but work against the achievement of the group goals. When this occurs, group output and group relationships are diminished.

1. *Aggressor*. We know from the previous chapter that aggression usually encourages defensive communication, not supportive communication. Aggressive people go over the line in criticizing other people's ideas and personality and minimizing their status in the group. Aggressive people promote themselves as being so smart and capable. "You guys don't know what you're doing. This is kindergarten stuff. Let me handle it."

2. *Blocker*. This member verbally opposes other people's ideas and makes disparaging comments about proposed actions. They do not mind holding up the group's progress and insist on having their own way. "You can if you want to, but I am not going to compromise my values. There is only one thing to do and it is not your crazy idea."

3. *Recognition-Seeker*. This individual gets the group to waste its time looking at him or her rather than work toward its goals. This person could get recognition by boasting about previous accomplishments or by telling people that he or she deserves the credit for the current group achievements. He or she would also brag about doing some task so well while other people in the group did poorly. "What can I say? I had a good month. I pulled the team through. I'm leading the team in every batting category."

4. *Self-Confessor*. Like the recognition seeker, this person gets the group to turn its attention away from completing its task to focus on him or her. He or she gives irrelevant, personal sob stories so group members will feel sorry.

"I can't help that I'm late. I had to stay up all night with my baby, then the car didn't start this morning. After I got a new battery I got stuck in traffic. Then the daycare called to say my baby was crying. Maybe they should have fed her."

5. *Playboy* (or playgirl). Most groups appreciate a little levity once in awhile but some members play around and joke so much that it interferes with meetings. This behavior suggests that the individual is not very involved with the group activity. "Jojean, tell the group what we did last Friday night after work. We closed that place. Left the Office at 12 PM. Great wine."

6. *Dominator.* This member is authoritative like some bosses can be as he or she tries to control the group time. He or she often talks on and on and interrupts if they want to control the discussion. "That ain't right, Sid. Let me tell you how it goes. It was about the time I went to college in California when we played video games on and on for days. You wouldn't have believed it. Anyway, I decided that I...."

7. *Special Interest Pleader.* This individual has his or her own private goals to achieve, not the groups. He or she earnestly argues for some action that purportedly fits the group's purpose but actually benefits a single person, a few undeserving people, or a particular organization at odds with the group's purpose. If the group supports the special interest pleader and the public later finds out, some of the supporters may be criticized.

Notice that special interest pleaders have a *hidden agenda* or ulterior motive for doing something that suits their own purposes, so they need to keep it secret or the group is likely to go against them. For example, a non-local politician seeking re-election may propose: "I think the indigenous people here deserve some protection and some special concessions. They have suffered for years. Fishing is their birthright, anywhere, anytime, including in protected waters." The hidden agenda is to get the votes of the indigenous voters during the next election.

Members enacting individual roles are commonly found in groups. Other members will have to work around them or get them to minimize their interference. Too many of these self-centered individuals in a group can drastically curtail the group achievement.

Benne suggests that groups in different stages of dealing with different problems may need more of some of the communication roles and less of other ones, so do not assume that all of the roles have to be manifest at the same time and used to the same degree.[2]

PRODUCTIVE WORK ENVIRONMENT

The physical environment and the communication climate influence the group's production.

1. *The Physical Environment.* This includes (among others) the room size, color, lighting, furniture placement, and seating arrangements. The *seating arrangement* is particularly influential on the interpersonal interaction between members and is something that group members can readily alter. With a *rectangular table* and the head person sitting at one end while the members sit on both long sides, only those people sitting directly opposite each other can easily communicate with each other. The person directing the communication is indirectly sitting off to their left or right and no one has a good, clear view of everyone,. This make it difficult for members to easily face and be close to the people they may desire to speak with, which increases the chance that they will not speak unless directly spoken to. Overall, communication is constrained. People sitting around a *square table* can most easily speak with those sitting directly across from them or to those who are at an angle to their immediate right or left side People sitting side-by-side rarely speak to one another about the group issue. Overall, there is an easier dialog between more members than when sitting at a rectangular table. An *informal* seating arrangement like might be found in someone's living room will probably bunch up a few members on a coach while the other members sit in clusters or singularly at random distances to the left, right, or opposite the couch. Mini-groups will form, with the people in clusters more easily speaking with each other. Overall group interaction is unlikely to occur.[3] In a *circle* seating arrangement, everyone can see everyone else so they have equal status. This provides the most ease for most members to speak with one another, so there is greater communication participation. As in the other arrangements, members are less likely to speak with people seated directly on their right or left sides.

2. *Communication Climate. Climate* refers to the intangible emotional atmosphere that group members sense in their interaction and work environment. Goldhaber describes communication climate as the "perceptions employees have of the quality of relationships and communication in the organization and of the degree of involvement and influence."[4] Members get a sense about which types of communication are and are not allowed so their behavior is altered in the group. The climate could be task-oriented but receptive to a small amount of jokes and laughter at the start of a meeting; the

climate could be foreboding and discourage any communication input from the members; the climate could be informal so as to allow members the use of first names when referring to each other, and so on.

According to Likert, organizational members perceive their relationships and experience as *supportive* when these elements help build or continue his or her own sense of individual significance and merit.[5] Supervisory personnel in the organization help provide a supportive climate when they exhibit the following characteristics:

> ... friendly ... helpful ... kind but firm, never threatening, genuinely interested in the well-being of subordinates and endeavors to treat people in a sensitive, considerate way. He is just, if not generous. He endeavors to serve the best interests of his employees as well as of the company.

> He shows confidence in the integrity, ability, and motivations of subordinates rather than suspicion and distrust.

> His confidence in subordinates leads him to have high expectations [of their] ... performance.

> He coaches and assists employees whose performance is below standard.[6]

A supervisor could also create a supportive climate by using the supportive-type communication suggested by Gibb[7] noted in Chapter 8: description, equality, spontaneity, provisionalism, empathy, and problem orientation.

To further enhance the group environment, Verderber suggests that groups create a sense of communication equality,[8] with all group members asked and allowed to participate in the discussions, and form everyone to listen to each member when they speak. Further, the group has to value each member's contribution (sincerely thank them for their input and attempt to incorporate their ideas into the problem solving discussion). Verderber concludes, "People will not participate if they fear personal attack; if they believe that their ideas will be belittled, ridiculed, or discounted, or if they feel that no one will intervene to allow their ideas to be heard."[9] If this latter climate exists, it is largely the fault of group leaders.

Both the physical circumstances and the communication climate influence and are influenced by each other as they create a favorable, not favorable, or somewhere in between environment in which the group members work. A number of productive communication elements have been provided which can, if applied, increase member production.

EFFECTIVE MEMBER COMMUNICATION

Certain communication behaviors by group members increase the chance that the group will achieve its goals.

1. *Communicate (and work) For The Group's Good.* It may seem so obvious as to not need stating, but be a team player. Ask yourself how you need to talk, about what, in what way to enable the group to reach its goals. Tell others what you know about the subject. Seek information that the group needs so it can make an informed decision. Unfortunately, it can be difficult to continue being a team player when other members try to fulfill their hidden agendas, but it can still be done and the group can be a success despite the self-centered followers.

An example of someone who worked and communicated for the good of the group is Bill Russell who played for the NBA Boston Celtics for 13 seasons from 1957-1969. During this time he and his teammates won 11 NBA championships (he was also selected 12 seasons to the All-Star Team and was the league's most valuable player 5 times). CNN/*Sports Illustrated* called him "… the greatest team player ever …." According to Russell, " …I decided early in my career the only really important thing is to win games. I wanted my career to be such that people would say, *He won championships*, and that's a historical fact …." In answer to a question about the qualities he admired in other players, Russell replied, "To watch skilled players use their skills to help their team win." "Oh yeah, [it's all about winning.] That's why they keep score. If it wasn't about that, you could substitute ballet for basketball because there's no goal—you're just making the moves."[10] Working in groups, the reader should expect to find some group members just "making the moves" with their mouths and their behavior, not helping the group achieve its goal.

2. *Focus On Results, Not People.* Emphasize the desired outcomes and how they might be achieved rather than on so-called people personalities (e.g,, "He's uptight."). As discussed in the previous two chapters, people respond more favorably to supportive communication than to defensive-arousing communication. Even if people dislike people they have to work with, this does not mean their co-worker's comments are a personal attack. Previous chapters in this textbook have provided methods of supportive communicating. If members get defensive without having a good reason, it will increase group tension and create a barrier to the group reaching its goals. If someone thinks your idea is a weak one, ask them why that is (who knows, maybe you will discover they do not have a good explanation).

3. *Be Objective.* Before jumping to conclusions as our minds are want to do, attempt to withhold judgment about a situation until a variety of members have offered their different points of view. According to Cragan, "Ideally, groups should only reach conclusions that have been rationally accepted by the group's members."[11] Differentiate between facts and opinions. Consider making provisional statements that make it easier for you and the rest of the group to critique the statements. Recognize that your own ideas will not always be the best ideas, so if you are going to be a team player and committed to the task, you will want to support the best ideas regardless of their source.

4. *Seek Group Decision Agreement.* Members tend to be more committed to decisions if they believe that their ideas have been fairly examined by the other members. Further, they will also be more dedicated if they agree that the decision agreed upon is the best one on which they can all agree.[12] When a group is committed to some action, it can quickly begin the action and be steadfast in completing it. The drawback to seeking consensus is that it takes a lot of time to get every member's input. If there is still no agreement, the group may attempt to put the proposed solution to a majority vote, which then creates some losers who may impede the progress.

5. *Verify Understanding.* Seek feedback, use active listening, observe the nonverbal communication, and be descriptive. It is insufficient to ask someone else if something you said was clear, for if they simply say, "Yes" or "I got it," you do not know what they "got. Ask them to briefly summarize what you said and what they think you meant by it. We, as listeners, help ensure understanding with our active listening so the speakers will know what we know.

6. *Beware of Groupthink.* Groupthink refers to unified group thought and agreement about a subject, revealing a lack of independent and contrasting ideas or courses of action. Group members respond to an issue in unison, self-censoring any discrepant personal thoughts, and do not debate or question each other's ideas. Members show high group cohesion and loyalty to each other. The group members act as if there is *a* group point of view, sometimes one pushed by the leader. What is the problem with groupthink? A narrow, simplistic, and parochial understanding of a given subject, and lacking objectivity and rationality, this will lead to an irrelevant and ineffective decision, doomed to failure.

Not all groups reflect groupthink, but different features of it are common, illustrated by the following statements: "go along with the boss," "go along to get along," "don't make waves," "don't worry, we know what we're doing," "We've got it all figured out," and "We have the moral high ground." Cragan reports that the more group members are friendly with each other and de-voted to a cause, the increased chance that their independent, critical thinking will be diminished and they will create illogical decisions.[13] If everyone is or seems to be thinking alike, it suggests that no one is doing any thinking.

To avoid groupthink, Janis recommends that the leader should assign ev-ery member to be a critical evaluator of the ideas presented, the leader should avoid advancing his or her own point of view but allow the group to have an open inquiry about it, the organization should create several groups to inde-pendently examine the problem situation and later combine their findings, , and members should occasionally discuss the group's status and positions with knowledgeable, trusted, non-group associates to get an outsider's view of the group proceedings.[14] Overall, groups need to encourage disagreements about ideas, assigned different members to act as devil's advocates, critique the pros and cons of every proposal, and do not let the leader dominate the group. Implemented decisions based upon untested and unchallenged ideas are usually found to be weak.

THE LEADERSHIP-COMMUNICATION CONNECTION

Leaders, as opposed to managers, establish is a direction for the group and a vision of what the group can become, and then communicate that vi-sion to the group members so they will cooperate with each other and with the leader to achieve that vision. According to Bennis, leaders have to be able to *articulate* their ideas, for if they cannot explain them to the group, then the leader will not get the members to work with him or her to reach the leader's, and ultimately, the group's, goals.[15] The leader has to make the group's mission understandable, has to convince the members to accept it, has to clearly explain how to correctly do a variety of tasks associated with accomplishing that vision,[16] and then has to repeatedly inspire the members with his or her communication to produce the change that is needed to achieve the vision. In short, the leader has to be an effective communicator. Thus, without setting the direction for the group and then communicating both what the group can become and how the group can achieve its goal, there is no leader.

Manager and other supervisory personnel are needed, for they organize and plan the work of group members, but they are not leaders.[17] Incidentally, as Phillips concluded after having observed hundreds of managers and super-visors in business organizations for many years, he "… can count on one hand the number of real leaders among them. Many of these men and women are corrupted by power; most tend to pressure or dictate when simple suggestions or recommendations would suffice."[18]

One political leader who gained a reputation as an effective leader was World War II (and during a period in the 1950's) Prime Minister of England, Winston Churchill. His vision, masterly communicated through his speeches, that England would prevail against all odds when Hitler and Nazi Germany were very close to defeating England, made all the difference.[19] According to Brendon, a biographer of Churchill:

> Churchill's greatest single contribution to the war was his oratory—the speeches he made while Germany was winning the battle of France and losing the battle of Britain. As President Kennedy remarked, he mobilized the resources of the English language, proving that the word was mightier than the sword.
>
> Never had a British leader so galvanized the nation by sheer force of rhetoric.[20]

Contrary to the idea that a leader should tailor his or her message to fit a particular listener or audience, Giuliani recommends that the leader "... present it so that it can be understood by whomever you're addressing. The goal should be to ensure your message gets through loud and clear to as many people as possible."[21] Since actions can speak louder than words, sometimes a leader should let his or her actions do the talking.

A more recent example of a leader communicating a vision is exemplified in the turn-around story of Continental Airlines beginning in 1995 after it had gone through three bankruptcies. Bethune suggests that leadership is "... to assemble the right team, set the big picture direction, communicate that, then *get out of the way.*"[22]

Additional Communication Skills and Qualities of Effective Leaders

1. *Sticks To His or Her Word.* This creates a sense of trust in the leader and encourages commitment in the followers to the leader's message.

2. *Is Tactful.* When necessary, carefully criticizes people's behavior, not their character.

3. *Tells Subordinates The Truth.* Increased respect and support results, even if the news is bad.[23]

4. *Admits Mistakes.* Be human; take responsibility. This reduces conflict by not blaming others and it increases believability with the group by conceding deficiencies.[24]

5. *Is An Effective Public Speaker.* This need is discussed above in the section defining leadership. Skilled extemporaneous speaking and storytelling are persuasive.

6. *Persuades Rather Than Forces.* Influence members with a friendly, open manner. Once coercion is used, the leader abandons leadership and becomes a dictator.[25]

7. *Listens Actively.* Genuinely listens and responds to members' needs and wishes.

8. *Fosters An Open Communication Climate.* Encourages subordinates to openly share their different problem-solving ideas, perspectives, and opinions.

9. *Gives Credit.* Publicly commends those who have helped achieve the group goals.[26]

10. *Is Consistent.* Communication is a package of signals so the leader has to responsibly guide his or her personal emotions to give everyone the same message.

11. *Humor Is A Plus* (not a necessity). An agreeable demeanor reduces group tension and takes the "edge" off the seriousness of required actions[27] and aids persuasion.

On this last point about humor, Johnson claims that both Lincoln and Reagan effectively used humor during their presidencies, particularly Reagan after he was shot and wounded in an attempted assassination. As he "… was in considerable pain and was wheeled into surgery, he said to the anxious team of doctors: 'I hope you're all Republicans [like I am].' And when his wife was first allowed to be at his side: 'Honey, I forgot to duck.'"[28]

LEADERSHIP STYLE COMMUNICATION

Another influence on group communication is the leadership style employed, generally categorized as being authoritarian, democratic, or laissez-faire. By listening to the group leader's communication, you can form a pretty accurate idea about which of the three different leadership styles he or she is primarily using.[29]

1. *Authoritarian Leader Communication.* The term *leader* is used loosely here since an autocratic or authoritarian head person does not fit the definition of "leader" provided previously in this chapter. The authoritarian's style of communication consists of giving orders, using one-way communication to direct all communication to and from him or herself while hampering or even preventing communication between group members. The leader

communicates to control and dominate discussions with group members; attempts to direct people in completing their tasks, rarely gives positive feedback; and uses poor listening. The leader requires absolute obedience to his or her authority, as opposed to individual freedom and group interaction. Obedience to the leader is rewarded and mistakes are punished. The authoritarian leader acts like a lone boss and minimizes relationships with group members. This leader decides what group members will do without seeking information or advice from them.

Ironically, with a leader skilled in the product or service provided by the group, the group may be highly efficient since solutions are reached relatively quickly by the leader, which in turn allows work production to increase.[30] Conversely, group members tend to be more hostile with each other and feel less personally satisfied with the outcome due to their small amount of participation. The authoritarian leadership style generally works best when "Group agreement is not required for implementation, [t]he group is very large, [t]ime for a decision is short [and] [t]asks are fairly simple."[31] This leadership style is ill-suited to organizations which operate in a highly dynamic environment for, as Lippmann suggests, "... the official cannot issue new commandments as fast as the inventors can invent. If he bases his decrees on yesterday's process, he must either suppress tomorrow's process or he must connive at disorder. The introduction of new methods cannot be coercively planned and directed."[32]

As the United States government increases in size and power over American citizens' everyday life (the Obama Administration health care bill is just one recent increase), citizens should expect more authoritarian leadership from the government (including Pres. Bush's Internet spying on Americas (continued and growing under Pres. Obama) and Pres. Obama's executive orders changing the health care law—a legislative function, as well as public statements by him that he would not enforce a marijuana law and a marriage law). According to Lippmann, "... the intellectuals who expound what now passes for 'liberalism,' 'progressivism,' or 'radicalism' are almost all collectivists in their conception of the economy, *authoritarians* (emphasis added) in their conception of the state, totalitarians in their conception of society."[33] This does not bode well for Americans who prefer the freedom and personal responsibility provided by an explicit, textual reading of the U.S. Constitution

2. Democratic Leader Communication. This type of leader gives some direction but encourages the group members to collaborate in setting goals and determining how to reach those goals. There is an effort to improve decision making by facilitating the communication between members so they will combine their knowledge. The leader provides suggestions for completing the task, rewards members' good work, and provides feedback about the group performance. The leader attempts to be good listener. Democratic communication has some drawbacks though, such as taking more time to accomplish a task (all that preliminary talk) and it is more difficult to execute than the other two leadership styles. Still, since members have greater participation in the decision-making process, more of their creative ideas can be shared and utilized, and they are more committed to accomplishing the group tasks. Hamilton suggests that the democratic leadership style generally works best when: "[g]reater employee satisfaction is needed, [g]roup commitment is needed for implementation, [t] asks are complicated and require lengthy discussion, [i]ncreased productivity is needed [and] [r]educed resistance to change is sought."[34]

3. *Laissez-Faire Leader Communication*. In some groups, the leader offers little or no direction for setting goals and procedures, thereby becoming a non-leader. Group members are left to their own devices and discretion as they work toward some largely indefinite and non-agreed upon goals. The communication is characterized by: indecisiveness and triviality from the leader, an avoidance of leader-member discussions, leader suggestions only when sought for by the members, infrequent leader feedback, infrequent or no leader rewards or punishment, and leader listening that runs the gamut from weak to good. Group members may enjoy the satisfaction of freely setting and satisfying their own goals but group cohesiveness and direction will probably be lacking so the group will be inefficient.

Former President Reagan may have been thought of as a laissez-faire leader since he did not involve himself in as much White House day-to-day affairs and in-fighting as did most presidents, but Noonan, who wrote speeches for him, found that everyone who worked for him knew his policies and the direction he wanted the country to go.[35]

4. *Leadership Style Effectiveness*. People might naturally suppose that the democratic leadership style is best and attempt to use the communication from that orientation in most situations they face. Hamilton cautions us about this assumption: "Selecting the wrong leadership style can result in an unnecessary waste of time, unacceptable solutions, unhappy or hostile employees, and resistance instead of commitment to an idea."[36]

Rather, each leadership style can be effective, depending on the situation and the qualities of the group members. When there are emergencies, the authoritarian style is very useful, but this does not mean that groups cannot have democratic style discussion in advance. When group members are skilled and motivated and working in an environment that has little change, the laissez-faire style can be effective, as it also can in community social groups that cannot order people around.. If a relatively fast-changing environment exists, requiring constant change and adaptation, and many members are on the job equals, the democratic leadership style will be needed for members to share ideas and coordinate their activities.

In summary of the above discussion about leaders and communication, certain leadership characteristics have been found to be effective for groups. Additionally, they tend to be what can be termed *group-centered*. As Likert concludes, "[g]ood communication and high performance go together."[37] This is why we need such communication from our leaders.

COMMUNICATION FLOW IN SMALL GROUPS AND ORGANIZATIONS

1. *The Serial Nature of Communication.* A message travels from one person to another, who then relays it to another, and so on. As we can observe in our own experience, most communication travels in this manner, the message going from one family member or co-worker or neighbor to the next. The message is reproduced as it is communicated from person to person until it stops with the final person. On each occasion as it is transmitted, some message details are omitted, others are distorted, new ones are added, some receive more emphasis and others less, and indefinite statements can become definite and definite ones become qualified..

The problem with such communication is that the message gets *distorted* along the way, with an increased probability of distortion the more times it is reproduced. People may then act on the basis of those distortions, leading to outcomes unrelated to the original message, and harmful to certain people, as well.

2. *Communication Networks.* Who speaks to whom, and how often? As a group develops over time, patterns are formed reflecting the flow or direction of communication between members, which in turn influence group productivity, cohesiveness, and member satisfaction.

Figure 10.1

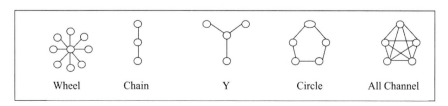

| Wheel | Chain | Y | Circle | All Channel |

The most common networks can be visualized and labeled as: the wheel (a center hub with spokes protruding outward), the chain, the Y, the circle, and the all-channel (a circle with internal lines, as well, criss-crossing within the outer circle), each with nodules representing people positioned along the lines. Depending on the existing network, members are able to communicate with certain other members.

The wheel, the chain, and the Y patterns reveal that individuals only speak to the person next to them on one side or the other so their sharing of information is limited, as is their influence over the entire group. These are highly centralized patterns since the person (typically the leader, or boss) in the middle or at the intersections is able to exert the greatest control over the flow of messages between members. Organizations such as the military, and to some extent universities, with different levels of command, have a centralized communication flow. Messages are supposed to flow from level to level and not skip any. A teacher might speak to a department chair, who speaks to an associate dean, who speaks to a dean, who speaks to a vice-president, who then speaks to the school president (or in the reverse order). On shared governance and faculty-union matters, universities emulate the all channel network. The Y-pattern solves group problems faster than the other patterns and has the fewest errors,[38] but it has the lowest group morale, a feature which was also noted about those serving under an authoritarian leader. Since the leader position person is very involved initiating and controlling so much communication, they have high moral. The wheel network is also fast since the central person simply has to speak to and is answered by each individual, which also made it the most accurate since there is no serial communication. On the other hand, the person at the center of the wheel is susceptible to information overload which can result in slow response times to information and the resultant missed opportunities to act.[39]

The circle and all-channel networks are decentralized since no one person controls all the flow and direction of communication. In the all-channel pattern, anyone may communicate with anyone else. These channels reflect high member morale, and as under the democratic leader style, they are effective for solving complex problems requiring a sharing of information. They just take more time in completing the problem solving.

Which communication network is the most effective? It depends on the complexity of the task and the time available. According to Goldhaber, "The decentralized network was found to solve complex problems not only faster, but with fewer errors than do other networks,"[40] while centralized networks are more effective for simple tasks. The all-channel network reports the highest level of satisfaction amongst its members,[41] while centralized networks report the lowest satisfaction.

PROBLEM-SOLVING DISCUSSIONS

Groups exist to resolve a problematic situation. Decisions have to be made. Even social groups exist to provide solutions for loneliness, boredom, lack of companionship, and so on, with the solution being some sort of fun or stimulating activity that brings people together and creates personal relationships. Since problem solving and the decision making incorporated in it are very common occurrences in stand-alone groups and within organizations, a general problem-solving guide is provided here.

According to Dewey,[42] individuals that follow a systematic guide for solving problems have an increased likelihood of both understanding the problems they face and creating more effective solutions for those problems. Although Dewey's *reflective thinking* guide[43] was meant to illustrate the general mental steps that his students (and people) followed in trying to individually solve problems, this guide has been adopted as a systematic tool for groups to use when discussing and attempting to solve problems.

Reflective thinking meant that people should think about and evaluate their thinking as they think so they can improve their thinking. This step-by-step procedure may be derided as being linear and non-representational of how people actually think but Dewey points out that people's thoughts do not follow this strict, step-by-step pattern.[44] Thoughts naturally jump back and forth between the steps he describes. He suggests that people initially familiarize themselves with the steps so the steps become, in effect, second nature. Then, as thinking about a problem occurs, the individual will "remember" to process thoughts that reflect each of the steps, thereby being systematic.

Brilhart reports of research support for groups using a systematic problem-solving guide: "One of the most common complaints about [group] discussions is that they are *not* organized, but jump back and forth among issues. Two recent studies have shown that perceived quality of discussions is related to how systematically they appear to have been organized."[45] Further, the author reports that those who are most successful in solving problems follow clearly defined steps when they attempt to solve such problems.

Reflective Thinking Sequence Decision-Making Guide

1. *Awareness of a Felt Difficulty*. Something seems to be wrong. Avoid jumping to conclusions. Gather relevant evidence about the situation. Describe the status quo. Be open-minded.

2. *Definition of the Difficulty*. Attempt a detailed explanation of the problem. Carefully judge the available evidence. [author's note: the term *problem* can be confusing so it is recommended that *problem* be followed by *outcome*

when the user refers to an unwanted, harmful effect, and the term *cause* be used when referring to a cause] Analyze and synthesize.

3. *Possible Solutions.* Create a variety of alternative solutions for the defined problem.

4. *Rational Elaboration of the Possible Solutions.* Analyze each proposed solution, including the implications of each one.

5. *Decision, Implementation, and Verification.* Select what appears to be the best solution, attempt to implement it as a test, and then verify that it resolves the problematic situation.

The problem solving process is an attempt to find and implement a solution that minimizes, bypasses, or makes irrelevant the cause or causes of the undesired problem outcomes, that provides a way to overcome the barriers to achieving the desired group goals.

Further Discussion of Dewey's Steps

According to Drucker, "Most books on decision-making tell the reader: 'First find the facts.' But ... one does not start with facts. One starts with opinions."[46] Relevant facts may be found later. First solicit people's opinions, and then caution them about people's tendency of seeking facts that fit their opinions and their initial conclusions, otherwise known as jumping to conclusions. Drucker finds that " ... effective decision makers have learned ... to start out with the assumption that the way the problem looks, in all likelihood, is not what it really is."[47] After compiling the existing informed opinions and facts about the problems outcomes and likely cause or causes of those outcomes, determine which conclusion or conclusions the opinions and facts logically lead to.

Drucker further suggests that groups should not follow common textbook advice to seek consensus but rather to air differences of opinions about the status quo and possible solutions.. Disagreements are important for a few reasons: they provide some defense against simply giving in to the special interest pleaders in the group or organization, they alone stimulate decision-making options in people's minds, and they arouse people's imagination.[48] The leader needs to both encourage people to disagree and then discover why they do.

Overall, Drucker concludes that clearly understanding the undesired outcomes, the symptoms, and the causes (namely, defining the problem) may be the most important element in making effective decisions,[49] for if the problem is not clearly understood, we would not expect to reach an effective decision for the problem. Even when a group reaches the point of making a decision, the decision-maker/group should ask whether a decision is really required.[50] Maybe nothing should be done.

Dewey's guideline [51] is provided in an expanded, outline form at the end of the chapter so it can be used as a group exercise or as an individual homework assignment for students to apply to some topic (one on cigarettes is provided). This author adds some additional details to step 2 from Kepner[52] that help define the problem, and slightly alter some of Dewey's terms.

ORGANIZATIONAL COMMUNICATION

Organization

An *organization* is two or more interdependent people whose interaction is guided by a structure created to coordinate their common goals within a larger, changing environment. To cope with the influence and uncertainty of the impinging, ever-changing environment, the members may adjust their actions and/or the organizational structure.

While people have organized themselves in a variety of ways within organizations, the traditional division of labor and chain of command seen in government, military, and educational institutions are very prevalent. An authority structure, often of successive levels or ranks, informs the organizational members who they are to interact with and how to accomplish the overall goals of the organization. Communication in the traditional organization is intended to follow the lines of authority in the hierarchy, and this is frequently accompanied by informal, non-prescribed communication. Even less-traditional organizations have some measure of authority and communication structure.

Organizational Communication

Following from the concept of an organization, *organizational communication* as "… the process of creating and exchanging messages with a network of interdependent relationships to cope with environmental uncertainty."[53] Within an organization, there is an ongoing sequence of information shared between people occupying various positions of responsibility in order for them to achieve their common goals while contending with constantly changing external and internal forces. External influencing factors include, among others, changes in: the overall economy, means of communication (i.e., telephone, internet, surface mail, mass media, and so on) government regulations, physical materials, public needs, available labor, predominant religious beliefs, and international competition. Internal factors include, among others, the organization's means of production and/or service, existing labor or union rules, physical means of internal communication, and so on.

Communication within an organization can be separated into the organizationally approved and created formal communication and the informal communication that arises from normal, personal interaction between people.

1. *Formal Communication.* This is approved communication that the organization has created to accomplish tasks that are expected to reach organizational goals. This includes the downward, upward, and horizontal communication that reflects the routes and types of communication occurring between people in organizations, according to the authority or network structure created by the organizations

Downward communication is the first type of formal communication examined. These are the messages from supervisory personnel to those lower in authority that direct the latter's task behavior. They originate with one manager and are sent to one or more subordinates, such as another supervisor with less authority or to regular organizational members (such as employees), according to the organization's hierarchy. Katz suggests that five types of communication messages go from superiors to subordinates:

- *job instructions*: "Please tell Joe to collect all the grades and deliver them to the Registrar."
- *job rationale.* Information that is used to help the person understand the purpose of their task and how it fits into the organization's overall activities or scheme of things: "Most of our students are on financial aid so you people in the Financial Aid office have to ensure that every available financial resource is used to provide students with the means to enroll in and stay in school or we will have to drastically curtail our university's operations."
- *procedures and practices.* Information about the organization's rules and procedures: "Employees experiencing flu-like symptoms of a runny nose, sore throat, cough, and having a temperature are required to stay home at least three consecutive days."
- *feedback* about member performance. Messages to subordinates about how well they did their job. "You never missed a day of work this past year, you advised all the school's new students, you supervised all of the student organizations, and you recruited fifty students from other colleges to attend ours. Excellent job."
- *indoctrination of goals.* Messages designed to encourage members to work hard and stay committed to accomplishing the organization's objectives: "Last year we had the highest graduation rate of seniors in 10 years. Let's top that figure this year, and then celebrate it."[54]

Typically, management does not give enough task justifications to subordinates to suit the subordinates so they do not respond to the tasks as seriously as they could. They may also feel some job dissatisfaction as they resign themselves to the task with, "Ours is not to reason why." Co-workers then are considered the best sources of information when management communication is of low quality.[55]

An atypical example of downward communication is illustrated by Continental Airlines under Bethune:

> First, when we had breaking news, we wanted to keep our employees in the loop. Employees had countless new places to turn for information about anything company-related they were hearing about. Instead of going to the water cooler or the Houston *Chronicle* ..., they could go to their daily update from corporate headquarters, which explained it. They could go to my weekly voice-mail message .... They could go to the monthly employee newsletter or the employee quarterly .... They had other internal resources to turn to for information. Second, when we said it, something remarkable happened. The employees believed it. After three years of experience with me at the top and my management team in place, they knew. We don't lie to them.[56]

Upward communication is a second type of formal communication. It refers to communication that goes from subordinates to superiors in the organization to provide information about employee performance, existing problems, and suggestions for improvement. It occurs in interpersonal interactions on the job, meetings, e-mail messages and letters, anonymous surveys about management, through formal grievances, and through chance meetings.

This communication is crucial for management since they need to know whether their downward messages were received, how subordinates interpreted them, and what the subordinates expect to do in response. Subordinates are often closer and more familiar with the current product, service, and customer than is upper management so they have insight that management needs for planning and decision-making. Management needs to hear these insights.

Bethune at Continental Airlines provides an example of an efficient upward communication structure.

> We have 800-number hotlines for our employees to call for information about ground safety and operational performance. We have hot lines for them to call for information about benefits, about payroll, about their 401(k) program. We have numbers they can call for nearly everything that comes up—anything they want to know more about or anything they want us to know.

And when we get employee calls, *we respond—fast*. They know that their questions and concerns aren't going into some black hole.[57]

When subordinates know that they can readily communicate with their superiors, then they trust and evaluate the superiors more favorably.[58] They think their superiors really value what they have to say and that the superiors are committed to make the group a success.

There are some inherent weaknesses with upward communication. First, managers are more used to telling subordinates what to do than they are to listening to them, so their listening is not as good as it should be. Second, employees know the messages they pass upwards may be used to control what occurs in the organization—including them—so they often omit saying anything that might hurt themselves, and may say things simply to ingratiate themselves to management. Third, supervisors may not like the objective reports of subordinates and might penalize them,[59] so employees learn to withhold information accordingly. Thus, employees "… prefer to tell the boss good news rather than bad news. And yet, to a boss, the bad news is infinitely more important."[60] When management does not hear the bad news, they cannot take immediate action to reverse the outcomes.

Executives can foster upward communication of bad news by creating an open door atmosphere that welcomes employee feedback about bad news, and by balancing bad news with good news to emphasize the importance of both.[61]

Horizontal communication is the third and last type of formal communication. This represents the messages going between people having an equal level of authority, such as between two teachers or two college deans at the same school, two first-line supervisors at a local retail store or two clerks at that same store, and so on. Horizontal communication usually consists of sharing information, coordination of activities, problem-solving discussions, and conflict resolution. It allows people in different parts of an organization to combine their knowledge and skills to accomplish a task, and when they successfully do this, they report higher worker satisfaction and morale.[62]

Unfortunately, the amount and accuracy of horizontal communication in organizations can be limited by inter-group rivalries. The reader might presume that everyone would work together fort he common, overall good, but that is often not the case. Individuals, groups, and managers often do not communicate all of their information to the rest of the organization due to competing interests as well as quests for power since information is power. Petty jealousies, individual likes and dislikes, and competition for organizational resources lead one or more department members to withhold vital information needed by another department, or even give them false information. This obviously hurts the organization as a whole and could easily cost for-profit organizations revenue.

2. *Informal Communication.* More communication occurs in an organization than just the task-related, official communication via sanctioned routes. People are social beings so many of them will develop communication contacts with other people in the organization that are not part of the organization's functional chain of command. People talk when passing in the hallway or while having coffee in the employee lounge. They also develop non-formal sources of company information when the formal communication is insufficient, slow, likely to be distorted, found to be ineffective in a crisis or solving a complex problem, or when individuals want to share personal information.[63] This type of informal communication is frequently termed the *grapevine*, in which people in informal relationships convey organizational and personal information among themselves.

Goldhaber summarizes the benefits of the grapevine.[64] First, it is fast since it is not constricted by a structure limiting who can speak to whom and when. Second, it is accurate (up to a reported 80+% for non-controversial information about the company). The idea that it is inaccurate stems from the fact that grapevine errors are occasionally so dramatic that people remember them over the multitude of accurate information. Third, the informal network can convey a great deal of information since more people exist in the organization than in the formal routes of communication. Fourth, the grapevine provides an unofficial way for employees to give management feedback. Fifth, people often put management instructions into more easily understood language.

The big drawback of informal communication networks is that they can convey rumors, which by definition are unverified information of uncertain origin. Such rumors can be embarrassing and even represent character assassinations. If the facts are contrary, the organization can provide them to reduce organizational uncertainty and personal anxiety.

If you do not like to receive rumors, you can directly and indirectly convey this to fellow organizational members. If you do not convey rumors yourself and if you respond neutrally to hearing them, you will significantly decrease the chance that other people will tell them to you.

Personal Networking

While some individuals in some departments in some organizations may find they can do their job by just interacting with their immediate department members, other individuals in other departments or in other organizations find that they need to collaborate with a whole variety of people throughout the organization to effectively complete their job. In this latter case, the individual member has to personally network with various people.

DeVito offers some networking principles, added to by this writer.[65] First, start with the people you know in the organization to see if they have the knowledge, skills, and/or resources you need to complete your job. Since many people respond to reciprocity, be prepared to offer them some knowledge, skill, or resource you have at your disposal that would help them do their job. If you do not, you can provide them with a small token of your appreciation. Second, ask them if they know any members outside your department who might be able to provide what you need, and arrange an introduction. Be even more prepared for reciprocity with people you do not know. See if you can create a mutually advantageous relationship. Third, consider which departments might have what you need, conduct some informal research about them, and then go in person to inquire of the secretary and staff members their organizational capabilities. Be very polite and respectful. Consider sounding provisional about the help you are seeking and then be descriptive about your specific needs. If they cannot help you but you are pleasant and sincere, they may direct you to someone within the organization who can help you, and occasionally someone outside the organization, if necessary. Fourth,, stay in contact. You have to make the effort to make the contacts and then stay in touch with all of your contacts, even if it means finding an excuse to briefly visit the different departments and individuals. Leave a small token like a coffee mug, etc., if you can. Fifth, ensure that they know what you can do for them. If you find you are able to help these other members, they may go out of their way to help you in the future. Overall, your networking efforts within the organization can help you do your job and do it better. Your contacts may also alert you to organizational job openings that might interest you.

Although employees in professional positions may not often think about it affecting their individual jobs, they also need to network with the support personnel in the organization. Be sure to sincerely communicate your appreciation to the parking lot attendant, the custodian, the delivery person, the building maintenance staff, the secretaries, the gardener, the warehouse staff, and so on. They do a lot of dirty jobs to help make your work environment more efficient and pleasant. Further, small and thoughtful, nonmonetary gifts may be appropriate, such as a plate of food given to them during their lunch hour, a bottle of cold water on a hot day, a birthday card, and so on.

CONCLUSION

In this chapter, small group communication is defined, common communication roles in groups are described, suggestions are made for creating a productive group environment, recommendations are made for effective participation in groups, three different leadership styles and their impact on group communication are explained, the importance of communication for successful leadership was explored, suggestions are provided for those leading a group meeting, communication flow in groups was described, and a problem-solving guide was offered as a structure for group discussions and problem-solving. Organizational communication was defined, as well as formal and informal networks within an organization. Upward, downward, and horizontal communication was described, and the chapter ended with suggestions for networking.

CHAPTER 10 HOMEWORK[66]
Dewey's Reflective Thinking Sequence
(or class exercise) Decision-Making Steps

Directions: Fill in the blank spaces on the problem-solving guide that follows with information about cigarette smoking or some other topic of your instructor's choice. See the pages following this guide for fact sheet to use as a basis of information about cigarette smoking.

Terms

1. Reflective Thinking: thinking about your thinking while you are thinking, to improve your thinking by using appropriate thinking assessment standards; to believe or disbelieve in something due to the support, evidence, proof, or witness of its existence.
2. problem (aka: *problem outcome*): an unwanted effect, perceived harms, a deviation from a desired set of conditions; a question, matter, situation, or person that is perplexing or difficult. In brief, a problem outcome is a bad result.
3. problem solving: any behavior which, through the manipulation of variables, makes the appearance of a solution more probable.
4. cause: anything producing an effect or result. A problem is an undesired result, while a cause is the stimulus for the result.
5. symptom: a sign; a circumstance, event, or condition that accompanies something and indicates its presence.

6. goal: a desired result or purpose, an objective, the hoped-for-condition/s.
7. solution/s: the answer to a problem; the process of solving a problem outcome.
8. Reasoning (common ones): cause-effect, effect-cause, sign, comparison, authority, example, generalization, criteria-to-application

Considerations

1. Do not confuse a problem outcome with its symptom/s.
2. Do not confuse a cause/s of the problem outcome with either the problem outcome or with the symptoms.
3. Do not confuse goals with solutions to achieve the goals.
4. Anticipate multiple causality.
5. Obstacles may be problematic, but not necessarily *the* causes. Obstacles are not problem outcomes.
6. The impact of problem solutions should alter/minimize/get around/ make irrelevant the causes so the desired goals are attained.

Overall Strategy: Find solutions that minimize, circumvent and/or counteract the causes so the desired goals/s can be reached.

Reflective Thinking Steps

1. *Felt Difficulty*—initial orientation to the topic (generate relevant evidence)
   a. Status quo: concisely describe the current situation—facts, stated opinions, etc., reflecting the significant differing points of view.

   _____

   b. Desired condition/s: list the goal/s, the hoped-for-condition/s, reflecting the significant differing points of view, from 1 side)

   _____

   (from 2nd side _____
   (from 3rd side _____
   c. Barrier/s: something that hinders or prevents achievement of the goal/s; reflecting the significant differing points of view.
   (from 1 side) _____
   (from 2nd side) _____
   (from 3rd side _____
2. *Problem outcome definition* (to be discovered/defined in completing the following steps)

a. Identity of the problem outcome (s), the existing and/or expected harm (s) - harmful effects. Be specific and concise.

   (1) Is: (now also insert this exact statement at the following places: steps 2.b., 2.c., 2.d., 2.e., 2.f., 2.g., 2.h., 3.)

   ___

   (2) Is Not: (what you think is not the key problem outcome/s)

   ___

   (3) Distinctive (what is unusual or stands out about the problem outcome/s? Anything revealing or strange?)

   ___

* Reminder: Reflect upon your evidence and reasoning.

b. Location of [stated problem outcome (s), from step 2.a.(1)].

   ___

   (1) Is: (where the problem outcome is located/found; the geographical location)

   ___

   (2) Is Not: (where the problem outcome/s is not located)

   ___

   (3) Distinctive: (what stands out about the problem outcome's location, where it occurs)

   ___

*Reminder: Reflect upon your evidence and reasoning.

c. Timing of [stated problem outcome (s), from step 2.a.(1)].

   ___

   (1) Is: (when the problem outcome/s occurs; year/month/day/hour/ period)

   ___

   (2) Is Not: (when time/s is not a factor in the problem outcome's occurrence)

   ___

   (3) Distinctive: (what stands out about when the problem outcome occurs)

   ___

*Reminder: Reflect upon your evidence and reasoning.

d. Magnitude of [stated problem outcome (s), from step 2.a.(1)].

   ___

(1) Is: (what is the size of the problem outcome/s; the extent (how much/often) it occurs)

_____

(2) Is Not: (what is not the size of the problem outcome/s (figures that are incorrect or irrelevant))

_____

(3) Distinctive: (what stands out about the size of the problem outcome/s)

_____

* Reminder: Reflect upon your evidence and reasoning.

e. Terms of [stated problem outcome (s), from step 2.a.(1)].

_____

define at least 3 terms that are critical for understanding the problem outcome (s), see, especially, your Identity statement)
(1) _____: _____
(2) _____: _____
(3) _____: _____

f. History of [stated problem outcome (s), from step 2.a.(1)].

_____

The harms occurring in the past, the ongoing problem outcomes, and their enlargement.

_____

g. Beneficiaries of [stated problem outcome (s), from step 2.a.(1)].

_____

A person or group that benefits from the bad situation existing or expected to exist, that may work/fight against you to keep it going?
(1) Is: (who and/or what group benefits by the problem outcome/s' continued existence)

_____

(2) Is Not: (who/what group does not benefit by the problem outcome/s' continued existence)

_____

(3) Distinctive: (what stands out about the person/group that benefits from the problem outcome/s)

_____

h. Cause/s of [stated problem outcome (s), from step 2.a.(1)].

_____

(see Barriers listed earlier for potential causes; look for underlying causes; verify the cause-effect/ problem outcome connection)

(1) cause 1: _____

(2) cause 2: _____

(3) cause 3: _____

* Reminder: Reflect upon your evidence and reasoning. [By this point, at least, verify whether you need to redefine the problem outcome/s stated in step 2.a.(1) and through this step. If so, start anew with step 2.a.(1) and recreate the succeeding steps in step 2.]

3. *Possible Solutions* for [stated problem outcome (s), from step 2.a.(1)].

_____

(list 3 possible solutions that can directly and reasonably be expected to resolve the stated problem outcome (s). A multi-faceted problem outcome will likely require a multi-faceted solution/plan). Solutions have to minimize/circumvent/counteract the causes listed in "h" above.

a. solution for cause 1 in #2 h above:

_____

b. solution for cause 2 in #2 h above:

_____

c. solution for cause 3 in #2 h above:

_____

4. *Analysis, reasoning, and implications* of each possible solution (plan) listed above.

* Reminder: Reflect upon your evidence/reasoning.

Analysis: the separation of a whole into basic parts for examination and interpretation. *Reasoning:* examining the relationship between and among actions, decisions, beliefs, etc. *Implications:* what is likely to result or enfold; the effect on a variety of phenomena.

a. solution #1 (strengths and weaknesses, pro/con statements of it):

_____   _____

b. solution #2 (strengths and weaknesses, pro/con statements of it):

_____   _____

c. solution #3 (strengths and weaknesses, pro/con statements of it):

_____   _____

5. *Decision, implementation, and verification* of the selected solution, including further analysis and how you might expect to verify that the chosen solution resolves the problem outcome.

* Reminder: Reflect upon your evidence and reasoning.

a. the best choice - why and/or how it is expected to resolve the problem outcome (s), including any additional reasons for choosing it.

_____

b. implementation and verification: explanation of how you might expect to put your solution (plan) into effect
(1) strategies for implementation:

_____

(2) verification (reasonable expectation; benchmarks that the plan is effective)

_____

CHAPTER 10 HOMEWORK
Problem-Solving Discussion about Cigarette Smoking

Your instructor may make this an individual, small group, or class-wide exercise.

Directions: To familiarize yourself with the small group problem-solving discussion steps presented in this chapter, use what you know about cigarette smoking to fill in each step in the expanded guide provided above. Supplemental information about cigarettes is provided below. You should not have to do any further cigarette smoking research to complete this.

Terms

1. *Cause-effect relationship*: the phenomenon is necessary and sufficient by itself to create the outcome. If applied to cigarette smoking, all smokers must get lung cancer. They do not.

2. *Correlation*: one variable goes along with and occurs as does another variable(s). This may *suggest* a possible cause. When applied to cigarette smoking, there has been a correlation of smoking with the incidences of cardio-vascular diseases.

Information that Makes Cigarette Smoking Appear Harmful

1. *National Cancer Institute Fact Sheet*.(2010)
   - cigarette smoking harms nearly every organ in the body and causes many types of cancer, including in the lungs and other airways, kidney, bladder, stomach, pancreas, and cervix.

- cigarette smoking or exposure to it cause an estimated average of 438,000 premature deaths per year in the America.
- of the premature deaths, about 40% die from cancer, 25% from lung disease, and 35% from heart disease.
- women smoking during pregnancy have an increased chance of delivering a premature baby and for their baby to die from Sudden Infant Death Syndrome.
- women smokers have an increased chance of experiencing menopause at a younger age
- in 1987, lung cancer became the leading cancer in females, passing breast cancer.
- tobacco smoke contains about 250 chemicals that are known to harm the human body, and about 50 of these chemicals cause cancer (carcinogens).
- the advertisements for the lesser amount of tar and nicotine in "light" cigarettes are misleading (for various reasons noted by NCI), and those switching from regular to light cigarettes inhale about the same amount of harmful chemicals.

2. *American Cancer Society* (2010)
   - cigarette smoking is the number one cause of cancer deaths in America.
   - tobacco use is the cause of about 1 out of every 5 deaths in America.
   - 46 million adult American smokers in 2008, about 20% of all American adults.
   - 20% of American high school students and 6% of middle school students smoked in 2007.
   - about one-half of all Americans that continue smoking will die from it.
   - about 443,600 Americans die every year from tobacco-related illnesses.
   - smoking cigarettes is a primary cause of heart disease, bronchitis, emphysema, and stroke.
   - tobacco use is correlated with reduced fertility in women and higher risk of miscarriage.
   - reports that adult male smokers died on average 13.2 years prematurely while female smokers died 14.5 years earlier than they otherwise would have.
   - cigarettes are addicting, and nicotine is the addicting element in tobacco. About 40% of smokers attempt to stop smoking cigarettes each year but just 4%-7% do it privately.

3. *Centers for Disease Control and Prevention (CDC)* (2010)
   - an estimated 3,000–6,000 nonsmokers die each year from environmental tobacco smoke.
   - 164,000 of the 514,000 expected cancer deaths this year are directly linked to cigarette smoking. ETS causes about 46,000 heart disease deaths/year.

- current patterns: 25 million Americans alive today will die prematurely from smoking
- per capita cigarette smoking dropped 41.6% from the 1963 high to 2004. Put in different numbers, in comparison to 2004, the 1963 consumption was 2.4 times higher.
- nicotine in cigarette smoke reaches the brain within 10 seconds.
- cigarette smoking causes about 90% of all lung cancer deaths in men, 80% in women.
- smoking men contract lung cancer 23 times more than do nonsmoking men; smoking women contract lung cancer 13 times as much an nonsmoking women.

4. *Additional information about cigarette smoking.*
   - some people consider cigarette smoke stinky; some people think it gives bad breath.
   - cigarette butt littering is common and unsightly; cigarette smoking is also a fire hazard.
   - it is a very difficult habit to quit.
   - smoking raises health care costs $75.5 billion/year according to the CDC; some state employees pay $7-40 bi-weekly or $182-1040/year more in costs.
   - On Guam, health care costs for groups of employees having smokers in them could be 10- 15% higher than groups that do not have smokers in them. (Pacific Daily News, November 7, 2005)
   - lower productivity of smokers costs businesses $92 billion/year according to the CDC. (Pacific Daily News, 2005)
   - 1998, government sued/won $206 billion from the tobacco companies, paid over 25 years.
   - cigarette packages have had a printed Surgeon General warning on them since 1968. - laws in various parts of the U.S. have banned smoking in public and even on private property (in private businesses operating on private property, including bars, parks, etc.
   - costly habit: someone (or couple combined) smoking 3 packs/day=1095 packs/year, or 50,370 packs over 46 years ending in the 1980's spent $33,190. If this was invested in Phillip Morris stock with dividends reinvested over 46 years it would have been worth over $2 million. (Stanley, 1996)
   - 2006 average Guam price $3.50x3 packs/day = $176,295+ over 46 years.
   - 2010 average Guam price $5.50x3 packs/day = $277,035+ over 46 years.
   - on Guam (2005), about 32% of the population smokes, including 26% of male youth and 34% of female youth. (2005)

- on Guam (2005), 23% of middle school and 31.6% of high school students smoked. Guam had the highest male smoking rate in the U.S., and 34% of the population smoked. (Pacific Daily News, 2005)
- the University of Guam banned smoking in August, 2006. The school receives cigarette-related research money.
- the Guam Community College banned tobacco and betel nut use on campus on June 1, (Pacific Daily News, June 2, 2007)

Information that Challenges the Conventional Wisdom about Cigarette Smoking or Provides Another Viewpoint

- anecdotal historical evidence suggests that the Andes Indians in South America smoked tobacco in approximately 3-5,000 B.C.; in 1492, Columbus found Caribbean Indians smoking tobacco; in 1612 the first American colonists grew tobacco at Jamestown; tobacco was a cash crop that helped the colonies survive; and that 5 million pounds of tobacco was used by Ben Franklin to secure a loan from France during the Revolutionary War. Thus, Americans can say that tobacco has been an important part of their culture.
- some state legislatures like Hawaii's have substituted the word "public places" in place of "private property" to convince the public that the state has some legitimate authority over personal conduct occurring on what is really private property. (Pacific Daily News, February 23, 2007).
- the main issue in the cigarette smoking debate is not smokers versus non-smokers rights but property rights—who has the authority to set the terms and conditions for entry onto someone's property. What gives non-owners the right to control someone business? While there may be some justification for banning smoking in what really are public places such as schools, courts, hospitals, and so on, non-owners are having the government stake a claim to private business owners' property. People who whine about smoke-filled bars should stay out of them. (Malone, 2007)
- for those who believed the 1950's advertisements that smoking cigarettes was healthy, they overlooked previous historical information. Cigarettes were referred to as *coffin nails* in a 1906 O. Henry short story; a dictionary listed the phrase *coffin nails* as dating to the late 1800's, and in 1900 the U.S. Supreme Court referred to cigarettes as having a harmful effect upon people. Since 1964 the U.S. Surgeon Generals have claimed that cigarettes are harmful, while the government subsidizes tobacco farming and receives billions of dollars in tobacco tax revenues. The EPA's 1993 fraudulent ETS report is small compared to the government's claim that smoking

costs the government money, given smoker's premature deaths (they collect little retirement, health care, and nursing home assistance) and that
cigarettes are the most heavily taxed consumer product. (Will, 1999)

- the January, 1993 EPA report on cigarette smoking revealed that women
  exposed to secondhand smoke (ETS) averaged just 1.19 times higher incidence of lung cancer as women who lived with non-smokers. This small
  amount is based on 30 studies, of which 6 showed no significant increase
  in lung cancer, none of the 11 U.S. studies met the study guidelines (7 of
  which had less than 45 subjects), and only 9 of the 30 studies showed a
  statistical significance of contracting lung cancer. From this, the EPA estimated that about 3,000 American nonsmokers got lung cancer each year
  from ETS. (Bernstein, 1996) - by about the year 2000, the U.S. government claimed that 4000,000 people die each year from smoking cigarettes.
  This figure originates from a computer-generated model which places
  every person's cause of death as smoking cigarettes if they ever smoked
  cigarettes in their life, even if they actually die from a brain aneurysm at
  80 years of age. Since one-half of the 400,000 people live to be 75+ years
  of age and 70,000 of them live past 85, who can be sure they died to soon?
  (Elder, 2000)
- R. Levy, a statistics professor, and R. Marimont, a mathematician and scientist, conclude that "… there is no credible evidence that 400,000 deaths
  per year—or any number remotely close to 400,000—are cased by tobacco.
  Nor has the estimate been adjusted for the positive effects of smoking—
  less obesity, colitus, depression, Alzheimer's disease, Parkinson's disease
  and, for some women, a lower incidence of breast cancer" (p.221) (Elder,
  2000)
- Federal Judge W. Osteen claimed that "EPA publicly committed to conclusion before the research had begun: adjusted established procedure and
  scientific norms to validate its conclusion, and aggressively utilized its
  authority to disseminate findings to establish a de facto regulatory scheme
  to influence public opinion" (p.222) (Elder, 2000) EPA head under Pres.
  Clinton is the same EPA head under Pres. Obama: Carol Browner.
- if an academic researcher used the statistical techniques used by the EPA
  in its secondhand smoke study, the researcher would be condemned and
  possibly fired. (Williams, 2006) The EPA lowered the study's confidence
  level to 90 from 95 to reach the conclusion that 3,000 people died each
  year from ETS, which doubled the margin for error and the probability
  that chance could have achieved the same result. (Williams, 2007d) the
  percentage of lung cancer deaths per year dropped about 16% in men and
  8% in women (Pacific Daily News, 2006).

- who decides which harm is more important and should be banned? Who decides who can harm themselves? A dictator decides this in a dictatorship and the majority decides this in a democracy. In a free society, an individual decides for him or herself. (Williams, 2001)
- property rights should determine who can smoke where in a free society. Permission to smoke or not is determined by the owner's permission. If nonsmokers do not like the smoking in someone's restaurant, bar, office, and so on, they can go elsewhere, just as the smoker can who may not want to visit a non-smoking establishment. (Williams, 2001)
- if nonsmokers can demand that people not smoke on other people's private property, cannot smokers demand that *they* be allowed to smoke on other people's property?
- some cities have banned outdoor and/or indoor smoking, even in one's own car. Watch out for the tyrannical strategy of removing liberties little by little, including those against smoking and trans fat. Why not ban supermarket food that is considered to be unhealthy and create laws about what can be eaten at home? (Williams, 2007a)
- is there a legitimate slippery slope argument when a government that would ban smoking on public and private property would also intervene in most aspects of our lives, such as requiring regular exercise and anything else considered important for good health? (Williams, 2006)
- Liberty and democracy are not the same and in individual cases could be the opposite. When there is liberty, the government protects the citizens against force and fraud but does not attempt to control the peaceful actions of the citizens. In a democracy, the majority rule of the people or through their representatives can grant or take away people's rights, the latter of which is tyrannical. (Williams, 2007c)
- property is a natural right or, in other words, an "unalienable right" under the pursuit of happiness noted in the Declaration of Independence. The means that the right to property does not come from government but precedes it. Therefore, government cannot (Constitutionally) take away the right to property, and government is established to protect this right. (Williams, 2007b)
- California passed a statewide ban on smoking in 1995. This and other bans take away the rights of individuals to decide how they want to live. This turns citizens into children since they are presumed to be incapable of making informed choices. (Gillespie, 2006)
- cigarette smuggling is the result of a carton of cigarettes selling for $160 in New York City and $35 in North Carolina. Is it the right of government to use its brute force to keep a New Yorker from choosing the cheaper

cigarettes from North Carolina in an attempt to avoid the government's confiscatory taxes in New York? (Williams, 2008)

- in a free society, who decides or should decide what a person eats (or whether they smoke cigarettes)? Why should someone take away the public's choices? Aren't adults responsible for their own lives and health? Why do some people want the state to control the rest of us? There is no end to what the government can ban. (Stossel, 2006)
- some people like smoke-filled bars. In a free society, why can't they have some? If you don't want to go to them, you don't have to. In our country, some people want the state to decide everything, but when this happens, minority groups lose their rights. (Stossel, [this is also known as a tyranny of the minority]
- the U.S. government is hypocritical for suing the tobacco companies since the military gave cigarettes for free in World War II to military people and it subsidizes tobacco farming. Further, the government does not have to pay billions for health care costs for smokers since they have a significant chance of dying early and not collecting government and other benefits. One calculation shows that each pack of cigarettes sold saves the government 32 cents. [this implies that as part of the general government revenue, cigarette taxes pay for schools, roads, and so on.] (Murphy, 1999)
- if everyone quit smoking, people would live longer and Social Security would become bankrupt sooner. We would have to work longer before retirement. (Mansnerus, 1996)
- taxes on cigarettes have helped states trying to balance their budgets. In 2009, 14 states raised taxes and by March, 2010, 2 other states raised theirs. Guam increased it previous tax [of $1.00+] by $2.00 per pack. (Pacific Daily New, March 27, 2010) In 2002, smokers in New York City paid as much as $7/pack, of which $1.50 went to the state and $3.50 went to New York City. The government makes the clear majority of money off this product {while the tobacco companies made about .25/pack]. Given the size of the taxes, it could be considered stealing. (Murphy, 2002)

Some Common Solutions Given for Cigarette Smoking

- increase further taxes to make the cost prohibitive to some percentage of smokers.
- create a more effective public awareness campaign against starting or continued smoking.
- ban cigarette advertising, including on billboards.
- ban tobacco sales to anyone under 18 years of age.

- ban smoking outright; make it illegal like marijuana, and so on. Make fines onerous.
- create a safe (or government approved marginally safer) cigarette using government subsidies or offer a cash prize for someone who can create a safe/safer cigarette.
- limit smoking to peoples' residences.
- ban all smoking around kids and ban it for all pregnant women.
- use or create further supplements and/or devices to help people quit, and offer these through peoples' health care plans.
- ban all cigarette vending machines and mail-order sales.
- offer employers tax incentives to ban smoking in their work places.
- offer tax incentives to all businesses which ban all smoking on their premises.
- exercise more
- ban tobacco companies from sponsoring sporting events
- repeal all smoking laws regulating smoking on all private property.
- pass a law that stipulates that private property owners will decide for themselves whether they will allow smoking on their own property (this would include their residence, their business, their shopping center, their warehouse, their vehicles, and so on).
- pass a law that attempts to prevent future tobacco lawsuits for health-related harms.
- repeal all prohibitions against tobacco advertising.

References for the Cigarette Information Above

American Cancer Society. July 5, 2010. http://www.cancer.org./Cancer/Cancercauses/ TobaccoCancer/CigaretteSmoking

P. Bernstein, *Against the Gods: The Remarkable Story of Risk.*(New York: John Wiley & Sons, Inc., 1996).

Center for Disease Control and Prevention, July 5, 2010. http://www.cdc.gov/tobaccon/ data_statistics/tables/health/attrdeath/index.htm

Center for Disease Control and Prevention, July 5, 2010. http://rex.nci.nih.gov/NCI_ Pub_Interface/raterisk/risks67.html

Center for Disease Control and Prevention, July 5, 2010. http://www.cdc.gov/tobacco/ data_statistics/tables/economics/consumption/in…

Center for Disease Control and Prevention, July 5, 2010. http://www.cdc.gov/tables/ data_statistics/sgr/2004/highlights/harm/indiex.htm

Center for Disease Control and Prevention, July 5, 2010. http://www.cdc.gov/tobacco/ data_statistics/fact_sheets/health_effects/tobacco

Center for Disease Control and Prevention, July 5, 2010. http://www.cdc.gov/tobacco/ data_statistics/fact_sheets/health_effects/effects

R. Dei, "Just for today, put away your cigarettes," *Pacific Daily* News, November 17, 2005.

L. Elder, *The Ten Things You Can't Say In America* (New York: St. Martin's Griffin, 2000).

N. Gillespie, "The race to ban what's bad for us," *reasononline* (December 11, 2006), http://www.reason.com/news/printer/117171.html

W. Malone, "Smoking debate is about property, not rights," *Pacific Daily* News (January 11, 2007).

L. Mansnerus, "Tobacco on trial; Making a case for death," *The New York Times* (May 5, 1996).

J. Murphy, "U.S. hypocritical for suing tobacco firms," *Pacific Daily News* (October 5, 1999).

J. Murphy, "Tide turns against American smokers," *Pacific Daily News* (September 2, 2002). *National Cancer Institute* (July 5, 2010), http://www.cancer.gov/cancer-topics/factsheet/Tobacco/cessation/print?page=

National Cancer Institute (July 5, 2010), http://www.cancer.gov/cancertopics/fact-sheet/Tobacco/women

National Cancer Institute (July 5, 2010). http://www.cancer.gov/cancertopics/fact-sheet/Tobacco/light-cigar

"Smokers' medical insurance bills may rise," *Pacific Daily News* (November 7, 2005).

"Percentage of cancer deaths falls," *Pacific Daily News* (September 8, 2006).

"Report: Fewer Americans are dying of cancer," *Pacific Daily News* (January 28, 2007).

"Hawaii bars want to bring back smoking," *Pacific Daily News* (February 23, 2007).

"College bans betel nut, cigarette use," *Pacific Daily News* (June 2, 2007).

"Cigarette taxes are gold rush for states," *Pacific Daily News* (March 27, 2010).

T. Stanley and W. Danko, *The Millionaire Next Door* (New York: Pocket Books, 1996).

J. Stossel, "In a truly free society, we don't all have to make the same decisions," *Jewish World Review* (November 30, 2005).

J. Stossel, "What will they ban next?" *Jewish World Review* (December 20, 2006).

G. Will, "Victims of 'Coffin Nails'?" *The Washington Post* (October 3, 1999).

W. Williams, "Who may harm whom?" in *Jewish World Review*, January 2, 2001.

W. Williams, "The slippery slope," *Jewish World Review*, June 14, 2006.

W. Williams, "Do-gooder tyrannical double-talk," *Jewish World Review*, January 10, 2007a

W. Williams, "Property rights," *Jewish World Review*, January 31, 2007b.

W. Williams, "Democracy of Liberty," *Jewish World Review*, February 28, 2007c.

W. Williams, "Phony science and public policy," *Jewish World Review*, April 11, 2007d.

W. Williams, "Cigarette smuggling," *Jewish World Review*, April 30, 2008.

REFERENCES

1.   K. Benne and P. Sheats, "Functional Roles and Group Members," *Journal of Social Issues*, *4*, (1948): 41-49.

2. Ibid.
3. R.Verderber, *Communicate!* (7th ed.) (Belmont, CA: Wadsworth Publishing Company, 1993).
4. G. Goldhaber, *Organizational Communication* (6th ed.) (Boston: McGraw-Hill, 1993), p. 65.
5. R. Likert, *New Patterns of Management* (New York: McGraw-Hill Book Company, Inc., 1961).
6. J. Gibb, "Defensive communication." *Journal of Communication 11* (1961): 141-148.
7. J. Gibb, "Defensive communication." *Journal of Communication 11* (1961): 141-148.
8. Verderber opt cit.
9. Ibid., p. 249.
10. "Mailbag: A Conversation with Bill Russell." *CNN/Sports Illustrated* (May 10, 1999), http://cnnsi.com/centurys_best/news/1999/05/06/russell/index.html
11. J. Cragan and D. Wright, *Communication in Small Groups: Theory, Process, Skills* (4th ed.) (Minneapolis/St. Paul: West Publishing, 1995), p. 106.
12. Verderber, op cit.
13. Cragan and Wright, op cit.
14. I. Janis, *Victims of Groupthink: A Psychological Study of Foreign-Policy Decisions and Fiascoes* (Boston: Houghton Mifflin Company, 1972).
15. W. Bennis, *On Becoming a Leader* (Reading, MA: Addison-Wesley Publishing Company, Inc., 1989).
16. M. McCormack, *On Communicating* (Los Angeles: Dove Books, 1998).
17. E. Stech, *Leadership Communication* (Chicago: Nelson-Hall Inc., Publishers, 1983).
18. D. Phillips, *Lincoln on Leadership. Executive Strategies for Tough Times* (New York: Warner Books, Inc., 1992), p. xv.
19. B. Biggs, *Wealth, War, and Wisdom* (Hoboken, NJ: John Wiley & Sons, 2008).
20. P. Brendon, *Winston Churchill: An Authentic Hero* (London: Methuen London Limited, 1985), p. 144.
21. R. Giuliani with K Kurson, *Leadership* (New York: Hyperion, 2002), p. 203.
22. G. Bethune, with S. Huler, *From Worst To First: Behind the Scenes of Continental's Remarkable Comeback* (New York: John Wiley & Sons, Inc., 1998), p. 43.
23. Phillips, op cit.
24. N. Qubein, *Get The Best From Yourself* (New York: Berkeley Books, 1986).
25. Phillips, op cit.
26. Qubein, op cit.
27. Ibid.
28. P. Johnson, *Heroes: From Alexander the Great and Julius Caesar to Churchill and De Gaulle* (New York: Harper Collins Publishers, 2007), p. 259.
29. M. Hackman and C. Johnson, *Leadership: A Communication Perspective* (5th) (Long Grove, IL: Waveland Press, Inc., 2009).
30. C. Hamilton, *Communicating for Results* (4th ed.) (Belmont, CA: Wadsworth Publishing Company, 1993).

31. Ibid p. 310.
32. W. Lippmann, *The Good Society* (New York: Grosset & Dunlap, 1943), p. 12.
33. Ibid., p. 49.
34. Hamilton, op cit., p. 310.
35. P. Noonan, *What I Saw of the Revolution: A Political Life in the Reagan Years* (New York: Random House, 1990).
36. Hamilton, op cit., p. 310.
37. Ibid p. 49.
38. Goldhaber, op cit.
39. Pearson and Nelson, op cit.
40. Goldhaber, op cit., p. 253.
41. Pearson and Nelson, op cit.
42. J. Dewey, *How We Think* (Boston: D. C. Heath and Company, 1910).
43. Ibid.
44. Ibid.
45. J. Brilhart, *Effective Group Discussion* (5th ed.) (Dubuque, IA: Wm. C. Brown Publishers, 1986), p. 291.
46. P. Drucker, *The Effective Executive* (New York: Harper & Row, Publishers, 1967), p. 143.
47. P. Drucker and J. Maciariello, *The Effective Executive in Action: A Journal for Getting the Right Things Done* (New York: Harper Collins Publishers, 2006), p. 171.
48. Drucker opt cit.
49. Drucker and Maciariello, op cit.
50. Drucker, op cit.
51. Dewey op cit.
52. C. Kepner and B. Tregoe, *The New Rational Manager* (Princeton, NJ: Princeton Research Press, 1981).
53. Goldhaber, op cit., p. 15.
54. D. Katz and R. Kahn, *The Social Psychology of Organizations* (New York: John Wiley & Sons, Inc., 1966).
55. Goldhaber, op cit.
56. Bethune, op cit., p. 199.
57. Ibid, p. 201.
58. Phillips, op cit.
59. Katz and Kahn, op cit.
60. M. McCormack, *What They Still Don't Teach You At Harvard Business School* (New York: Bantam Books, 1989), p. 234.
61. Ibid.
62. J. DeVito, *Human Communication: The Basic Course* (11th ed.) (Boston: Pearson Education, Inc., 2009).
63. Hamilton, op cit.
64. Goldhaber, op cit.
65. DeVito op cit.
66. Dewey, op cit.; Kepner and Tregoe, op cit.; R. Paul, *Critical Thinking: How To Prepare Students For A Rapidly Changing World* (Santa Rosa, CA: Foundation for Critical Thinking, 1993).

CHAPTER ELEVEN

Intercultural Communication

Intercultural communication is simply the communication interaction between two or more people who are of different cultures. This can be illustrated by the interaction between someone born and raised in Japan of Japanese decent and speaking Japanese as a first language and someone similarly born and raised in Italy of Italian decent speaking Italian as a first language.

As a foundation for discussing intercultural communication, *culture* will be defined and described. Then an overview of the connection between culture and communication will be explored, followed by a brief review of *communication* itself. The next section will examine cultural influences on communication, followed in turn by an overview of nonverbal communication differences between cultures. Lastly, some barriers to intercultural communication will be described and some strategies proposed.

Separate from the above sections of chapter reading material, there is a discussion of a few controversial cultural issues just before the chapter reference list. Unless specifically assigned, the reader may decide to skip over these.

OVERVIEW OF CULTURE

1. *Definition of Culture.* The patterns of behavior and rules for communicating exhibited by a group of people living in a given place over a period of time that remain largely unchanged, differing from the behaviors and communication rules of people living in another place and/or time. [1] It includes the group of people's values, beliefs, religion, laws, artifacts, and language.

2. *Culture A Shared Design for Action.* Culture is an overall design that provides a shared set of rules and action for its members to follow. It provides

guidelines for noticing and interpreting what is meaningful and how members are to respond with their behaviors to that meaning. To the extent that culture group members share the same "game plan" and "plays," these members can predict what each other are likely to do and say. When it comes to observing or being involved in *inter*cultural interactions, we have to know the *other* culture's rules and their meaning for those rules if we expect to reasonably predict what they will do and say.

According to Hall, "…anthropologists do agree on three characteristics of culture: it is not innate, but learned; the various facets of culture are interrelated—you touch a culture in one place and everything else is affected; it is shared and in effect defines the boundaries of different cultures."[2]

3. *Culture is Learned, and Through Communication.* Barnlund suggests that it is through our use of symbols, which includes our language system and other codes (math, music, and so on), that each new generation learns its culture.[3] A culture promotes shared meaning through its language,[4] so in essence, "culture is communication."[5]

Thus, if culture is not innate but is conveyed and learned through language and other symbolic forms, then we cannot tell by looking at someone's physical features such as skin color, body shape, or hair texture to know whether they are one culture or another. For example, if a boy or girl who is born in America has one parent who is not American at all and if this parent immediately leaves and does not raise the child, then this parent imparts nothing of his or her foreign culture to the child. The child may look, for example, similar to people in Korea, Italy, or Kenya but this child is not one-half Korean, one-half Italian, or one-half Kenyan. Being raised in America by an American, he or she will learn the American culture and be an American regardless of appearance.

If culture is not innate, then how can *typical* Americans claim they are a certain other culture if: these Americans' ancestors arrived in America generations ago, these ancestors did not speak English, (even British English has many differences with American English), the ancestors held different beliefs upon arrival than do current Americans, they followed different social interaction patterns in their homeland, they were accustomed to different laws, and so on? This does not mean that there will be no identifiable characteristics that link a given person today with some distant ancestor (such as work habits or manner of speaking), but those traits are often overshadowed by normal differences in personality traits between any two people. This general conception recognizes that there are groups of people like the Amish in America that have held onto many traditional practices,[6] and regions of the country—particularly the South[7]—that preserved communication and other cultural traits originating in Great Britain.

Even on the island of Guam, an American territory far out in the western Pacific, situated close to the intersection of an imaginary line going due south from Tokyo and a line going due east from Manila, how different can the people and culture there be from the average differences amongst Americans country-wide and given the regional differences that exist when: nearly everyone on Guam speaks English, Guam has the same basic American public school system with an elected board, the same school books and teachers having passed the same basic classes and educational standards as those in the states, with the basic religions and traffic laws found in the states, with a court system operating with the same structures and on the same principles as those in the states, with typical stateside fast-food restaurants and grocery stores, with local people joining and serving in the U.S. military with no apparent difficulty, with one Chamorro becoming a Marine Corps general and another a Navy admiral, with Air Force, Navy, and National Guard installations similar to those elsewhere, with community centers, with politicians such as mayors, legislators, governors, and lieutenant governors elected by the same voting process as in the states, with semi-pro baseball and football teams, with the same almighty dollar and clothes fashions (sorry, grass skirts are not currently in style), with public and private school kids who had fundraisers to send money to Hurricane Katrina victims in New Orleans and earthquake victims in Haiti, with local politicians sending money to Washington hoping for political favors, with the U.S. Postal System, with deer and wild pig hunting, with the pervasive federal welfare system, and so on? If local Chamorros go on vacation, they invariably say they are going to the mainland that requires twelve flying hours alone just to reach the West Coast. Their moving to a city on the mainland and living there is apparently no more challenging for them than it is for anyone else in America moving to a new city. They readily attend universities in other parts of the country. "Where America's day begins" is a popular slogan on Guam. This does not mean there are no differences between Guam and any other part of America. For one, locals on Guam show a great deal of respect for elders and for their family. More than a few who do leave Guam miss their families and the island so much that they have to return. For another, it is highly doubtful that any other place in America provides more and varied food at celebrations (as well as the frequency of celebrations) than do Chamorros and Filipinos on Guam—and everyone is invited. Anecdotal evidence suggests that college students in the States do not know the friendliness and friendships they are missing by not attending school on Guam. Overall, though, given the definition of *culture* provided at the beginning of this chapter and the list of cultural features listed earlier in this paragraph, Chamorros are, to a significant degree, Americans. This does not mean that they cannot refer to themselves as Chamorros, appreciating some of the distinctions they bring to the entirety that is America.

4. *Cultural Components Are Inter-related*. Characteristics of a given culture do not exist in isolation from each other but are inter-connected.[8] For example, Althen suggests that certain American traits are connected to other traits: what might be seen as excessive individualism is connected to freedom, materialism is connected to hard work (and a higher standard of living), the impersonal response of organizations is connected to the efficiency of those same organizations, and so on.[9] Further, a change in any one element in the system has a rippling effect across the system, as what might be visualized when a pebble is thrown into a lake. If individuality becomes valued less, then there would be a decreased desire for and effort made to provide people with the freedom to express their ideas openly. With little or no individuality, there would be little or no need for or expression of individual ideas.

5. *Language-Thought Connection*. According to Steinberg, there is a long-standing belief that our thinking (cognition) is significantly influenced by and even dependent on our language.[10] This is illustrated by the Sapir-Whorf hypothesis that Hoijer summarizes as the notion that "… language functions, not simply as a device for reporting experience, but also, and more significantly, as a way of defining experience for its speakers."[11] From this idea, we could get statements such as: "If you do not speak Spanish then you cannot think like we Mexicans (and you are not a real one)," or "If you do not speak Chamorro (the combination native and Spanish language of the indigenous people in the Western Pacific, Marianas Islands spoken today) then you cannot think like we Chamorros." This claim is then used to claim that there is a Mexican, Chamorro, or whatever language point of view of history and interpretation of life in general that "outsiders" cannot know and therefore cannot evaluate. Although this language-thought notion was created long before the multicultural and diversity proponents came to the fore, it helps their cause for it suggests that "outside" speakers cannot tell whether a culture is not just as good and as valid as other cultures. A cultural criticism by a non-speaker must be inaccurate for the non-speaker would be inhibited and blinded by his or her own language-induced thinking to clearly "see" the evaluated cultural artifacts for what they "really" are.

Steinberg provides three basic claims of the language-thought relationship and his critique of them: (1) Language is a fundamental basis of thought; (2) The language system per se provides specifics of one's view of nature, and (3) The language system per se provides specifics of one's culture.[12]

Claim #1 suggests that *language is a fundamental basis of thought*, a common point of view of language theorists such as Vygotsky, Sapir, and Whorf. This means that "... the language system, with its rules of vocabulary, forms thought or is necessary for thought."[13] Steinberg provides some evidence in opposition to this claim. First, deaf children who have not acquired language have been found to act as logically as do hearing children. Second, if language is a fundamental basis of thought, then people speaking multiple languages should have as many systems of thinking (and by extension, personalities) as they do languages. If this was the case, their individual mental systems would have difficulty transferring knowledge between each systems for thinking is supposed to be specific to each language. According to Steinberg, "No evidence of the malfunctioning and other sorts of problems for multilingual persons which the theory predicts has ever been offered to support the theory."[14] Furthermore, Steinberg cites the example of two brothers he knows who spoke three different languages from birth and yet these boys reveal no differences in values, beliefs, perception of the world, and other potential cultural differences with English-only speaking kids of a similar age.[15]

Claim #2 holds that a language system provides specifics of one's view of nature. This means, according to Steinberg, that "... one's knowledge of vocabulary or syntax influences one's perception and understanding of nature."[16] There are some counterarguments for this claim. First, a person's vocabulary has not been found to affect his or her perception but it may help them remember information. While it has been suggested that the Eskimos' language helps them perceive different types of snow that other language speakers would be unable to perceive, this type of information can be readily gained from personal experience as shown by English-speaking skiers, such as this writer, who are able to notice different forms of snow despite their lack of words that distinguish between the forms. Second, if a language system shapes the way we perceive the world around us, we would expect to have as many "conceptual perceptual systems" as we have languages. As noted for Claim #1 above, there has been no evidence to support the idea that multilingual people have multiple and different perceptual insights of the world.[17]

Claim #3 suggests that our language system provides specifics of our culture. Even if language is somewhat distinct from thought, nevertheless, knowing a language will itself condition one's cultural beliefs, social beliefs, and/or views of the world. From this idea, we get statements such as, "This is how _____ speakers view the _____ situation," and "You cannot know how we _____ speakers think or feel if you do not speak our language (with the implied message that: you outsiders have nothing legitimate to say about our culture and our beliefs so keep quiet)." If language does influence our point of view of life and much that is within it, then there should be differences between speaker of different languages in their basic religions, philosophy, political structures, and social interactions, and within each spoken language, there should be similarities among the speakers. The following from Steinberg are some objections to this idea.

First, people speaking the same language have been found to have widely disparate views about life. Among English-only speakers in America, for example, it is easy to find variances in religion (Catholics, Baptists, Mormons, etc.) and politics (conservative Republican, Libertarian, far-left Democrat, etc.). Even within the same family there can be marked religious differences so there is not a language-religion view connection. Second, a language can remain basically the same over time but the worldviews of the speakers can change. If our worldview changes, how can we be getting it from our language that has stayed the same? According to Steinberg, China provides clear counterevidence to Claim #3 for its primary political philosophy changed three times in less than one hundred years, "...from Feudalism (under the Manchus) to Capitalism (under Chiang) to Communism (under Mao)."[18] Third, people with different languages can have similar worldviews. For example, you can find Catholics among different language speakers around the world, you can find socialistic governments around the world, you can find people speaking different languages using the scientific method, and so on. Thus, a given language system does not affect or determine our worldview. Fourth, a given language can describe many different views of the world although Claim #3 suggests that it should only form a specific view of the world. As Steinberg notes, "...the Bible of the ancient Hebrew peoples and the Communist Manifesto of the Europeans have had their essential ideas translated into most of the world's languages. The theories being assessed are unable to account for such a phenomenon."[19] Fifth, multilingual people have not been found to have distinct worldviews associated with their different language systems. If they did, they would have to accept the competing views as true.

As Steinberg argues, the language-thought connection that has been presumed to exist is highly in doubt.[20] Someone speaking a given language does not have a unique language-dependant insight to any existing or pre-existing reality. Further, presumed "outsiders" can speak passionately and accurately about another group's experience.

OVERVIEW OF COMMUNICATION

As Chapter One suggested, communication is the process of sending and receiving of messages, not meaning. Meaning exists in people's minds, and only the individual creates his or her own meaning. People, in varying degrees of accuracy and completeness, attempt to communicate that inner meaning via messages they send to others. They can gain an idea about the success they have had in conveying their meaning by evaluating the receiver's response to those messages. In short, messages provide a clue to the meaning the message sender has created within him or herself.

To gain a sense of the meaning of the clues, we have to have a common basis for interpreting them. According to Barnlund, "...to make thoughts and feelings intelligible to other people, we must use and respect the same rules for articulating and interpreting meanings."[21] Culture provides the common basis, the set rules that are the same for its members, to enable them to create a similar interpretation. Culture creates a "meeting of the minds" in our interactions with other cultural members, a common basis for understanding each other.

Communication is also equated to culture since it is through communication that the individual and each new generation learns his or her culture.[22] Communication and culture cannot be conceptually separated for they are so intertwined. Similarly, Hall suggests that "... what gives man his identity no matter where he is born—is his culture, the total communication framework: words, actions, postures, gestures, tones of voice, facial expressions, the way he handles time, space, and materials, and the way he works, plays, makes love, and defends himself."[23]

Intercultural Communication

This is the person-to-person, small group, or public communication occurring between people who are of different cultures.

It is difficult enough to communication effectively with someone from your own culture. In an intercultural communication situation, the differences are magnified and agreement is much more difficult even if the two of you speak a common language. There will be the additional difficulties in reaching agreement about nonverbal communication messages. What one culture finds as meaningful can be simply noise (and meaningless) to another culture.

Effective intercultural communication depends upon reducing uncertainty levels between the communicators. Knowing something about each other's culture, the verbal language, and the nonverbal language, will likely reduce uncertainty and allow each person some basis for predicting and controlling for the subsequent communication.

Overall, our given cultures provide us with a system to communicate with one another as well as meaning for the communication that occurs. Barnlund refers to culture as the "Mediating Factor,"[24] for it acts as a intermediary between any two people, guiding their communication according to cultural expectations.

The following sections provide some information about culture and communication differences that exist between cultures that can enable a communicator to anticipate how both they and the other person are likely to respond.

CULTURAL INFLUENCES AND THEIR COMMUNICATION CORRELATES

1. *Individualism and Collectivism.* One way to differentiate cultures and their accompanying communication is by placing the cultures on an individual-collective continuum. Although every culture has a mix of people, on one end would be those cultures whose members place more emphasis on the achievement of individual goals and a lesser amount of emphasis on achieving group goals, such as in the United States, Australia, and Great Britain. Those cultures on the other end of the spectrum exhibit more group-oriented achievement and a diminished effort to satisfy individual achievement, as shown in Venezuela, Columbia, and Pakistan.[25] Countries falling in the middle range of these two extremes are Israel, Spain, and India. Separate from their political structure, most of the countries and cultures give priority to group authority and desires rather than to individual autonomy.[26]

Individualism

In an individualist society such as America, children are referred to as individuals, distinct from their siblings or other kids, so they learn they have a self-identity. "Billy, go pick up your clothes." "I (Mary) would like my favorite ice cream, vanilla." Sure, they are part of some group such as a family or a class and they have to participate in some group activities, yet they come to know that they clearly separate from others. It long has been an ideal to be an independent, personally responsible individual that is able to live life on his or her own terms.[27] Individuals have their own unique beliefs, values, goals, immediate desires, and conscience. Individuals have to speak for themselves for no one else can do it for them. How can others know them unless the individual tells others about themselves? So of course there is "I-" and "me-centered" talk. We say *we* want to grow up to be a ____. We share our successes (and often thank those who have helped us). We tell our family that we like prime rib so they make that on our birthday. We are not offended if one American wants a coke and another a 7-Up. We do not react to this talk as "self-centered" though we can recognize when people are "full of themselves."

Obviously, some of our individual desires will be in conflict, but disagreements are expected and verbal conflicts can be viewed as productive.[28]

This idea of individualism carries over into U.S. military operations, as Schweikart suggests, that was evident in the 2003 war in Iraq where:

> ... officers adapted new tactics in the field without fear of reprisal, [which] spoke volumes about a key American military trait—that of empowering the troops. Exercising their individual initiative ... presumes that officers and troops have ... the incentives to exercise their own judgment. Unlike any other military culture in history, American fighters are trusted to adapt and overcome—the field manual be [condemned].[29]

If we are individuals and we have to speak about ourselves, then clear and direct speaking is valued so listeners can more accurately know what we are conveying (Chapter Six emphasis). According to Barnlund, individualism and the expression of that quality is stressed in America:

The ability of every person to act as his or her own advocate, to articulate personal opinions trenchantly and persuasively, is cultivated throughout the education process. The constant encouragement to express one's self, to be heard and felt .... Rarely does one gain a position of power without a gift for articulating ideas clearly and eloquently.[30]

Due to this individualism, Americans can largely *write* their own life story, and many literally do it, as well. President Obama's life was not preordained—he wrote it (with some early family help, of course). He has also cultivated an expressive, articulate voice. This is respected in America.

While there is individualism in America, it has diminished over time. According to Codevilla, "In 2008, some 13 million American children were on welfare, and 28 million—9.4 percent of all Americans—received food stamps."[31] Eighty-five different welfare programs exist, beginning with those enacted during the 1930's.[32] A woman on welfare with two kids in twelve states receives 90 percent of the average local wage, while this same family unit receives more than the after-tax earnings of the average worker in four other states and Washington, D.C. Further, the family receiving benefits from just five welfare programs has greater benefits than the person who has a minimum-wage job in any of the fifty states. Thus, many Americans have given up their self-reliance, individual initiative, and overall personal responsibility and independence. Rather, they rely on the U.S. government to take, through taxes, the earned income of working Americans (yes, many working Americans are also subsidized in varying degrees). To what extent can people who receive either all or nearly all of their income or income-in-kind from taxpayer subsidies be an advocate for their own personal life? How can they express their independent voice, speak about personal responsibility and individual goals, or persuasively argue for individual liberty? Ironically, Codevilla finds that approximately "… 40 percent of those eligible for benefits do not take advantage of them because they are too proud to become part of a culture of dependence so at odds with normal American ways."[33] Some Americans still ascribe to Emerson's self-reliance.[34] According to Brinkley, "…the real reason that the War on Poverty lost its popularity is because deep down inside most Americans is an admiration for those who have overcome difficulties and risen to achievement by their own efforts."[35] Thus, the unpopular and failed War on Poverty had its name changed to the guilt free and merit-implied term *entitlements*.

Collectivism

Collectivist cultures provide a stark contrast to individual cultures. The members give priority to harmonious communication and interdependence.[36] The group members' communication reflects cooperation talk to satisfy the group's needs and achieve its goals. There is an emphasis on having a group interpretation of the group's status quo and goals.[37] According to Gudykunst, "Children in Japan are taught not to call attention to themselves or take the initiative verbally. Rather, they are taught to foster *enryo*, ritualized verbal self-depreciation used to maintain group harmony."[38] Japanese go out of their way to be in agreement with their group members since expressing displeasure about something can destroy a lifelong friendship.[39] Since collectivist cultures like Japan have more shared agreement about their language and culture than do individualistic cultures, they can be more circumspect in stating their opinions, trusting the other communicator/s to figure out what is not directly said, such as displeasure.

Further, since the collectivists such as East Asians desire to achieve harmony in their communication, they also emphasize face-saving. This attempt to preserve a positive, public image of someone results in little or no questioning of superiors, few public arguments, and an attempt to avoid saying "no." It would be embarrassing if a teacher or political leader could not give a legitimate answer since they are supposed to know, so they are not asked. Arguments signal discord between individuals and are thought to upset the group harmony. Lastly, the Japanese want to avoid hurting the other person's feelings so they have developed sixteen different ways to express *no* without directly saying it.[40]

While there is more group-centered emphasis in some cultures, some of this group solidarity is an appearance. Such is the case in Japan where individuals are loyal to their groups because (when) it satisfies personal goals.[41]

Further, even apparent collectivists are not necessarily group centered outside their immediate group, for during World War II with America, the Japanese Army and Navy did not commonly work together.[42] The emphasis on achieving group goals in Japan is also at least a little simplistic for someone or a relatively few number of people instigate and at least indirectly direct the agenda of a given group. While a group leader's motivation may be to do things for the good of the group, individual and self-serving goals cannot be ruled out.[43]

Groups, particularly the family, are very important to Filipinos for these groups provide them an identity and help them with life's difficulties.[44] The more groups someone is connected to, the greater potential for personal prestige and help. In conversations, Filipinos are expected to be loyal and supportive of those members in their groups. As Gochenour concludes, "Maintaining good relations with other people is more important than being 'right' or getting a particular task accomplished."[45] One way they do this is by being polite. Barnlund also finds the Japanese to be very polite.[46]

So what do you do as an *individual* if you discover your intercultural stranger is from a collectivist culture? Collectivists tend to be indirect so you will have to listen for hints of some preference or viewpoint they have. With Japanese, especially, the American can act a little more polite than usual, be a little less assertive about a point of view they hold, ask fewer questions, speak less about their successes and personal affairs, slow down their rate of speaking, vocally analyze a topic of discussion less than would be normal, and avoid asking for clear, concise language.[47] While in individualistic cultures like America people readily express their feelings, people in collectivistic cultures withhold these until they think they know the other person.[48] Communication is not a one-way responsibility. The collectivistic stranger (such as a Japanese) will have to recognize that the American is just being their typical more open and direct self. Filipinos, while collective, are different from Japanese. Filipinos may ask relative strangers what the stranger paid for something, which Americans (and Japanese) would consider a private matter, and if the stranger (American) is married, as these inquires reveal the Filipinos interest in the other person.[49]

2. High-Context and Low-Context Cultures. According to Hall, "'Context' is the information that surrounds an event ..."[50] and informs people (in varying degrees) about the meaning of the event and the communication occurring therein. On the basis of their cultural preparation for interpreting the situations in which they find themselves, people will have an idea about what to pay attention to and what can be overlooked. The idiosyncrasies of the encounter, such as the purpose of the interaction, the physicality of the setting, the relationship with the people present, and the actions that are occurring provide people with information from which to draw meaning, including what communication is expected and acceptable. We know from Chapter One that the context influences our communication. We adjust our communication in part according to the situations we are in. What differs between cultures is that they vary on a continuum about the degree to which they expect to be informed more by the context itself (and their preparation for communicating in that type of context) and the degree to which they are dependent upon their own and surrounding people's communication for the meaning they draw from the situation.

High-Context

For example, Japanese are said to already know what they are supposed to say in a variety of situations and when in a given one, the context alerts them to the appropriate message to use.[51] This is categorized as being *high-context*. In these cultures, we might say that the culture provides a high amount of information for most contexts people find themselves in, with little need to be informed at the moment with explicit, verbal messages. Members are "schooled" by those in close personal relationships with them[52] as they grow up in their culture to communicate such-and-such messages at funerals, other specific messages at weddings, other messages at sporting events, and so on. It is as if the high-context individual's communication is programmed into them, awaiting the appropriate setting in which to call up the stored message. Either by knowing what they are supposed to know or by being able to figure out the situation they encounter, a high-context listener is expected by the speaker to perceive what the speaker's feelings are, be they happy, sad, pensive, or whatever.[53] The speaker does not have to be direct and explicit. The listener examines the implicit, nonverbal messages to tip them off as to what the speaker is implying and what would be appropriate to say in response.[54] High-context cultures include, among others, Japan, China, Korea, Arab, and Latin-American countries.[55]

One liability for high-context members is that in an unfamiliar circumstance, they may not be able to effectively adapt. In this event, Japanese (for example) may just keep silent.[56] Given the implicit, indirect, ambiguous, and fewer verbal messages from high-context people, low-context people may perceive the high-context members as "… non-disclosive, sneaky, and mysterious."[57]

Low-Context

Americans, on the other hand, do not have as much stored, situation-specific information to use in their communication encounters so they have to depend more on verbal interaction to acquire the bulk of their information. They are considered *low-context* for the context provides very little information (relatively speaking) to guide their communication and meaning creation. According to Hall, this leads Americans to think it is necessary to know what the purposes and expectations are of the circumstance if someone wants them to decide on and/or take a certain course of action.[58] "This need for detailed background information stems from the fact that the American approach to life is quite segmented and focuses on discrete, compartmentalized bits of information. Americans need to know what is going to occur before they commit themselves.[59]

Although low-context cultures such as America do recognize different contexts and know some appropriate communication to use in many contexts, they do not feel entirely constrained by the expectations. For example, we know the proper communication decorum to use during a church service. Still, members of low-context cultures have to explicitly communicate with each other to co-create meaning since they do not share sufficient message and meaning similarities as do those from group-centered cultures. There has to be a great deal more emphasis on clear, verbal communication. If there is not, Americans will likely say, "Don't beat around the bush" and "Get to the point." Other, and even slightly more, low context cultures include Switzerland, German, and the Scandinavian countries.[60]

To communicate with low-context people can require some extra effort by high-context people who " ... are apt to become impatient and irritated when low-context people insist on giving them information they don't need."[61] With the greater amount of information that low-context think they need to get from and give to each other, high context culture people often perceive them as too talkative and redundant. On the other hand, Hall finds that "... low-context people are at a loss when high-context people do not provide *enough* information."[62]

In summary, Gudykunst characterize the communication of high-context peoples as "...indirect, ambiguous, and understated, with speakers being reserved and sensitive to listeners. Low-context communication ... [is] direct, explicit, open, precise, and consistent with one's feelings."[63] The author suggests that high-context peoples use high-context messages most of the time when they communicate. Low-context peoples use low-context messages most of the time but will use high-context messages depending upon the person they are with. For example, Americans do not have to be so explicit in their communication with their close family members and friends. A certain glance or indirect comment by the sender may be all that is needed between two close Americans for the receiver to get the idea.

High-context cultures are also collectivist cultures, and low-context cultures are individual cultures.[64] Thus, America is relatively low-context and individualistic while Japan (and to a lesser extent, the Philippines) is high-context and collectivist (group-oriented).

3. *Power Distances.* This characteristic reveals the extent to which the least powerful group of people in a culture accept any existing political, financial, and/or social power differences among the greater population. Hofstede reminds us that, "Authority survives only where it is matched by obedience."[65] How do the least powerful communicate with the most powerful, and vice versa? A cursory understanding of history and geography illustrates that distinct class systems with their separation of power between classes have existed in many places for most of recorded human history.

　　We know that communication is transactional so if the least powerful alter their part of the transaction by not verbally going along with the system, the system will not go along as it has or the most powerful will sanction the least powerful. In high power distance cultures, there is widespread acceptance of the power differences revealed through communication transactions by the least powerful with those who are in the most powerful political, economic, and/or social positions. Hofstede notes that coercive (presumably physical and/or legal force) and referent (charismatic) powers are common in high power distance cultures.[66]

　　People in low power distance cultures, such as America, view each other as individual, equals who are fulfilling roles (such as supervisor) that have more or less power available to the position. People tend to emphasize the use of legitimate or expert power in their interactions, as opposed to referent power (more fitting a class society) or coercion (individuals dislike bossiness or force).

　　What is the impact of power distance on communication? In the high power distance cultures, there are hierarchical power and status distances, which means that those in superior positions frequently give orders and the subordinates carry them out and without question.[67] Hgh power distance cultures are found in Malaysia (with a large Muslim population), Guatemala, Panama, Philippines (with Muslims primarily in the south), Mexico, Venezuela, Arab countries, Ecuador, and Indonesia (the largest Muslim population in the world).[68] Thus, the top nine cultures with recognized (and accepted) power distances are either former Spanish colonies or Muslim countries. Gochenour suggests that the Philippines is hierarchical, and amongst the countries noted above, people prefer autocratic and paternalistic bosses and employers.[69] There is more of telling people what to do and the least powerful accepting orders at face value. There is greater emphasis on the less powerful people communicating respect to the powerful. Teachers in high power distance cultures are respected both in and outside of school, never criticized, and are viewed as a "guru" imparting personal wisdom to the students. Parents in high power distance cultures expect more obedience from their kids than do parents in low power distance cultures.[70] Even though America is not a high power-distance culture, we can see some power distance in typical American families between parents and their children in which the children tend to use deferential communication toward their parents, and they do not (excepting extreme cases) order their parents around

In those cultures identified as having low-power distance, such as Austria, Israel, Denmark, New Zealand, and to a lesser degree the United States,[71] the disparity between the social and economic power between cultural members is markedly less than in the high-power distance cultures. There is less presumption of expecting to and actually telling people what to do. In America, there is more of a presumption of equality of individuals, as persons, so there is no power position respect to show, only common courtesies. According to D'Souza, "Bill Gates could not approach a homeless person and say, 'Here's a $100 bill. I'll give it to you if you kiss my feet.' Most likely the homeless guy would tell Gates to go to hell!"[72] Further, "America is the only country in the world where we call the waiter 'Sir,' as if he were a knight."[73] As another example, Schweikart suggests that "...most Americans in the military are equal, as General George Patton learned in Sicily in 1943 when he struck a pair of enlisted men in two separate incidences at Army hospitals"[74] for which he was ordered to apologize to each soldier and his command was taken from him. A doctor observing Patton asking one of the soldiers for forgiveness wrote, "I kept thinking, 'My Lord, here is a three-star general apologizing to a lowly private soldier.' I could not imagine anything similar happening in any other army."[75] Employees may question their bosses (in a respectful manner), and they often want to be told why they have to do what the bosses want. American students in class are expected to ask questions when they do not understand something. They may argue with teachers (particularly in an argumentation, logic, or law class which may require it), express class criticisms, report criticisms of teachers to a school principal or college dean, and show no particular respect to teachers outside school (teachers may be no more insightful about the world outside school than the general population).

Americans tend to be informal in their communication because they see each other as equals, including those in superior business, political, and education positions. As the old sayings go, "He has to put his pants on just like me, one leg at a time" and "He has to wait in line, just like me." The British historian Keegan suggests he found this orientation on his visit to the White House. Notice the low-power distance illustrated in Keegan's description below.

The President [Bill Clinton] is cocooned by perfection. He is not, however, allowed to think for one moment that he is royal. Head of State he may be, but his fellow citizens speak their minds directly and unaffectedly. At my [English] palace evening the guests spoke hesitantly and into the middle distance. In the White House, the President's guests addressed him over dinner face-to-face, and made polemical points.

I was, I realized, present at an occasion when the American voice makes the American mind unequivocally clear to the chief of the nation. I could imagine no similar occasion in England. We defer, not only to our hereditary but also to our elected leaders; collectively, we are as independent and as difficult to govern as any people on earth; individually, we shuffle and stumble our words and bob our heads and hope we have not broken any of the rules. There are no rules between Americans, except those of the common politeness that ought to govern free people.

It was I who had "sirred" and "Mr. Presidented" in a reflex of the manner I would have used at home. The Americans had "Mr. Presidented" also, but as the preliminary to statements of what he ought to say, what he ought to think.

I had seen the President as a first among equals, a relationship that is the essence of the American political system.[76]

It does not appear to be an accident that the cultures that are most individualistic are also likely to have a low-power distance orientation. The stressing of individuality means that everyone is equal, so no one would have any presumed personal power over anyone else.

NONVERBAL COMMUNICATION

Intercultural strangers would be expected to use different nonverbal messages and have differing meanings for at least some (if not many) of those, which in turn are likely to become a basis for misunderstandings. For example, what Americans label as the "A-OK" hand gesture is interpreted with hostile meanings in at least a few cultures. There are an endless number of message examples that can be considered inappropriate by intercultural strangers.[77] Since people creating nonverbal messages are typically unaware of many of their own messages, as well as those of culturally different people with whom they are unfamiliar, they usually do not realize when their nonverbal communication is inappropriate unless the other person indicates it in some way. If we think we might make mistakes, we tend to avoid strangers.[78]

Fortunately, we can learn some of the basic gestures and other nonverbal communication rules of people in other cultures. *Emblems*, for example (briefly discussed in Chapter 7) are a type of hand gesture that translate directly into a word or phrase so they are observable and clear.[79] We can anticipate the use or not of certain emblems depending on the host culture's rules, thereby avoiding some of the simpler or more obvious misinterpretations, blunders, ill will, and conflicts between strangers. The section below provides the reader with some examples of nonverbal meaning differences for messages that exist in different parts of the world.

While it is easy to say that participants in intercultural communication situations need to *be flexible* with their communication and adapt, it may or may not be easy. We could easily have a strong aversion to people standing too close to us, to touching us or in certain places, to speaking very loudly to us, to using a gesture toward us that we interpret as profane, and so on. Someone telling you to be flexible is unlikely to diminish your anxiety in the moment. Still, all you can do is try to adapt to the extent you can. You do not have to do everything everyone in host culture is doing. Many people present will recognize that you are a visitor and would not know or do everything they do. Is your Italian brother-in-law going to get mad if you do not kiss him on both cheeks upon greeting? If you do not bow or bow correctly, are the Japanese you meet in Japan going to be mad at you? People know there are cultural differences and if they get the sense that you are trying to perform some common courtesies, they are generally pleased.

By the same token, we should not readily assume that we can do "over there" what we do at home. We could do a little research about the place before we visit it. Unless people are sure about a culture's rules for using emblems, Galllois recommends that intercultural travelers carefully communicate ideas, feelings, and attitudes with words instead of gestures.[80] This is not easy since feelings can be difficult to describe in an understandable way.

Sample of Nonverbal Messages and Meanings (Axtell[81])

1. The action of a newly arrived Korean store owners/employee to America (including Guam) when giving change to customers who have made a purchase: no smile or thank-you and they place the change on the counter (not into your hand). American (and Guam) interpretation: rudeness, unfriendliness, does not want my business.

2. American OK hand gesture (ends of thumb and index fingers touching, other fingers slightly bent or straight)
   • America: OK, good job, completed the task, settled the concern, agreement.

- Mediterranean Sea area (parts of): zero (France: zero or worthless).
- Latin America: up yours (like American middle finger).
- Germany: crude message for female genital area.
- Tunisia: I will kill you.
- Japan: money.

3. American two-fingered "V" gesture, palm towards audience/receiver: victory or peace. In England, with palm toward the person making the gesture: up yours/American middle finger.

4. Japanese (and South Korean) listeners' reaction to your speech in Japan (or Korea), during which their eyes may close and heads nod, as if they are sleeping during your speech. Meaning: concentration and possibly agreement. They are listening.

5. Japanese male reaction to an American male putting his arm around the Japanese's shoulder while talking or walking in Japan: embarrassment, American should not be touching him.

6. American pretending to be shoveling dirt or snow while you speak to him (or her): disbelief, he thinks you are "full of baloney."

7. In many parts of the Middle East and Far East, showing the sole (bottom) of the shoe to people: it is dirty, insulting.

8. Signaling "I see a pretty girl" in:
- Italy: index finger corkscrewing into one facial cheek.
- Greece: male strokes his chin with 1 hand, as if stroking a beard.
- Brazil: form a telescope with both hands, hold over one eye, observe the desired object.
- France: kiss the fingertips of 1 hand in the direction of the pretty girl, then open the fingertips, grunt, maybe say "magnifique" (this can also indicate good food, wine, etc.).
- U.S: whistle.

9. Cheek kissing among males in Eastern Europe, Italy, France: greeting, respect, friendship.

10. Spitting or blowing the nose directly onto the ground in public in China: hygiene and getting rid of evil spirits.

11. Thumbs-Up (four fingers in a fist position with the thumb pointing up) in America: good job, success. In Australia: up yours, like the American middle finger.

12. Frenchman pretending to play the flute: disbelief of what you are saying.

13. Butt-pinching (formerly) in Rome (remember, when in Rome,...): compliment, pretty lady.

14. American "come here" gesture with arm outstretched, palm up, fingers scratching motion. To Australians and Indonesians: "come here, dog."

15. Staring at people in Japan, Korea, and Thailand: rude, offensive, and disrespectful. This is normal in Saudi Arabia.

16. Jews pointing to the palm of their hand while listening to someone speak: disbelief, grass will grow on his or her palm before what is said will occur.

17. Filipino girls and/or women walking arm in arm in the Philippines (and on Guam): closeness, friends, sisters, mother and daughter. Male hand-holding is common in the Middle East, parts of Korea, China, and Indonesia: friendship.

18. Picking your nose in someone's direction in Syria: go to hell.

19. Showing public affection in Saudi Arabia (kiss, hug): forbidden, may be arrested. This is also unacceptable (especially kissing) in Japan, Korea, and China.

20. Smiling in Japan may indicate happiness, anger, confusion, apology, or sadness.

21. Silence a virtue in China and Japan; comfortable for them. Americans are uncomfortable with silence. They think they must talk.

22. An open mouth, revealing teeth: impolite in Japan (notice how they cover their mouths when laughing). No sneezing or blowing your nose at business meetings or at social gatherings.

23. Posture in Japan and Korea: do not slouch or put your feet on a table or stool; walk and sit upright, solid-appearing.

24. Americans gesture with their arms. This is socially and in business impolite to Japanese.

25. Pointing towards something in the Philippines: with the lips. In the U.S.: with fingers (Japanese consider this rude, as do some people in the U.S.).

26. Drinking tea in Hong Kong: do not touch your served tea until the host begins to drink.

27. Shaking hands while greeting:
- America: use a firm grip (a limp hand implies the person is weak, uncertain, effeminate).
- Russia: use a strong, firm grasp, followed by a bear hug.
- Middle East: use a gentle grip.
- Japan, Korea: use a gentle grip, joined by a slight head bow (but not required for outsiders).

28. Nodding the head in an up and down direction means "yes" in America, "no" in Turkey, Iran, and some other places.

29. Americans stand 24-30" apart, Asians further apart. Latin Americans, Middle Easterners stand closer.

30. Use of left hand in the Middle East: never use it (they wipe their butt with it). Leave it at your side. Shake hands and give things to others only with the right hand.

31. Admiring a person's kids in the U.S.: do not pinch the kid's cheeks.

32. Hello, goodbye gesture is common in Europe: extended arm, palm down, with hand movement up and down at the wrist.

33. Touch: there is more of it in Korea, Indochina, Italy, Spain, Puerto Rico, and some other places. There is little or none in Japan, U.S., Australia, and some other places. There is a middling amount in France, China, India, and other places.

34. Giving and receiving business cards (meishi) in Japan: have information about yourself in English on one side, in Japanese on the other. Exchange cards early in the introduction, presenting the card with both hands, the card grasped between the thumbs and forefingers, with the lettering facing the receiver, slightly bowing. Give and receive like this. Study the other person's card for a few seconds to read their name, title, company name, and address. Then shake hands (gently) and bow again. Handle (treat) the other's card with respect—do not write notes on it in front of them.

Guam Examples

35. Greeting an elder (or even an older adult) Chamorro on Guam: with your right hand, take an elder's available hand and while bowing slightly, bring the back of it to your nose as if you are smelling it. *Amen*, meaning to inhale the elder's wisdom, is a sign of respect. This is frequently followed by a kiss on the cheek if the elder is of the opposite sex. Filipino variation: holding the back of the elder's hand to your forehead, again taking in their wisdom.

36. Chad nod (head nod) on Guam: a form of greeting or "Hi" to a friend, a challenge to a disliked person. Tilt the head backwards with the chin jutting forward, looking at the person of interest, and for a friend, probably accompanied by a smile and an eyebrow flash.

Upon entering another culture, or when interacting with someone from another culture, people cannot be expected to know very many of the other culture's gestures and other messages. It would be helpful if major violations are avoided.

Time

According to Hall, time talks.[82] How we respond to time provides a clear nonverbal message to those with whom we interact. Hall categorizes cultures' time orientation as being either *monochronic* (M-time) or *polychronic*.(P-time).

People in *monochronic* cultures such as Americans and Northern Europeans generally pay attention to, schedule, and do one task at a time for serious matters (such as business). Americans divide the available time, which brings order their lives—time for work, time for family, time for play, time for church/community, and so on. Even within each of these activities, we generally segment our time. People are expected to be prompt, on time for the agreed-upon activities. Americans do not want to "waste time," particularly at work where "time is money." Americans and Northern Europeans think of time as tangible, something that can be saved, spent, or lost.[83] The more we "use our time wisely," the more we can accomplish. The more we accomplish, the more money we may make or the improved quality of life either we or someone else may experience. People should be well organized and follow a schedule to accomplish necessary tasks and not waste other people's time. The reason we pay such close attention to time is to allow us to be efficient (the quickest way, be it cleaning the house, paying the bills, completing taxes, getting food prepared or buying it (fast food), getting to the vacation destination, starting a potential romantic relationship (speech dating, anyone?), and so on). Other countries that particularly emphasize M-time are Germany, Switzerland, and Scandinavian countries.[84]

"Polychronic time" reflects an almost opposite use of time from M-time. Activities are done on a more ad-hoc basis, multiple activities may be scheduled or occur at overlapping times, and things get done when they get done. Someone's attention may shift from one incomplete task to another activity, and then maybe back to the first one. Latin American and Middle Eastern countries illustrate this time orientation. It may seem that they will start or finish projects "when they get to it." Actions seem more the result of spontaneous choices.[85] Interruptions are common and business appointments may be put aside for several hours while something else considered more important in the moment is dealt with.[86] For M-time people, time in P-time cultures seems to stand still. It is relaxing for Americans and Northern Europeans to visit P-time countries on vacations since these countries are more "laid back" with time than are their own cultures.

As it might be imagined, M-time and P-time people have difficulty working together. American culture places a high value on results, 'getting the job done,' and expects everyone to pull their own weight to finish in the shortest amount of time. For P-time Filipinos, they think that maintaining harmonious group feelings is just as important as achieving a goal. In Japan, M-time is adhered to for appointments and scheduling activities (business first, and this includes golf) while P-time is followed for most other situations.[87] When people from cultures with different time orientations work together, conflicts can easily occur over time work habits.

There are strengths and weaknesses to both time orientations. M-time is not biologically natural[88] but a cursory glance around the world and over the last one hundred-plus years reveals that M-time cultures have greater economic production and higher standards of living. M-time cultures should have advantages over P-time cultures when fighting a war for "he who gets there first and with the most" has a significant advantage. Losing wars have serious consequences for the losers. On the other hand, there are many working people in America and Northern Europe that appear to be living in a rat race, which creates social problems and physiological stress. While P-time cultures appear to be more socially humane as individuals are allowed to focus on human needs in the process of completing business activities, a general sense of history shows that the economies in Southern Europe, the Middle East, and Latin America were weaker during most of the 20th century than were M-time economies. People from P-time countries often emigrate to M-time countries for a "better life."[89]

Space

In the chapter on nonverbal communication there was a discussion about proxemics and peoples' use of space in daily interactions. Space "talks" even if we do not "hear." It is very easy to make space mistakes in other cultures because cultures differ in their use of space and our use of it largely occurs outside our awareness.[90]

Althen places cultures into one of three groups.[91] People from Latin America and the Middle East stand so close together when speaking that their toes may even touch. At this distance you can readily smell the other person's breath and their body odor, as well as touch them in many parts of their body. Americans occupy the middle range, standing about an arm's length (2 to 2.5') away from each other when talking. According to Hall, when Latin Americans speak to Americans at a close distance, Americans back up. To Latin Americans this suggests Americans are "…distant or cold, withdrawn and unfriendly."[92] Watson's proxemic study of Americans and Arabs found that Arabs interacted at a closer distance.[93] Japanese and Chinese stand even further apart when speaking (space permitting). Barnlund reports that in a study of same-sex Venezuelans, Americans, and Japanese, the Venezuelans stood 32.2" apart, the Americans 35.4" apart, and the Japanese 40.2" apart.[94] When Americans speak to Japanese, they stand too close to suit Japanese and may be considered too intimate or pushy. Ironically, when Japanese sit and speak English with each other, they sit at a similar distance as Americans.[95] The use of space is such a subtle behavior that we are normally unconscious of our use of it, but when someone uses it differently than we, we are usually uncomfortable. Gudykunst reports people's individualism-collectivism orientation is related to their response when people violate their space.[96] People from individualistic cultures are inclined to respond aggressively. People from collectivistic cultures typically back away and respond passively.

Touch

As noted in Chapter 7 Nonverbal Communication, people are very sensitive to touch. It is used in various contexts and implies different meanings. As might be expected, the contexts, actual touching behaviors, and meanings differ from culture to culture. It was also reported that touch can elicit a strong emotional response. We know that American women react angrily to strangers or even casual friends or co-workers touching them, particularly in sensitive areas. This could get the "toucher" arrested. Both Americans and Japanese can be ranked as noncontact cultures.[97] Still, in a comparison between these two, the least-touched Americans report being touched more than the most-touched Japanese.[98] Arabs, Latin Americans, and Southern Europeans are ranked as high contact cultures.[99] We could expect that someone from one of these areas, while interacting with Americans, would touch the American more than the American is used to so the American would feel uneasy and possibly withdraw. In America, with groups of people coming from around the globe, Americans of English descent touch less than Italian-Americans or African-Americans.[100]

BARRIERS TO INTERCULTURAL COMMUNICATION

In addition to the previous information in this chapter that may be used to aid intercultural communication effectiveness, there are also some general obstacles that increase misunderstandings and make the sharing of meaning more difficult in intercultural encounters. DeVito describes six of these,[101] suggesting that if we can overcome these barriers, we will increase our communication effectiveness.

1. *Ignoring Differences Between Yourself and the Culturally Different.* This occurs when a person mindlessly assumes that similarities exist and differences do not, particularly regarding values, attitudes, and beliefs. When we communicate the idea that similarities do or should exist, we are implicitly communicating that our ways are the correct ways and that the other person's ways are unimportant. For example, since Americans generally believe that everyone is born equal, they do not readily defer to people or like public displays of respect given to them[102] when the showing of respect is common around the world (bowing to kings, queens, sheiks, emperors and showing

respect in other ways to higher status people). When Americans do not show the expected respect, foreigners get upset with them. On the other hand, foreigners who get upset with Americans about this are also ignoring the differences between themselves and Americans. Ideally, we would recognize differences and attempt to be appropriately flexible.

   2. *Ignoring Differences Among the Members of the Culturally Different Group.* This is stereotyping. There are differences within every cultural group. Not all Filipinos, Japanese, and so on are alike. Within a country, people may vary by region or island. There are also gender differences within each culture. When our messages leave unstated the differences between people in a given group, we are stereotyping. We almost always do this without mental awareness of it, operating on "auto pilot" generalities. When people are labeled and treated like the label—the stereotype—they often object. It is as if they are being treated like an object.

   Many people claim that diversity exists betweens groups of people, that one group of, say, ___-Americans is different from the rest of Americans. This implies there is a commonality among those in the given group, different from the entire country. To refer to what is most common among these group members, or at least a large portion of them, would not be in error.

   When a foreigner stereotypes Americans in our presence, we can recognize the validity (or not) of the generalizations and know that we, individually, probably differ in some respects. That foreigner did not know us before so how could they know our individuality?

   3. *Ignoring Differences in Meaning in Verbal and Nonverbal Behavior.* Within *human communication* as this text emphasizes, it is suggested that meaning does not exist either in the words or the nonverbal messages used but in the minds of the interacting individuals. In an interaction between people of different cultures, we can expect that there will be meaning differences between people as they interpret the existing verbal and nonverbal messages. We are not usually mindful of how the other person is interpreting the situation so we overlook potential differences and this leads to misunderstandings between us.

   For example, Althen finds that people from countries such as Germany and Brazil think that politics is a great topic to discuss in informal situations but they usually overlook that Americans have a different sense of politics and are taught not to discuss it unless they know a person well (and even then they may avoid it).[103] These two points of view about the meaning of *politics* can lead each side to think something is wrong with the other side. Typical Americans think *money* is a private matter while a Filipino from the

Philippines thinks otherwise and may ask the American, "What did you pay for that?"[104] Americans consider this an intrusion into their privacy that the Filipino has ignored. From the Filipino point of view, the Americans are misinterpreting what is to them a feeling of interest in the American.

While different cultures may have language terms for what we call *men, women, children, family, religion, sports, work*, and so on, and may even use these exact words when speaking English with us, we should not assume they have a similar meaning in mind. If we are able to see how they interact with the people, beliefs, or concepts these words symbolize, we are very likely to see a range of different behaviors suggesting that different cultures have different meanings for these terms. Further, it can be recognized that there are meanings differences for nonverbal messages, too, as the earlier section in this chapter illustrates.

4. *Violating Cultural Rules and Customs.* Each culture has its own unique rules for acceptable communication, and being natural to them, they think that the rules are correct. For example, typical Americans expect to look at each other when they speak to each other, while Japanese, Koreans, and Thai expect to avoid direct eye contact when communicating—they think it is rude when Americans and others violate this rule.[105] Arabs and Latin Americans expect to stand closer to those with whom they are communicating than do Americans so when they stand close to Americans, Americans feel uncomfortable. There are virtually an endless number of customs around the world and no cross-cultural books citing those of each culture, so we can expect that the other person will not share all of our social rules and values. When rules are broken, it can be understood as a sign of offense or disrespect. If the person with whom you are interacting has a different reaction to your behavior than you do, he or she may have a different set of rules. Ask them about this if you can.

5. *Evaluating Differences Negatively/Ethnocentrism.* When we notice differences between our own and another culture, our first impulse is to think that something is wrong with the other culture since our own culture is so natural to us. If we follow this reaction with a depreciating statement about the culture to our intercultural partner, they are likely to become defensive.[106] As an alternative, we could use supportive climate language. Even if our impression seems justified at first glance, it can easily be simplistic, overlooking other more justifiable features of the culture to which the feature before us is inter-related. Americans debate ideas, even between parents and their children.[107] This would be interpreted as disrespectful to many people in Asian cultures, but to Americans it is a part of being an individual and thinking for

themselves. Some foreigners may disparage the general American tendency to not communicate what foreigners believe is appropriate respect for their esteemed people, when to Americans, everyone is equal and deserves nothing more than common politeness. These foreigners will probably not make this connection in the moment, and even if they did, they still believe in the inequality of people.

This leads into the second part of this barrier, ethnocentrism, evaluating the values, beliefs, and behaviors of our own culture as being superior to those of another culture. Since all we know is what we know and what we generally know is our own culture, we would expect to use it as a benchmark for evaluating other cultures. The same tendency occurs in people in other cultures as they assess the cultures they come in contact with or speak about.[108] A superiority orientation tends to be simplistic in understanding and interpreted as condescending.

Still, there are obvious cultural differences around the world whose manifestations make life much more unpleasant for the people living within those culture. It is not ethnocentric to say so, and people living in those places frequently agree. Americans know that there are some weaknesses in America, such as in the public education system. Crime led to a great deal of suffering from the mid-1960's to the early 1990's. In some parts of the world, normal sexual practices have significantly increased the spread of AIDS in these places. Corruption and dishonesty are almost a way of life in some countries and these hurt the economies of these countries and the standard of living for people there. Any member of a culture that has sexual practices that do not easily spreads AIDS or is in a significantly less-corrupt country would not be ethnocentric to believe that their culture was superior on those artifacts to countries having the opposite traits. If many other things are equal, life in a culture having little or no corruption is better than life in a culture having a great deal of corruption.

Would it have been ethnocentric for the Indians and Arabs that initially used what came to be called Arabic numerals to evaluate the pre-existing Roman numerals as inferior and their own as superior? Would it have been ethnocentric for people then and later living in what is present-day Italy to maintain their Roman numerals simply "because they are ours so they are better"? Could we begin to imagine what life would be like for Italians today if they continued exclusive use of Roman numerals rather than having switched to the obviously better system? As discussed in greater detail in the additional material at the end of this chapter, some cultural groups obviously do some things better at a given point in time than do other groups and it is hardly ethnocentric to mention these strengths and the redeeming outcomes of those strengths.

While it may be ethnocentric to expect everyone in the world to speak your language, should it be considered ethnocentric to expect everyone in a given country such as America to speak the common and established language? How else can they be expected to communicate with each other? English has been the *lingua franca* in America since before the Revolutionary War. Is it ethnocentric for immigrants to America in the late 20th century and thereafter to presume to primarily or solely speak their native tongues in public and expect and/or demand that 250-plus million other Americans accommodate their languages and even create situations that force these other Americans to speak the more recent immigrants' tongues?

For those who think having multiple public languages is a trite issue, they may be reminded of the trouble in Belgium in the 1960's and 1970's when Flemish speakers refused to speak French and the French speakers in Canada in more recent times refused to speak English.[109] French-speaking Quebec seriously considered seceding from Canada around the year 2000. Does America really want a divided country like in Belgium and in Canada, in this case between English-speaking regions and primarily Spanish-speaking regions in America? Mexifornia through Mexitexas, anyone? Was not the Civil War fought in part because a divided country cannot expect to hold itself together, at least in a crisis?

We also know from the cultural elements mentioned earlier in this chapter that the cultures in America and in Mexico, the country of origin for most of the Spanish-speaking peoples in America, differ quite a bit when it comes to individualism and collectivism, high-context and low-context, power distances, and uses of time, space, and touch.[110] Is it ethnocentric for those who identify with Mexico to presume to change these American cultural values, beliefs, and communication behaviors to fit Mexico's image? Is there not an underlying assumption within those who have come to America from Mexico that America is superior to Mexico for they have, according to Hanson, "vot[ed] with [their] feet to reject Mexican culture.... [Mexican immigrants] saw America as antithetical to their homeland and thus their last and only hope."?[111]

Since so many newer arrivals to America speak little or no English,[112] and they have been encouraged to speak Spanish in America, are we adding a "tower of Babel"? How are Americans ethnocentric to expect foreign immigrants to speak English if they, the immigrants, want to participate in the public marketplace?

Consider a different, potential ethnocentrism issue. Should a tourist or hoped-for emigrant from Country A visiting or residing in Country B be expected to follow the host country's laws? Push-come-to-shove, whose culture rules? If a local person would be fined and/or jailed for a certain behavior, should the visitor be treated likewise? How far will you go to allow the visitor's religious or sexual practices, social customs, and so on? Do they have "cultural" immunity?

It is in every culture's long-term interest to recognize critical weaknesses in the culture and correct them. We read about failed cultures in our history books. If it takes someone outside the culture to point out a culture's weaknesses, even as he or she points out his or her culture's superior ways, we do not have to simplistically and defensively label them ethnocentric.

6. *Culture Shock.* We would expect to be surprised by some things that occur in other cultures, but culture shock means being exposed to a cultural situation so very different and unsettling that it leads us to experience a strong emotional reaction—extreme bewilderment, embarrassment, frustration, fear, and so on We may fear being laughed at or belittled in public (lose our *face*, as noted in Chapter Nine), robbed, going to jail, and so on. We may experience a mental block with our emotions overriding our clear thinking, resulting in an extreme response such as yelling, physically hitting someone, being totally silent, or running away. We may give up in our attempt to communicate in a civil manner or even at all.

It is easy to scoff at others' fears when facing new situations but to the uninformed and inexperienced visitor, "local" messages and meanings can be startling. Perceived aggressiveness, use of space, touch, eating practices, and so on in other cultures can be in stark opposition to the religious and social customs of someone's own culture. For example, sanitary conditions differ around the world, including the handling of food and toilet facilities. People in some places eat markedly different food. Business practices vary widely, as do relationship and sexual practices. Americans will verbally challenge each other in public in ways that if it happened to an East Asian, it would be quite shocking. Any one of these can become a culture shock to a visitor and lead to extreme personal discomfort. Advance knowledge can provide partial preparation for expected communication and behavior. Having a "local" contact to explain what transpires can also help the visitor minimize culture shock.

ADDITIONAL STRATEGIES FOR
EFFECTIVE COMMUNICATION

Since it would take many years for an intercultural visitor to learn how to effectively communicate with people in a different culture, Gallois and Callan provide a list of general guidelines that a newcomer can use to decrease some of the misunderstandings and misbehavior.[113]

1. *Keep An Open Mind*. Remind yourself that people's meanings for their words and nonverbal behaviors may differ from yours. Avoid assuming each of you know what each other means.

2. *Watch What Other People Do, and Listen Carefully*. If you are treated like other people, you are probably seeing the practice of a general rule. Combine the verbal and nonverbal messages in an attempt to form a more complete understanding of what is occurring.

3. *Be Prepared to Explain in Detail What You Say and Do*. Your own cultural members will be familiar with your cultural rules but since nonmembers will not, you will need more explanation.

4. *What You Do Not Learn by Observation Will Need to be Learned by Asking*. Ask why someone said or did what they said or did. Consider that there may be alternative explanations.

5. *Be Mindful of Your Communication*.[114] Prepare as much as possible in advance of entering another culture to both learn and form some educated guesses about its rules and values.[115] When in the culture, verify the accuracy of your knowledge to reduce some of your uncertainty.

6. *Be Patient, Expect to Make Mistakes, and Give the Other Person the Benefit of the Doubt*. Slow down the communication. When mistakes occur, talk about and try to repair them. Do not be so quick to condemn the other person's apparent meaning—you could be inaccurate.

7. *Increase Politeness*. To the extent you are able to convey what that other culture evaluates as politeness, this helps smooth over misunderstandings. Politeness minimizes a perceived threat to other people's public image and their self-esteem. It suggests to people that you have good intentions and that you are willing to work with them to have effective communication.

8. *Know Your Own Inviolate Values and Behaviors*. You may refuse to say and do things that are in stark opposition to your own values and/or behaviors, yet recognize that viable alternative explanations may exist. Realizing where you will not compromise can help you see just where you can change to meet the demands of an intercultural situation.

Summary

Culture has been described as a group of people's distinctive system of inter-related behaviors existing over a period of time, and is conveyed and learned through communication. Intercultural communication was defined as the communication between people of different cultures, and this chapter examined a number of ways by which cultural factors influence the communication of those within the culture. An alternative to the language-thought connection was provided, suggesting that our thinking is not as closely tied to our language (and culture) as often thought. The cultural differences of individualism/collectivism, high- and low-context, and power differences and their impact upon communication were described An overview of differing nonverbal communication gestures, proxemics, eye behaviors, and the use of time, space, and touch were illuminated. Lastly, some key barriers to intercultural communication were described and guidelines provided for creating more effective interactions. The overall goal of intercultural communication is for our communication with culturally different people to become more interpersonal.[116]

Intercultural communication has been a fact of life for about as long as people have been living on the earth. In varying degrees, people have found ways to communicate that have allowed them to make do with the limitations of their own culture's message system. It is a bit of a marvel that people of nationalities that fought each other in Europe and in other places in times past have been able to come to America and interact in a civil manner.[117] That anyone would want to alter the key conditions that created this outcome is somewhat of a mystery.[118]

If those who speak a given language, such as English in America, have a hard enough time understanding each other and getting along, what could we expect of their interaction with non-speakers of English in America who have come from cultures very different from America and who are attempting to maintain their or their ancestors' culture and language? Americans do not have to leave America to have to overcome the intercultural barriers noted in this chapter for one or more ethnic groups and immigrants (and some of their offspring) are behaving and speaking in ways foreign to the larger population in America today.[119]

SELECTED CULTURE ISSUES

1. *Universal Values, Universal Criteria.* It is commonly said in discussions about intercultural issues that there are no universal values. Without such universals, any evaluation we might make of another culture is really only relevant to our own culture. Cultural relativism suggests that we cannot legitimately judge as right or wrong, or as good or bad, the values, behavior, and tangible outcomes of other cultures because we would only be using our

own culture's "yardstick" (criteria) to do so, criteria that are only applicable (relevant) to our own culture. Each culture can only be evaluated in terms of its own criteria. Since we cannot judge ourselves as being culturally superior, then we can only conclude that all cultures are equal to the rest. In late twentieth and early twenty first century America, this means that any identifiable cultural grouping in America has a legitimate right to exist apart from the mainstream culture, as does any culture existing anywhere in the world. Newly arrived immigrant groups should be free to practice their non-American culture in America since all cultures are equal.

If this is the case, then how do we account for what occurred after the initial formation of the United Nations in 1945? Eleanor Roosevelt, the widow of President Franklin Roosevelt, chaired a U.N. committee in 1947 that created a Universal Declaration of Human Rights that specified basic principles of behavior for both country-to-country interactions and the behavior of individual countries toward their own inhabitants.[120] Members of the committee included "...Christians, Muslims, Hindus, Jews, atheists, and agnostics; communists, socialists, liberals, and fascists; Western and Eastern nations; colonial powers and recently decolonized nations."[121] A group of internationally recognized writers and philosophers that included Mohandas Gandhi concluded, "...it was possible to identify values that cut across all national, ethnic, religious, and regional boundaries."[122] In brief, the group told the U.N. committee that cultures share certain principles. The committee then used these universal values to draft a Universal Declaration of Human Rights, summed up below:

> ... the right to live, the right to protection of health; the right to work; the right to social assistance in cases of need; the right to property; the right to education; the right to information; the right to freedom of thought and inquiry; the right to self-expression; the right to fair procedures; the right to political participation; the right to freedom of speech, assembly, association, worship, and the press; the right to citizenship; the right to rebel against an unjust regime; and the right to share in progress.[123]

The committee's declaration based on the universal values was non-binding but it had been created by a consensus of the cross-cultural United Nations committee members. When voted on by the entire United Nations General Assembly, there were no votes against it, eight countries abstained (the U.S.S.R. some Eastern-bloc (then Communist) countries, Saudi Arabia, and South Africa), and the rest of the U.N. voted in favor of it. Thus, the existence of universal values has been affirmed, which undermines the notion of cultural relativism.

Regardless of what value terms we ascribe to them, peoples' behaviors reflect what they desire. This is particularly noticeable when it comes to movements of people around the world. Many people "vote" with their feet by leaving their country and culture of origin because they foresee a better life for themselves in a different culture elsewhere, be it for health, education, property rights, freedom of speech and religion, and so on. It is not inconsequential or immaterial to people's lives to recognize that people have more control over their personal destiny in some cultures than in others, that people have more available nutrition and food and shelter (a higher standard of living) in some places, that there are more economic options and earning power in some places, that there is more religious freedom in some places, that there are more life choices to be whomever or whatever they want in some cultures than in others, and so on. Many people around the world have been and are aware of these differences.[124]

It is not an overstatement to say that many people in many different countries around the globe want what is provided by Western culture.[125] Western societies certainly appear to provide more of the U.N. values and rights than virtually anywhere else, as well. Americans are well aware of the seemingly countless Cubans, Jamaicans, and Haitians who over the years have risked drowning in their makeshift boats (and some have drowned) to reach Florida, but we have not seen the reverse exodus by Americans (or anyone else) to such places. According to Sowell, "The movement of immigrants is overwhelmingly from other cultures to Western cultures. Virtually the whole human race has voted with their feet as to which economic and other benefits they prefer to have."[126] There may be 20 million illegal aliens in America from Mexico (primarily) and countries to the south. There are a sizeable number of Muslims in France and other Western European countries. Filipinos work in a variety places around the globe and such immigrants have been readily seen filling medical field (among other) jobs in America. People from many sub-Saharan African countries emigrate to the West. Many Micronesian Islanders have moved from Yap, Palau, Chuuk, Phonpei, Kosrae, and the Marshall Islands to Guam, Hawaii, and the mainland. We can infer from people leaving their cultures that they are making judgments about their life and their culture, that they do not believe that at least certain cultural features are relative, and that they find some cultural features in other cultures more desirous than some of those in their own culture.

Even within a country that has the basic U.N. human rights, there may be significant cultural features in a given locale that minimize these, which in turn becomes an impetus for them to move elsewhere. According to Dr. Robert Underwood, President of the University of Guam, former Guam Representative to Congress, and long-time Chamorro educator on Guam, local college graduates on Guam "should take a look at their fellow classmates and recognize that they will never see half of them again here in Guam. It is a startling figure and it is a sober reality. That is the true evaluation of life on Guam.... When our own young people decide to leave and not come back, that speaks volumes about our current condition."[127] As of the 2000 Census, there were 65,000 people of Chamorro ancestry on Guam, 19,000 on Saipan, and 93,000 in the states.[128] Dr. Underwood does not specify the reasons for this exodus. Maybe the "local" culture stifles the local economy and limits job growth (in part from valuing a *pare* or patronage system of awarding jobs), forcing people to relocate to find work. Maybe the "local" culture does not make local business opportunities attractive enough for outside investors and entrepreneurs to enter the local economy (maybe there is too much red tape or even corruption), thereby limiting job growth. Maybe the "local" health care is insufficient in some respects due to some features of the local culture (such as unskilled professionals, political interference, or plain mismanagement), forcing still more people to relocate closer to more comprehensive care. Maybe the "local" culture does not create the "human capital" necessary for creating wealth and a vibrant economy (the value of hard work and educational attainment may be lacking). Any number of reasons could exist for people in a "local" culture to evaluate some other place as exemplifying more of the universal human rights that they would like for themselves.

2. *Cultural Inequality.* As noted previously, cultural relativism suggests that all cultures are equal, an idea reinforced by those touting multiculturalism and diversity,[129] so it would seem to be anathema to suggest that cultures differ, and as such, are unequal in some important aspects. As the immediate section above suggests, people around the world judge and make comparisons all the time, and sometimes they reach the conclusion that their own culture is unequal to another one. According to Sowell,

> one of the clearest facts to emerge from ... worldwide histories of various racial and ethnic groups is that gross statistical disparities in the 'representation' of groups in different occupations, industries, income levels, and educational institutions have been the rule—not the exception—all across the planet.[130]

Groups, and the cultures of which they are a part, clearly reveal disparate artifacts and outcomes. Although the Portuguese governed Brazil for hundreds of years, they did not do much to create a thriving economy, but rather, it was the German, Italian, and other immigrants beginning in the late 1800's that did. Something similar happened in Argentina where the

Spanish did little but raise cattle. Immigrants to Argentina created agriculture and industry.[131] A similar story was repeated in Peru where the descendants of original indentured Chinese and Japanese laborers become prominent in retail businesses. Sowell suggests that "[w]hat all these groups brought was not wealth but the ability to create wealth—whether on a modest scale or a grand scale, whether through specific skills or just hard work. They did not share the Spanish and Portuguese disdain for manual labor, or for commerce and industry, or for thrift."[132] In America, Sowell records that "... Italians were noted for their diligence and sobriety—the latter often contrasted with the drinking of the Irish—but also for a lack of initiative that required them to have considerable supervision."[133] The Italian immigrants, to a great extent, rose economically in America by acquiring blue-collar job skills as opposed to getting professional jobs requiring education. The Irish, both in Ireland, England, and America were different than most other Europeans, living in poverty for generations. They were not self-reliant or business entrepreneurs, but performed a great deal of unskilled labor. Excessive alcohol consumption occurred amongst Irish in both Ireland and elsewhere, and as late as 1970, Irish in Ireland spent more of their income on alcohol than did people in any other European country. Due to alcoholism, Irish had a high rate of rejection from the U.S. military in both World War I and II. Even at the publication date of Sowell's book (1983), Irish Americans were the biggest drinkers in America.[134] Their frequent arrests for drinking and fighting led to many of them being hauled to jail in police panel trucks referred to as "Paddy Wagons," and the term is still in use today for police vans and similar vehicles. Even with the Irish American success in gaining some political power around 1900 and the patronage jobs which came with that, it did not boost their low financial well-being. Remarkably, Irish Americans did transform themselves during the post-World War II years and finally equaled or surpassed the national income average.[135]

According to Hanson,[136] culture is the greatest determinant of economic and military development. This can be seen by comparing the significantly different economic outcomes existing between essentially the same people, speaking the same language, living in the same region, such as those in North Korea versus those in South Korea, or those living in East Germany versus West Germany between 1945-1991. While there were some dialect differences, Hong Kong with its British culture until 1993 and particularly post-WW II, could be compared to Communist China. Different outcomes can also be seen when comparing side-by-side countries around the world.

Cultures vary in some other obvious and important ways, as well. Although bribery and corruption, for example, are culturally acceptable in some places and a way of life in other places, this does not mean that they are not economically harmful. Solache claims that a bribe culture can hinder a country's economy and efficient government service. The "local" people have to live with the outcomes.[137] The Philippines has a noticeable amount of corruption, as does Mexico.[138] While these cultural artifacts are common around the world, they are more prominently practiced in some places than in others. In Transparency International's corruption ranking (the higher the number, the more perceived corruption), Haiti ranks at 168 with only 9 countries in the world considered more corrupt.[139] The Philippines ranks 139. Mexico tied with 6 other countries at 89 (about midpoint on the scale of countries). By comparison, America came in 19th on the least corrupt end of the scale, and the U.S. territory of Puerto Rico placed at 36. Haiti's high level of corruption is joined by an extremely high crime rate. Williams suggests that Haiti is a poor country because it limits economic freedom, and it might be added that few investors would want to do business in a place where police have difficulty enforcing the law.[140] Overall, Haitians enjoy few of the U.N.'s human rights.

Mere biases and supposed differences in perception do not prevent such legitimate observations of other cultures. In fact, in most, if not all cases, outsiders do not have to do the evaluating for invariably there are "insiders" who say their own culture has deficiencies. That outsiders notice the same shortcomings does not automatically make their observations biased. Dr. Underwood, in pointing out the existence of official corruption on Guam, notes that it is rarely condemned.[141] This behavior is a cultural artifact, as is the common response of those accused of corruption: blame the federal government of being out to get the Chamorro people. Dr. Underwood is not only a Chamorro insider speaking about Guam, but he also disagrees with Guam government officials (almost the entirety of whom are Chamorros) "… who suddenly hide behind cultural explanations … for personal malfeasance of duties and responsibilities."[142] He believes this behavior is harmful to local life (culture) and disagrees with those who justify such behavior. Speaking about a different cultural artifact, another experienced educator and insider on Guam, Dr. Yamashita states that "…having an unstable education system is a Guam thing," and she wishes that accountability (which she implies is not a cultural artifact) would take its place.[143] Another harmful Guam cultural artifact relates to food, as it does for some other groups in America. A local Guam historian, Benigno Palomo, laments the Chamorro love of high fat and high cholesterol food, an obvious barrier to good health that leads many Chamorros to acquire diabetes, gout, and high blood pressure.[144] Emphasizing the same culture-food connection is an article by Martinez in the local paper entitled "Eat, drink and be culture."[145] Pacific Islanders on the island of Saipan (near Guam) have an even higher incidence of diabetes. Another Chamorro, Tony Artero, claims that "negligence is the standard of practice in

practically every area of [Guam's government],"[146] staffed primarily by Chamorros. He also claims "this culture of handout, corruption, and cover-ups is
keeping Guam in a downward spiral."[147] These are just a few more examples
to show that cultures are not the same (equal), and there are cultural insiders
who say that the cultural practices are harmful. A cultural "outsider" could
easily say the same thing. Incidentally, the above comments are not to suggest
that Guam is a terrible place to live, only that there are some distinctions.
Given the various problems that exist in many parts of America, people on
Guam can conclude that they are lucky to be on Guam.

Should not those who say that all cultures are equal be obliged to describe
the significant ways cultures are equal? Do the different ethnic groups in
American high schools study the same amount of hours, achieve the same
grades and SAT test scores, have the same graduation rates from high school
and college, and earn the same academic credentials from college? Are all
ethnic groups equally represented in all career fields, work the same number
of hours, have the same employment rate, and achieve the same incomes? Are
all ethnic groups equally willing to work at low-paying, dirty jobs, or do some
groups of people think some types of jobs are "beneath" them so they avoid
them? Do members of all ethnic groups commit the same amount and types
of crime? Do all ethnic groups have the same size of down payment, amount
of assets, and credit score when they seek a loan to buy a house? Do people
from each ethnic group have the same life expectancy and do they equally
contract the same amount and types of diseases? Do the top American high
school students score the same on international math and science tests as
do high school students in other countries? Are all governments around the
world equally efficient? This list could go on. Those who say that cultures
are equal should provide clear and substantial evidence that different ethnic
groups in America and different cultures around the world are equal in important human endeavors.

Many cultures throughout history have willingly borrowed cultural artifacts from other cultures, deeming them more valued than some of their own.
This borrowing implies perceived inequality on the borrowers' part.

It may be suggested that those cultures in a given place and time that do
not "get with the program," whatever that "program" might be in the world's
long-standing globalization, are jeopardizing their own existence. Cultures
that have not successfully adapted to their environment can be read about in
history books.

3. Exceptionalism. Not only are cultures different and unequal, some cultural features set a culture quite apart from other cultures and may even provide favorable outcomes for culture members. People around the world could

probably find aspects of their own and other cultures that they particularly like, and some of these may be rare in the rest of the world.

Is there anything culturally exceptional about the English-speaking peoples? Hannan[148] claims that three political structures can trace their origin to England, including the rule of law, representative government, and personal liberty. This means there is equality before the law, jury trials with the presumption of innocence, and that the government, too, must abide by the law; that there are elected legislatures answerable to the citizens and a democratic government; and there is freedom to live your own life, including to say what you wish, freedom of the press, religion, and assembly, free contracts, open markets and private property ownership ("a man's home is his castle"), freedom to use and dispose of your personal assets as you wish, freedom to work and be hired or fired freely by those for whom you work (their freedom). The individual is valued, a secular government was created, and a strong middle class evolved.

To put England within the larger context of Western Civilization that stretched over time from the ancient Greeks and Romans to Western Europe and America in the 16th through 20th centuries, have there been any significant features of Western Civilization that other cultures around the world have gravitated to? Yes, particularly the values listed in the preceding paragraph articulated in the UN's Declaration of Human Rights: the right to work, property, religion, freedom of thought, self-expression, free speech, free press, assembly, association, fair procedures, and the right to rebel against an unjust regime (noted in the Declaration of Independence.) Furthermore, world emigration has largely been to Western Europe and America.

Sure, Western Civilization peoples were primarily Caucasians, just as the people of ancient China who invented paper and other artifacts borrowed by later Western Europeans and still in use today were Chinese, and those in the great kingdoms in Africa's past were Africans. Could we have expected otherwise? Should China, Africa, and Western Civilization be held in contempt today for their general lack of diversity with the present day application of the word?

With the unique cultural elements cited above, the Anglosphere, those places in Western Europe (primarily) adopting these principles, and some well-known, former English colonies are the freest and most prosperous cultures in the world.[149] Should Americans be ashamed and embarrassed about freedom, the rule of law, and representative government? According to Sowell, America has been the exception in the world when it comes to government oppression, violence, carnage, poverty, and general squalor, yet "Most Americans take our values, traditions and institutions so much for granted that they find it hared to realize how much of these things are under constant attack in our schools, our colleges, and in much of the press, the movies and literature."[150] We have had a culture war since the 1960's (termed a "counter culture" at the time) with overt attempts by America's critics in America to change the fundamental culture elements listed in the preceding paragraph, resulting in a significant degradation of them through a radically transformed and expanded U.S. government

According to Eberstadt, "From the founding of our state up to … recently—the United States and its citizens who peopled it were regarded, at home and abroad, as 'exceptional' in a number of deep and important respects."[151] Chua finds that a majority of "Americans still believe in America's exceptionality,"[152] and, it may be added, despite the continuous denigration of and hostility toward America's superiority. American still offers opportunities for people to create their own lives, unbridled by ethnic or cultural baggage, and despite the ever-growing regulations and barriers created by the federal government. Many (not all) foreign born and first generation Americans have prospered and, along with many existing Americans, achieved the American Dream of career aspirations and upward mobility. Sowell reports that more than 75 percent of Americans earning in the bottom 20 percent range in 1975 had increased earnings that placed them in the top 40 percent of income before or by 1991. Taxpayers whose income placed them in the bottom 20 percent of income earners in 1996 had their incomes rise 91 percent by 2005, while the top 1 percent of income earners had their incomes drop by about 25 percent in that period.[153] Sowell found that "… from 1967 to 2007, real median household income rose by 30 percent.…"[154] Voegeli reports on a study finding that two-thirds of sample children born in the 1950's and 1960's had more real income in the 1995-2002 period than did their parents in the 1967-1971 period, and adjusting for smaller households and other variables by 2000, " … the proportion of Americans who had a higher income by 2000 than their parents did some thirty years earlier rises to 81 percent."[155]

While no one will claim that a hypothetical married couple, both of whom worked full-time at a Federal minimum wage of $7.25/hour and were raising two kids in 2014 were wealthy, their $30,000 2014 income put them above the poverty line of $24,250 (and just at it in 2015), which may be considered exceptional in comparison to the grinding poverty suffered by so many low-income people around the world. It also makes a great deal of financial difference in which state minimum wage earners reside. People do not have to have great intellects to avoid poverty in America for " … only 8 percent of Americans who (a) finish high school; (b) marry before having a child, and (c) postpone marriage until after the age of twenty wind up impoverished."[156] These three, plus working full-time at any job and avoiding criminal behavior minimize the incidence of poverty, let alone the opportunity to increase job skills at readily available low cost or subsidized post-high school education training programs. [157]

Unfortunately, not all Americans or immigrants use the existing opportunities (such as education) to become financially independent and live the lives they most desire. While there are many and varied explanations for this, Kimbro provides a relevant response gleaned from his interviews with many black American millionaires: that "Every life is full of opportunity."[158] There are opportunities presented to us every waking moment, but that we will say "yes" to them and work from there. "Wealth is less a matter of circumstance than it is a matter of knowledge and choice."[159] We can choose the opportunities that will put us on the path to financial independence and minimize our dependence upon government entitlement/welfare programs that take from taxpayers and transfer to other Americans what amounts to be approximately 70 percent of yearly government revenue (largely taxes).[160] America is still the land of opportunity.

Another cultural artifact that is exceptional about America is the amount of work that people put into their jobs. As reported in January 2015, Americans work more hours than those in any other economically developed country, toping #2 Japan by 137 hours per year (2.63 hours/week), Britons by 260 hours, and French people by 499 hours (approximately 2 months of working 8 hours/day, or 1.6 months at 10 hours/day).[161] This has been referred to as the Puritan work ethic and is a key factor for upward mobility and a higher standard of living. It is said that with hard work, anyone can succeed. Try, try again. As synthesized by Chua, "Work hard during the week, and you can play hard on the weekend, work hard for years, and you can have the house and cars and family you dreamed of."[162] America honors those who have successfully overcome the odds through their own hard work. Within America itself, some groups of people work more at their education and/or careers than do other groups, and these prominently include Chinese, Koreans, Indians, Mormons, and Jews,[163] so it should not be a surprise that they are overly represented as academic and business successes. No person or group "owns" the work ethic so it is readily available to all.

America's work ethic is closely related to and may be thought of as necessary for the self-reliance and independence that has historically set America apart from many other countries.[164] Emerson wrote about the value of self-reliance back in 1841,[165] not many years after de Tocqueville noted this exceptional quality of Americans to depend upon themselves for their life's achievement.[166] Today, Americans cannot legitimately cite self-reliance as a distinct cultural feature since " ... more than half of all American households receive ... [entitlement/welfare] transfer benefits from the government." [167] Moreover, " ... social welfare programs are no longer reluctantly defended, but instead positively celebrated as part of the American dream...."[168] Fortunately for our economy, enough Americans are still attempting to be business entrepreneurs and/or work long and productive hours.

Within America and many other cultures, planning for the future and completing steps toward accomplishing goals makes the achievement of those goals more likely. This is particularly true for those seeking advanced education and training necessary to reach some future goal. Yet to complete any such education or training, at least at the highest level, requires a great deal of individual impulse control for there are always distractions and temptations to give up, particularly when there is a difficult task. This behavior came under direct attack in 1960's America and thereafter, with the ideas of "if it feels good, do it," "live for the moment," and "Tune in, turn on, drop out." This permissiveness, in contrast to controlled behavior, privation, and adversity, was considered necessary for happiness, for we were all supposed to "be happy!" As it turns out, those individuals or groups of people who reject this now mainstream orientation and instead practice discipline toward achieving their long-term goals have been most successful in education and income acquisition.[169] With all the pressure on teenagers to enjoy alcohol and sex, Asian American teens have much lower rates of heavy alcohol and drug use than do others, and teenage Asian American girls have far fewer births than do girls in other ethnic groups. "Because giving birth for teenage girls, and being convicted of a drug crime for teenage boys are so highly correlated with adverse economic outcomes later, Asian Americans' impulse control in these domains contributes to their disproportionate success."[170] As with the work ethic referred to in a previous paragraph, no one "owns" impulse control, but those who practice it will probably both think of themselves and be thought of by others as outsiders.

Summary

America's exceptionalness still has drawing power, given the number of people around the world who wish to become American emigrants. Still, it is sobering to consider that the U. S. government is not following the rule of law (4th Amendment and presumption of innocence) with its brazen spying on most, if not all Americans (among its other lawbreaking); that individual equality before the law is frequently superceded by a subjective group animus spoils systems; that personal property has frequently not been sacrosanct under eminent domain applications or with whatever EPA powers EPA decides to grant itself, that people's income and wealth are hardly considered *theirs'* when the government decides what it will take and what it will allow people to keep (a disciplined, hardworking American couple earning $150,000/year can expect to lose about one-half of that to federal, state, and local governments, while tax freedom day in 2014 averaged April 21 per taxpayer when all government taxes due for the year had been hypothetically paid, but as late as May 9 for those in Connecticut)[171]; that free contracts are nullified by the government as in the General Motors and Chrysler bankruptcies in 2009 or in many of the housing foreclosure during 2009-10; that employers are almost completely constrained in their hiring and firing practices by government regulations, in addition to mandated employee retirement contributions and employee healthcare contributions that many of them are forced to make; and there has been a general loss of individual freedom in the face of a huge and growing government. The list can go on. America has become significantly less exceptional (free) after 1965 and more like the collectivist cultures and governments in Europe.

4. *Cultural Nostalgia.* It is easy for people living in one age, such as in the present time, to romanticize that arbitrarily selected ancestors lived in a cultural nirvana. These current people presume to be omniscient of that former culture and time, and yearn for a present-day reincarnation of at least selected parts of that former culture, as if the previous culture could exist in the current world.

What evidence exists, and what evidence is provided by those espousing multiculturalism that there was, for example, greater respect accorded others who had earned it, that there was greater affection between people, that there were more intimate (non-obligation) human bonds, and that people were more successful in fulfilling other basic human needs?

The past is past. Barring a "dark age" occurring, people alive today cannot expect to live even remotely like some selected ancestor of one hundred plus years ago. Yet, as D'Souza points out, this has partly been the position and direction given by those espousing multiculturalism in America[172]—be *your* culture, the culture of your ancestors (whichever one, a subjective decision)— and *not* the generalized American culture that has been predominant over the last 200-plus years.

There is a huge liability to accepting this multicultural idea. According to Sowell, claiming as heritage discarded beliefs, behaviors, and creations of earlier generations is self-defeating:

> ... there is no need for nostalgia to corrupt history for rejected cultural artifacts to be resurrected at public expense, much less imposed on others for obligatory admiration. Above all, there is no need to encourage those who have progressed by cultural borrowing to retrogress by painting themselves into their own cultural corner and taking upon themselves the arduous

burden of advancing solely by what their own subgroup can accomplish in isolation from the wider world which has long been the cultural resource of peoples, nations, and whole civilizations.[173]

Thus, the practical outcome for those in America who look to the distant past for their culture, possibly on some other continent, would be to turn away from, among other things, the progress in the last seventy-five years alone in medicine, nutrition, transportation, and the higher standard of living. Many women in Micronesia, for example, would have to "return" to the "men's house" where they would satisfy men's basic cravings while men would have to build huts and canoes with old-fashioned implements. Women around the world would have to forgo caesarian births and strictly deliver children the old-fashioned way or die trying. A hand-to-mouth existence would prevail, and so on. Are people cognizant of what would actually await them if they were able to "go back" to what previously existed, and would they really desire this?

For better or worse, cultures do not remain entirely the same since the environment around them is always changing, forcing the cultures to change (if they are to remain viable). According to Makihara, a seventy-year old Ainu (indigenous Japanese) in Japan suggests, "It's not like we can make a living off salmon from the river any more. Our customs died because they were no longer needed."[174] Some people in America today could say the same thing in reference to many customs of their various ancestors. Another Ainu, a thirty-year old man, adds, "It seems a fraud to preserve the Ainu language and customs when we don't use them anyway."[175] Rather, *culture* is what we do in the here and now, the present, and not necessarily the heritage of our ancestors.

5. *Diversity.* Differences, in this case, presumed racial or cultural group differences, are praised by those who favor a multicultural America,[176] yet should any real or imagined group differences or ethnic physical appearance take precedence over individuality, equal opportunity, merit, and intellectual diversity at institutions of higher education in America?

Even if we claim that there are existing cultural differences among distinct ethnic groups in America and these differences are important, we know from the first pages of this chapter that we cannot tell someone's culture by his or her physical features. For example, is not the generalized American middle class with its middle class values composed of people from every ethnic and religious group in America? What are the big differences between those with individual initiative and self-sufficiency whom value individuality, hard work, education, an intact family, community volunteerism, planning and working toward the future, and private property? Thus, simply choosing people for college admissions or employment hiring and promotion based upon their appearance does not reveal the candidates' cultural diversity, so those presuming to select for cultural diversity face an indeterminate task. Physical "diversity" selections are likely to simply be a way for those who want proportional ethnic representation in college and in business to achieve their quota goals. In this case, real diversity of individuals and ideas becomes a moot point for college admissions.

According to Williams,[177] there is little respect for actual racial, sexual, or political differences and a great deal of emphasis on conforming to politically correct ideas on college campuses. The preponderance of college faculty is Democrat with some departments being 100 percent registered Democrats. Stated similarly, this idea of cultural diversity has become aligned (ironically) with " ... a rise in *political uniformity*," and " ... the promotion of a left-wing ideological agenda."[178] Ideas and beliefs of fundamentalist Christians, Constitutional traditionalists, Libertarians, and conservatives in general are rarely sought or respected.

As practiced in most colleges, diversity works in opposition to equal treatment of individuals. Admissions and promotion by merit, and academic standards suffer as a result.[179] A racial (and gender) "spoils system" rewards the designated diverse students by admitting some of those with lesser grades and test scores. Williams[180] reports that some minority applicants to the U.S. Naval Academy are admitted despite B and C high school grades and a 500 score on each portion of the SAT while non-athlete white students with similar merit are not. Further, some minorities are allowed to enter the academy after earning a C average in one year of remedial work at a Navy prep school. If some of these minorities are later charged with violating an honor code, they are usually cleared. This double standard is resented by some other minority students and by white students who maintain meritorious standards. According to Williams, "Diversity is simply the old racism in a new guise, spiced up with a touch of sexism. Diversity is a call for race-conscious decisions in hiring, promotion and college admittance policy. Diversity management success is measured by the numbers. A wrong (low) number of minorities or women invite the wrath of the state."[181]

While diversity is routinely touted by many college presidents and colleges spend millions of dollars on diversity programs, the schools' conspicuous sports teams "...are the least diverse and least inclusive"[182] on campuses, making administrators appear disingenuous about the issue. Similarly in professional sports, there is a lack of diversity. About three-fourths of the NBA and two-thirds of the NFL players are black. If diversity is so valued and beneficial, why is it not practiced and enforced in all areas of endeavor, on and off campus?

Hanson suggests that "diversity" is an updated euphemism for the pre-vious euphemism "affirmative action," itself a euphemism meant to cover up "quota," a word denoting an obvious act of discrimination.[183] With the meaning and justification of "difference," there is no need to cite historical discrimination as a way to justify current discrimination so the "crass" tit for tat justification stays largely hidden. All that is needed to put diversity treat-ment into effect is to simply look at someone's physical features.

According to Hanson, the future result of this racial meddling "...will not be a multiracial population bound by a common culture and swirling continuously in a melting pot, but something akin to the Balkans, Iraq, or Rwanda, where our appearances and self-claimed identities are essential, not incidental, to our characters—a nightmare of endless competitive claims that can only end in violence and chaos."[184] This is echoed by Voegeli, citing Florida, "The more diverse or integrated a neighborhood is, the less socially cohesive it becomes."[185] Sowell claims those who think that promoting a real (or imaginary) group identity is beneficial to a civil and productive society are overlooking "... the tragic historic consequences of Balkanization in many parts of Asia and Africa, as well as in the Balkans themselves."[186]

Thomas questions the historical evidence of diversity: "Did diversity build and sustain America through world wars and economic challenges? No, it was a firm set of principles held by patriots of many races who were willing to pay the price in money and blood."[187] Overall, the practice of determining competence by skin color promotes separateness, divisiveness, and is counter to the basic principle of equal treatment before the law[188]

Summary of Selected Cultural Issues

The America Codevilla found as an adolescent immigrant boy in the 1950's has changed in unimaginable ways. Now, he writes, "... the character [and by extension, culture] of the American way of life is up for grabs perhaps more than ever before."[189] The common position in Communication text-books on the cultural issues of universal values, cultural equality, relativism, and diversity reflect part of the change to which Codevilla speaks. The extra readings herein provide a different point of view.

REFERENCES

1.   D. Klopf, *Intercultural Encounters: The Fundamentals of Intercultural Communica-tion* (3rd ed.) (Englewood, CO: Morton Publishing Company, 1995).
2.   E. Hall, *Beyond Culture* (Garden City, New York: Anchor Books, 1977), p. 16.
     E. Hall, *Beyond Culture* (Garden City, New York: Anchor Books, 1977), p. 16.

3. D. Barnlund, *Communication Styles of Japanese and Americans: Images and Reality* (Belmont, CA: Wadsworth Publishing Company, 1989).
4. Ibid.
5. E. Hall and M. Hall, *Hidden Differences: Doing Business with the Japanese* (New York: Anchor Books, 1987), p. 3.
6. T. Sowell, *Race And Culture: A World View* (New York: BasicBooks, A Division of Harper Collins Publishers, Inc., 1994).
7. T. Sowell, *Black Rednecks and White Liberals* (San Francisco: Encounter Books, 2005).
8. Hall (1977), op cit.
9. G. Althen, *American Ways.* (2nd ed.) (Yarmouth, ME: Intercultural Press Inc., 2003).
10. D. Steinberg, "Language and Thought." in *Psycholinguistics: Language, Mind, and World.* (London: Longman Group Limited, 1982).
11. H. Hoijer, "The Sapir-Whorf Hypothesis," in *Intercultural Communication: A Reader* (2nd ed.) (Belmont, CA: Wadsworth Publishing Company, Inc., 1976), p. 151.
12. Steinberg, op cit., p. 101.
13. Ibid., p. 105.
14. Ibid., p. 107.
15. Ibid.
16. Ibid., p. 108.
17. Ibid.
18. Ibid, p. 111.
19. Ibid., p. 112.
20. Ibid.
21. Barnlund, op cit., p. xiii.
22. Ibid.
23. Hall (1977), op cit., p. 42.
24. Barnlund, op cit., p. 31.
25. W. Gudykunst and Y. Kim, *Communicating With Strangers: An Approach to Intercultural Communication* (Boston: McGraw-Hill Companies, Inc., 1997).
26. G. Hofstede, *Culture's Consequences: International Differences in Work-Related Values* (Thousand Oaks, CA: Sage, 1984).
27. R. Emerson, *Self-Reliance. An Excerpt from Collected Essays, First Series* (Rockville, MD: Arc Manor, 2007).
28. Barnlund, op cit.
29. L. Schweikart, *America's Victories. Why the U.S. Wins Wars and Will Win the War on Terror* (New York: Sentinel, 2006), p. 100.
30. Barnlund, op cit., p. 44.
31. A. Codevilla, *The Character of Nations: How Politics Makes and Breaks Prosperity, Family, and Civility* (2nd ed.) (New York: Basic Books, 2009).
32. M. Gross, *National Suicide: How Washington Is Destroying the American Dream From A to Z* (New York: Berkley Books, 2009).
33. Codevilla, op cit., p. 266.

34. Emerson, op cit.
35. D. Brinkley, *Brinkley's Beat: People, Places, and Events That Shaped My Time* (New York: Ballantine Books, 2003), p. 63.
36. Klopf, op cit.
37. Gudykunst and Kim, op cit.
38. W. Gudykunst and T. Nishida, *Bridging Japanese/North American Differences* (Thousand Oaks, CA: Sage Publications, Inc. 1994), p. 29.
39. Barnlund, op cit.
40. K. Ueda, "Sixteen ways to avoid saying 'no' in Japan," in *Intercultural Encounters With Japan: Communication-Contact and Conflict* (Tokyo: The Simul Press, Inc., 1974).
41. Gudykunst and Nishda, op cit.
42. Schweikart, op cit.
43. K. Wolferen, *The Enigma of Japanese Power: People and Politics in a Stateless Nation* (New York: Alfred A. Knopf, 1989).
44. T. Gochenour, *Considering Filipinos* (Yarmouth, ME: Intercultural Press, Inc., 1990).
45. Ibid., p. 16.
46. D. Barnlund, *Public and Private Self in Japan and the United States* (Tokyo: The Simul Press, Inc., 1975).
47. Barnlund (1989), op cit.
48. Gudykunst and Nishida, op cit.
49. Gochenour, op cit.
50. Hall and Hall, op cit., p. 7.
51. Ibid.
52. Ibid.
53. Hall (1977), op cit.
54. Klopf, op cit.
55. Gudykunst and Kim, op cit.
56. Hall (1977), op cit.
57. P. Andersen "Explaining intercultural differences in nonverbal communication" in *Intercultural Communication: A Reader* (6th. ed.) (Belmont, CA: Wadsworth Publishing Company, 1991), p. 294.
58. Hall and Hall, op cit.
59. Ibid..
60. Hall (1977), op cit.
61. Hall and Hall, op cit., p. 11.
62. Ibid.
63. Gudykunst and Kim, op cit
64. Hofstede (1991), op cit., p. 28.
65. Ibid.
66. Ibid.
67. Ibid.
68. Ibid.
69. Gochenour, op cit.

70. Hofstede (1991), op cit.
71. Ibid.
72. D'Souza, op cit., p. 78.
73. Ibid.
74. Schweikart, op cit., p. 109.
75. Ibid.
76. J. Keegan, *Fields of Battle: The Wars for North America* (New York: Vintage Books, 1995), p. 59.
77. Gudykunst and Kim, op cit
78. Ibid.
79. C. Gallois and V. Callan, *Communication and Culture: A Guide for Practice* (Chichester, England: John Wiley & Sons, 1997).
80. Gallois and Callan, op cit.
81. R. Axtell, *Gestures: The Do's and Taboos of Body Language Around the World* (New York: John Wiley and Sons, Inc., 1991).
82. E. Hall, *The Silent Language* Garden City, New York: Anchor Books, 1973).
83. Hall (1977), op cit.
84. Hall and Hall, op cit.
85. Gudykunst and Kim, op cit.
86. Klopf, op cit.
87. Hall and Hall, op cit.
88. Hall (1977), op cit.
89. D'Souza, op cit.
90. E. Hall, *The Hidden Dimension* (Garden City, New York: Doubleday & Company, Inc., 1966).
91. Althen, op cit.
92. Hall (1973), op cit., p.185.
93. M. Watson, and T. Graves, "Quantitative Research in Proxemic Behavior." *American Anthropologist*, New Series 68, 4 (Aug. 1966): 971-985.
94. Barnlund (1989) op cit.
95. Gudykunst and Nishida, op cit.
96. Gudykunst and Kim, op cit.
97. Barnlund (1989), op cit.
98. Barnlund (1975), op cit.
99. Althen, op cit.
100. Klopf, op cit. Klopf, op cit.
101. J. DeVito, *Human Communication: The Basic Course* (5th ed.) (New York: HarperCollins Publishers Inc., 1991).
102. Althen, op cit.
103. Ibid.
104. Gochenour, op cit.
105. Axtell, op cit.
106. DeVito (1991), op cit.
107. Althen, op cit.

108. A. Hill, J. Watson, D. Rivers and M. Joyce, *Key Themes in Interpersonal Communication* (Berkshire, England: Open University Press, 2007).
109. Gallois and Callan, op cit.
110. S. Huntington, *Who Are We? The Challenges to America's National Identity* (New York: Simon & Schuster, 2004).
111. V. Hanson, *Mexifornian: A State of Becoming* (San Francisco: Encounter Books, 2003), p. 79.
112. Ibid.
113. Gallois and Callan, op cit.
114. Gudykunst and Kim, op cit.
115. Gallois and Callan, op cit.
116. Ibid.
117. D'Souza, op cit.; A. Schlessinger,Jr., *The Disuniting of America: Reflections on a Multicultural Society* (New York: W.W. Norton & Company, 1992).
118. Huntington, op cit.
119. Hanson, op cit.
120. A. Petigny and J. Zeitz, "Disunited Nations: Why the UN was in Trouble from the Start." *American Heritage* 54, 4 (New York: American Heritage, Inc., September, 2003): 55-60.
121. Ibid, p. 57.
122. Ibid.
123. Ibid, p.57
124. D'Souza, op cit.
125. Ibid.
126. T. Sowell, "Death of the west?" *Jewish World Review* (January 24, 2002), p. 2.
127. R. Underwood, "Brain Drain Says Volumes About Guam Condition" *Pacific Daily News* (June 5, 2005).
128. Chamorro people. (2010, July 19). In *Wikipedia, The Free Encyclopedia*. Retrieved 10:46, July 27, 2010, from http://en.wikipedia.org/w/index.php?title=Chamorro_people&oldid=374250835
129. D'Souza, op cit
130. T. Sowell, *Migrations and Cultures: A World View* (New York: Basic Books, A Division of Harper Collins Publishers, Inc., 1996), p. 372.
131. Sowell (1994), op cit.
132. Ibid., p. 35.
133. Sowell (1996), op cit., p. 164.
134. T. Sowell, *The Economics of Politics and Race: An International Perspective* (New York: William Morrow and Company, 1983).
135. Ibid.
136. V. D. Hanson, "Culture and candor," *nationalreviewonline.com*, August 2, 2012.
137. S. Solache, "Bribe Culture Hinders Mexico." *Pacific Daily News* (September 5, 2006).
138. J. Murphy, "Corruption is a Plague not only in the Philippines, but also in Guam." *Pacific Daily News* (April 4, 2005); Codevilla, op cit.

139. "Corruption perception index 2009," in *Transparency International*, http://www.transparency.org/policy_research/surveys_indices/cpi/2009/cpi_2009_table.

140. W. Williams, "Haiti's avoidable death toll," *Jewish World Review* (January 26, 2010).

141. R. Underwood, "Corrupt Officials Can't Hide Behind Culture." *Pacific Daily News* (February 22, 2004).

142. Ibid

143. A. Yamashita, "Accountability Needs to be Part of Guam's Everyday Culture." *Pacific Daily News* (June 15, 2001).

144. B. Palomo, "Celebrations Raise Likelihood of Poor Eating, Disease Among Chamorros." *Pacific Daily News* (December 5, 1999).

145. L. Martinez, "Eat, Drink and be Culture." *Pacific Daily News* (August 20, 2007).

146. T. Artero, "Negligence is Standard Practice in GovGuam." *Pacific Daily News* (August 17, 2009).

147. T. Artero, "Give Deeds to Land Trust Leaseholders." *Pacific Daily News* (March 13, 2010).

148. D. Hannan, *Inventing Freedom: How the English-?peaking Peoples Made the Western World* (New York: HarperCollins Publisher, 2013).

149. Ibid.

150. T. Sowell, *The Thomas Sowell Reader* (New York: Basic Books, 2011, p. 7).

151. N. Eberstadt, *A Nation of Takers: America's Entitlement Epidemic* (West Conshohocken, PA: Templeton Press, 2012, p. 24).

152. A. Chua and J. Rubenfeld, *The Triple Package: How Three Unlikely Traits Explain the Rise and Fall of Cultural Groups in America* (New York: The Penguin Press, 2014, p. 219).

153. T. Sowell, *Intellectuals and Society* (New York: Basic Books, 2009).

154. T. Sowell, *Basic Economics: A Commonsense Guide to the Economy* (New York: Basic Books, 2011, p. 217).

155. W. Voegeli, *The Pity Party: A Mean-Spirited Diatribe Against Liberal Compassion.* New York: Broadside Books, p. 128).

156. Ibid, p. 93.

157. W. Williams, "How not to be poor," *Liberty Versus the Tyranny of Socialism.* (Stanford, CA: Hoover Institutional Press, 2008).

158. D. Kimbro, *The Wealth Choice: Success Secrets of Black Millionaires* (New York: Palgrave Macmillan, 2013, p. 5).

159. Ibid, p. 2.

160. Eberstadt, op cit.

161. G. E. Miller, "The U.S. is the most overworked developed nation in the world—where do we draw the line?," *20somethingfinance.com/American-hours-worked-productivity-...*January 17, 2015).

162. Chua, op cit., p. 208.

163. Ibid.

164. Eberstadt, op cit.

165. R. Emerson, "Self-Reliance," *Collected Essays, First Series* (Rockville, MD: Arc Manor, 2007).
166. A. de Tocqueville, *Democracy in America* (New York: New American Library, 1956).
167. Eberstadt, op cit., p. 25.
168. Ibid., p. 26.
169. Chua, op cit.
170. Ibid, p. 133.
171. K. Pomerleau and L. Stone, "Tax freedom day 2014," *taxfoundation.org*, March 1, 2015.
172. D'Souza, op cit.
173. Sowell (1996), op cit., p. 385.
174. K. Makihara,"The Plea of the Ainu." *Time* (January 6, 1992), p. 53
175. Ibid.
176. D'Souza, op cit.
177. W. Williams, "Diversity." *Jewish World Review* (January 16, 2002).
178. J. Kerwick, "'Diversity': The idol of academia," *Daily Mailer,FrongPage*, frontpagemag.com, June 26, 2014.
179. Williams, op cit., January 16, 2002.
180. W. Williams, "The Racism of Diversity." *Jewish World Review* (July 22, 2009).
181. Williams (2002), op cit., p. 1.
182. W. Williams, "We need diversity," *Jewish World Review* (January 27, 2010), p. 1.
183. V.D. Hanson, "Diversity, inc.," *National Review Online* (December 28, 2011).
184. Ibid, p. 5.
185. Voegeli, op cit., p. 81.
186. Sowell (1994), op cit., p. 31.
187. C. Thomas, "E. Pluribus Diversity?" *Jewish World Review* (November 12, 2000), p. 2.
188. D'Souza, op cit.
189. Codevilla, op cit., p. ix.

CHAPTER TWELVE

Public Speaking Subject
Selection, Audiences, and Research

There is so much to know and do all at once to be an effective speaker. Since that is a impossibility, the public speaking material and speeches will have to be provided in pieces and in stages over the following chapters as you come to acquaint yourself with speaking before a crowd. In this chapter, there will be an overview of the need for public speaking, some common myths about speech making, speech apprehension, the overall speech preparation steps, and the initial speech preparation steps including selecting a subject, clarifying the speech purpose, and analyzing the audience. The chapter will end with a brief about research.

THE NEED FOR PUBLIC SPEAKING

Our country and culture depends upon people speaking in the public marketplace of ideas so we can be informed about the issues of the day, be those issues people's lives, proposed government action, products and services that we might purchase, and so on. We need a seemingly endless supply of bits of information to help us navigate our way through life's daily quandaries. We get some of that information either directly or indirectly from someone speaking to a public somewhere, about which we are enlightened later.

Growing up with public speaking and freedom of speech probably does not seem like a big benefit to us, but to those people in human history who did not have this right and the opportunity, it typically spoke of a highly constrained life. It ought to give all of us pause when citizens in America, even public officials, are not allowed to speak at public forums in America.

ing list provides some additional reasons we speak:

- to learn more about ourselves and what's around us
- to gain a insight to what might happen to us in future situations and then prepare for that
- to increase the chances that our communication skills will help us reach our goals in life
- to satisfy other's goals, as much as we are able
- to work effectively with others
- to create and maintain the type of friendships we have or would like to have with others
- to enjoy ourselves, to entertain others, even relax with funny stories

We have a mind. We have our own individual and unique thoughts. We have our likes and dislikes, what we think we need in life, and our goals. If we don't speak up, who can speak for us? Our voice has to be heard.

PUBLIC SPEAKING MISCONCEPTIONS

It is common when observing people who are good at their craft to make inaccurate assumptions about the craft and the performance of the individual. Such applies to speaking.

First, it is not a misconception that speaking before a group can be a nerve-wracking event. It is a misconception that the anxiety people typically feel is completely harmful and cannot be controlled. People in most, if not all, endeavors use the adrenalin produced in anxious situations to achieve outstanding performances. They have learned to concentrate their focus on what they were doing and allow few, if any, thoughts about what observers might be thinking.

Second, people are not born as good public speakers. Good public speaking takes effort, clear and mindful thinking, and practice to achieve superior results. We hear someone at a one-time event and are impressed, but we are unaware of the typical years of "growing" pains the speaker suffered through and the countless hours of refining his or her ideas.

Third, you are unlikely to go from being a poor speaker to a great one after performing the speeches required for this class. This introduction to speaking is just that. You should learn the basic principles of effective speaking that will act as a foundation for your increasing competence in the future. You will have to gain additional practice that benefits from insightful observations of weaknesses that can be overcome with each additional event. You can become comfortable speaking before others.

SPEECH ANXIETY

As noted above, speaking before a crowd typically leads to a great deal of anxiety in people. People fear it and rightly so, in a sense, for who wants to make a fool of themselves in public? Further, the classroom grade evaluation adds additional pressure.

If we have to give speeches, we have to find a way to minimize and even control our fears.

The following provide a variety of methods which people have found to be effective in controlling their speech anxieties.[1] They are easier said than done, but with attention and practice they can work.

1. *Think Positive.* If you choose a topic you have a positive regard for you will not have to manufacture enthusiasm for it. Further, feelings are contagious, both for the speaker's delivery and for the listener's response. An audience's enthused response, in turn, can stimulate you to become additionally enthused as you deliver the speech, thereby reducing an existing anxiety.

Some people report that purposely thinking positive thoughts about the outcome diminishes their anxiety of performance. They may simply think, "I can do it." Added to this, people may take time to visualize their selves delivering the speech in an effective manner. We cannot deny that we are the ones in control of our thoughts so we do not have to dwell upon doing poorly.

2. *Be Prepared.* Knowing that we have adequately prepared ourselves is comforting. On the other hand, we have every reason to feel nervous if we are not prepared. Little, if anything, can allay that. With practice we gain a sense that we are going to be OK. The activity can even become routine as our training takes over some of our performance. Consider practicing the speech ten times once it is in its final form.

Your appearance also needs to be prepared for the occasion. While in class you may be allowed to dress in your normal attire, audiences outside of class will be more critical of whether you look the part. If you do not, your believability will suffer

3. *Be Realistic About Your Expected Performance.* The speeches you deliver in front of the class may be the first (and last) ones performed in your life. As much as perfection should be your goal, it is unrealistic to expect that either during the speech or in retrospect you will judge yourself as perfect. Speaking is an acquired skill (so is enjoying it, for most of us). While you are probably taking the class to fulfill a college requirement, you are also taking the class to learn and improve. As you gain experience, your skill level is likely to rise. Challenge yourself to do better with each succeeding speech.

4. *Familiarize Yourself With The Setting.* Even if you cannot change how the room or place is arranged, knowing how it is set up can provide some comfort. This is especially so with speaking occasions held away from places you frequent. Pay particular attention to the available lighting so you will be able to read your notes and to the sound system so you can know how close to the microphone you need to be to sound loud enough for everyone. Visit the setting the day before or earlier the day of the event so you can practice with the lighting and sound system. Some women have stood behind the podium in advance to determine whether they should wear high heels that allow their selves to be clearly seen over the top of it.

5. *Use Relaxation Techniques.* Some students like to take some slow, deep breaths at their seat before getting up. Once in front they can take another one before they begin. A friendly gaze at the audience can have a calming effect on the speaker. An open posture that allows you to turn and shift slightly to one side, then the other, dissipates some anxiety. Tightly squeezing the rear of the podium where it cannot be seen can direct some tension away from your voice. It is also relaxing to gaze about the entire room, picking out a friendly face on the sides and in the middle who offer reassurance.

These methods can be used in combination or in their entirety. Since a multitude of anxious thoughts and feelings typically run through a beginning speaker's mind before and during a speech, these methods may take some experimentation and practice until they are perfected.

SPEECH PREPARATION STEPS

The following list provides an overall look at the common steps speakers can follow in preparing to deliver a speech. This list also gives an overview of what will be covered in more detail in this and in the subsequent chapters.

1. Select the topic and purpose
2. Analyze the audience
3. Research the topic
4. Develop the thesis and main, supporting points
5. Support the main points with information
6. Organize the body of the speech
7. Construct the conclusion, introduction, and insert transitions
8. Outline the entire speech

9. Word the speech
10. Rehearse the speech

SUBJECT SELECTION, PURPOSE, AND OCCASION

You have to choose to speak about something. The elements in this section should inform the choices you will have to make about what is and what is not to be included in your speech. Bear in mind that effective speaking requires a listener-centered orientation. What can you say, with what style, organization, and arguments, and delivered in which fashion, that will encourage your listeners to perceive both you and your message as credible? What can and will they find meaningful in your speech? As you consider your subject selection, speech purpose, and the speech occasion, what choices can you make about these factors that are likely to lead to mutual understanding with your audience?

The elements of *subject selection, purpose, and occasion* are combined, along with audience analysis hereafter since they are interdependent and thus, inform each other.

1. *Speech Purpose.* In general, is your speech supposed to inform, persuade, or satisfy a special occasion? These are the *general purposes* that provide a particular orientation to how a topic is covered. The *informative speech* is designed to help the audience understand a concept, person, or action. The *persuasive speech* tries to influence the audience's behaviors—to get them to believe something and to take some action. The *special occasion* speech varies according to the context as it attempts to get the audience to feel good about something or someone. It varies in emphasis from promoting good will, to courtesy, to entertaining. Notice how many graduation speeches do not emphasize graduates or graduation, and thus do not fulfill their intended general purpose.

It is not enough to have a general purpose. Each speech requires a *specific purpose* to help the speaker clarify his or her focus on the topic. The specific purpose narrows the topic area to a specific aspect of that area (examples provided on the next page). You cannot cover the entire area of cancer or even skin cancer in a 6-8 minute informative speech. The specific purpose provides the exact, concrete goal the speaker wishes to achieve.[2]

For example, the *general speech* purpose may be to inform the audience about skin cancer. The *specific purpose* may be: I want my audience to know how to protect themselves from contracting skin cancer. If the general purpose is to persuade the audience about some aspect of skin cancer, the specific purpose could be: I want my audience to use skin protective devices. If the general purpose is to provide a good will speech about skin cancer, the specific purpose could be: I want my audience to feel glad that people can beat skin cancer.

Complete the following for your own speeches:

The *general purpose* of my speech is to (choose): inform, persuade, or provide good will.
The *specific purpose* of my speech is to (see Subject Selection next page).

When you are clear about the specific purpose, it can be used to guide you in choosing what is relevant for your speech. As the material for a speech is gathered, the speaker-to-be has to verify that it fits the specific purpose.

2. *Speech Occasion.* There are a variety of speaking events, ranging from classroom presentations to wedding celebrations to awards ceremonies to business luncheons to political rallies, and so on. Each conveys certain expectations about which topics can be broached and how they can be appropriately discussed. You expect an up-beat feeling at a political campaign rally where the speaker lauds the candidate (possibly him or herself). Business people who have just finished lunch enjoy a humorous expose about some aspect of business, especially something they have accomplished. Each different occasion suggests its own theme, tone, and language style.

The occasion usually suggests the *time* available for the speech. Your instructor is likely to give you a specific time frame, to allow you to both satisfactorily complete the assignment and allow class time for other student speeches. Remember that audience attention typically wanes after 20 minutes and you'll notice audience din after just 10 minutes. As a general rule outside classroom requirements, shorter is better. If your boss or organizational leader tells you that you have 10 minutes to speak, attempt to finish the speech in eight minutes. No one at a wedding, funeral, business luncheon, or awards ceremony is going to tell you afterward that your six minutes speech was two minutes too little. Ironically, shorter speeches are more difficult to prepare since more preparation time is needed to winnow out the least important information.

3. *Subject Selection.* You have to choose a topic or find a point of view about the topic chosen for you about which you are interested. If you are, you are likely to better prepare for it and reveal your interest in it with your speech

delivery, which in turn will increase the chance that audience members will be more attentive listeners and find it of interest.

Your interest. Begin this process by listing your favorite topics on a piece of paper. What subjects do you discuss with your friends? Which books, magazine, or newspaper stories catch your attention? What do you spend your money on? If you are not that interested in the topic, you will not work as hard to prepare the speech and both you and your audience will notice your lack of interest, diminishing their interest and attention.

For example, assume you listed the following topic areas as of interest to you: music, sports, family, money, cars.

Next, be more specific about each of the topics:

Table 12.1

Music	a) the benefits of an ipod	b) internet music sites
Sports	a) the love of competition	b) teams to join
Family	a) importance of family	b) family history
Money	a) becoming a millionaire	b) money and happiness
Cars	a) the 1950's styles	b) racing cars

Ask yourself if you are interested in any of the sub-topics, and if not, extend your list of general and sub-topics until you can find a few of interest.

Your audience's interest. Ask yourself if you think your audience would be interested in hearing about the specific topics from your final list, as well. Attempt to find one that suits both you and your audience. Eliminate those you think the audience would not be interested in hearing. People usually pay more attention to topics that are about:

- happy things in life or doing fun activities
- feeling safe and secure in their daily life and being that way in the future
- being healthy
- achieving personal goals, especially in school and jobs they might have in the future
- some new toy, tool, fashion, entertainment equipment, car, and so on
- a solution to a know problem they do or will face

The time. Lastly, ask yourself if the selected topic makes sense as something that people talk about in the time allotted? Can you speak in depth about the topic within the classroom time requirements? Two, four, six, eight minutes? If not, choose another topic from your list that you have enough to talk about for the time limit. Eliminate those topics deemed inappropriate for the occasion or too large in scope. Verify whether your speech topic fits the general purpose.

AUDIENCE ANALYSIS

Audience analysis is the process by which you determine what characterizes your audience in relation to your speech topic so you can decide what you should say to effectively communicate your ideas to them. To do this, you have to make some educated guesses about your listeners. Are there any clues that can tell you something about them and what their reaction might be to the topic of your speech? Knowing what they know about the topic, you can avoid boring them or wasting your time trying to persuade them of something they already believe in. Below are just a few common audience categories to examine.

1. *Age.* What does the age of your audience suggest to you about their knowledge and point of view of the speech subject? People your parents' age may be interested in knowing what food might lead to diabetes or aggravate their diabetes, but people your age are probably interested in what tastes good, especially desserts. Retired people on fixed incomes may hate inflation but most college students probably have little emotional response to it. Knowing your listeners' ages, will they be interested in your speech topic? Would they rate it favorably or unfavorably?

2. *Gender.* While males and females are similar in some respects, they differ in others. What do you need to say to keep both the males and females listening to your speech? Are there some topics that males are not interested in, and others females are not interested in or topics they both are interested in? While few males get nursing degrees, most college graduates can appreciate the difficult graduation requirements and the necessity of having nurses. Speakers might remind themselves to avoid stereotypes in their speeches. In a speech about breast cancer, what do you need to say to attract and maintain the interest of male audience members?

3. *Religion.* Although people can get very emotional about religious topics, religions do provide a great deal of meaning and direction to people's lives.

Knowing your audience's religious beliefs, how can you expect them to react to what you have to say about your chosen topic? If Guam or your city is about 90% Catholic (or some other religion), what does that tell you about your audience's knowledge about and attitude toward your topic? What if you wanted to talk about gambling, nativity scenes on public property, or saying "Merry Christmas"? What would you expect Protestants to know and believe about abortion or birth control? Since religion can be a touchy subject, be sure to discuss it with respect and fairness.

4. *Occupation and income.* People in different occupations and income brackets typically have different interests and lifestyles. They read different books (if they read at all), they take different vacations, have their children attend different schools, they spend differently what money they have, and own different symbols and assets of wealth (among other things). While college graduates as a whole earn more than non-college graduates, assembly-line union workers may earn more than teachers. If you were to speak to an audience comprised of both groups, what would you say about a proposal to build a new high school that would appeal to both of them, and what would you add to answer specific concerns of each group of audience members?

Overall, your audience analysis should inform you what to say and how to say it to your audience so the speech will be of interest and of relevance to their lives. You must speak to them where they are in terms of knowledge, beliefs, attitudes, experiences, and so on.

RESEARCH

You have to have something to say about your topic. You need relevant information to illustrate, explain, and otherwise support your main ideas. Education is structured in a way to force students to discover information on their own and submit it according to some structured format. Research can provide students with the requisite information they need to complete the speaking assignments.

There are many pitfalls in doing research. The source of information could be biased or be deficient in their information. The information could be dated and thus superseded by more current findings. There is an endless amount of information but there is not an endless amount of knowledge. Acquiring or believing in some information can be toxic, so as to lead the holder of that information to reach an inaccurate and harmful conclusion. There can also be such an enormous amount of information on a topic that the reader cannot organize it or reach a firm conclusion about it.

1. *General research principles.* First, compile what you know about the topic, including the nominal who, what, where, when, why, and how information. Include your own experiences on the subject. Second, acquire some general information about the subject. Encyclopedias are helpful here and loaded onto many computers. Stories from your local newspapers or national magazines can provide quick and general information, along with specific sources of more in-depth information. Lastly, look for specific and focused sources of information. These will provide the specialized and most likely expert information. Attempt to find what recognized experts in the field say about the subject (and why they say it). Overall, expect to compile much more information than you will end up using. In the process of learning more about the topic and refining your ideas, you will discard extraneous and less important information.

2. *Information sources.* The introduction part of this research section noted some problems with sources of information. The researcher needs a healthy dose of skepticism about the validity (legitimate evidence and logical reasoning) and reliability (repeatable findings) of the information they acquire. Physical repositories of physical information (books in libraries) have long held both credible and non-credible information. The main difference between a library book or printed journal and many Internet sources is the intermediary publishing organization that filters some of the information (some books and articles are not printed, ostensibly because they are of lesser value, and there are editors that filter some information provided on websites). We cannot deny that there is a great deal of information on the Internet yet the source or credibility of the source is often unknown. Of course, we never knew if books in libraries or stories in print news publications, or even film documentaries, were credible, either, given all the misleading information in some of them that we know after-the-fact. On the other hand, there has been some legitimate filtering process. That being said, what should you do?

Search out libraries for all the books, other printed sources, and film archives available that you can read or see on the speech topic given your time constraints. Compare the information presented. Scan these for recent and both cursory and in-depth information about the subject. One advantage of printed materials in libraries is that you can quickly look over the table of contents, the index, and chapter material to see if it is of use. Examine encyclopedia articles as a source of general information. Mix primary sources with secondary sources of information. Perform an Internet search via Google (for example) for resources about your subject. Be very clear about keywords and subject categories for you can easily generate more sources of information than you can evaluate or that can be of use to you.

The Internet has greatly aided our connections with knowledgeable people around the world. Many sources of information provided on the Internet offer a way to e-mail the writers, researchers, and experts directly to get a response to specific questions and statements. They know they are speaking to the world when they post their information. By the same token, interview people in person in your community who are authorities on the subject you will speak. Be sure to take accurate notes, as well as the date, time, and place of the interview.

A book such as this could go on and on about sources of information. Students are likely to do what is quickest and will provide sufficient information to satisfy the course assignments (as they have for a millennium). That being the case, an in-depth understanding of logic, research methods, statistics, and widespread reading is absolutely essential for determining what is legitimate information and what is not.

Be sure to take accurate citations of your sources to use either in the text of your speech or made available as references that would allow you to answer questions about them. .

CONCLUSION

Speak about what interests you. Know your general and specific purposes and fit your subject into that. Get and maintain the audience's attention by tailoring your speech to fit their interests, concerns, and their relationship with the topic. You do not simply say what you think the audience wants to hear but entice them to hear your point of view on the subject by making a connection between what they know and value with what you know and value. You can only identify with your audience and they identify with you if you know your audience. This is the purpose of audience analysis. You cannot help but generalize your audience characteristics, but you can work at making good generalizations. Build upon these generalizations by finding and using good sources of relevant information.

Public speaking has a high fear factor rating within nearly everyone. With practice and attention to key details, people can become effective speakers and even enjoy it.

CHAPTER 12 HOMEWORK
(or class exercise):

1. a. List the three most common and important characteristics shared by the class (such as religion, age, etc.) and briefly explain how these would be important to a speaker (in short, what is the significance of each of these three for a speaker?).
   b. List three topics that you consider to be inappropriate subject matter for class speeches and explain why.

2. Create a list of ten subjects you are interested in, then list two sub-areas within each subject for which a more specific speech might be given. Examples are provided in the section on *Subject Selection* discussed earlier in this chapter.

3. Critique your first speech by reviewing the video copy made of it. You may find this in the audio-visual section of the library (or some other place designated by your instructor). In one-half to one page, note the strengths and weaknesses of your speech based upon the guidelines you were to follow for this speech.

MEMORABLE MOMENT SPEAKING ASSIGNMENT

This is a 2-3 minute speech that focuses on one event, be it exciting, embarrassing, scary, or other. You have told your friends and family members many stories about your experiences. Now tell one of these to us. We cannot expect you to know much about speech making at this point in the class, but you should be able to do the following.

Guidelines

1. Choose an event that you well remember and could easily talk about right now.
2. At home, consider writing down the time order of events to verify your details are in order. Be descriptive of what occurred rather than simply say "It was fun/exciting/boring/etc." By how you describe the event, we should know if it was fun, scary, embarrassing, or whatever. Verbally go over the details to verify the content, order, and length
3. Begin the speech with the first detail of the story (e.g., "One day when I was 7, my cousin and I ...."), then continue on with the details of the

story so we can imagine being there. Do not begin the speech with: "This is about the most memorable/scary/etc. moment in my life."

4. Be succinct with the content of the story, telling us just what we need to know without the unnecessary details. Of course the story has to be at least 2 minutes long. Do not add unnecessary details to meet the minimum time. If the story is too short, choose another one.

5. Practice at home speaking in complete phrases or sentences. Avoid pausing where there would be no comma or period (e.g., "When I was ... 7, my cousin ... and I ...went ....). If you errantly pause, avoid filler words or sounds such as: uh, um, well, and uh, like, you know, etc.

6. With your voice, make some changes in loudness, rate, pitch, pauses, and tone of voice to help convey the meaning and feeling of the story. You already do this when you tell stories to your friends and family as a way to create a mental picture of what has occurred. For example, when people are excited they speak faster, when scared they often use a higher pitch, and so on.

7. Do not give away in advance a surprise that may come up later in the story.

8. In your concluding sentence (or two), use your voice to combine with your words to give us the idea that you are about to finish. Usually, people speak slower and with a lower pitch. When you have given us the final word, avoid saying "The end", "Thank you", "The moral to the story is ....", or "That was the most exciting ..." We should already know this by how you spoke.

9. A brief outline can be used. A complete written account of the story is not allowed. Remember, this speech is about one event that you have probably already told to someone else, so a complete account is not needed. We want you to speak to us, not to your notes.

Evaluation: time (2-3 minutes), loudness and vocal changes, organization, succinctness, phrasing, use or not of filler words/sounds, and conclusion (what and how it is said).

SAMPLE MEMORABLE MOMENT SPEECH[3]

It was on December 12th, 1999, and I was ready to run the Honolulu Marathon.

Before the 5:00 AM cannon blast to start the race, I was with eight runners from Guam and about 30,000 from all over the world. We saw the most beautiful five-minute fireworks display that shot over Ala Moana Beach Park opposite the well-known shopping center.

My friend, Mary, cheered me on as I waited to start. "Go, Madeline!" The rain poured on us while we waited ten minutes to begin moving after the runners in front first took off. There were so many people around us.

As I began my run, I told myself to stay relaxed, not to increase my speed, and drink a lot of water to prevent "hitting the wall."

The five-mile-point was Kapiolani Park at the lower end of Waikiki, right before the run up and around Diamond Head Crater. Even though I felt strong, relaxed, and very prepared for this race, my nerves got the best of me and brought on the urgency to find a pit stop. I didn't see any portable johns but I did find a small bush and that was all I needed.

By this time, the Guam group was about five miles ahead of me so I was on my own. I remember saying a prayer and asking our Lord to stay close to me because I felt lost among the 30,000 people. I managed to bring my stress level down and I had a consistent, strong run all the way up the Diamond Head pass and over to Highway 1. While on H-1, I heard a voice. "Hey Maddy, is that you? Slow down so we can run with you." It was unbelievable. My adrenaline and prayer had spurred me on to reunite me with my group. What are the chances of that happening?

My friend and I were running side-by-side through Hawaii Kai and down to Kahala Ave. On and on we went, one grueling step after another, as the route led to Hawaii Kai and circled back to Kahala Ave and Diamond Head Road toward Waikiki. At the twenty-six-mile point we were both exhausted but at the Kapiolani Park finish line we held our hands in the air together as we completed the race! I had been able to finish in the top ten percent of my age group with a race time of 4:49:56.

After the event, I had to show Mary the bush in the park I had used as my pit stop early in the race. I looked all over for it but could not find it next to the race route. There was no bush where I had stopped. Did I moon thousands of people at 5:30 AM?

Table 12.2

Speech 1: Memorable Moment Name _____ Time (2-3 minutes)_____	
Organized: from the beginning to the end Introduction: avoided mentioning type of story	0 1 2 3 4
Delivery: loud enough, varied voice to convey emotions	0 1 2 3 4
Phrasing: words grouped into thought units, phrases, or sentences -- given the content. Choppy?	0 1 2 3 4
Inarticulate/filler words (um/uh/and/you know/ok/etc.)-	0 1 2 3 4
Eye contact: from the beginning to the end	0 1 2 3 4
Succinct: told as briefly as possible, given the event Too long? Too short?	0 1 2 3 4
Conclusion: rate & duration appropriate to the ending, Tone of voice fitting, avoided "moral of story"	0 1 2 3 4
Amount grade lowered due to excessive shortness or length?	
[0-inadequate, 1-adequate, 2-good, 3-very good, 4-excellent]	Grade_____

REFERENCES

1. M. Griffin, *Public Speaking Basics* (Lanham, Maryland: University Press of America, 2009).
2. Ibid.
3. M. Torres. Unpublished speech, University of Guam, Mangilao, Guam, February 3, 2005.

CHAPTER THIRTEEN

Creating A Main Idea, Supporting

Your Idea, And Using Presentation Aids

If we want people to listen to and understand us, we have to be understand-able. This means we have to be clear with the focus of our speech. We need to have an over-arching idea to which everything we say relates and is in logical concert. A well-written thesis, or main idea, is the foundation of the clarity and organization we seek in a speech. To justify, support, and/or illustrate our main idea, we need to create separate supporting points that give focus and depth to the thesis. To help clarify the supporting points, some sort of presentational aid may necessary.

THE THESIS

As noted above, the thesis is the fundamental center point. Everything said in a speech needs to evolve from it and revolve around it. According to Grif-fin, "The thesis is the yardstick by which ideas and information are evaluated and determined to be relevant to a particular speech. It is the foundation of meaning for an individual speech and serves to coalesce the speaker's ideas."[1] It is the basic idea of the speech that the speaker wishes the listener to accept.

Where can you find your central idea? Think about the subjects you are interested in. If you are interested in nutrition and your specific purpose is: I want inform my audience of the healthy food available at typical Thanks-giving dinners, your main idea might be, *Thanksgiving dinners can provide a healthy diet.* If your specific purpose is to persuade your classmates to join the school soccer team, your main idea (termed a *proposition*) might be: *You should join the school soccer team* Thus, you find your thesis within the subject matter about which you will speak.

1. *Characteristics of a Well-Written Thesis* (criteria list). For your thesis to be clearly and easily understood, it should exhibit certain characteristics and avoid others. It should be: a briefly worded grammatically complete sentence with only one key idea, a clear and simple declarative statement (no question), purposive (show an intention), direct—not indirect (as in, *is not*), written for audience acceptance (worded to interest, not anger or insult), and should avoid figurative language (abstract and unclear), vague (such as clichés), general (unmodified subjects such as *day* need *cold day, summer day*, etc.), or ambiguous words (*cute, affordable*, etc.). Do not define terms in the thesis (can do so shortly thereafter), avoid using the personal pronouns "I/me" (redundant), avoid comparisons (they lengthen, complicate, and raise two different ideas in the thesis), and avoid compound phrases (they extend the length and detract from directness, and no commas). The thesis subject should be placed near the beginning of the sentence so the listener immediately knows the subject. While there is no set length to a thesis, 15-20 words is normally long and 10 or less is excellent. Informative speech theses should avoid persuasive words (such as *should, must*, and so on) and promises.

Create a central idea after you have completed your initial research so you can have an informed understanding about the point of view you will express. Limit your speech so that everything you plan to say goes with the main idea. If your point is that sports provide good exercise, avoid discussing the character-building aspect of sports or professional salaries.

2. *Corrected Poorly Worded Thesis Sentences.* After reading, in turn, the three thesis statements below, note their weakness/es and how they can be correctly rewritten.

(1) Thesis: Hawaii has many places to visit but you cannot expect to travel on $25 per day.

a. Weakness: there are 2 different speech topics here (Hawaii places and travel on $25/day), travel seems vague since the more apparent idea is daily vacation expenses, *you cannot expect* is indirect and not entirely purposive, and *places* needs to be modified (and preceded) with a word such as *exciting*

b. Acceptable: Hawaii has many exciting places to visit.

(second main idea) People can easily explore the Hawaiian island of Oahu on $25/day.

(2) Thesis: Football playing is crazy, kind of like being nuts, I think you will come to agree.

a. Weakness: *crazy* would offend some lovers of football (audience acceptance) and *crazy* is unclear. Avoid comparisons, multiple phrases, figurative language (*nuts.*), run-on sentence, and a promise/persuasion attempt (*think you will ... agree*).

b. Acceptable: Continual football playing typically leads to long-term physical deterioration.

(3) Thesis: Let me discuss about academic majors (a major being a specific discipline).

a. Weakness: Personal pronoun *me* and the sentence is not grammatically correct (discuss about). Also, there is no purpose: what about academic majors? Further, do not define terms.

b. Acceptable: There are many college academic majors from which to choose.

SUPPORTING THE THESIS SENTENCE

Once you have formed your thesis sentence, you have to think about what you will say about it that makes it understandable and justified. This requires that you create additional specific ideas, or points, that give support to the thesis. Information that you present under each of these supporting points will further explain and demonstrate the sound basis of the thesis. These main supporting points cannot be just anything about the thesis but should in unison make the thesis appear thoughtful and complete.

1. *Finding Supporting Points for the Thesis.* Ask *what* or *how* about an information speech thesis (and *why* of a persuasive speech proposition) as a technique for generating information about the thesis. From this information, see if there are three different ideas that, on their separate merit, explain and justify the thesis. For example, if you want to speak about the public health system, you might create the thesis: *Guam Public Health provides needed services for senior citizens.* Next ask yourself: *what* needed services? Now list ideas that answer that, such as: dental care, medical care, wellness counseling, psychiatric care, immunization, prescription drugs, lab testing, podiatry, and x-rays.

Use the following guidelines to evaluate the supporting main points initially created.[2]

- combine points having a common focus, eliminating points with less relevance.
- use the 3 most important points (the third one helps put the other two in contrast).

- may word the points in parallel) style (college graduates can ..., college graduates can).
- avoid a single lead-in phrase preceding the points that presumes to individually refer to each point. For example, "Jason's Restaurant is a financially successful eating establishment … since *it is a great place to* work, entertain, and baby sit kids. Rather, each point should have its own wording that allows that point to be read directly from the thesis and sound like a complete idea. Combined with the thesis, the first point wording might be, "Jason's Restaurant is a financially successful eating establishment … since *it is an easy place to* work." The thesis combined with the second point might be, "Jason's Restaurant is a financially successful eating establishment … since it is a fun place to entertain." Combined with the third point, "Jason's Restaurant is a financially successful eating establishment … since it has a safe place to baby sit kids." All together, "Jason's Restaurant is a financially successful eating establishment since *it is an easy place to* work, *it is a fun place to* entertain, and *it has a safe place to* baby sit kids."
- avoid an added phrase after the supporting points are listed that is used to explain the points: "… since you can walk, bike, or drive *to the beaches there.*" Rather, change to "…since you can walk to the beach, ride your bike to the beach, or drive to the beach."
- verify your main points do not overlap each other in meaning, but are separate and discrete. Avoid saying, ": … since football is *fun, exciting, and entertaining.*
- ensure that each main point fits the thesis. For example, if you say, "Scooters are convenient for driving through city traffic," you cannot support it by saying that they are economical.

Now going back to the previous thesis, *Guam Public Health provides needed services for senior citizens*, you might select the three points that focus on *dental care, medical care, and wellness counseling.* Combined, the thesis and points would read: *Guam Public Health provides needed services for senior citizens, such as dental care, medical care, and wellness counseling.*

Notice that you will use a few words to connect the thesis with the main points. These include examples like: such as, due to, since, because, including, and so on.

Applying these ideas to the thesis sentences corrected on the previous page, some supporting points added to them might be written as follows:

(1) c. thesis plus 3 supporting points: Hawaii has many exciting places to visit, including … the Arizona Memorial, Waikiki Beach, and the Ala Moana Shopping Center.

c. second thesis plus 3 supporting points: People can explore the Hawaiian island of Oahu on $25/day if they camp at public beaches, ride *The Bus*, and only eat at restaurants during happy hour.

(2) c. thesis plus 3 supporting points: Continual football playing typically leads to long-term physical deterioration such as immobility, uncontrolled speech, and dementia.

(3) c. thesis plus 3 supporting points: There are many college academic majors from which to choose, including those in business, those in education, and those in science.

Fitting the Thesis Plus Supporting Points Fit Into An Organized Speech

In a normal outline, the thesis and main supporting points would be placed as follows:

- Introduction, with supporting statements.
- Body.
- Thesis statement, followed by 3 main supporting points (combined in one sentence).
- Definition of terms (if any in the thesis (only) need defining).
- Statement of 1st main supporting point, with supporting statements.
- Statement of 2nd main supporting point, with supporting statements.
- Statement of 3rd main supporting point, with supporting statements.
- Conclusion, with supporting statements.

SUPPORTING AND AMPLIFYING YOUR IDEAS

There are two general types of statements used when we attempt to inform or persuade others, whether we are engaged in normal, everyday, informal communication or are delivering a prepared formal speech before an audience: one, claim, or conclusions we want our listeners to accept, and two, the justifications we provide for those claims. The emphasis in this section will be upon the various ways speakers can validate, illuminate, and even heighten their ideas. While people will occasionally understand and even accept without question a speaker's claims, most listeners will usually require some further explanation, clarification, and/or elaboration of what they hear so they can better understand the speaker's point of view. They may even want the speaker's ideas substantiated before they will accept them. Further, the speaker may have a reason to magnify his or her ideas, such as to emphasize its importance, increase the likelihood the listener will remember or respond to it, or even to accept the idea. The following methods fulfill these purposes. They also act as evidence for a speaker's claim (conclusion), they may complement each other, and are often combined.

1. *Statistics.* These are numerical data which summarize information used to emphasize the state of a certain situation which the speaker thinks is meaningful. The numbers may emphasize how something is small or large, is increasing or decreasing, or how two different phenomenon are similar in size. Figures by themselves tell little so the speaker has to establish their significance. Although the use of statistics gives weight and authority to generalizations, do not merely cite figures (or even say that "they speak for themselves") but explain their importance. Verify that they are accurate, recent, specific, from a reliable and preferably unbiased source, and drawn from a sufficiently large group (sample) being measured. If exactness is not needed, round off figures to the closest relevant whole number.

Books such as *How to Lie with Statistics*[3] or *Damned Lies And Statistics: Untangling Numbers from the Media, Politicians, and Activists*[4] can give the reader some insight to how people manipulate numbers for their own self-serving purposes. Lomborg finds that the statistical evidence used by many environmental and media outlets as a basis for their doomsday messages about our environment is, in fact, selective and misleading.[5][6] As a former member of Greenpeace and a left-wing statistics teacher at a university in Denmark, he was surprised to discover that the statistical data largely support conclusions *opposite* those of the environmental alarmists. For another example, to simply focus on the significant fact that America's national debt in 2009 was $12 trillion dollars while overlooking the $57 trillion dollars in *unfounded future obligations* of government programs such as Social Security, Medicare, and Medicaid[7] is misleading. Statistical misrepresentation is much more common than most people realize.

2. *Testimony.* This is the citing of someone's opinion or conclusion about something observed or collected together and could take the form of a *quotation*. The testimony could be from a witness or authority. State how the person is a relevant and reliable witness and/or the basis of their expertise. Opinions do not prove anything since they are interpretations about facts, beliefs, or other states of existence. The best testimony comes from those who have firsthand knowledge, are capable of accurately observing the phenomenon, or are experts in the subject matter being discussed and whose background qualifications are known and respected.

Maybe Dr. Patrick Moore[8] is one such person. He earned a Ph. D. in ecology and environmental science (a relatively unknown specialty at the time) and then became a co-founder of Greenpeace (which later became the world's foremost environmental group) in 1971. Here is someone educated in the field and worked on the inside from the beginning. He knows the issues, the places, the dates, and the players. Fifteen years later he left Greenpeace when it left science (incidentally, there were no scientists on its board on his leaving). What could we, or anyone you know, say to challenge his testimony given below? What about the University presidents, professors, media people, and some of your acquaintances who repeat sensational environmental story lines and slogans, and speak so highly of the environmental movement to which Greenpeace is intimately connected and how we have to do this and that to save the planet? Have they actually researched the subject? Which insiders have they worked with, on what issues? Yes, we should evaluate Moore's work on its merit. According to Moore:

> Greenpeace became increasingly senseless as it adopted an agenda that is anti-science, antibusiness, and downright antihuman.[9]

> Many of the [peace movement's anti-American, neo-Marxist members] joined the environmental movement .... To a considerable extent the environmental movement was hijacked by political and social activists who learned to use green language to cloak agendas that had more to do with anticapitalism and antiglobalization than with science or ecology.[10]

> The environmental movement has unfortunately become ... partly a political movement that aims to influence public policy, but is also partly a religious movement in that many of its policies are based on beliefs rather than scientific facts.[11]

Thus, Moore provides us with some powerful testimony that refutes the conventional wisdom about environmentalism, and especially of Greenpeace. His conclusion is supported by the statistical information about environmentalism referred to Lomborg in the previous section.

Sowell suggests that we be skeptical of the very common "expert" testimony given by people speaking outside their field of expertise.[12] Leckie concludes that this "is an American weakness. The success becomes the sage. Scientists counsel on civil liberty; comedians and actresses lead political rallies; athletes [used to] tell us what brand of cigarettes to smoke."[13]

Sowell also cautions us to be wary of "experts" whose ideas have not been verified and those "experts" who cannot be held accountable if they are inaccurate, such as those in academia.[14] According to Biggs, "...there is increasing evidence that relying on expert opinion for advice is a loser's game. ...[It] should be ignored as random blather because experts are even less accurate than non-specialists in guessing what is going to happen."[15] Stossel suggests that we receive, and unfortunately believe, all too much "expert" testimony that turns out to be false and misleading.[16] Williams reports that "95 percent of what you read about economics and finance is either wrong or irrelevant."[17] Feynman (referred to in Chapter 8), interviewed claims that "…most experts, whether in the stock market, education, sociology or some parts of psychology, don't know more than the average person…. [T]hey follow certain methods and have results. But they are really practicing what I call 'cargo-cult [or typewriter] science.'"[18] Tetlock says something similar about the predictions of political experts and our political leaders, whose judgments he found *on whole* to be very inaccurate.[19] Feynman makes a similar statement about politics: "Politics offers another good example. We all know that they don't know what they're doing in Washington…. A lot of experts have studied these subjects. But they know much less than they will admit."[20] For a good reason, Samuelson titled his book *UNTRUTH: Why The Conventional Wisdom is (Almost Always) Wrong.*[21]

Imagine you are a travel agent in Oakland, California who has been to American Samoa and disagrees with Margaret Mead,[22] the most esteemed anthropologist in America.[23] Will academia and the public believe you or Dr. Mead about the Samoan culture? The travel agent was vindicated when the Australian Anthropologist Freeman published his work, *Margaret Mead and the Heretic: The Making and Unmaking of an Anthropological Myth,* revealing her preconceptions, oversights, and inaccurate generalizations.[24]

In addition to the recommendations for responding to testimony listed in the first paragraph above, minimize the accepting of inaccurate testimony and verify that enough testimony has been presented. Be careful not to take the source's words out of context. Feynman, suggests that to "…distinguish between what is valid information [from experts] and what is cargo cult, people need use only common sense. They need to look at the effects of policies…. Another way of evaluating ideas [from experts] is to ask yourself, 'How did they find that out?'"[25] Further, "[I]f an expert … [has an idea] that cannot be explained, then be suspicious. I know very few examples of knowledge that cannot be explained."[26] If at all possible, avoid the trap of responding to the "expert" in terms of the label "expert" (the intensional reality) and simply reflect upon the legitimacy of his or her statements and the outcomes of those statements (the extensional reality). Any appeal the expert makes to his or her expertise is an effort to intimidate the listener or get the listener to focus on the label, not the substance of what the expert is supposed to explain—but may be incapable of.

3. *Examples.* These are a brief case in point of an event, concept, or occurrence that is used to clarify something and help prove some point, suggesting a representation or pattern of something.

An *Illustration* is a more detailed story of what did or could occur.

Both examples and illustrations can be either real or hypothetical. Examples can be either detailed or not, depending upon the audience's familiarity with subject or circumstance, and multiple examples may be used as deemed necessary for audience understanding or persuasion. Verify the examples or illustrations are relevant and representative of the situation or idea, and are highly probable if predicted to occur. The use of extreme or uncommon examples exhibit gross stereotyping and will lower the speaker's perceived credibility.

A *Specific Instance* is a brief references to something you expect your audience to be familiar with so you do not have to give much description of the event, person, place, or process.

4. *Comparisons.* Also known as analogies, they attempt to equate two or more phenomena as a method for determining which one is superior or to increase the listener's understanding of an otherwise unknown phenomenon. On the basis of what is already known about the recognizable or first phenomenon stated, listeners are expected to understand the unknown or second one being cited. The usual outcome is that a product, service, concept, or occurrence discussed by the speaker is deemed more desirous than another. The two phenomena being compared need to be clearly alike in enough significant aspects and this should exceed the importance of any existing differences.

Recognize that no two things are exactly alike (such as the many types of apples) and people tend to be indiscriminate in what they compare. The most common term for weak comparisons is "comparing apples to oranges." This was revealed in the *Sexism* section of Chapter Six with the typical comparisons made between male and female incomes, supposedly indicating sexism

Contrasts are statements that emphasize the differences between phenomena—those qualities that set them apart. They help show what something is not. Ensure that at least one phenomenon is familiar to the listeners, and that the distinctions clearly separate the two.

5. *Definitions.* These attempt to reveal the fundamental character of it. Speakers may do this by citing the etymology (origin or derivation) of the word, or by placing it in a class with like phenomena. Words can also be defined by stating what they are not, or by providing an application example (operational definition).

Is there a difference between the dictionary definitions of "tax" and "penalty" to guide our thinking about whether Obamacare "taxes" or "penalizes" those who do not buy mandated healthcare? Are Americans "greedy" like some big government proponents say when these working Americans want to keep a large part of their legally earned money? Do you think the government can legitimately define and should enforce what is "greedy" or not? What is "entitlement," and why is the government "entitled" to both create "entitlement" programs and decide which people are "entitled" to receive other people's property, which the government forcibly takes? Thus, the words speakers' use and the stated or contextual meanings suggested for those words is crucial for explaining a given point of view of a speaker.

Descriptions are explanations used to give clarity to a term, concept, process, event, or proposal. Be concise in using these supporting devices so time is not wasted and the audience does not become bored.

6. *Restatement.* This is the repeating of an idea in different words to help your listeners remember it.

Application: Supporting Elements Used in a Single Topic.[27]

Thesis: Soybean products provide significant benefits (basic information taken from "The world's healthiest foods."[28])

1. *Statistics.* U.S. farmers grow just over 50% of the world's soybeans, making it an important export crop. Further, one cup of soybeans provides over 50% of the daily value for protein.

2. *Testimony.* Dr. Madeline Horinouchi, University of Guam Extension Agent: "Soybeans are one of the healthiest and cheapest sources of nutrition in the world for humans and livestock."

3. *Example.* Soybeans provide protective effects against heart disease, cancer, and osteoporosis and lead to longer life.

Illustration. Imagine having a Type 2 diabetic person in your family who has problems with meat protein. Then you discover that soybean protein and fiber prevents high blood sugar levels.

Specific Instance. Remember the soy burgers served at John Perez's Welcome Back Party?

4. *Comparisons.* Soybeans can be thought of as meat that is boneless and without fat. It can even look similar when it is fashioned into hot dogs, burgers, and steak.

Contrast. Unlike meat that contains saturated fat and cholesterol, soy protein tends to lead to lower cholesterol levels and a lesser amount of diabetes, heart disease, and strokes.

5. *Definition.* A leguminous plant cultivated in China over 13,000 years ago, its seeds are used as a source of nutrition by both people and animals, and its bush for soil improvement.

Descriptions. Soybeans are edible seeds of green, yellow, brown, or black color, about one-fourth inch wide, that grow in pods on a bush that typically stands five feet tall. They can be found in various forms, including fresh, dried, as soymilk, nuts, or flour, and processed as tofu.

6. *Restatement.* Soy products are a very important source of high quality food and a meaningful source of income for U.S. farmers.

7. *Presentational Support Material. Audio-Visual Aids*[29] Audio-visual aids are used to gain attention, maintain interest, and both clarify and reinforce the speaker's ideas. They can make the supporting facts clearer, more vivid, and convincing. They use tools such as the chalkboard, poster paper/board, projectors, and music players and include printed material such as handouts, charts, graphs, diagrams, maps, or pictures, as well as models, special clothing, and actual people or objects.

When considering the use and selection of presentational aids, answer the following:

    a. Is the aid necessary for the critical idea to be understood?
    b. Is the aid, and the message of the aid, relevant?
    c. Does the aid reinforce the idea under consideration?
    d. Is the aid appealing?

Rules for use of presentational aids:

    a. Ensure the entire audience can easily see it.
    b. Ensure the visual aid is visually appealing (e.g., use vivid colors instead of weak pastels).
    c. Use few and simple words on it.
    d. Put only 1 idea or 1 closely related sets of ideas on each chart.
    e. Do not stand between your listeners and the visual aid.
    f. Be sure you can easily handle the visual aid.
    g. Do not unnecessarily leave your aid in view when it will otherwise be distracting.
    h. Speak to your audience, not simply to your visual aid.
    i. Never pass around any material during your speech.
    j. Ensure that the time and cost of creating the aid is justified.
    k. Do not project text (especially via Power Point) upon the screen simply to read it, or leave it in sight thereafter when the discussion has changed.
    l. Be prepared with backup equipment and/or parts. Ensure you can change bulbs in the dark, and have a flashlight ready.
    m. Consider using simplified backup posters in the event a projector or computer fails.

CONCLUSION

Speech time and listener attention is limited. Speeches need a guiding theme for speaker focus that leads to listener clarity and understanding. Correctly written thesis sentences along with their supporting ideas provide these outcomes. Further, it is in both the speaker's and the audience's interests that the speaker provides adequate justification for the conclusions he or she wants accepted. Inaccurate, incomplete, unstated, and/or irrelevant supporting information may initially be overlooked by the audience but in the long run (at least) it nearly always harms the speaker's credibility.

CHAPTER 13 EXERCISES[30]

Thesis Characteristic Review (criteria list): briefly worded, grammatically complete sentence, one idea, clear and simple declarative statement, purposive, direct— not indirect (as in, *is not*), for audience acceptance, avoids figurative, vague, and general language or ambiguous words, avoids definitions, personal pronouns (I/me), comparisons, and compound phrases. The main subject should be placed near the beginning of the sentence, the thesis should ideally be 10 words or less (baring exceptions), and avoid both persuasive words and promises.

A. *Poor Thesis Sentences.* After reading the statements below, list their weakness/s and rewrite them in a correct manner.

1. Bad things happen to your body when you eat a lot of fat.

     a. weakness: _____

     b. rewrite: _____

2. The FDA policy to cut the amount of salt in food is a nutty movement.

     a. weakness: _____

     b. rewrite: _____

3. The benefits of owning land in San Francisco.

     a. weakness: _____

     b. rewrite: _____

4. Giving children an allowance (an amount granted) is not a good idea.

    a. weakness: _____

    b. rewrite: _____

Skip to Exercise C next page, then come back here to complete Exercise B.

B. *Thesis Sentences Needing Supporting Points:* Using the thesis sentences previously rewritten in Exercise A above, add appropriate main points. First transfer the correctly rewritten theses from above to here.

    1. Poor thesis: Bad things happen to your body when you eat a lot of fat.

        b. rewrite: _____

        c. rewrite, with 3 main points added: _____

    2. Poor thesis: The FDA policy to cut the amount of salt in food is a nutty movement.

        b. rewrite: _____

        c. rewrite, with 3 main points added: _____

    3. The benefits of owning land in San Francisco.

        b. rewrite: _____

        c. rewrite, with 3 main points added: _____

    4. Giving children an allowance (an amount granted) is not a good idea.

        b. rewrite: _____

        c. rewrite, with 3 main points added: _____

C. *Examples of Thesis Sentences with Unacceptable Supporting Points*

    1. Pearl Harbor, Waimea Bay, and Dole's pineapple fields are fun places to visit in Hawaii.
       Weakness: Begin the sentence with the thesis, followed by the supporting points.

2. Being a car mechanic is a very demanding profession since you always
   have to keep up-to- date about how to fix cars, you have to work on
   cruddy cars in greasy shops, but you might be well paid.
   Weakness: point #1 is not concise, point #2 has 2 ideas and uses vague
   terms, and point #3 is not written in parallel style or in a parallel sense
   with the viewpoint of the 1st two points.

3. Playing professional football may be detrimental to your health, since
   it can lead to injuries, head injuries, and sore muscles.
   Weakness: points #1 and #2 are not parallel, "injuries" overlaps "head
   injuries," point #3 does not fit the thesis since "sore muscles" does not
   reinforce "detriment" for sore muscles are temporary and therefore not
   considered a health issue.

D. *Supporting Information*[31]: Describe what type of support information (statistics, testimony, etc.) it would take to convince you that the following claims
are true (not that they are). Answer in the space next to the claims.

1. People on Guam are very friendly.
2. Legalized gambling provides an overall economic benefit to those places
   allowing it.
3. More than just Lee Harvey Oswald (if he did participate) fired shots at
   JFK that fateful Dallas day in November 1963, when JFK was killed.
4. The legal alcohol drinking age in America should be a uniform 18 years
   of age.
5. Marijuana has no deleterious effect on our body.

Supporting Material Being Used: Identify the type of support material being
used in the following examples. Choose from among: description, explanation, definition, comparison, contrast, example, illustration, specific instance,
statistics, testimony/quotation. Answer in the left margin.

1. The $.75 that bought one Hershey's candy bar in 2005 would have
   bought fifteen of them in 1970.
2. Osama Bin Laden is a hero to Muslims in the Middle East since he at-
   tacked Western nations.
3. The earth is round. A Continental flight attendant told me.
4. President Reagan's decisive actions quickly won the final stage of the
   Cold War with Russia.
5. Stock brokers must follow one basic rule: they have to earn money for the
   firm.

CHAPTER 13 HOMEWORK
Thesis Sentences[32]

Directions. Rewrite the following poorly written thesis sentences following the thesis sentence characteristics *criteria list* provided on the first page of this chapter. Keep the length to about ten words or less. If any sentence has *two separate main ideas, create two separate thesis statements* and three separate supporting points for each of them. No research should be necessary other than a cursory look at a dictionary or an encyclopedia.

To each complete sentence thesis, provide three reasonable, parallel, non-overlapping main supporting points, and be concise with these. Use connecting words like *since, due to, because, including,* etc. between the thesis and the three supporting points. Avoid using the multiple supporting points as a way of producing a complete sentence ("Baseball is challenging, relaxing, and inexpensive.") or using a plural reference in the thesis statement ("There are three criteria for determining an effective baseball pitcher."). Although technically correct, students are not challenged if they are allowed to create theses like these.

Find the sentence weakness/es first to insure you avoid the same thing in your rewritten thesis. List the words that are flawed, accompanied by their weakness (only use the list of thesis criteria at the chapter beginning). Follow exactly the directions for the *a, b,* and *c* sections noted below for each thesis and put an *a, b,* and *c* on your page with each separate number.

1. Problems of fad diets.
   a. Weakness/es?
   b. Create a grammatically complete-sentence thesis (with a period; no supporting points used here)
   c. Copy exactly the complete-sentence thesis from *b* above and add 3 reasonable-sounding supporting points that fit each other and support the thesis idea.
2. How is life in Kansas?
   a. Weakness/es?
   b. Create a grammatically complete-sentence thesis.
   c. Copy the complete-sentence thesis from *b* and add 3 reasonable-sounding supporting points.
3. I will convince you that anyone who thinks America's educational system is great is an idiot.
   a. Weakness/es?
   b. Create a grammatically complete-sentence thesis.

   c. Copy the complete-sentence thesis from *b* and add 3 reasonable-sounding supporting points.

4. President Harding was not as bad a president as his biographers made him appear.

   a. Weakness/es?

   b. Create a grammatically complete-sentence thesis.

   c. Copy the complete-sentence thesis from *b* and add 3 reasonable-sounding supporting points.

5. Flying airplanes is for the birds; I think I'd rather drive on my vacation.

   a. Weakness/es?

   b. Create a grammatically complete-sentence thesis.

   c. Copy the complete-sentence thesis from *b* and add 3 reasonable-sounding supporting points.

REFERENCES

1. M. Griffin, *Public Speaking Basics* (Lanham, Maryland: University Press of America, 2009), p.15.
2. Ibid.
3. D. Huff, *How to Lie with Statistics* (New York: W.W. Norton & Company, Inc., 1954).
4. J. Best, *Damned Lies and Statistics: Untangling Numbers from the Media, Politicians, and Activists* (Berkeley: University of California Press, 2001).
5. B. Lomborg, *Cool It. The Skeptical Environmentalist's Guide to Global Warming* (New York: Alfred A. Knopf, 2007).
6. B. Lomborg, *The Skeptical Environmentalist: Measuring the Real State of the World* (Cambridge, UK: Cambridge University Press, 2001).
7. M. Gross, *National Suicide: How Washington is Destroying the American Dream From A to Z* (New York: Berkley Books, 2009).
8. P. Moore, *Confessions of a Greenpeace Dropout: The Making of a Sensible Environmentalist* (Vancouver, B.C.: Beatty Street Publishing Inc., 2010).
9. Ibid, p. 1.
10. Ibid, p. 5.
11. Ibid, p. 27.
12. T. Sowell, *Intellectuals and Society* (New York: Basic Books, 2009).
13. R. Leckie, *Helmet For My Pillow: From Parris Island to the Pacific* (New York: Bantam Books Trade Paperbacks, 2010), p. 7.
14. Sowell, op cit.
15. B. Biggs, *Wealth, War & Wisdom* (Hoboken, NJ: John Wiley & Sons, Inc., 2008), p. 9.
16. J. Stossel, *Myths, Lies, & Downright Stupidity* (New York: Hyperion, 2006).

17. W. Williams, "Economic Myths and Irrelevancy." *Jewish World Report* (November 4, 2009).

18. A. Sanoff, "A Conversation with Richard Feynman." *U.S.News & World Report* (March 18, 1985), p. 79.

19. P. Tetlock, *Expert Political Judgment: How Good Is It? How Can We Know?* (New Jersey: Princeton University Press, 2005).

20. Sanoff, op cit., p. 79.

21. R. Samuelson, *UNTRUTH: Why the Conventional Wisdom is (Almost Always) Wrong* (New York: ATRANDOM.COM, 2001).

22. C. Petit, "An amateur who refuted Margaret Mead." *San Francisco Chronicle* (April 5, 1983).

23. M. Mead, *Coming of Age in Samoa: A Psychological Study of Primitive Youth for Western Civilization* (New York: Morrow Quill Paperbacks, 1928).

24. D. Freeman, *Margaret Mead and the Heretic: The Making and Unmaking of an Anthropological Myth* (Ringwood, Victoria, Australia: Penguin Books, 1996).

25. Sanoff, op cit., p. 79.

26. Ibid., p. 80.

27. Griffin, op cit.

28. "The world's healthiest foods." *The George Mateljan Foundation*, 2001-2007.

29. Ibid.

30. Ibid.

31. Ibid.

32. Ibid.

CHAPTER FOURTEEN

Organizing the Speech

Listeners more easily follow, understand, and remember an organized speech. Having some structure also aids the speaker in preparing what to say, when, and how. Further, an organized speech can usually be presented in less time than an unorganized one. Of course, the structure has to represent some recognizable logic that makes sense for the subject, occasion, and purpose. A well-organized speech makes the speaker appear more believable to the audience.

Thus, the overall question the speaker needs to ask him or herself is, what overall arrangement will help the thesis become clear and the subject matter understood by the audience? To this end, this chapter will cover basic organizational patterns, outlines, introductions and conclusions, and transitions.

BASIC SPEECH STRUCTURE

A. Introduction
B. Body of the speech
C. Conclusion

While this structure provides a general form, it provides little insight about what to do in each of these sections. The structure of the body, or main part of the speech, is discussed below.

ORGANIZATION OF THE IDEAS IN THE BODY

There are a number of organizational patterns that can be followed when arranging ideas in the body of the speech. Which one is followed depends on the speech topic and the purpose of the speech.

1. *Chronological Order.* This one is useful when the speaker wants to describe events or processes occurring over time, especially when demonstrating either how to do something or how something works (e.g., the Demonstration Speech). The main points of the subject are put into a sequence according to when they occur. The following provide some examples

Historical Period Topic: Government executive control on Guam, 1898-present.

1. U.S. Navy Admirals Oversee Guam, 1898-1951
2. Limited Democracy During the Early Years of the Compact 1951-1970
3. Guam Elects its own Governors 1970-present

Construction Topic: (process) House painting.

1. Preparation
2. Painting the Large Surfaces
3. Painting the Trim
4. Cleanup

2. *Spatial Order.* This structure is useful for describing physical places. The main points are arranged according to where they exist. For a speech about America's Pacific Islands, they might be ordered thus:

1. Hawaii
2. Johnston, Midway, and Wake
3. American Samoa
4. Guam

Spatial Order exercise: fill in the following outline spaces:

Table 14.1

1.	Gateway Arch
a.	Toronto
b.	United States
2.	Sears Tower
a.	St. Louis
1)	Canada
2)	Chicago
b.	Wrigley Field/Cubs baseball team
1)	Montreal

3. *Topical Order.* This pattern places speech ideas into a grouping of topics that are then sorted into some logical order. The ordering of topics often allows some speaker flexibility since topic areas may be independent of each other. A speech about the main components of a car could start with the engine or body or suspension or transmission, but there would be some justification for discussing the car engine first since it provides the power, then the transmission which transfers that power to the wheels, then the body, and finally the suspension which provides a smoother ride for the body.

Suppose you want to give a speech about cars. What car topics would you discuss and how would you arrange them? First, list what you know about cars. Next, narrow down the list to fit the purpose, audience, information availability, personal interest, and time limit. Then create an informative speech thesis sentence about that aspect of cars upon which you have decided to focus. Finally, you create and organize the main points about cars that fit your thesis. Main ideas can be generated by asking yourself *what* or *how* in regard to the thesis.

Topical Order exercise: assume the thesis sentence about cars is: *Buying a car is relatively easy.* List aspects of cars and their ownership that influence people's car-buying decisions:

Table 14.2

color	purpose	insurance	affordability	parts availability
make	price	2wd/4wd	safety features	used/new condition
mpg	engine	wheel base	cargo capacity	extended warranty
size	seating	2/4doors	down payment	transmission type
loan	loan	mileage	accessories	warranty

Then sort the ideas according to which seem to fit together and which over-arch other ones. The following outline provides one possibility.

1. (1st major point)__Affordability_
   a. (sub-point)__Price_____
   b. (sub-point)__Down payment___
   c. (sub-point)__Loan_____
2. (2nd major point)__Make_____
   a. (sub-point)__Model_____
   b. (sub-point)__Color_____
   c. (sub-point)__Safety features__

3. (3rd major point)__Accessories_
   a. (sub-point)__Power features__
   b. (sub-point)__CD player,_____
   c. (sub-point)__Chrome rims___

Verify the chosen supporting points fit the thesis and follow from it. Does it make sense? *Buying a car is relatively easy if you determine affordability, decide on the make, and choose your accessories.* If these were the important factors for you, knowing them would make buying a car much easier.

Notice that you are likely to have listed ideas that do not seem to fit the overall structure and that you thought of additional ideas during the organization process. This is typical. Remember that time constraints will limit what you can cover.

4. *Problem–Solution Order.* People spend a great deal of their time discussing problems they face, so this is a useful pattern for describing such problem and then providing solutions for them. The speaker may want to persuade the audience that his or her solution should be accepted.

  1. Description of the Problem (harms)
  2. Possible solutions
  3. Best solution

Application.

1. Many Americans are overweight (Problems)
   a. Increased heart attacks
   b. Increased diabetes
   c. Increased medical costs

4. Americans can lose weight (Solutions)
   a. Diet
   b. Exercise
   c. Supplements
   d. Follow the _____ diet

5. *Causal Order.* A *cause* is an agent or condition that brings about a particular result. It is a stimulus for a given outcome. The object of this pattern is to clarify both the causes and the effects. When people are unhappy with certain outcomes, they seek to alter what is responsible for them (which can be a separate informative speech or even a persuasive speech).

1. Cause/s (present conditions or causes; reasons for)
   a. one specific one
   b. another specific one
   c. another specific one
1. Effects [of the conditions or causes; adverse effects (typically harms)]
   a. one specific outcome
   b. another specific outcome
   c. another specific outcome

Application

1. There are several key factors that account for teen pregnancy
   a. lack of social sanctions against it
   b. peer pressure to engage in sex
   c. government social support services

2. Effects of teen pregnancy
   a. many single mothers raising kids
   b. increased anti-social behavior in the community
   c. increased tax burden on working people

In summary, these organization formats are for arranging main and sub-ideas in the body of the speech and are always used in conjunction with a separate introduction and conclusion.

ORGANIZING THE ENTIRE SPEECH: THE MOTIVATED SEQUENCE

As the chapter initially described, the basic speech structure requires an introduction, then the body of the speech, and lastly a conclusion. In an attempt to tailor the speech toward a given audience, the *Motivated Sequence* was created.[1] By specifying speech duties that both followed an interconnected logical pattern and stimulated a psychological reaction in the audience to act, this sequence helps ensure speaker success in persuading an audience to believe in something and/or act in some desired fashion. In other words, by speaking to the needs of an audience (problems they are experiencing), the speaker maintains audience attention, creates speaker credibility, and primes (motivates) the listeners to seek information that will satisfy their concerns (needs). With that information, they are prepped and stimulated to act.

Table 14.3

The basic speech structure	*becomes* (for persuasive speeches)
A. Introduction	A. Attention Step
	B. Need Step
B. Body of the speech	C. Satisfaction Step
	D. Visualization Step
C. Conclusion	E. Action Step

Explanation of The Motivated Sequence Steps (as follows).

A. Attention Step: Get the audience interested in the speech so they will want to listen.
B. Need Step: Describe how the audience is or will be harmed by some phenomenon.
C. Satisfaction Step: Satisfy (resolve) the harms by providing a solution or plan of action.
D. Visualization Step: Describe both the good and bad results that can be expected ahead.
E. Action Step: Specify an action/behavior wanted from the audience.

Modification of the Motivated Sequence for Informative Speeches

A. Introduction
    1. Attention Step: Get the audience interested in the speech so they will want to listen.
    2. Need Step: Describe how the audience is or will be harmed by some phenomenon.
B. Body/Satisfaction Step: Satisfy the harms by providing solution information.
C. Conclusion: Give final comments to end the speech.

The Motivated Sequence for informative and persuasive speeches will be discussed in greater detail in a later chapter. One informative example is provided below.

Sample Motivated Sequence Informative Speech Outline

A. Introduction
    1. I couldn't wait to graduate from high school so I could go to college and learn the wonders of the world. I looked forward to being more on my own.

2. Yet, college can be stressful due to competition for grades, majors, and scholarships which is correlated with binge drinking, drug use, junk food consumption, little sleep, and subsequent low grades and irritability. Some drop out, realizing a bleaker future.
B. Satisfaction Step
   1. Thesis: You can keep your body in peak physical condition during college by maintaining a healthy diet, exercising regularly, and getting sufficient sleep.
   2. Definitions (if any): peak physical condition
   3. 1st major supporting point: First, maintaining a healthy diet
   4. 2nd major supporting point: Next, exercising regularly
   5. 3rd major supporting point: Lastly, sufficiently sleeping
C. Conclusion
   1. Summary: You can be in top physical shape in college by maintaining a healthy diet, exercising regularly, and getting sufficient sleep.
   2. Further Thought: College can be a wonderful time in your life as your work toward a career and writing your own story. Being fit helps get you where you are going.

OUTLINE FORM AND SYMBOLS

The outline of a speech shows its basic parts and their order. The order of the speech parts reveals their relationship to each other and implies their relative importance. Creating a speech outline tests the speaker's knowledge on the topic and provides a tangible representation of ideas for the speaker and/or instructor to critique in advance of delivering the speech. At a glance, a reviewer can form a sense of the proposed speech. Further, an outline can be used to speak from when actually delivering the speech.

While convention dictates the use of Roman Numerals (I, II, III, IV, etc.) when listing major headings, they are not used here since their use is cumbersome. Consider how the first major point in the speech body might look in outline form (from the earlier car example):

1. Affordability
   a. Price
      (1) Dealer costs
         (a) Transportation

Following the *Motivated Sequence* for informative speeches, the outline symbols might look like (with the accompanying format words):

A. Introduction
  1. Attention Step: statement
     a. supporting statement
     b. supporting statement
  2. Need Step: statement
     a. supporting statement
     b. supporting statement
B. Body/Satisfaction Step
  1. Thesis
  2. Definitions
  3. Statement of 1ˢᵗ major supporting point
     a. supporting statement
     b. supporting statement [and so on]
C. Conclusion
  1. summary
  2. further thought

TRANSITIONS

To help the audience follow the progression of the speech, certain words and phrases can be used between the major sections of the speech and between the supporting points, especially within the body of the speech. These transitional words and phrases act as guides or sign posts, linking the parts of the speech together for both the audience and the speaker. The following are common transitions:

Table 14.4

first	however	similar to…	Not only…but also…
second	similarly	nonetheless	Neither…nor…
third	moreover	subsequently	In the final analysis…
since	therefore	in contrast to…	On the other hand…
thus	furthermore	As we can see…	More important than…is…

THE INTRODUCTION

When you speak, you want your audience to listen to what you have to say. To achieve this, you have to speak to their interests as these relate to the speech topic. It is during the introduction that your audience forms a first impression of you that will influence their reception and perception of the rest of the speech. Make sure your first few sentences are memorized, you look at the audience while you speak them, and you use a full voice. In the speech preparation process, you create your introduction after you have created the body and your conclusion.

Functions of the introduction: gain attention, orient the audience to the topic, and establish credibility. The methods below satisfy one or more of these functions.

Common faults: Do not apologize, rely on gimmicks, or preface your introduction.

Methods of Introduction.

1. Personal reference or greeting
2. Reference to the subject or occasion
3. Startling statement
4. Illustration (story)
5. Humor
6. Quotation
7. Question (rhetorical)
8. Presentational aid

1. *Personal Reference or Greeting.* Make an interesting comment about your own response to giving the speech, such as being excited about it. You can also extend a warm greeting to the audience, thanking them for providing you the opportunity to speak. If appropriate, you can state your qualifications to speak on the topic.

2. *Reference to the Subject or Occasion.* You may make an intriguing remark about the subject you will discuss, or a thought-provoking comment about the occasion. You might mention something provocative about how the subject was chosen or how you were chosen to speak.

3. *Startling Statement.* By definition, what is said in this instance would have to catch the audience's attention. Some kind of strong or extreme piece of information or point of view would do this. Provide a remarkable or little known but influential fact or statistic.

4. *Illustration.* A brief, detailed, dramatic story that is relevant to your speech and in good taste. It would be fitting to tell such a story about

audience experiences and/or your own. The story, seemingly over, could again be referred to as the real ending.

5. *Humor.* People love humor, and humor in the introduction immediately sets an audience at ease as well as creating a bond with them. Ensure that the humor fits the subject, occasion, and audience. Do not make a joke just to make a joke, and an ineffective joke at the beginning can almost kill the rest of the speech.

6. *Quotation.* To motivate the listeners to ponder the subject, you can use a quote that is catchy and consistent with your point of view. The source of the quote should be respected by the audience. If the audience does not like the messenger, they are very unlikely to accept the message.

7. *Question.* Speakers frequently make rhetorical questions (outward audience responses are not intended) with the hope it will encourage the audience to begin thinking about the speech. However easy they are to form, they are often boring so their use should be limited and combined with other methods of introduction.

8. *Presentational Aid.* Visual aids, recorded sounds, or even your own style of delivery could get the audience's attention.

THE CONCLUSION

It is in the conclusion that the last statements are made, so you will want to use it to reinforce what you have said earlier. To do so, first restate your central idea and the key points so these will be remembered. Then make one last comment, preferably memorable, about the topic. Do not say/ask: "Are there any questions?" Few speaking situations actually allow for this. Further, knowing your topic and your audience, you should have anticipated their questions and answered them during your presentation.

Function of the conclusion: summarize the speech and provide closure The methods below can be used in combination to satisfy one or both of these duties.

Common faults: Don't apologize, introduce new material, or drag out the conclusion.

Methods of Conclusion.

1. Summary
2. Question
3. Quotation
4. Statistics
5. Refer back to what was said in the Introduction
6. Refer to (likely) future events
7. Pose a challenge (persuasion)
8. State a personal intention (persuasion)

1. *Summary.* Restate the main supporting points, along with the thesis. This is virtually mandatory since speakers want to ensure that these are fresh on the audience's minds after the speech ends. In the conclusion, summarize first and follow it with other methods of conclusion.

2. *Question.* A rhetorical question can also be used in the conclusion. Again, do not be boring and do not use these by themselves. You present a stronger position by declaring what something is than by asking a question about it.

3. *Quotation.* A relevant statement that emphasizes a key idea, stated by a credible person.

4. *Statistics.* These can make a dramatic statement from a brief, numerical fact.

5. *Refer Back to What Was Said in the Introduction.* This can add emphasis to what was earlier said by restatement or can finish a story begun in the introduction, tying the speech together.

6. *Refer to Likely Future Events.* This is an attempt to get the audience to envision a highly probable outcome so the speaker's ideas have some justification and the audience knows what to expect. This method can simply be informative about what is probable, yet the outcome may also be so desired by the listener that the listener may be persuaded to accept the prerequisite belief or agree to perform the specified action. The Visualization Step in the *Motivated Sequence* exists for this latter purpose.

7. *Pose a Challenge.* As an attempt to motivate their audience to act, speakers will call them to do some action. To "challenge" someone is easy to do—simply

say it. For it to be meaningful, the speaker will have had to have spoken to the audience's needs, described legitimate solutions, visualized realistic outcomes, and then provided relatively easy and practical actions for success.

8. *State a Personal Intention.* This is another inducement to action, hoping that by you telling the audience what you will do (and possibly by yourself if need be), some of them will follow. Project a strong image, describe a clear path, and say "go" and some people are likely to follow you. You hope people will not want to be left out, will not want to be left behind, or will feel guilty if they do not join you.

Use both the introduction and conclusion methods in combination, a minimum of 2-3 different methods in both the introduction and in the conclusion.

CONCLUSION

Organization benefits the speaker when arranging the speech and the audience when hearing it. Different organizational patterns fit different types of speeches and purposes. A clear and appropriate organization will also help the audience remember the speech. Transitional statements aid in the flow of ideas, keeping the audience on track as it follows the speech. Introductions get the audience's attention and create an interest for what is to follow. Conclusions wrap up the speech, reminding the audience of the main idea/s, plus leave the listeners in the desired mood.

CHAPTER 14 HOMEWORK[2] #1
(or class exercise)

Directions: Provide a brief outline example of *each one* of the basic organizational orders cited in this chapter (chronological, spatial, topical, problem-solution, and cause-effect). Organize the main and sub-points just as the chapter examples illustrate. Choose topics from the following.

See the following page for blank outline forms to fill in.

> Computer viruses (location, harms, or transmission)
> Social Security (history, purpose, or problems)
> Single-parent families (history, circumstances, or problems)
> Dream interpretation (explanation)
> Skin cancer (stages, locations, symptom, or problems)

Fetal alcohol syndrome (stages, location, symptoms, or problems)
Student financial aid (application stages, use of, likely problems)
Dieting (choose one) (steps, reasons, or problems)
Honolulu (or city/state of your choice) (places, activities, education, or
      problems)
Diabetes (stages, places in the body affected, causes, or problems)

CHAPTER 14 HOMEWORK #1
(or class exercise) Outlining. Fill in the spaces.

Table 14.5

Historical Order (or)	Process Order
1.	1.
2.	2.
3.	3.

Spatial Pattern topic/statement: _____

1. _____

      a. _____
      b. _____

2. _____

      a. _____
      b. _____

3. _____

      a. _____
      b. _____

Topical Pattern thesis: _____

1. _____

      a. _____
      b. _____

2. _____

    a. _____

    b. _____

3. _____

    a. _____

    b. _____

Problem-Solution Pattern topic/statement: _____

1. _____

    a. _____

    b. _____

2. _____

    a. _____

    b. _____

3. _____

    a. _____

    b. _____

Causal Pattern topic/statement _____

1. _____

    a. _____

    b. _____

2. _____

    a. _____

    b. _____

3. _____

    a. _____

    b. _____

CHAPTER 14 HOMEWORK #2
(or class exercise) Introductions and Conclusions[3]

Directions. In both the Introduction and Conclusion provided in the sample speech below, clearly write next to the beginning of each sentence the type of method being used.

Methods of Introduction

1. Personal reference or greeting
2. Reference to the subject or occasion
3. Startling statement
4. Illustration (story)
5. Humor
6. Quotation
7. Question (rhetorical)
8. Presentational aid

Methods of Conclusion

1. Summary
2. Question
3. Quotation
4. Statistics
5. Refer back to what was said in the introduction
6. Refer to (likely) future events
7. Pose a challenge (persuasion)
8. State a personal intention (persuasion)

Sample Speech

A. Introduction
   1. Attention Step. I walked briskly along Tumon Bay at 6 AM, the pink sunrise filtering through the palm trees onto the glassy water. It was amazing to see so many other people walking or jogging through the warming, slightly salty air. Scores of people in kayaks paddled inside the reef. As Moses liked to say, "It's another gorgeous day in paradise."
   2. Need Step. Unfortunately, people on Guam have significant health-related problem outcomes. My neighbor was overweight and died in his late 50's, leaving his wife and kids traumatized. According to Dr. Nikki Rivera, "Obesity, diabetes, and gout are very prevalent and their

symptoms are extremely debilitating." The Annual Guam Physical Fitness Report claimed that 75% of those who are either teenagers or older were found to be in poor physical condition.

B. Satisfaction Step (body)

    1. Thesis. Jogging is advantageous for your health, since it leads to reduced weight, increased cardio-vascular strength, and enhanced overall muscle tone.

    2. Definition of terms: none.

    3. Reduced weight.

    4. Increased cardio-vascular strength.

    5. Enhanced overall muscle tone.

C. Conclusion

    1. Jogging improves people's overall bodily fitness by bringing about reduced weight, increased cardio-vascular strength, and enhanced overall muscle tone. As doctors note, with just 20 minutes a day for 6 months at what is a brisk pace for your condition, you'll become fit.

    2. As an extra bonus, people have been found to experience a "work-out high" when they exert their bodies. Being drenched in sweat just adds to the feeling of accomplishment.

CHAPTER 14 HOMEWORK #3
(or class exercise) Developing an Introduction and Conclusion[4]

Directions: For the following topic, with the body of the speech outlined, create an appropriate introduction and conclusion. Use the outlined example in the chapter as a guide.

A. Introduction
   Attention Step:

_____

   Need Step:

_____

Body

1. College students can effectively manage their time by setting realistic goals, getting organized, and avoiding procrastination.

2. Terms

3. Setting realistic goals

    a. *realistic* definition

    b. *goals* definition

    c. determining objectives

    d. determining what's attainable

4. Getting organized
   a. making lists of tasks
   b. scheduling time to do each
   c. checking them off on completion
5. Avoiding procrastination
   a. focus each day on what has to be done
   b. avoiding interruptions
   c. completing tasks immediately
C. Conclusion
   Summary:

Further Thought:

REFERENCES

1. D. Ehninger, B. Gronbeck, R. McKerrow, and A. Monroe, *Principles and Types of Speech Communication* (10th ed.) (Glenview, Il: Scott, Foresman and Company, 1986).
2. M. Griffin, *Public Speaking Basics* (Lanham, Maryland: University Press of America, 2009).
3. Ibid.
4. Ibid.

CHAPTER FIFTEEN

Wording the Speech and Delivery

Speaking is a one-time occurrence requiring instant intelligibility. The words chosen by the speaker have to be instantly understood by the audience as they are spoken or their intended meanings will be missed.

This liability is partially due to the reality behind the communication principle that we send messages but meanings are cognitively created by each individual. Being different people with different experiences and a different vocabulary developed with that experience, we have differing notions about the meaning/s associated with a given word and an experience. This aspect of meaning overlaps with the symbolic nature of language. Words are symbols that represent some thing; the symbolic representations in our minds are not exactly the object or concept to which the speaker refers. Further, people do not have a perfect match in their minds for words used between each other.

Thus, speakers have to consider how the listeners will conceptualize the words spoken, and then choose those words that will stimulate listener interpretations that are as close as possible (overlap) to what the speaker is thinking. The question for the speaker is, how to frame the message to increase the chance that the listeners will create the desired meaning/s within each of them? In this chapter, the emphasis is on the words chosen for the speech.

Each speaker brings his or her existing vocabulary to the speaking moment. The Public Speaking portion of the class is not going to increase very much anyone's storehouse of known words and how to put them together. Still, the individual speaker can reflect upon his or her wording choices and make some educated decisions.

GUIDELINES[1]

1. *Words Have to be Simpler Than in Writing.* This aids listener comprehension as well as speaker memory and pronunciation. This does not mean that a speaker should never use words conveying broad concepts or of unknown definitions to the audience. Speakers are encouraged to define largely unknown words in the content of the speech so as to educate (uplift) the audience. Speakers can also increase their own vocabulary by searching for words new to them that better fit the concepts in their speech.

2. *Words Should be Specific and Descriptive.* In general, these simpler words should be as specific and as direct as possible to aid the listeners' understanding. Seek clear language. Slang, by its nature non-standard, abstract, and typically short-lived, is not descriptive. Certain political demands or even legitimate concerns for some listeners' feelings may compel the speaker to be ambiguous and abstract to minimize objections. This should be done cautiously to avoid being labeled indecisive.

3. *Select Words for Their Imagery.* For those who have or can develop the artful skill, words selected for their imagery can be very effective in conveying the feelings and ideas of the speaker. Vivid language will emphasize descriptions and actions. This also increases the audience's attention during the speech and their later memory of it.

4. *Be Exact.* Additional clarity can be gained by using exact numbers, accurate descriptions of objects and events, correct source quotations, and the avoidance of jargon. Exact numbers and accurate descriptions make very definite points and imply that you are clear about the concepts and/or people being described. Misquoting a source suggests sloppy preparation or even bias on your part. Jargon is fine for an audience that understands it (such as automobile terms for an audience of mechanics) but unclear and possibly deceptive for use with the general population.

5. *Sentences Have to be Shorter.* Use fewer words in a given sentence than you do in writing so the audience can easily follow your speaking and the ideas conveyed. This will also aid you in speaking complete sentences without pausing.

REHEARSAL

You may remember from Chapter 12 that sufficient speech preparation can reduce speech anxiety. Rehearsal provides additional benefits. It helps you become more comfortable with your material, it aids your memory, it provides you with an additional opportunity to discover organizational, logical, and delivery weaknesses, it allows you to time your speech to fit the occasion, and to see if you can integrate any presentational aids in a seamless manner.

Rehearse your speech at least a few days in advance of the speech occasion so you will have time to incorporate any desired last-minute changes. Verify correct pronunciations in the dictionary (for those who know how to interpret them) and/or from people who work in your subject field. Be sure to practice pronouncing people's names. Ask friends, family, or roommates if your visual aid is appealing and large enough to be easily seen from the distance the audience will be, and practice in front of them, if possible. Also practice delivering the speech in front of a mirror to monitor your eye contact, body movements, and expressions. Attempt to practice in advance in the very place you will deliver the speech to increase your level of comfort and make any adjustments to the setting. Ensure you have sufficient lighting to refer to your notes and that the podium can be placed as close to the audience as is possible.

Consider practicing the speech ten times once it is in its final form. Practice over and over, using your eyes (not your head) to look down at your notes. Keep your speaking toward the imagined audience. If you do this with your script prepared so that it has every new sentence printed on a new line with double-spacing between them, you can become skilled in glancing at your notes and speaking entire phrases and sentences toward your audience.

Your appearance also needs to be prepared for the occasion. While speaking in class you may dress in your normal student attire, consider that audiences outside of class will be more critical of whether you look the part. If you do not, your believability will suffer.

DELIVERY[2]

This is the moment at which the audience comes in contact with the content of your thoughts and your feelings about them. How you create this transmission will influence the audience's receptivity of your speech. A well-delivered speech of average content can be perceived as better than a poorly delivered speech with excellent content.

1. *Eye Contact.* An audience wants a speaker to speak to them, not to some notes on a podium (or even to a teleprompter). If listeners are not looked at while they are spoken to, they will typically think about something aside from the speech. If someone does not have enough confidence and good will toward the listener to look at whom he or she is speaking to, the listener will not give much credence to what the speaker has to say. Thus, the speaker has

to make continual eye contact with the audience, gazing around the group as he or she speaks to them. This requires that the speaker is very familiar with his/her speech material and adept at handling any notes that are referred to during the speech. An added and no less important aspect of eye contact is the receiving of audience reactions to the speech. A flexible speaker can alter what he or she is about to say and even adjust his or her voice to effectively respond to the audience. A speaker can sense a positive regard from the audience that in turn increases speaker energy in delivering the speech.

2. *Conversational Style.* To ease the flow of ideas from speaker to listener, speakers should speak to their audience as they would be speaking in a one-to-one basis with their friends during a normal conversation. This will increase the likelihood of the listener presuming that the speaker is speaking directly to him or her, not at him or her. A normal conversational voice makes the thoughts of the speaker more believable. While people do use incomplete sentences while speaking in one-on-one encounters, be sure to speak in complete phrases or sentences with that personal tone of voice. Speaking in a conversational style can be relaxing to the speaker.

3. *Pronunciation.* A speaker's believability will diminish in the audience's mind if the speaker mispronounces words that are spoken. It can seem as if the speaker does not know what he or she is talking about. Still, unless the speaker has completed a voice and diction class, he or she will not know how to interpret the pronunciation guide for pronouncing a given word. The speaker should know whether they know a word's correct pronunciation. If there are doubts about a word, the speaker can ask knowledgeable people how they say the word, especially words used in given career field. A separate voice and diction class will provide knowledge and skill in both correctly articulating Standard American Speech sounds and pronouncing words.

4. *Stand Up and Move.* Speakers need to stand up straight. Slouching over and leaning on the podium conveys a lack of vitality and over-casualness. People will not take you seriously. Keep your hands either at your side or resting on the rear edge of the podium where you can easily move them to make gestures. Never put your hands into your pockets, and jingling of keys and coins is a great distraction. Women should ensure their hair does not fall in front of their eyes nor bracelets rap against the podium. While standing, occasionally shift your weight from side to side, alternately taking a one-half step toward the right and then to the left. This conveys energy and helps your blood circulation. Avoid rocking back and forth, which is also distracting.

5. *Gestures.* Moving your hands in a natural-appearing manner can help you emphasize your key points and keep you feeling loose. As you practice at home in front of a mirror, experiment with moving your hands and arms in different ways that compliment what you are saying. This should be done in conjunction with shifting your position towards different parts of the audience. Position your hands on the rear of the podium where they are easily moved as desired.

6. *Vocal Changes.* Speakers need to vary their loudness level, their pitch, and their speed of delivery to communicate the meaning and feeling for that which they are saying. Monotone deliveries are considered boring and listeners will stop listening to the speaker. In advance, practice changing your loudness, pitch, and rate of speech according to the ideas you are presenting, as a way to emphasize them. Listen to yourself, tape record yourself, or have a friend or family member listen to you to give you feedback on these. Do you sound alive? Do you sound like you believe in what you are saying?

Overall, speakers need to convey the idea that they are comfortable with their speaking and they can deliver their message in a dynamic manner, which aids the audience in both understanding and accepting the thoughts of the speaker.

MODE OF PRESENTATION

Speaker preparation and use of notes vary according to situational demands and speaker preferences. Some adaptation may be necessary.

1. *Impromptu.* In this situation, the speaker uses no notes nor has any preparation and speaks immediately on some topic. This is sometimes termed speaking "off the cuff." It is not uncommon for a student to be called upon in class to briefly speak about a topic under discussion or in the assigned reading. Thinking on your feet is a useful skill. Potential speakers may want to learn about using an introduction, forming a central idea, creating multiple supporting points, use of evidence and reasoning, and how to construct a conclusion to help them effectively present this type of speech. People in a variety of government and business occupations are sought by the media to provide an impromptu (and concise) response about a current issue.

2. *Extemporaneous.* This type of speech should be well prepared. The speaker will have an outline to follow to ensure that the major sections of the

speech are covered--many fill-in words and even some explanations may be omitted on the outline. If the speaker is well prepared, this is the most life-like and seemingly spontaneous of speeches, for which audiences are more likely to listen. With an outline, constant eye contact with the audience, and an accurate reading of the audience response, a speaker can easily adjust the emphasis of his or her speech delivery. This type of speech encourages the use of a conversational voice, which appeals to listeners.

3. *Manuscript.* This type of speech preparation requires a great deal of detail to ensure that what a speaker wants to say is written down in just the desired way because it is read from during the speech. This is helpful when there is a time limit and when the speaker has ideas that he/she wants to con-vey in just a certain way (especially controversial ideas). The liability of using a manuscript is that the speaker may speak to his/her script as he/she reads it rather than toward the audience. Lack of speaker eye contact will lead the audience to evaluate the speaker negatively and to daydream. Those speakers following this type of preparation have to know the speaking material so well that they can glance at the script and then speak it to the audience.

4. *Memorization.* In this situation, the speaker commits the speech to memory. This could take the form of memorizing every word or memoriz-ing the organization of the main ideas and like the extemporaneous speech, add the words needed to complete the phrases and sentences. It is impressive when speakers speak in an organized, detailed fashion without using notes. The liability of this style of delivery is that the speaker cannot easily adapt to the audience, and such speeches are invariably spoken in a stilted, robot-like manner. They rarely sound conversational or personable and do require a great deal of time to commit to memory. Further, the speaker may forget to say something deemed important.

CONCLUSION

Everyone comes to the speaking event with a different vocabulary. Each speaker can use this individuality to encourage his or her listeners to create a meaning in their mind that is similar to the speakers. This is not easy but that is part of the speaking challenge, and certainly requires audience analysis. Learning dictionary meanings (including any change over time), increasing our vocabulary, and correctly pronouncing words is an ongoing, lifetime pro-cess. Connecting with the audience through the symbolic interaction of our word choices, delivery, and body movements is necessary for the audience to get *it*, our basic idea and point of view. Given the varied speaking situations and demands we face, we also need to be skilled and comfortable with the impromptu, extemporaneous, and manuscript methods of delivery.

CHAPTER 15 HOMEWORK #1
(or class exercise) Slogans

A slogan is a verbal or written phrase expressing an individual's or group's aspirations, revealing an intended goal. It is often a repeated phrase in an advertising campaign to promote a person, group, product, or service. It could be a rallying phrase for those people supporting a team or cause.

1. Write down a slogan you have encountered (such as for a political candidate, a cause, a product, a service, a place, an organization, or an event).
2. Describe the imagery the slogan raises in your mind.
3. Provide an evaluation of the effectiveness of the imagery and the slogan itself.

The following slogans provide examples and can be used for this assignment.

Political: Delucchi Works (for Senator); Bring the Republicans (or Democrats) back.
Cause: Responsible drinking, not age. (lower the legal drinking age to18)
Product: Moving You Toward Your Dreams; Building for Generations; We Eat Our Own Cooking.
Service: Building Trust When You Need Coverage and Care. (insurance, medical care)
Place: Where (Business X/City Y/Country Z's) Day Begins.
Event: A Game to Remember; The Greatest Moment in Sports.
Organization/team: Cougars With An Albany High. (high school sports team)

CHAPTER 15 HOMEWORK #2
(or class exercise) Word Pronunciations

List five words you hear used for which the pronunciation is uncertain to you. From an *American Heritage Dictionary* (or one specified by your teacher), also write down the pronunciation form of each word. Your instructor will collect these and write the pronunciations on the board, helping everyone to correctly pronounce the words. The words submitted may be compiled and later distributed to the class.

CHAPTER 15 EXERCISE #3
Impromptu Speech

The instructor may collect an object from each student, put them in a bag, and have students pick something from the bag. Then they will be asked to give a 1-2 minute impromptu speech on that object. Be advised that preceding this exercise, students need to be familiar with creating an introduction, a body of a speech including a main idea with supporting points, and a conclusion. Students need to concentrate on speaking in complete phrases and they accomplish the organizational and informational goals of this speech.

REFERENCES

1. M. Griffin, Public Speaking Basics (Lanham, MD: University Press of America, 2009).
2. Ibid.

CHAPTER SIXTEEN

The Informative Speech[1]

The purpose of the informative speech is to provide information on some topic to a greater depth and breadth of understanding than what is known by the majority of your listeners. It should be enlightening, educational, and possibly instructive. It can occur in different speech forms, including lectures, reports, and instructions. It may primarily provide an explanation, a definition, or a demonstration of some phenomenon.

REQUIREMENTS

Since this speech is informational, its most important quality is clarity. To achieve clarity, your thesis will need to be simple and direct. (see Chapter 13). The organization will have to be clear (see Chapter 14). Key terms will have to be understood so they may need to be defined. The wording of the speech will have to be descriptive and specific (see Chapter 15). You will need sufficient, clear, and relevant evidence to illuminate and validate your two, three, or four main supporting points. Presentational aids may be needed to clarify one or more of your main points (see Chapter 13). Your listeners will have to aurally identify what you say, so speak loudly and with appropriate pronunciations. Since each audience is different, you will have to tailor your overall message to suit each one's comprehension level and knowledge of your topic.

The informative speech should also be concrete, filled with facts, descriptions, and names about the specific object, concept, or instance being discussed. The speaker's goal is to stimulate a conception in the listener's mind that is close to the existing reality being referenced. It is fine to use more abstract terms for concepts that you have determined your audience already understands. In a 6-8 minute speech you should not use more than three main supporting points, for you will not be able to provide enough depth that would be informative for your audience.

People learn about new concepts by associating them with what they already know so you can compare and contrast new with known information. You can also use examples and definitions. Detailed descriptions help listeners recognize something for what it is.

Notice that audience analysis is crucial to conceptually reaching your audience where it is on the subject. Review Chapter 12 as necessary. Being informative to your audience requires that you sufficiently research the audience and the topic. If you have adequately shown your audience that the subject matter impacts their lives, they will more readily listen to the information you provide about their needs, goals, and/or solutions to achieving those goals.

Review of Organizational Patterns for Informative Speeches. See Chapter 14 for details.

1. Chronological Pattern (Historical or Process order)
2. Spatial Pattern
3. Topical Pattern
4. Problem-Solution Pattern
5. Causal Pattern
6. Motivated Sequence Pattern (the Body may follow a time, spatial, or topical pattern).

DEMONSTRATION SPEECH

This is a type of informative speech in which you explain and show an audience how to do something. People often show and are shown how to complete a task so such speeches are necessary. While a given process may appear simple and matter-of-fact, many observers are unable to successfully complete a task on their first effort after having been shown how. Effective teachers (and listeners?) do not seem that common, whether they are demonstrating how to prepare a certain dish of food, how to correctly write a thesis sentence, and so on.

In this speech you physically show and explain to your audience how to do something. You have to *do something* and talk about how to do it while you do it. For example, bring the ingredients to class and *make the cake*. For such a speech at work, you will need to have all the necessary supplies and equipment. This speech also emphasizes the use of introductions and conclusions, organization, transitions, physical movement, and verbal descriptions.

The time allowed for this speech in a classroom setting may be only *5-6 minutes* so you cannot do something that is complicated or time consuming.

It is possible that you may select a process that can have separate stages partially completed at home that can be individually completed in class, showing how each stage is done. Subject selection is crucial for fitting the time limit. There should be no 4 minute or 7 minute speeches if 5-6 minutes is the parameter. Your grade will be lowered for being too short or too long. Be sure to time yourself at home to ensure you can do the demonstration plus the introduction and conclusion in time allotted.

As noted above, you will need to bring all the necessary presentational aids to the speaking site (e.g., class), such as the object(s) you will be using and necessary tools to complete the task. Extension cords, tape, cutting boards, and special surfaces may be needed. Ensure the objects and tools used are all large enough to be seen by the entire audience (class). For demonstration purposes you may need to also have and use substitute equipment and/or supplies to ensure that everyone can see everything.

You should expect to follow a *time pattern* in organizing and delivering your demonstration, beginning with the first step in the process and continuing through the last one. Be clear about the sequence so you do not have to backtrack or entirely omit an important step in the process. As you go from step to step, use transitions such as: *first ...., second ...., third .... for the next step ...., as you can see...., also consider...., not only ... but also ....,* and so on.

To aid you in your organization, follow the steps below:

A. Introduction.

   The purpose of the introduction is to get the audience's attention and orient them to the topic. Begin by describing a situation in which your listeners can visualize wanting and needing to know how to do the process you are about to demonstrate. *Do not begin your speech with*: "Today I'm going to show you how to make a ____." This is boring. Create an interesting scenario here with your verbal description to gain the listeners' attention and convey the speech topic. Consider something like: "Last Saturday I was swimming at ____ Beach with a friend, enjoying the cool, gentle waves, the warming sun, the laughter of kids on the beach, when all of a sudden ...." After finishing this scenario, state the purpose of the speech: "If you are ever in this situation, you will want to know how to ...." or " ... so today I will be demonstrating how to ...." Added to this, state the reasons for wanting to know how to do what will be demonstrated.

B. Body.

   At this point, go through the steps in the process, showing the class how to do each one. This is not simply an informative speech in which you tell us how to do something. You have to actually show the class how, describing each step in the process. If the speech is about six minutes long, you should expect the body of the speech to be about four minutes long.

1. Begin with an overview. Give a general description of what you expect to do. Be concise.
2. Describe and point to the objects to be used. Define any key terms, materials, and/or equipment the audience will not know.
3. Start with the 1st step in the process. Be sure to explain *how* and *why* to do each action and clearly show this to the audience.
4. 2nd step
5. and so on through the last step These steps should take from 3.5-4 minutes to complete.

If you are doing something that you have described and still need to continue doing it a little longer (such as some final mixing) you may have time to describe the process at work, the history behind it, or some other interesting fact. Your grade will be lowered if you are silent at any point.

C. Conclusion.
The purpose of the conclusion is to wrap up the speech and then end. The speech is not over when the last step is completed. Do not say: "That's it" and simply hold up the completed object. There is a three-part conclusion. First, summarize the key steps in the process. Second, remind the audience of the good reasons for doing the activity. Third, close with a final thought.

D. Further Comments.
Be organized. Have materials ready to use when you set them out before you begin the speech. Quickly set them up or your grade may be lowered. Do not waste class time writing on the chalkboard—do it in advance or even on poster paper. Again, verify your audience can clearly see the objects, tools, and process of demonstration. You may need larger-sized substitutes. Bring towels to clean up any mess. Do not use something noisy like an osterizer to make crushed ice since it is so loud your speaking will not be heard (you have to continually speak). Have the ice already crushed. Businesses have time constraints, as well, so people at work do not want to sit around while you get ready and if you are unorganized.

1. *Examples of Suitable Topics* (verify with your teacher). These include food dishes like cakes, cookies, lumpia, corn soup, fried bananas; financial topics like balancing a checkbook, filling out a tax form, completing a loan

application; physical health topics like basic exercises, weight lifting, stretching; physical hobbies like dancing, massage, self-defense; arts and crafts topics like paper mache flowers, soap balls, knitting/ crocheting, or homemade greeting cards; emergency procedures like CPR, first aid, Heimlich maneuver, or tourniquet; humorous topics such as cheating on tests, getting out of a driving ticket, and so on.

2. *Examples of Topics That Have Frequently Failed.* Try to avoid these, such as computer use, playing a guitar, card games, female facial make-up, and the origami crane. This demonstration speech *is not a performance*, so do not sing to the class, play a guitar song, etc.

3. *Examples of Products Not Allowed.* These include anything with alcohol or tobacco, or actual firearms (verify school rules).

4. *Using Visual Aids.* This was covered in Chapter13 so review their use there. They are used to gain attention, maintain interest, and both clarify and reinforce the speaker's ideas. They can make the supporting facts clearer, more vivid, and convincing. Remember, you should only use one if you determine it is necessary for the process to be understood and completed.

A sample Demonstration Speech and a sample Demonstration Speech evaluation form are provided latter in this chapter, as well as a Demonstration Speech Assignment.

MOTIVATED SEQUENCE: INFORMATIVE SPEECH[2]

This organizational pattern for informative speeches can be used for either speeches of description that describe people, objects, events, or processes, or speeches of definition that make a statement of significance about some concept or term.[3] Description speeches will typically answer some or all of the following information: who, what, why, where, and when.

Definition speeches focus on answering *what* and are particularly useful for "… explain[ing] a difficult or unfamiliar concept …."[4]

This textbook is emphasizing the use of Monroe & Ehninger's *Motivated Sequence Pattern*[5] for informative and persuasive speeches. Immediately below is a description and explanation of this pattern's steps for an informative speech. The body of the speech follows a topical pattern. An illustration of these steps is provided by the *Breast Cancer* outline that follows the initial explanation of steps.

A. Introduction
  1. *Attention Step.* An opening statement to get the audience's attention and give then an idea about the topic of your speech. *Do not begin* by saying "My speech is about ...." This is boring and unorganized. Use multiple introduction methods described in Chapter 14. Avoid common mistakes such as: apologizing, prefacing your speech, or a gimmick that does not relate to your topic. You will be speaking about harms related to your topic in the next step, so omit such references here. Begin by referring to a situation going well in relation to the topic.
  2. *Need Step.* This is where you speak to the concerns (needs) of your audience in relation to your speech topic so they will want to listen to what you will later say that will satisfy the concerns. What is the audience lacking that it has a need to satisfy? For example, does it have any physiological needs such as food or shelter, any safety need such as physical protection, any social needs such as companionship, sexual attraction, or prestige, any financial needs such as an emergency savings account or sufficient income to repay student loans, any autonomy needs such as freedom or independence?

Describe to the audience how it suffers or can be expected to suffer from a loss of something it deems important (such as the needs noted above), or that it will not gain a desired goal, with the result that it will motivated to satisfy what is lacking. Provide evidence about the multiple ways an existing situation such as obesity, illiteracy, crime, and so on, imperil the audience, that the situation is a threat to their money, property, job security, life itself, health, happiness, education, family, and so on. *Do not state that the audience needs to know something or suggest here any causes or solutions for the harms experienced.* To make your case about a problematic situation, do exactly the following.

  a. Problem statement: a clear, concise *general* statement about the *existence of some suffering.* For example, many retired people are financial poor.
  b. Illustration: a concise, detailed story showing someone in a given circumstance is *suffering.* For example, poor, retired Mr. X suffers bouts of hunger and pain when he has no money for the additional food and medicine he needs, and he is also a burden on taxpayers for the minimal public assistance he gets. (avoid causes and solutions)
  c. Ramifications: additional examples, statistics, testimony, visual aid, and so on that show how wide/deep are the harmful effects. For

example, cite a social worker about elder people's difficulties experiencing a hot summer and a survey about how many poor retirees exist. Attempt to describe how the subjects in your speech suffer physical and/or emotional pain. (again, avoid discussing any causes or solutions)

    d. Pointing: a concise statement to the audience that they, too, are or will suffer. For example, tell the class that they have older relatives who are likely to need help so they, the class, will have to come to their relatives' aid with physical and/or financial support. This is likely to put a burden on the students' completing their schoolwork or having sufficient income to pay for their own meager necessities.

B. Body (*Satisfaction Step*) (this main step consumes about three-fourths of the speech time)

    1. Thesis: a concise sentence of your main idea, followed by your major supporting points.

    2. Definition of terms, if any of the words in your thesis (only) may be unclear to the audience. Terms in the supporting points should be defined when they are discussed.

    3. Statement of the 1st major supporting point (idea), preceded by a transitional word.

      a. supporting statement for that (possibly define a word used as a supporting idea)

      b. another supporting statement (testimony, quotations, examples, statistics, illustrations, definitions, comparison/contrast, restatement, specific instance, personal experience)

    4. Statement of the 2nd major supporting point, preceded by a transitional word.

      a. supporting statement for that

      b. another supporting statement

    5. Statement of the 3rd major supporting point, preceded by a transitional word.

      a. supporting statement for that

      b. another supporting statement

C. Conclusion (to wrap up your speech and help your audience remember your thesis and major supporting ideas)

    1. Summary (restate your thesis with slightly altered words conveying the same idea, followed by your three major points)

    2. Further thought: final remark about your topic (2-3 sentences). Remember to leave them in the desired mood. Avoid common mistakes: do not bring up new ideas, do not keep talking and drag out the speech, and do not apologize. Avoid explicitly persuasive words such as *remember*, *do this/that*. Review the conclusion methods in Chapter 14.

CONCLUSION

Most people will provide a variety of informative talks throughout their lives. Some of these have been or will be informal as we show our family, friends, or co-workers how to do something, or provide them information about a topic. On other occasions, we may have to provide formal presentations to work groups, community organizations, or the public at large to explain an important concept, person, or event. This chapter has stressed the use of the time organizational pattern when delivering one type of informative speech, the demonstration speech, and the motivated sequence pattern for organizing the strictly informational speech.

CHAPTER 16 EXERCISE #1
Informative Speech Outline. Create an Attention
and Need Step for the following.

A. Introduction
   1. Attention Step:

     _____

   2. Need Step:
     a. _____

     _____

     b. _____

     _____

     c. _____

     _____

     d. _____

     _____

B. Satisfaction Step (body)
   1. Thesis statement: Students can effectively manage their finances if they avoid impulse buying, follow a budget, and minimize expensive social activities.
   2. Definitions (if any in thesis need it):_____
   3. Statement of 1st major point. Begin with a transition word:
     First, students can avoid impulse buying. No Ross or K-Mart, only household necessities, put off purchases, discuss logically and justify beforehand.

    4. Statement of 2nd major point. Begin with a transition word.
Second, they can follow a budget. Define "budget," prioritize needs. Distinguish between wants and needs, only food/shelter/gas, live with family

    5. Statement of 3rd major point: Begin with a transition word.
Third, they can minimize expensive social activities. Define "expensive." Rent videos, play video games, potluck meals, cook at home, go to the beach or Mia's.

C. Conclusion

    1. Summary: Thus, students can successfully control their use of money if they avoid impulse buying, follow a budget, and minimize expensive social activities.

    2. Further thought: This can be good practice for the future as they learn how to live within their means. This, in turn, will provide money needed for life's daily needs, emergencies, a wedding, a house, children's college tuition, and even investing for retirement.

CHAPTER 16 EXERCISE #2
Need Step. Create an appropriate
Need Step for the following. Introduction

Attention Step. Vacation, here I come! Boy, I can see myself sipping those tropical drinks.

Need Step. [potential suffering on a vacation, what might be lost or not gained—such as health, safety, money/savings/personal possessions, companionship, adventure, control over events]

a. _____

b. _____

c. _____

d. _____

Body
Thesis: Hawaii is an exciting place to visit ....
Conclusion

CHAPTER 16 HOMEWORK #1
Specific Purpose.

Directions: Given the following topics, create a specific purpose for one demonstration speech and (separately) for one informative speech of either description or definition. Review Chapter 12 as needed. *Topics*: Thanksgiving or fiesta food, use/abuse of drugs or alcohol, land use/return of excess military land to local communities, university tuition costs, student loans.

Chapter 16 Demonstration Speech Assignment

Directions: Create a 5-6 minute demonstration speech following the guidelines presented in this chapter. Surprisingly, many students do not practice or time themselves in advance. Speeches over six minutes will be stopped and the student will be graded on what was presented up to that point, as well as for what was not completed. If there is class time and it is apparent that the student will finish shortly after six minutes, the speech *may* be allowed to continue but will be graded lower for being overtime. The instructor will not be a timekeeper for the student. This is excellent time management practice for the business world outside of school. A sample Demonstration Speech is provided later in this chapter.

Chapter 16 Informative Speech Assignment [6]

Directions: Create a 6-8 minute informative speech following the guidelines presented earlier in this chapter. This speech should provide greater depth and breadth of understanding on the subject than what is known by the majority of your listeners. *Do not* tell the class (audience) something you can expect it already knows, such as a health topic you all learned in ninth grade. Audience analysis is crucial for determining this. The speech should be enlightening and educative. As previously stated, in a 6-8 minute speech you should not use more than three main supporting points for you will not be able to provide enough depth that would be informative. The time spent on the supporting points in the body of the speech should be 3.5 to 4 minutes.

Transitional words and phrases are required in this speech as you introduce each of the main supporting points. You are likely to use transitional words and phrases in other places, as well. Review Chapter 14 for examples.

Your instructor may or may not require that you use a visual aide. If you choose to use one, verify that its use is necessary and ensure that you follow all the guidelines noted in Chapter 13.

Your instructor may also require that an outline be submitted either before and/or at the time you deliver the speech. It will probably follow the Motivated Sequence steps, as illustrated multiple times in the chapter and in the blank form near the end of this chapter.

CHAPTER 16 HOMEWORK #2
Informative Speech Outline

Directions: For your Informative Speech, follow the *Motivated Sequence* steps explained earlier in this chapter and illustrated by the *Breast Cancer* speech located later in this chapter. At least three days prior to your speech, submit an outline of your speech *on the form* provided later in this chapter so your instructor can give you with some feedback on your thesis and other preparation. This is an *outline*, so be concise. A final, corrected copy of this outline form is due at the time of your speech. This final copy will be graded.

SAMPLE DEMONSTRATION SPEECH
Clam Chowder

[Set-up before the speech actually begins: ensure the table is arranged to suit this speech. Everything should be open or unwrapped, ready to use, and placed on the side of the table. Do not leave the finished product in sight. For cost and ease of demonstrating, the speaker may reduce all of the amounts by about one-fourth (e.g., 1 potato). The speaker should pre-cook the separate ingredients since this can't be done in 5-6 minutes, using these to actually put together later in the speech. Clear, glass-type cooking pots allow the audience to see how something is cooking and mixed. Be prepared, think through every step.]

A. Introduction

It was a cool evening as I headed home after work, wondering what to fix my family for dinner. What would be different, something we usually only get at special times at restaurants? Clam chowder! I can make it on thirty minutes, it's a meal in itself, it tastes better and is cheaper than what is served in restaurants, and apart from a few items, it is healthy. I always keep the ingredients on hand except for the cream so I just need to stop at the store to buy that.

B. Body

    1. In the kitchen, assemble the ingredients and implements on the countertop and stove: 3-6 oz. cans minced clams, 1-6 oz. bottle clam juice, 4 oz. frozen sliced bacon, 1 medium onion, 4 cloves fresh garlic or 2 tsp. minced garlic, 4 medium russet potatoes, 3-8" carrots, 2-12" stalks celery, 3-8" zucchini, ¼ tsp. salt, ¼ tsp. black pepper, ¼ tsp. celery seed (if not, dill), 1 Tbl. olive oil, 1-4 oz. stick butter, 16 oz. heavy (whip) cream, cutting board and knife, medium pot, vegetable steamer, large pot, can opener, medium size stirring spoon, and soup ladle.

[speaker should not place any items or equipment across the front of the table which will later block the audience's view of the preparation]

    2. Place vegetable steamer basket into medium pot, fill with water to cover the 3 legs, place on the stove at high heat. Wash potatoes, carrots, and celery (no peeling). Vegetables will be cut small to increase the likelihood when later eaten that they will be mixed in with clams. Cut the potatoes into 3/8" cubes, place in steamer, cut carrots in 1/8" pieces and place atop potatoes, covering with the lid. When water comes to a boil, reduce heat to medium and tilt lid slightly.

[speaker should scrub one potato and carrot, explaining how and why as cutting both of them; rinse. Place these into the steamer and pretend to cook. Have some of each in a baggie already cut and precooked that you can later poke with a toothpick to show just done.]

    3. Large pot: put olive oil in the bottom, slice and chop frozen bacon slices into ¼" pieces and place in pot, turn on high heat, slice onion in ¼" by ¼" pieces and put atop bacon, reduce to medium heat, add finely chopped garlic to spread out its flavor, stir so bacon doesn't stick and burn. Remove from heat when onion is translucent. Add butter, cut up into 4 separate pieces. [speaker should slice and chop just 2 sections of bacon and onions, explaining how and why they are done that way, then put pre-cooked bacon, onion, garlic, and melted butter into pot]

    4. Slice each zucchini and celery lengthwise in 4 equal pieces, chop zucchini cross-ways in 3/16" pieces and set aside, chop celery in 1/8 in pieces and set aside.

[speaker should slice 1 each zucchini and celery, and only chop 1" of each for demo purposes]

5. Check doneness of potatoes and carrots with a toothpick, remove from heat when barely done, scoop and add (without the steamer water) to the big pot, on top of the butter/onions/garlic/bacon.

[speaker should poke 1 each piece of pre-cooked potato and carrot to show doneness]

6. Open the cans of minced clams and drain the juice only into the large pot. Add the bottle of clam juice, the zucchini, and the spices.

[speaker should have the cans opened before the speech begin and at this time pretend to slightly open one. The speaker may use a can of tuna in place of costlier clams, draining the tuna water into the pot, and use water instead of costlier real clam juice, labeling a small bottle of water as "clam juice."]

7. Turn on the heat under the large pot to low, stir all the contents to mix thoroughly. Cook for 3 minutes, stirring constantly, just enough to cook the zucchini a little and mix all the flavors.

[speaker will do this for about 5 seconds]

8. With the contents warm, add the finely chopped celery and cream and stir thoroughly. The celery will add a little crunch in addition to its taste and nutrition. Stir intermittently for 3 minutes, just to warm the cream. Do Not allow this to boil for the cream will curdle.

[speaker may add milk for demonstration purposes]

9. Add the clams and stir thoroughly for one minute. Remove from heat. Cooking the clams too much can give them a rubbery texture.

[speaker may add the drained tuna for demonstration purposes]

10. Serve with a soup ladle in a soup bowl.

[speaker should ladle some into a bowl for the audience to see]

C. Conclusion

In summary, assemble all the necessary ingredients, tools, and cookware. Wash and cut up the potatoes, carrot, zucchini, and celery, steam the potatoes and carrots in one pot, cut up the bacon, onion, and garlic, placing them in oil in a large pot to sauté, add butter to the sauté, put the cooked potatoes and carrots on top of them, add the clam juice, zucchini, and spices, stir to mix, cook slightly, stir in the celery and cream, cook slightly, add the clams, cook slightly, then remove from heat.

This is a delicious substitute for the local favorite, corn soup. It is inexpensive, quick, easy, and nutritious, given all the vegetables. Outside the canned clams, clam juice, and heavy cream—which are available at many stores, most people already have all of the items at home.

Instead of the Friday Night Seafood Buffet at the Hilton, consider the Friday Night Chowder at Cruz's House of Clams.

SAMPLE INFORMATIVE SPEECH OUTLINE
Breast Cancer[7]

A. Introduction
1. *Attention Step.* Looking good, Hollywood! People like favorable comments about their health and appearance, in turn radiating these to others who compliment them and are drawn to them. Most women are especially mindful of their appearance.
2. *Need Step.*
   a. Yet for some women, feeling attractive can be a thing of the past if they develop breast cancer, "…probably the most … feared disease among American women."[1]
   b. One of my aunts got breast cancer, forcing her to have a breast removed. Leave from work cost $3,000 and her insurance co-pay was $1,500. She thinks she is a freak and sobs in silence. It pains her to vacuum and miss playing with her kids in the ocean.
   c. 274,900 women are likely to be diagnosed in 2006, with 41,000 expected deaths.[2] The 'cure,' losing a breast, is devastating. Guam 2002: 26 reported cases, 7 died. Herceptin costs $2,000/week for 1+ years, is only 20-30% effective.[3] "At … birth, a baby girl has a 1-in-8 chance of [getting] breast cancer at some point [in] her life."[4]
   d. Women by age 18, like those in this class, are at such risk. While men are unlikely to get it, the females in your lives may well develop it.

Table 16.1

Demonstration Speech
Name: and Topic:_____
Time (5-6 minutes):_____

Introduction: Gained attention, orientation to topic • interesting illustration/scenario (yes/no) • purpose of the demonstration clear (yes/no) • reason/s given for needing to know (yes/no)	0 1 2 3 4
Visual Aids/materials to be used were described, large enough, not hidden, properly referred to	0 1 2 3 4
Demonstration was organized, 1st step to last	0 1 2 3 4
Conclusion: Summary of steps + reasons for knowing/doing Future use; voice conveyed a sense of finality	0 1 2 3 4
This *was* a *demonstration* speech -- subject selection	0 1 2 3 4
Expect the audience to be able to now do it	0 1 2 3 4
Eye contact: spoke to the audience, not to the aid	0 1 2 3 4
Phrasing: spoke with complete phrases	0 1 2 3 4
Inarticulate sounds/filler words (um/ur/and uh/OK/etc)	0 1 2 3 4
Pauses: enough, correct length, no extended silences	0 1 2 3 4
Loudness: all was heard, varied, no fading out	0 1 2 3 4
Pronunciation (if a criteria)	0 1 2 3 4
Overall time (5-6 minutes) if too long, how much grade is lowered if too short, how much grade is lowered	
[0-inadequate, 1-adequate, 2-good, 3-very good, 4-excellent]	Grade_____

B. Body (*Satisfaction Step*)
  1. *Thesis* Women can increase their chances of surviving breast cancer if they discover their susceptibility, get a regular diagnosis, and seek proper treatment.
  2. *Definition of terms:* none needed.
  3. First, discover their susceptibility.
     a. heredity: 5-10+% of women, ask female family members about family history.
     b. age: high risk over age 50, age 44 for those with hereditary breast cancer.
     c. lifestyle factors: diet, exercise, weight gain, smoking, alcohol.
  4. Second, get a regular diagnosis.
     a. self breast exam: once/month, do one week after menstruation for those in menses.
     b. clinical breast exam: once every 3 years age 20-40, once a year thereafter.
     c. mammograms: annually at age 40, younger (maybe at 25) for those with genetic risk.
  5. Lastly, seek proper treatment.
     a. lumpectomy: removes tumor and some tissue, preserves breast, often with radiation.
     b. mastectomy: removes part or all of the breast, reconstruction option, often radiation..
     c. systematic therapies: chemotherapy, hormone therapy, immunotherapy.
C. Conclusion
  1. *Summary.* Therefore, if they discover their susceptibility, get a regular diagnosis, and seek proper treatment, women can minimize or even avoid life-threatening breast cancer.
  2. *Further Thought.* Breast cancer is not pleasant to think about but all women are at risk, and there is increased risk since women are living longer. Early detection can save a life, and secondly that self-confidence that compels the interest and admiration of others.
D. Sources
  1. "Baffled by choices," *AARP Magazine*, September/October, 2006.
  2. "Dear Annie: October is Breast Cancer Awareness Month," *Pacific Daily News*, October 11, 2006.
  3. G. Doleno, "Drug offers hope for breast cancer patients," *Pacific Daily News*, October 20, 2005.
  4. *The Harvard Guide to Women's Health.* Harvard University Press, 1996.

CHAPTER 16 HOMEWORK #2
Motivated Sequence Informative Speech Outline Form. Use this.

This initial outline will be due 1 week before the speech, to be returned to you for final revisions.

A. Introduction
   1. *Attention Step* (Do not mention problems/harms here, but describe a situation going well that relates to the topic. Be interesting)

   _____

   2. *Need/Problem Outcomes Step*: Here you have to show the audience that it lacks (has a need for) something (such as: safety, physical health, financial security, happiness, career goals, power, etc.) by pointing out negative outcomes (harms) that affect it (*suffering* from crime, death diabetes, job loss, lack of entertainment, increased school costs, physical injury, etc.).
      a. Make a general statement about people suffering in some way that relates to a specific topic.

      a. _____

      b. Provide a brief story (illustration) which describes various, specific ways someone is suffering from a certain problem outcome/harm (e.g., having a family and then becoming unemployed).

      b. _____

      c. Provide ramifications of the problem outcome. Describe how the stated harm (such as sudden unemployment for a married man or woman) is creating suffering (another illustration, specific examples, statistics, testimony, definitions, visual aids) for your audience. Only list data here.

      c. _____

      d. State clearly to the class (your audience) that these problem outcomes currently *harm them* or will do in the future (they are suffering now or will suffer in the future (e.g., by losing a job).

      d. _____

B. *Satisfaction Step* (Body of the speech should last about 4 minutes in a 6 minute speech.)
   1. *Thesis statement* (Provide a grammatically complete sentence first, omitting persuasive words like *should*. Then use connecting words like *since, due to, because, including*, etc., followed by three concise, main, supporting points which can be generated by asking *what* or *how* in reference to the thesis.

   _____

2. Definitions of terms (if there are any key terms in the thesis only that the audience needs to understand? Don't define the supporting points here.

———————————————————————————————————

3. Statement of 1st major point (state exactly as with the thesis above, *precede it* with a transitional word/phrase)

———————————————————————————————————

supporting info (list here; possibly define)

———————————————————————————————————

4. Statement of 2nd major point (state exactly as with the thesis above, *precede it* with a transitional word or/phrase)

———————————————————————————————————

supporting info (list here; possibly define)

———————————————————————————————————

5. Statement of 3rd major point (state exactly as with the thesis above, *precede it* with a transitional word/phrase)

———————————————————————————————————

supporting info (list here; possibly define)

———————————————————————————————————

C. *Conclusion*
   1. *Summarizing statement* (restate the thesis with slightly different words having the same meaning, and add the three points *stated exactly* as they were stated accompanying the thesis and as used in the body)

———————————————————————————————————

   2. Further thought/concluding remarks (give 1 of the 2-3 sentences you expect to use; avoid persuasive words like *remember, must, do this/that, I'm going to,* and so on)

———————————————————————————————————

D. Sources:

Table 16.2

Informative Speech Evaluation
Name: _____

Topic: _____

Time (6-8 minutes):

Intro: Attn. Step (gained attention, topic reference, credibility)	0 1 2 3 4
Need Step (statement, illustration, ramifications, pointing) a. b. c. d.	0 1 2 3 4
Body: Thesis (clear, appropriate, w/3 supporting points)	0 1 2 3 4
Main points (coherent, organized, unified) Definition/s 1. 2. 3.	0 1 2 3 4
Development/support: specific, relevant, sufficient valid reasoning 1. 2. 3.	0 1 2 3 4
Transitions used, and at key places between main points	0 1 2 3 4
Conclusion: 1. Thesis reference, summary of main points 2. Further thought 3. voice - sense of finality	0 1 2 3 4
Visual aid: helpful purpose, used effectively	0 1 2 3 4
Subject selection: suits audience/occasion	0 1 2 3 4
Eye contact and appropriate use of notes	0 1 2 3 4
Delivery: phrasing, loudness, rate, pronunciation	0 1 2 3 4
Fit time limit (6-8 minutes) or not	0 1 2 3 4

[0-inadequate, 1-adequate, 2-good, 3-very good, 4-excellent]   Grade____

CHAPTER 16 EXERCISE #3
Sample Informative Speech Outline to Correct. *Obesity in Children*

Table 16.3

Directions: Determine what is wrong with the outline in the left-hand column then fill in the right side with appropriate information to make it an acceptable outline.

A. Introduction	A. Introduction
1. *Attention Step* Illustration of field trip to Jose Rios Middle School and the recognition of obese kids	1. *Attention Step*
2. *Need Step* (harms the audience can expect) Parents should become aware and be knowledgeable about ways to prevent obesity in their children.	2. *Need Step*
B. *Satisfaction Step* (body of speech)	B. *Satisfaction Step*

1. Why don't children exercise anymore?
    a. Hi-tech electronics for entertainment
    b. Statistics about TV time
	1. *Thesis statement*

2. Good nutrition diet
    a. Parents should be aware of proper amounts and nutrients for the child
    b. Child-growing needs
	2. Definition of terms (if necessary)

3. Why obesity happens
    a. Lack of exercise
      1) Shortage of school budget
      2) Competition in schools
	3. Statement of 1st major point

b. Nutritional influence
      1) parents are always on the go
      2) children easily influenced
      3) skipping breakfast
	4. Statement of 2nd major point

c. Lack of stable food environment	5. Statement of 3rd major point

4. Solutions
    a. Promotion of good exercise
    b. Promotion of good nutrition
    c. Promotion of stable food environment
    d. Doctor evaluation
    e. Weight reduction
    f. Stabilization of diet
	C. Conclusion 1. Summary
	  2. Further thought

REFERENCES

1. M. Griffin, Public Speaking Basics (Lanham, MD: University Press of America, 2009).
2. Ibid.
3. J. DeVito, Human Communication: The Basic Course (10th ed.) (Boston: Pearson Education, Inc., 2006).
4. Ibid., p. 365.
5. D. Ehninger, B. Gronbeck, R. McKerrow, and A. Monroe, Principles and Types of Speech Communication (10th ed.) (Glenview, Illinois: Scott, Foresman and Company, 1986).
6. Griffin, op cit.
7. Ibid.

CHAPTER SEVENTEEN

Special Occasion Speeches

Good Will, Courtesy, Entertain, Introduction

These speeches emphasize common identities and values that join people together as a group. They promote and strengthen group members' common beliefs and goals, which in turn increases their positive regard of themselves.

According to Osborn, the ceremonial speech answers four basic questions[1]: Who are we? Why are we? What have we accomplished? What can we become together? In focusing on what an individual or group has accomplished, this speech also promotes these actions as a standard for the group to follow in the future.

There are two basic aspects to ceremonial speeches: identification and magnification.

IDENTIFICATION

This is the recognition among people that they share something in common. The speaker's goal is to illustrate and magnify those beliefs and experiences that he or she jointly holds with the audience. Many politicians are known to do this, so voters will see them as just like themselves. The audience will not feel as one with the speaker and legitimize their being together in that context if the speaker does not promote identification. This is achieved through stories, recognized heroes, and renewed commitment.

1. *Through Narratives.* This is telling a story about a shared past event, including times of difficulty and discouragement, followed by moments of success when members of the group (now hearing the speech) made significant contributions.

2. *Through Hero Veneration.* For this, the speaker names those people in the organization or public who made superior and unusual contributions to the product or event. Ensure that all deserving people are acknowledged and that the audience agrees that those named are deserving.

3. *Through Renewed Group Commitment.* Describe the importance of the group, both individually and collectively. Visualize for the audience the improved future conditions that can be achieved if the group commitment continues. Explain how this benefits them and the community. Challenge them to not be satisfied with the present success, but to build on that to shape the future to achieve even greater goals. Remind them that competition rarely rests.

MAGNIFICATION

Enlarge the worth of some person or event. According to Osborn, this can be accomplished by explaining how:[2]

- The person or group had to overcome obstacles
- The accomplishment was unusual
- The performance was superior
- Their motives were pure
- The accomplishments benefited society

Comparison and contrast of events and people's actions can promote magnification by making the selected features stand out. This magnification should increase as the speaker moves toward the conclusion (arrange successes from earlier and smaller ones to later and larger ones).

Save the best stories, the most illuminating details, for the end of the speech. The impact of the stories should never diminish as the ceremonial speech reaches the conclusion.

TYPES OF SPECIAL OCCASION SPEECHES

There are a variety of ceremonial speeches, including: Speeches of Good Will (including Introduction), Courtesy (Welcoming, Acceptances, and Toasts), and Entertaining/After Dinner.

1. *The Good Will Speech.* Given its title, the purpose of this speech is to increase the listener's appreciation of a person, product, service, or procedure.

The speaker wants the audience to view the subject more favorably. To accomplish this, the speaker will have to be both informative and persuasive, emphasizing identification and magnification.

The occasions of these speeches are symbolic, and the speeches themselves tend to be standardized. Good Will speeches include, but are not limited to, farewells, wedding anniversaries, funerals, fund-raising campaign kickoffs and celebrations, beginning or end of the year events, political rallies, awards banquets, and other celebrations.

The manner of speaking is very important on these occasions. The speaker's tone of voice should be consistent with the context. Anniversaries, funerals, and the beginning of an event or campaign can be formal and even subdued. Some humor may aid in the identification and magnification. Levity in a eulogy can also help inspire a positive view of what the deceased experienced and what the future holds for the deceased and those present. Anniversaries tend to have even more light-heartedness to balance the serious appreciation of those being honored.

If you are an important subject in the speech, be sure (with modesty) that the audience has been sufficiently informed that the work you do or the service you provide is of value to them, that it makes their lives happier, more productive, interesting, or secure in some way.

2. *The Courtesy Speech*. These include welcoming speeches, acceptance speeches, and toasts. At group functions, someone like a supervisor, coach, or announcer typically greets newcomers or visitors. In this way, the group gets to know a little about the strangers and they are made to feel more welcome and comfortable. Awards acceptances are also pretty common, and those receiving an award usually give a short acceptance speech, thanking the group for the honor as well as giving credit to those who helped make the achievement possible. Toasts are given at nearly every wedding, either by the best man and/or the maid of honor. These express gratitude and admiration for what the subject has done. Toasts may also be given after the completion of negotiations between competing groups, such as foreign countries, in the hope that they will have continued good relations.

3. *The Entertaining/After Dinner Speech*. The After Dinner Speech exists to give pleasure to a group of people after they have eaten. It is humor with a message. Its theme should relate to the purpose of the group's existence. It should not be too serious or substantive in detail, as if the speaker is trying to prove a substantive issue. The speaker should also avoid attempts to get the listeners to reconsider their values or significantly change their beliefs or behavior. Further, this is not a situation to engender anger or negativity. Rather, this speech should help the audience recognize and enjoy their existence,

accomplishments, and/or their goals. The after dinner speech should help clarify the group's purpose and encourage it to continue in its efforts.

Humor places people at ease, so it is necessary in most after-dinner speeches. Find humorous stories to tell about the group's experiences, which in the telling create a closer relationship between the speaker and the group.

Not everyone considers him or herself humorous or a joke teller, but anyone can survey group members in advance for funny incidences that have occurred. Groups especially like it when the jokes poke fun at management mistakes that came to no harm. Be careful about offending people, so give humor careful consideration. Consider discussing your comments beforehand with those about whom you are planning to say a joke. Speakers may find it safer to joke about themselves as related to the group's activities and purpose. Self-depreciating humor can even increase the audience's perceived credibility of the speaker. Use the humor to make a point, not just humor for humor's sake.

Stories (real or imagined) are typically used by after-dinner speakers, yet other humorous devices can be useful, such as puns, witty descriptions and illustrations, humorous lines of poetry, indirect reference (allusions) to famous people or events, and even indirect references to local people and topics. Former President Kennedy was known for using witty comments during his speeches and press conferences. Former President Reagan was known for his Irish jokes and funny allusions to former Hollywood actors and their movie lines, including his own. Although it was not in an after-dinner speech, speaking in the second debate he had with former Vice-President Mondale in 1986, Pres. Reagan, who was 75, said he would not use his opponent's youth, age 58, as a campaign issue. Even Mondale laughed.

The after-dinner speech should have the basic speech parts that include an introduction, body, and conclusion. Get the audience's attention immediately since many in the audience may be talking to other members at their tables or still eating. Use stories to establish a light-hearted mood and to carry a message. Build the stories and comments along a common theme towards the conclusion. Use a brief conclusion that sums up (probably with humor) the overall idea. Remember to be brief, so anything over eight minutes should be considered long and five minutes should be fine.

Barrett suggests that the following criteria be use when creating an after-dinner speech:[3]

- Choose a theme that is suitable to the audience and the occasion.
- Plan carefully and follow the selected them; avoid irrelevant detail.
- Develop the theme with appropriate material, being careful to eliminate any that may offend or otherwise distract listeners.
- Give special attention to transitions, which connect and give coherence to ideas.

- Use only your kind of stories or humor, that which is easy for you to do.
- Be brief, especially if in doubt as to the amount of allotted time.

4. *Speech of Introduction.* This type of Good Will speech is given immediately before the featured speaker presents his or her own speech, to create in the audience a favorable image of both the featured speaker and his or her message. The introduction is normally delivered by a member of the group that has arranged the speech occasion. To be effective, the introduction speech needs to stimulate a desire in the audience to want to hear the featured speaker. Inform or remind the audience of the speaker's position and accomplishment in the community and/or within the organization. Your role is not to air your own views on the subject to be discussed by the main speaker or call undue attention to yourself. You are only the speaker's advance agent and your job is to sell him or her to the audience.

Speeches of introduction help create a friendly relationship between the speaker and the audience and they dispel any potential fear about the unknown person and/or their topic.

The two speaker goals and responsibilities are:

- arouse the listener's curiosity about the speaker and/or subject.
- generate audience respect for the speaker to help his/her message acceptance.

PREPARATION STEPS

1. *Purpose and Manner of Speaking.* Know your function. You are providing a service, which is to create for the speaker a position of prominence. Do not draw undue attention to yourself.

2. *Formulating the Content.* Learn about the speaker, his or her background and biographical data. Arrange a personal interview, if necessary. Be certain all your information is accurate. Know how to correctly pronounce his or her name.
   a. Be brief. As a general rule, saying too much is worse than saying nothing at all. Two to three minutes in length should be sufficient.
   b. Talk about the speaker. Who are they? What is their position in education, business, the community, etc.? Summarize the speaker's primary qualifications to speak on the announced subject but do not overdo it to the point of embarrassment. Avoid simply stating a long list of details about the main speaker's life or retelling some funny experiences you previously had with the speaker. You can use humor if it is in good taste.

c. Emphasize the importance of the speaker's subject and describe how it is relevant to the audience's interests. Only make general comments about the speaker's topic area. Do not praise or blame the speaker's ability as a speaker. Let the speaker emphasize his or her own knowledge and skills.

ORGANIZING THE SPEECH OF INTRODUCTION

1. Use a brief opening to get the audience's attention and interest.
2. Develop 2-3 main points of interest about the speaker, including the importance of the topic.
3. Finish with a key statement about the person and a reference to his or her topic.

For the final statement of your speech, you should make a statement to let the speaker know that the time to speak has come. For example, you might say, "Now to speak to us about _____, Mr./Ms._____" or "Let's give a warm welcome to Mr./Ms._____" After this conclusion, turn toward the speaker and lead the audience's applause.

CONCLUSION

Speeches of Good Will, Courtesy, Entertainment, and Introduction stress the characteristics that people have in common, including who they see themselves being and what common values they share as a group. These types of speeches draw attention to and fortify the beliefs and goals shared by the group members. With such speeches, these members feel better about who they are and what they have succeeded in doing.

Chapter 17 Homework #1: Speech of Introduction

1. For the Speech of Introduction, submit a 1-2 page biography of yourself one week before the speech is to be given. This can be accurate, partly true and partly fantasy, or entirely fantasy. Your biography will be given to a classmate who will introduce you. They will decide whether to use all, part, or none of what you write down.

Chapter 17 Special Occasion Speech Assignment

This is a 2.5-5 minute speech in which you will stress the significance of a person, group, idea, phenomenon, goal, event, place, or action (or some combination of these). In so doing, the identity and value of that being accentuated is celebrated and reinforced among the audience.[4] The speech should encourage the members to be more appreciative of what they have in common and even what they may become in the future.

The following is a brief summary of the special occasion speeches described in this chapter.

Good Will speeches include, but are not limited to, farewells, wedding anniversaries, funerals, fund-raising campaign kickoffs and celebrations, beginning or end of the year events, political rallies, awards banquets, and other celebrations. Overall, this speech should increase the listener's sense of value for the person or phenomenon.

Courtesy speeches include welcoming speeches by a supervisor, coach, or announcer, and acceptance speeches by those receiving an award, and toasts. Toasts are given at nearly every wedding and sometimes after the completion of negotiations between competing groups, expressing gratitude and admiration for what the person or group has done as well as positive expectations for the future relationship.

The Entertaining or After Dinner Speech functions to give pleasure and ease to a group of people, often after they have eaten. It is humor with a message, helping the audience recognize and enjoy their existence, accomplishments, and/or their goals.

The Speech of Introduction can be and is used prior to the occurrence of most of the ceremonial speeches noted above. This speech is given immediately before the featured speaker speaks, to create a favorable image for both the featured speaker and his or her message. It should stimulate a desire in the audience to want to hear the featured speaker.

Manner of Speaking

The manner of speaking is very important on these occasions. The speaker's tone of voice should be consistent with the context. Anniversaries, funerals, and the beginning of an event or campaign can be formal and even subdued. This does not mean there cannot be some humor to aid in the identification and magnification. Levity in a eulogy can also help inspire a positive view of what the deceased experienced and what the future holds for the deceased and all those present. Anniversaries tend to have even more light-heartedness to them to balance the serious appreciation of those being honored.

Conclusion

Ceremonial speaking, according to Osborn and Osborn, answers the following four questions: who are we, why are we, what have we accomplished, and what can we become together?[5] They enhance our appreciation of some entity, idea, or action. They illuminate and/or reinforce the audience's reason for existence.

SAMPLE SPECIAL OCCASION SPEECH
Good Will—Award [6]

Thank you, Mr. Iseke and you in the audience for that warm welcome of introduction. I would also like to thank you for this beautiful medal of accomplishment.

I am very excited to accept this special medal for finishing in the top 10% of women at the master's level in the Honolulu Marathon.

I have been a member of the Guam Runner's Club—your club—since 1998. We have 500 dedicated runners who come out rain or shine. For some of us, running provides a time to relieve stress from work; for others, to socialize; for still others, to primarily enjoy being outdoors. It's amazing to think that we can even become addicted to sweating, as if we don't already get enough of it in our daily lives. I am delighted to say that while we all run for varied reasons, we have one overall goal and that is to stay healthy. One specific running goal I had for this last year was to enter and finish a marathon before I turned the age of 50 years young. I am happy to have finally done that,

During my 8 months of training for the marathon, my trials were many. They began with waking up at 4:45 to meet friends three times a week for a 5 AM fun run. Oh, the days I craved to just turn over and go back to sleep in that warm soft bed. Still, with great difficulty, I was able to ease toward the edge of the bed and then onto the floor. Later, when I stepped into the pot-holes and tripped on the deep cement cracks of Guam's streets and sidewalks, I became discouraged. Upon running up Nimitz Hill, I would think, "Why am I doing this?" There were some moments of success when my body felt strong enough to run 10-18 miles and call them an easy run.

I am not the star today, for every runner in this room who accomplishes a goal should be recognized. You are setting a good example for people of all age categories that health is the answer to living a happier life.

I would like to recognize Dr. Youngberg, who was my personal preventive care specialist. He diligently researched supplements that would enhance my endurance and recommended proper food nutrients for energy that would keep me healthy while running 35-40 miles a week.

He repeatedly encouraged me to stick with it. If all runners can support at least one new person in taking up the sport, we would create a positive image for our community and help an ever-widening group of people with their health.

Guam's Runner's club was gracious to acknowledge me as the oldest woman to finish the marathon. I share this medal with each one of you, especially those who have striven for a dream.

Thank you very much.

SAMPLE SPECIAL OCCASION SPEECH
Good Will—Eulogy

Dave's Auto: Closed for Renovation, June 30, 2008.

I first met Dave as he had a 4 o'clock martini at my brother John's house where he gave me an "Ace high and a big Richmond hello." It wasn't 4 pm yet. John said it was 4 pm somewhere. They said they needed a "tune-up" before going to a party, probably at Denny & Mary's. John liked 3 eye-drops of vermouth with his glass of pre-chilled gin. Dave liked them so dry that he simply called up a bar to see if they had any vermouth in stock. The jokes and boasts were flying fast and furious between the two as they pounded their drinks.

I saw him next when he hired me to work at *Dave's Auto* in San Ramon alongside his friend, The Greek. I learned about building VW engines and Indians from Bearcat Creek. I also learned about measuring. Dave normally used feeler gauges to check clearances between car parts, but sometimes he insisted that I know the difference between the thickness of a blond hair and a redhead hair to adjust the gap accordingly. Some parts had to be as close as a "gnats [orifice]." Others were "kyled" or didn't pass the "smell test." Once when I asked him how hard I should tighten down a particular bolt, he made a vague reference to honeymoons. If something was "rode hard and put away wet," well, that wasn't supposed to be good for cars and horses.

On a couple of occasions he enjoined me to take a New Year's day evening lap in his freezing San Ramon swimming pool, followed by a hot tub with Tommy and Jim Beam. Then he had me up to his Occidental property during the winter where the thing to do was to take a scalding hot bubble bath in claw-foot tubs positioned under ferns and redwoods as torrential rain cascaded onto your head, and shout "Herrrr - maaann!" No worry about keeping cool the beer and martinis alongside. If the fire under the hot water heaters died down, it was simply "more oil" to "give it a hot spark." No sense letting all that dirty, old motor oil go to waste.

I was surprised one hot afternoon after working with Dave on some "beater" of a car (Aunt Eleanor's?) when he offered me a *lawnmower* beer.

Lawnmower beer? His strategy was simple and frugal. He said you don't much taste or appreciate your first beer in that thirsty situation, so you might as well drink the cheapest one available (like Brown Derby or Olympia). Follow it up with a fine imported Belgium beer to sip and enjoy. He then made the exhaling, relief sound of a horse shaking its head and letting some saliva fly, followed with an "Easy big fellah."

No one mimicked effeminate men like Dave. He liked to talk that way to truck drivers he could reach at night with his CB radio from his property, getting them all riled up. When he told us gay content jokes, he had us laughing through our tears when he gave the punch line to, for example, "The first coat's dry" and "Let the man rob the train the way he wants to." And he did.

Zucchini. He could never get enough of it. He must have dreamed of it the way young Navy men used to dream of you-know-what in Subic Bay, the Philippines (no, he dreamed of San Miguel when he was there and snuck some back aboard the ship). When I made him clam chowder, I put zucchini in it just for him. He called it a number "10." He rated some place at Bodega Bay a 9.5. Spenger's got a 9. When I camped with he and Tom at Smith Valley, Nevada, along with Denny and others, we ate nothing but zucchini, bean sprouts, tofu garden burgers, wheat bread, and a whole-grain cereal. My mouth salivated smelling Denny's and Jim Carey's steaks and John Ford's lobster cooking. I had to "shaken the bush, boss" 6 times a day with that stuff. Good thing Carey installed that seat over the sagebrush.

No one at Smith Valley in the 80's ever topped Dave's hot tub on wheels. He and Tom drove Denny, Jim, and others around the desert camp with a bathtub full of water sloshing around, set high in the rear of a VW dune buggy. Baths were taken in 1, agitating lap around the sage brush campsite while the bathees drank their favorite liquor (Denny liked one-half gallons of Crown Royal). The next day, Dave climbed 600 yards up a mountain nearby and set out a bowling ball he'd painted white just for us to have some target practice on. Everything from 2" .38 snubs to .22, .357, and .44 mag pistols to 30-06's and assorted police long arms rang out from the ragged firing line. Dave retrieved the ball the following day. The cops weren't very good marksmen.

Dave was meticulous with how he wanted things done. How he fixed and guaranteed the fixing of all those cars over all those years, how he painted his houses, how he hot-water mopped with TSP his garage floor 3 times/day, how he raked the gravel at his old campsite, how he "filleted" (16" exact), split, and stacked firewood, how he constructed the train site outside his house, how he built the bocce ball court, and in what order and how much he drank of his favorite beverages. His standards were high for himself, and he expected them of others, too.

Boy, he liked to run, anywhere, anytime, but especially scenic parks inhabited by "monkey women." He'd stop working on cars or some other job just to go on a "run date" with Tom, Jeff, Joe, even Janet. The San Ramon-Alamo ridge, the Dipsea, Armstrong Redwoods, even the "Bongo Straights" if he had to while at the firehouse. He ran so much he hurt his back, but he kept on running, running so fast the bounds couldn't catch him, down the Occidental to the Gulf Sebastopo.

Now the running is played out.

Oh, we're adults, we're supposed to know this is what happens.

But no, not to us, not to our "one for the road" Dave, not now.

He was supposed to be around a good long while, like his parents.

He prepared himself for that, and prepared us, too. No one really *likes* skim milk, but he drank it. Now, to our consternation, we won't have the consolation of one last "good mornin" from him while he's chewing some food and sipping a cup of Peet's, or one last "goodnight" with an E&J nightcap.

We're cheated, through no fault of his. Gone in a flash. That's the shock we feel.

And sadness about the expectations no more.

For what he'll miss of our continued lives, and we to miss of him without him.

Often the life of the party and in his own way, of our lives. That's the rub, our missing-to-be.

Bye Dave. It's a cliché, but we will miss you. That missing will go on until we are all missed.

We are also filled with sadness for your kids, Tom, Shelley, and Theresa, your brother Denny and sister Janet, all of their families, and your many other relatives. We wish them well

SAMPLE SPEECH OF INTRODUCTION[7]

Good afternoon graduates, family members, friends, faculty, Board of Regents, and distinguished guests.

Many University of Guam students select majors that will help fulfill their career goals and their financial dreams. It was 20 years ago when a UOG Communication major said in an informative speech that, "the cure for diabetes should be vital to you." His listeners knew it to be true since so many on Guam and in Micronesia suffered from it, but what was the answer? Fortunately, that answer was vital to that speaker.

After graduating from UOG, this person attended Loma Linda Medical Center for Preventive Medicine in Southern California where he began a

Table 17.1

Special Occasion Speech Name and Topic: _____ Time (2.5-5 minutes): _____	
Introduction (gained attention, subject clear)	0 1 2 3 4
Body: *magnification* of event/service/person/group; interesting facts; magnification built toward conclusion [if entertaining speech, support materials entertaining]	0 1 2 3 4
Identification (bond created, w/stories, heroes, renewal)	0 1 2 3 4
Conclusion (reference to theme, finality-voice)	0 1 2 3 4
Common theme throughout	0 1 2 3 4
Good Will speech enhanced audience's appreciation of a specific phenomenon	0 1 2 3 4
Entertaining speech (humor tasteful)	0 1 2 3 4
Language clear, concrete, vivid	0 1 2 3 4
Eye contact & appropriate use of notes	0 1 2 3 4
Delivery: voice used expressively, phrasing	0 1 2 3 4
Fit time limit (2.5-5 minutes) or not?	
[0-inadequate, 1-adequate, 2-good, 3-very good, 4-excellent]	Grade_____

20-year journey around the world teaching and researching preventive medicine. We know that doctors do not get rich working for SDA and that is not their goal, anyway. We also know that medical facilities and living conditions can be deplorable in many parts of the world, but that is where the people and diseases largely exist. This doctor wasn't doing his research in the Mayo Clinic. Following many setbacks and the constant budget constraints we all recognize, and with the continual mentoring of Dr. Wes Youngberg, he made a breakthrough in his quest for a diabetes cure. For this he was awarded the 2025 Nobel Prize in physics and given a $1.5 million religion award by the Seventh Day Adventists.

When asked in Sweden how he did it, he replied, "Many people don't realize that science basically involves assumptions and faith. Wonderful things

Table 17.2

Speech of Introduction

Name and Topic: _____

Time (2.5-5 minutes): _____

Opening statement: gain attention/interest, eye contact, loud clear voice, welcome speaker	0 1 2 3 4
Development of the person's background: expertise, knowledge, skills, experience (not embarrassing extent)	0 1 2 3 4
Importance and/or appropriateness of the person and the subject of the speech they'll give	0 1 2 3 4
Organization of the information	0 1 2 3 4
Conclusion: reference to what the person will immediately speak about; increasingly firm voice with a sense of expectancy/excitement	0 1 2 3 4
Anticipation created for the introduced person	0 1 2 3 4
Eye contact	0 1 2 3 4
Phrasing: fluid or choppy; filler words/sounds	0 1 2 3 4
Delivery: loudness, rate, word emphasis, sincerity	0 1 2 3 4
Style: words chosen to convey ideas & feelings	0 1 2 3 4
Conciseness; length (2-3.5 minutes) fit (or) not	
[0-inadequate, 1-adequate, 2-good, 3-very good, 4-excellent]	Grade_____

in both science and religion come from our efforts based on careful observations, thoughtful assumptions, logic, and faith." He cited his 2010 discovery of Master Principles as an example. While sitting on a park bench reading the Bible verse in the book of Matthew 21, verse 22, it states: "All things, whatsoever ye shall ask in prayer, believing, ye shall receive." This guided his behavior as he concentrated his efforts toward synthesizing what became the Principles.

We are very fortunate to have our UOG alumnus deliver the Commencement Address at this Spring, 2026 graduation ceremony. Anchored in his faith in a largely secular world, with perseverance to help change for the better the lives of millions and even billions of people, he will describe the journey that made his dream come true, just as it can for our current students. This will help our UOG students see how they, too, can achieve their goals after leaving this campus.

Members of the University of Guam family and community, someone who will share how the Bible sparked his dream for success, speaking on the topic, *Follow Your Dreams*, I am honored to present Dr. Hawley Iseke, Jr.

[turn toward the side—this imaginary person—and clap moderately enthusiastically]

REFERENCES

1. M. Osborn and S. Osborn, Public Speaking (2nd ed.) (Boston: Houghton Mifflin Company, 1991).
2. Ibid.
3. H. Barrett, Practical Uses of Speech Communication (5th ed.) (New York: Holt, Rinehart and Winston, 1981).
4. Osborn and Osborn, op cit.
5. Ibid.
6. M. Torres, unpublished speech, University of Guam, Mangilao, Guam, April 19, 2005.
7. M. Torres, unpublished speech, University of Guam, Mangilao, Guam, March 10, 2005.

CHAPTER EIGHTEEN

The Persuasive Speech[1]

Persuasion is a common aspect of communication since people attempt to predict and control their environment. In the classroom setting, persuasion is the conscious verbal and nonverbal attempt by a speaker to bring about some desired action from an audience (normally, other students). You may want to convince your audience to vote for a certain candidate (check their name on the ballot), follow a certain food diet in their daily eating, avoid alcohol binge drinking, and so on. While it is common to speak about using persuasion to change someone's beliefs, attitudes, or point of view about some person or phenomenon, there is no way to confirm such changes without seeing the behavior that suggests such changes (and even that is not foolproof). While we would not expect it in classroom speeches, there are coercive regulations or laws combined with persuasive messages outside the classroom.

Self-centeredness in this application should not suggest a negative connotation since it is natural for people to seek to satisfy their individual desires. It is unlikely to be considered immoral if you attempt to persuade a family member to loan you $10 for gas or to give you a ride to school, or to convince an employer to hire you for a job (and so on).

While most students will not have to give formal persuasive speeches outside of the class, persuasive speeches are common during our daily everyday lives. Politicians give such speeches frequently. People in sales give such presentations to groups of people in an attempt to get the audience to buy their health care plan, their computer software package, their fleet of trucks, and so on. Persuasive speaking is an important part of a religious leader's activities. Attorneys deliver persuasive speeches to juries. Notice that even if you give no other formal persuasive speech in your life, you will frequently be on the receiving end of such communication.

Knowing about how persuasion in speeches occurs can help you become a critical listener.

To persuade people, you have to provide them with an answer to a need of theirs, a justification to act. The listener has to be convinced that your belief, cause, person, or product will significantly improve his or her life. Otherwise they will have little reason to act. This requires you to be familiar with the audience's needs, desires, attitudes, knowledge, and previous behaviors, so you can refer to these in relation to the action you desire of the audience. With your audience analysis (including relevant motivation appeals), you can illuminate what you together have in common. This will increase the likelihood that listeners will identify with you and follow your prescribed action/s to satisfy something lacking (a need) in their lives. Your illumination of an audience need and a solution to satisfy that need will increase the audience's motivation to act. Your convincing listeners that you have a significant amount of similarities helps assure them that your specified action is the right thing to do.

People tend to change little by little, sometimes with sudden shifts and sometimes not at all. Simply hearing a speech rarely moves a person to act. Thus, think of planting a seed in the audience's mind that will be able to grow over the years. A strong attempt to change your listeners may easily backfire, as when parents attempt to force their son/daughter to stop being a friend with some other boy or girl. People who are authoritarian, dogmatic, or deeply committed to a cause tolerate little change and will require a sustained campaign to be persuaded.

PLANNING STEPS

1. Clarify your persuasive goal: the specific action you desire of your audience
2. List the key characteristics of your listeners as revealed by your audience analysis (e.g., age, gender, values, etc.) that give insight to their potential motivation to act as you desire. Can you cite harms they are likely to experience when their needs and desires are not satisfied?
3. Find enough legitimate evidence that can be discussed in the time allotted for the speech.
4. Verify your reasoning (by analogy, authority, cause-effect, generalization, etc.) is sound.
5. Create a solution and a plan of action that can reasonably be expected to resolve the difficulty they experience.

WORDING OF SAMPLE PERSUASION
SPEECH PROPOSITIONS

1. Your should take proper care of your teeth to have a healthy smile, avoid general health problems, and save money.
2. You should abstain from premarital sex to avoid unwanted pregnancies, to avoid sexually transmitted diseases, and to avoid a forced marriage.
3. You should avoid smoking cigarettes since _____, _____, and _____.
4. Puerto Rico should become a state since/due to/because of _____, _____, and _____.
5. You should eat healthily to _____, _____, and _____.

ORGANIZATION OF THE PERSUASIVE SPEECH:
THE MOTIVATED SEQUENCE[2]

1. *Attention Step*. You have to initially say something in some appealing manner about the topic to be discussed so the audience will want to listen to you.

2. *Need Step*. Describe how the audience is either currently suffering a loss or will suffer in the future from some unsatisfied need or desire, such financial independence, physical safety, or companionship. Point out various ways the audience is losing something, such as a revered tradition, adventure, or sexual attraction. Describe how the audience will not gain something it desires in the future, such as individual freedom, loyalty, or prestige, and so on.

3. *Satisfaction Step*. Provide listeners with information (a solution) that shows how the harms can be minimized or overcome. Create a proposition statement here along with three main supporting reasons for following it.

4. *Visualization Step*. Specify the benefits of incorporating the solution you propose as well as the negative (possibly ongoing) outcomes from not following the general idea in the Satisfaction Step. Do not simply reiterate what has just been said in the Need and/or Satisfaction Step but describe more specific, tangible outcomes. Use examples and illustrations of what can be expected, expert testimony and statistics about likely future outcomes, and so on.

5. *Action Step*. Tell listeners exactly what behaviors to perform so they will be satisfied. Choose some simple, physical actions that are well within their capability and both easy and convenient for them to accomplish in the everyday life. Although you have created your speech in hope that the listeners will follow your actions, you may simply but importantly have moved the listeners one step closer to actually achieving the desired outcome.

See the Persuasive Speech outline at the end of this chapter for an illustration of these steps.

BUILD YOUR CREDIBILITY

To increase the likelihood that you will be persuasive, your audience will have to believe in *you* as a person. For an audience to consider you credible, they evaluate what they perceive to be your character, intelligence, good will, and dynamism. Other terms for these factors are trustworthiness,/honesty, expertise, competence, sincerity or concern for others, and charisma, attractiveness, or personal energy. Your credibility is in the eyes of the beholder—the audience.

The following are some methods for enhancing your credibility.

1. Character/honesty. Refer to values, beliefs, and actions of yours that are esteemed and common among your listeners, refer to memorable accomplishments revealing personal integrity but without boasting, use highly credible authorities to substantiate your conclusions (claims), and discuss more than one side of any debatable points to increase your perceived fairness.

2. Intelligence/competence/expertise. Refer to your relevant experiences and successes. Show that your speech is well organized, and use valid evidence and reasoning to support your claims. Show that your recommendations follow generally accepted criteria; explain how they will solve the problems you have identified. Document the variety of sources of information you use. Use clear, simple visual aids when fitting, and deliver your speech in a calm and forthright manner.

3. Good will/sincerity/friendliness. Show personal warmth toward the audience by looking at them and speaking with both a friendly and sincere tone of voice. Give recognition to anyone who has helped you accomplish a relevant project. Refer to past, present, and/or future suffering by your audience. Speak in a respectful manner despite possible differences of opinion; sound as if you are open to correction and criticism should you be questioned.

4. Dynamism/charisma/energy. Speak vividly and create clear images. Use active rather than passive verbs, and concise wording as well as an animated body, direct eye contact, and upright posture. Dress appropriately for the occasion; and sound like you are enthused about the audience, the occasion, and the subject matter.

RESPONDING TO THE AUDIENCE'S GENERAL PREDISPOSITION/S[3]

In general, an audience will have one of five general attitudes toward your topic and your purpose. Speakers can counteract these predispositions with the suggestions provided.

1. *Interested but undecided what to do.* Review for your audience the relevance of the subject to their lives, describe a few possible solutions, and then emphasize the one you think is most suitable for both you and them. Reinforce the benefits of the solution you propose.

2. *Favorable but not aroused to act.* Verbally reinforce the audience's beliefs in the subject, then emphasize what is not being satisfied among its primary needs. Describe the harms they are experiencing and/or will face in the future and how specific actions will minimize or stop them.

3. *Interested in the situation but hostile.* They are hostile to your proposed belief, value, or action. Verbally confirm the good feelings listeners have about the topic, then review their suffering under the status quo. Enhance your own credibility by the methods noted earlier in this chapter. Appear fair in your discussion of different points of view of the topic. Effectively refute existing hostility by citing legitimate evidence and respected authorities. Follow this with a small range of possible solutions and use counter evidence to show that only one is a viable one.

4. *Apathetic toward the situation.* In this case, expect that you will need multiple speaking occasions to arouse them. Humor can help get their attention. Keep your message simple and direct. Clearly explain how the current situation and subject matter impinges upon their lives. Avoid being overbearing in your tone (do not sound "preachy"). Visualize for them the tangible and realistic benefits they could receive by their specified involvement with the current situation.

5. *Hostile to any change in the status quo.* This is the supreme challenge you will face as a persuader. You are likely to get little, if any, hearing from such an audience. A third party may be needed to even force such people to attend your speech. They will have numerous counterarguments against your presumed position before you have begun speaking and may blame you for making them be there. Expect that in their minds, they will be thinking that you cannot convince them. To overcome this, you will probably have to have the personal ability to satisfy one key need in their lives that is outside the speech context. You cannot make the situation complicated since they will have no motivation to process a range of variables.

The use of humor can easily backfire if your listeners interpret it as manipulative or irrelevant to their lives (people who are on the defensive or upset about something do not interpret something said about a change as a joking matter).

Keep the speech short and direct. Initially speak to their current position. On future occasions target the message closer and closer to your position, describing the common ground you share with them. They have to perceive that there is obvious benefit for mentally aligning themselves with you. As with the previously noted predispositions, use legitimate evidence and cite respected authorities.

CONCLUSION

Persuasion is an inherent aspect of our communication and is used in our lives as we negotiate our daily actions with each other. In speeches, there is a conscious attempt to encourage a certain action from the listeners. Speakers will typically be more successful if they attempt to get their listeners to take small steps in the direction of the ultimate goal. Make sure that these small steps are easily performed and within the listeners' capabilities.

CHAPTER 18 PERSUASION SPEECH ASSIGNMENT

This is a 6-8 minute speech in which you will attempt to alter some set of beliefs, values, and/or attitudes that may reasonably be expected to lead to some audience change of behavior. Follow the steps listed on the *Persuasive Speech Motivated Sequence* outline form provided later in this chapter. The *Safety Glasses* speech outline provides a model.

Your instructor may or may not permit the use of a complete speech manuscript. Using a detailed outline and being extemporaneous will help you be more persuasive.

Be sure to use your audience analysis. Review the audience's knowledge of the topic, their general predisposition toward it, their reference groups, the audience's ability to understand what you are saying, and how credible your orientation toward the topic is likely to seem to them.

Organization of the Persuasive Speech: Monroe and Ehninger's Motivated Sequence[4]

1. Attention Step
2. Need Step
3. Satisfaction Step
4. Visualization Step
5. Action Step

Change

Your attempt to get the audience to change some aspect of their behavior may require you to reinforce some existing mindset. Review the suggestions in the audience's predispositions section previously noted in this chapter. In addition, refer (appeal) to the audience's long-standing beliefs, values, knowledge, and/or attitudes. For example, the audience may need to be reminded of the value of the group and its causes so that they will once more contribute their time, energy, and money to the tasks needed doing.

Changes in beliefs, values, or attitudes cannot be known apart from behaviors that seem to emulate them. Thus, your goal is not just to change someone's belief about something but use that mental change to bring about the behavior you want. You cannot be sure a mental change has occurred so you can only infer such from behavioral changes you witness.

CHAPTER 18 HOMEWORK

For your Persuasion Speech, submit to your instructor one week before your speech an outline of you speech that specifically and completely follows the steps on the persuasion speech outline form provided in this chapter. Your instructor can then provide you with some feedback about your proposition, basic information, organization, persuasive appeals, and especially the

Visualization and Action steps. This is an outline, so be concise. A final, corrected copy of this outline (to be graded) is due at the time of your speech.

SAMPLE PERSUASIVE SPEECH OUTLINE:
Safety Glasses

A. Attention Step
  1. I woke this morning to a sunlight-filled room, my eyes well rested, my vision clear. I gazed out the window at the blue sky over Pago Bay and the gentle aquamarine water moving rhythmically back and forth along the palm-tree lined shore. Another day in paradise.

B. Need Step
  1. Still, not everyone can enjoy my experience for more than 2,000 Americans each day sustain an eye injury.
  2. When an air conditioning installation man drilled a hole through my cement wall, he struck a steel bar and a piece of it floated into his left eye. When it would not wash out, he went to a clinic to have an eye surgeon pick the piece out of his eye with a needle, apply a few drops, then patch his eye. He missed work the next day, costing him $120 in lost wages plus the $250 he paid the clinic.
  3. According to OSHA, eye injuries in the workplace lead to more than $300 million/year in medical costs, worker compensation, and production losses. A university study reports just over one-half of eye injuries each year occur to those under 25 and over 100,000 of these injuries are in sports or recreational pursuits. People may lose their sight in one or both eyes, be unable to work at some jobs, drive, or cook, and so on.
  4. On Guam, most college students such as you work both at home and on paid jobs. You also enjoy sports and recreational activities so you are at risk of suffering an eye injury.

C. Satisfaction Step
  1. You must wear safety glasses to protect your eyes, including on the job, at home, and in public.
  2. Safety glasses: specially constructed glasses that protect the eyes from the impact of flying objects.
  3. First, on the job.
     a. chemicals
     b. metal and wood splinters
     c. swinging and falling objects

4. Second, at home.
   a. trimming grass and foliage
   b. house repairs
   c. vehicle repairs
5. Third, in public.
   a. sports
   b. recreational activities
   c. motor vehicle traffic
6. Internal Summary: It is essential that you use safety glasses on the job, at home, and in public.

D. Visualization Step
   1. Remember who and what you saw at your surprise birthday party, the daily looks of love on the faces of your family and friends, your favorite ring or car, the perfect paint job you did on your sister's room, the icing on your cake at your sister's wedding? The sunset out over the Philippine Sea as you dig your feet into the sand along Tumon Bay? The money you have to loan your brother from not having to spend it on medical bills and vision-impaired glasses? Can you even imagine the darkness that would descend unnecessarily over your world if your eyes were impaired? Now helpless and dependent, the record playing over and over in your mind about what you could have easily done differently that certain day?

E. Action Step
   1. Ask your employer to provide you with safety glasses, and wear them. Purchase them, if necessary.
   2. Buy your family safety glasses for $10 each at any hardware store. Insist that everyone wear them when doing any kind of project or playing a game needing eye protection. Lead by example. Put extra pairs in your car glove box for when you're out in public. The next time you are overlooking the bay, any bay, consider the beauty of what you see.

F. Sources
   1. "Eye injury prevention month," *Federal Occupational Health*, U.S. Dept. of Health, 2011
   2. "Eye and face protection," *OSHA*, http://www.osha.gov/SLTC? Eyefaceprotection/index.html.
   3. "Eye injuries," University of Michigan Kellogg Eye Center, http:/www.kellogg.umich. edu/patientcare/conditions/eye.injuries.html

CHAPTER 18 HOMEWORK
Persuasive Speech, Motivated Sequence[5] outline form

A. Introduction
   1. Attention Step. Do not mention problems/harms here, but describe a situation going well that relates to the topic. Be interesting.

———————————————————————————————

   2. Need (problem outcome) Step. Show the audience that it lacks (has a need for) something (such as: safety, physical health, financial security, happiness, career goals, power, etc.) by pointing out negative outcomes (harms) that affect it (*suffering* from crime, death diabetes, job loss, boredom, increased school costs, physical injury, etc.).
     a. Make a general statement about people suffering in some way that relates to a specific topic.

———————————————————————————————

     b. Provide an illustration (concise detailed story) which reveals the resulting suffering or loss experienced by someone.

———————————————————————————————

     c. Provide ramifications of the current or expected loss—additional illustrations, specific examples, statistics, testimony, and definitions revealing that people are suffering, or will not gain something they need.

———————————————————————————————

     d. State clearly to the audience that they are or will be harmed, will suffer.

———————————————————————————————

B. Satisfaction Step
   1. Proposition, using words like *should*, followed by answers to what, how, or why (reasons for the proposition)—3 concise, main, supporting points.

———————————————————————————————

   2. Definitions of terms (any key terms in the *proposition only* that the audience needs to know.

———————————————————————————————

   3. Statement of 1st major point (stated exactly as it is above, preceded by a transition).

———————————————————————————————

   supporting info (list here; possibly define)

———————————————————————————————

Table 18.1

Persuasive Speech
Name and Topic:_____
Time (6-8 minutes): _____

1. Attention Step (gained attention, orientation to topic, credibility)	0 1 2 3 4
2. Need Step (statement, illustration, ramification, pointing—harms) a. b. c. d.	0 1 2 3 4
3. Satisfaction Step: Proposition (clear, appropriate, w/3 supporting points)	0 1 2 3 4
Satisfaction Step (reasons/plan clear, points coherent, organized, unified) Definition/s:	0 1 2 3 4
Development (logical support: specific, relevant, sufficient, valid) a. b. c.	0 1 2 3 4
Transitions used between points _____ other _____	0 1 2 3 4
Internal summary of proposition plus points	0 1 2 3 4
4. Visualization Step: benefits of reasons, practicality of plan a. Positive b. Negative	0 1 2 3 4
5. Action Step: specific actions, vivid, final appeal, voice finality a. b.	0 1 2 3 4
Eye contact and appropriate use of notes	0 1 2 3 4
Delivery: phrasing, loudness, rate, pronunciation	0 1 2 3 4
Subject Selection: analysis - audience/occasion	0 1 2 3 4
Visual Aid: helpful purpose, used effectively	0 1 2 3 4
Fit time limit (6-8 minutes) or not?	
[0-inadequate, 1-adequate, 2-good, 3-very good, 4-excellent]	Grade_____

4. Statement of 2nd major point (stated exactly as it is above, preceded by a transition).

_____

supporting info (list here; possibly define)

_____

5. Statement of 3rd major point (stated exactly as it is above, preceded by a transition).

_____

supporting info (list here; possibly define)

_____

6. Internal Summary (restate the proposition with slightly different words and same meaning, and add the 3 points/reasons exactly)

_____

D. Visualization Step. Describe the consequences of doing what is asked for in the Satisfaction Step. Do not merely repeat information given earlier.
   1. Benefits (pro)

_____

   2. Undesirable effects if not done (con)

_____

E. Action Step. The specific actions you desire of the listeners. Ask for what is within their power to do, convenient and easy for them to accomplish.

_____

F. Sources.

REFERENCES

1. M. Griffin, Public Speaking Basics (Lanham, MD: University Press of America, 2009).
2. D. Ehninger, B. Gronbeck, R. McKerrow, and A. Monroe, Principles and Types of Speech Communication (10th ed.) (Glenview, IL: Scott, Foresman and Company, 1986).
3. Ibid.
4. Ibid.
5. Ibid.

Index